LIVIN' LOUD

ART*itation by*

CHUCK D

& The Near DEF Experience

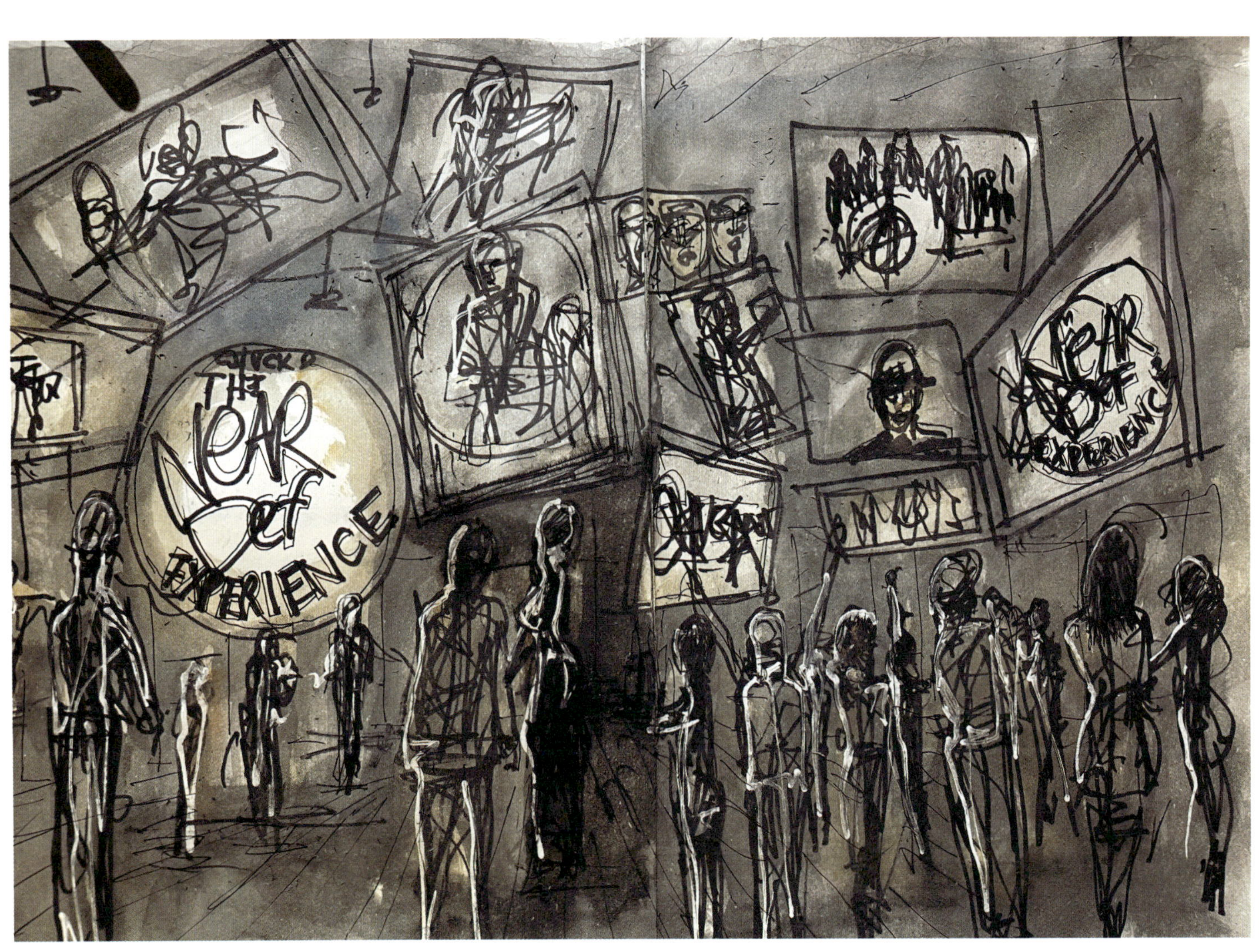
EXPERIENCE
EXPERIENCE

LIVIN' LOUD

ART*itation by*

CHUCK D

& The Near DEF Experience

GENESIS PUBLICATIONS FINE LIMITED EDITIONS SINCE 1974

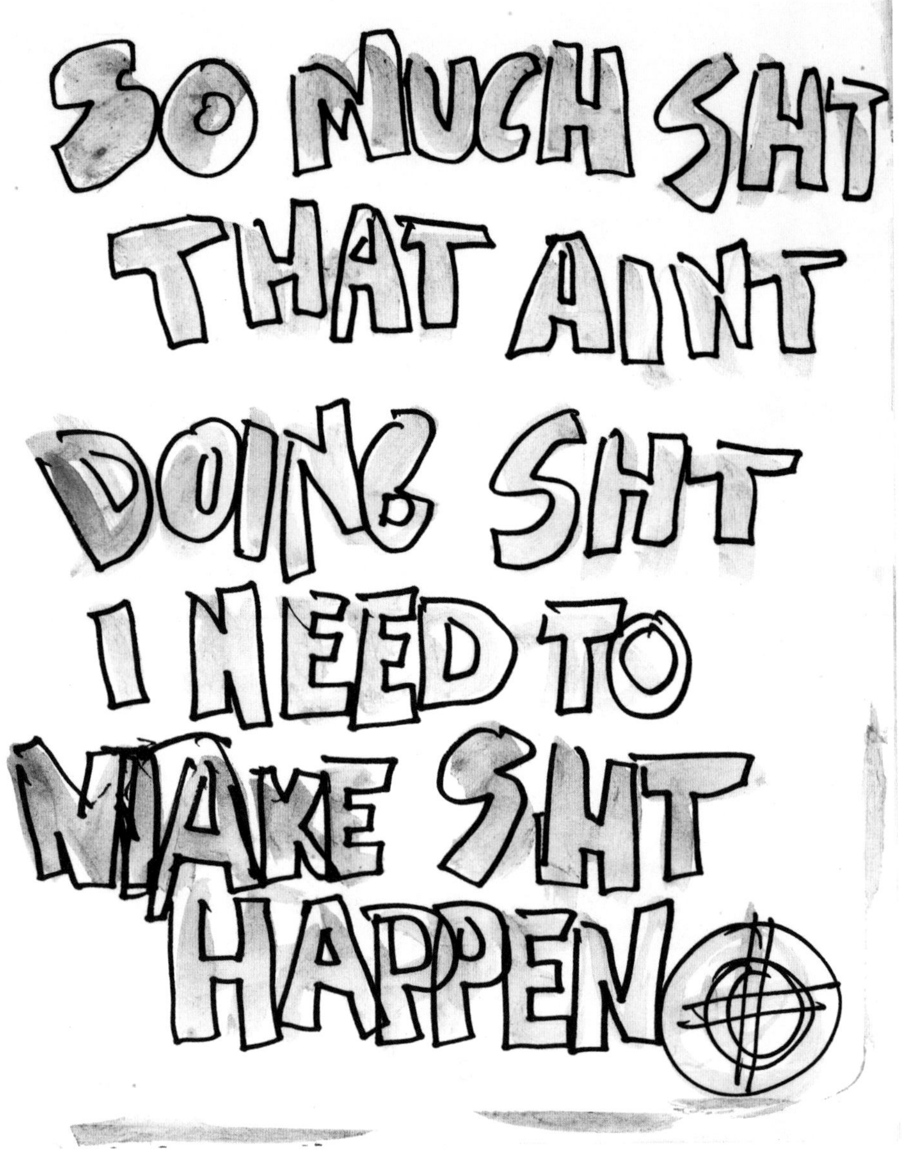

1 3 5 7 9 10 8 6 4 2

This book first appeared as a limited edition of 1,200 numbered copies, signed by Chuck D

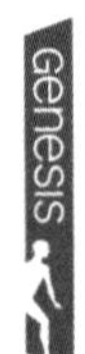

www.genesis-publications.com

ISBN: 978-1-905662-76-0

Genesis Publications Ltd
Genesis House
2 Jenner Road, Guildford
Surrey, England, GU1 3PL

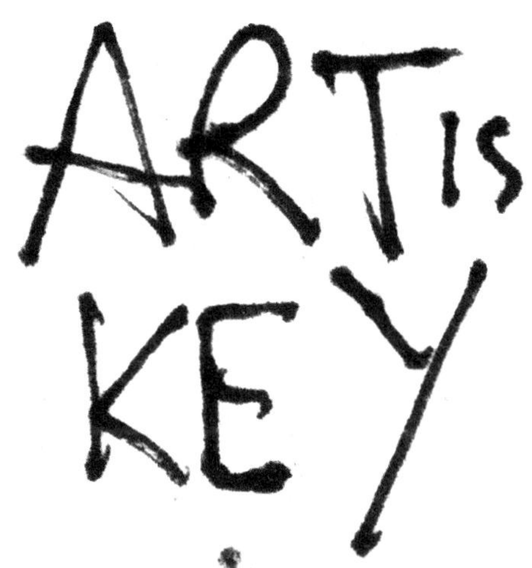

To me art is anything at any time. It's the thing that drives my life.

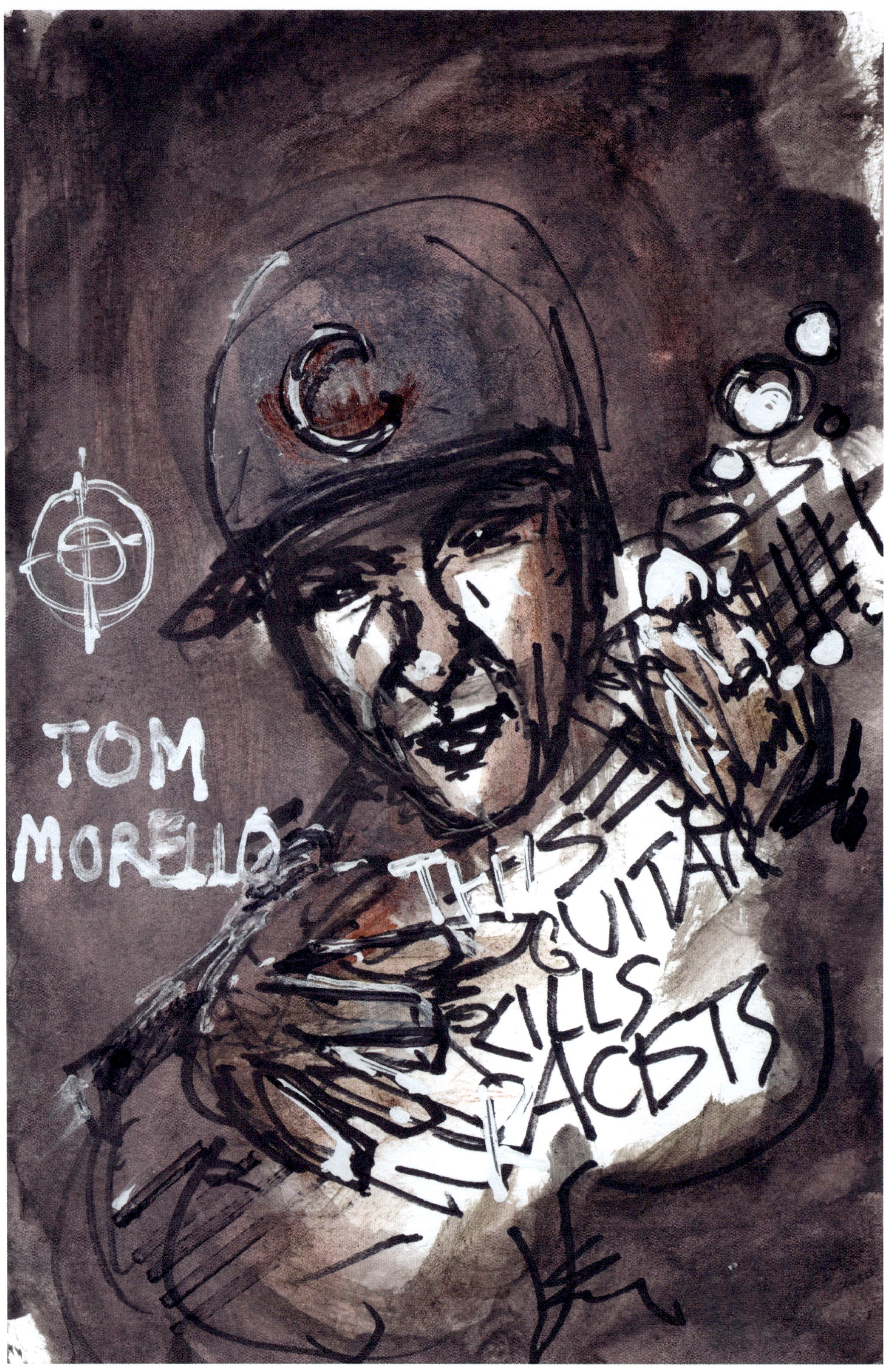
TOM
MORELLO
THIS
KILLS

FOREWORD **TOM MORELLO**

Chuck D, 'The Hard Rhymer', is a transcendent musical artist of the twentieth and twenty-first centuries. He's an apex talent: a hip-hop icon, a lyrical visionary, a commanding MC, a fiery activist and a devastating frontman all rolled into one. But – surprise! surprise! – he's also as gifted a visual artist as he is a microphone master. From the iconic Public Enemy logo to the incredible sketches I witnessed him effortlessly draw every day while on tour, I am amazed and in awe of his talent. Whether he focuses this talent on music, sports, political satire or even landscapes, Chuck is able to channel in his drawings the immediacy, nuance, humanity, righteousness and power of his greatest recordings.

INTRODUCTION **CHUCK D**

In school we had the art contest and the poetry contest. I was an art student, so I didn't really bother with writing any poetry until I was 20 years old. It took off from there.

We had to endure three-and-a-half-hour life drawing sessions with a nude model, just trying to figure out at 18 years old why we were stuck there for so long. We all had to be pros. My expression came through graphic arts. It's no different from why a lot of people got involved in graffiti. I went to Adelphi University to become a commercial artist, left after a year, but later went back as I could see a way to apply graphic art to hip-hop.

As a college student during Jimmy Carter's presidency, I was able to vote for the first time – for Angela Davis in 1980. I was already expressing my political viewpoint through my art and graphics, so the bridge into music was a natural next step. First I expressed myself with my head and my hands, and then later with my voice.

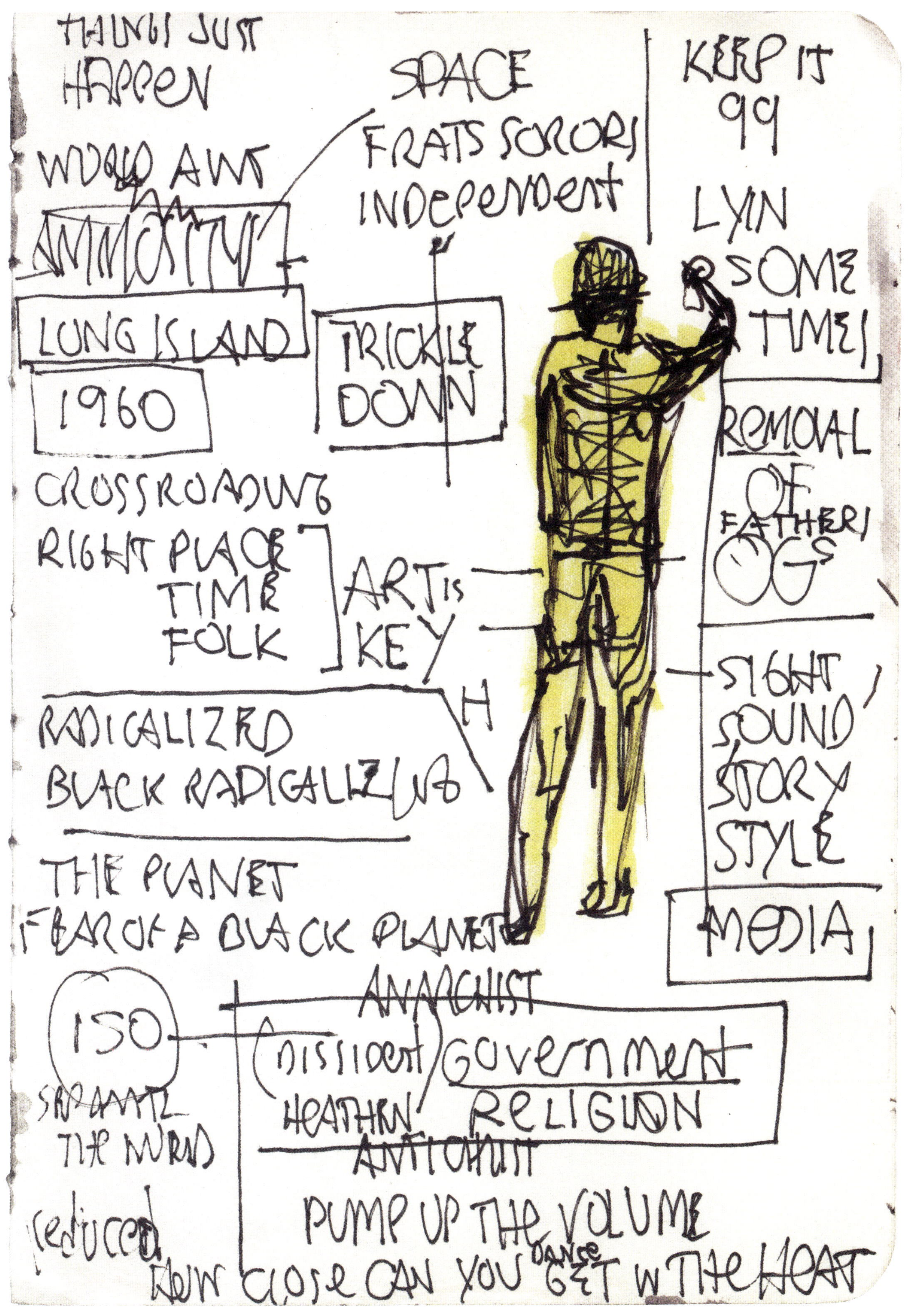

THINGS JUST HAPPEN
SPACE
FRATS SORORS
INDEPENDENT
KEEP IT 99
LYIN SOME TIMES
ANIMOSITY
LONG ISLAND
1960
TRICKLE DOWN
REMOVAL OF FATHERS
OGs
RIGHT PLACE TIME FOLK
ART IS KEY
SIGHT SOUND STORY STYLE
RADICALIZED
THE PLANET
FEAR OF A BLACK PLANET
MEDIA
ANARCHIST
150
DISSIDENT
GOVERNMENT
HEATHEN
RELIGION
ANTICHRIST
PUMP UP THE VOLUME
reduced
HOW CLOSE CAN YOU DANCE GET WITH THE HEAT

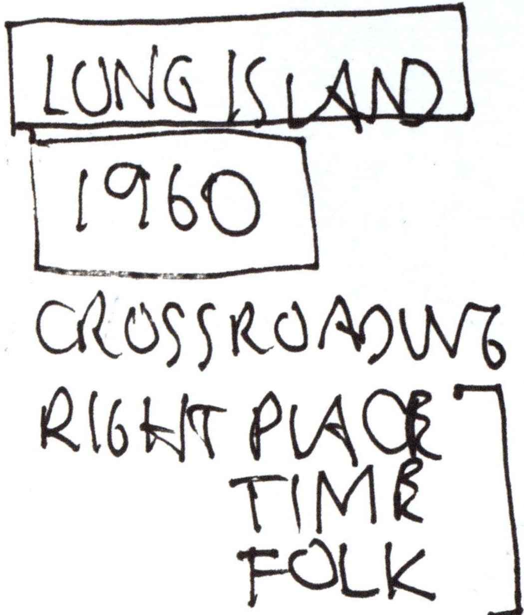

I was born in 1960 in Flushing, New York and I grew up in Roosevelt, Long Island. The music of the household was Stax, Motown, Atlantic, some jazz records – James Brown, Ike and Tina Turner, Aretha Franklin and Curtis Mayfield were like aunts and uncles to me. My mother always played music while I was doing chores. So, when I had to work but I wanted to go outside and play these people were talking to me from that turntable in the back room. Their words were heard and respected in the crib.

The music of that time was the sound of inspiration, hope, faith and charity – all coming from the jewels of soul. Living my first 10 years in the Sixties, I saw music as a portal to black inspiration and pride.

Motown is in my blood. Before you had an iPod or streamed music on a phone, these records already lived inside my head and rode on my imagination. Songs like 'Smiling Faces Sometimes' from the Undisputed Truth. It's just in there. 'Fingertips' by Stevie Wonder, I've known it since I was three years old. It's embedded.

I grew up in New York, so pop radio meant everything. Gladys Knight and the Pips were played next to Steely Dan. When you find out an artist is from New York, you start to hear it in their music. People like Frankie Lymon, you really get a sense of what the music is about and where it comes from. You can almost smell the hot dogs when you listen to 'Under the Boardwalk' by the Drifters.

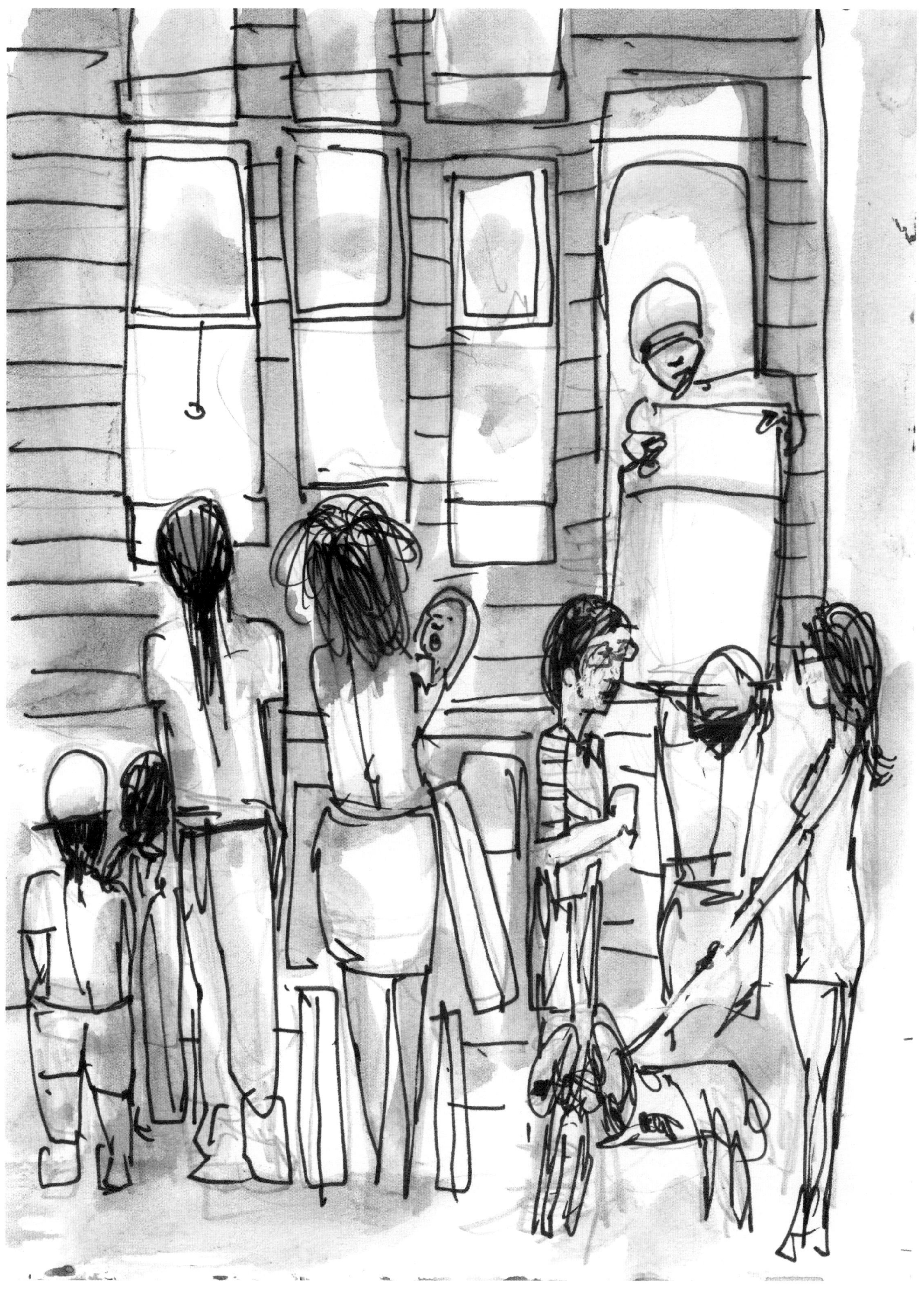

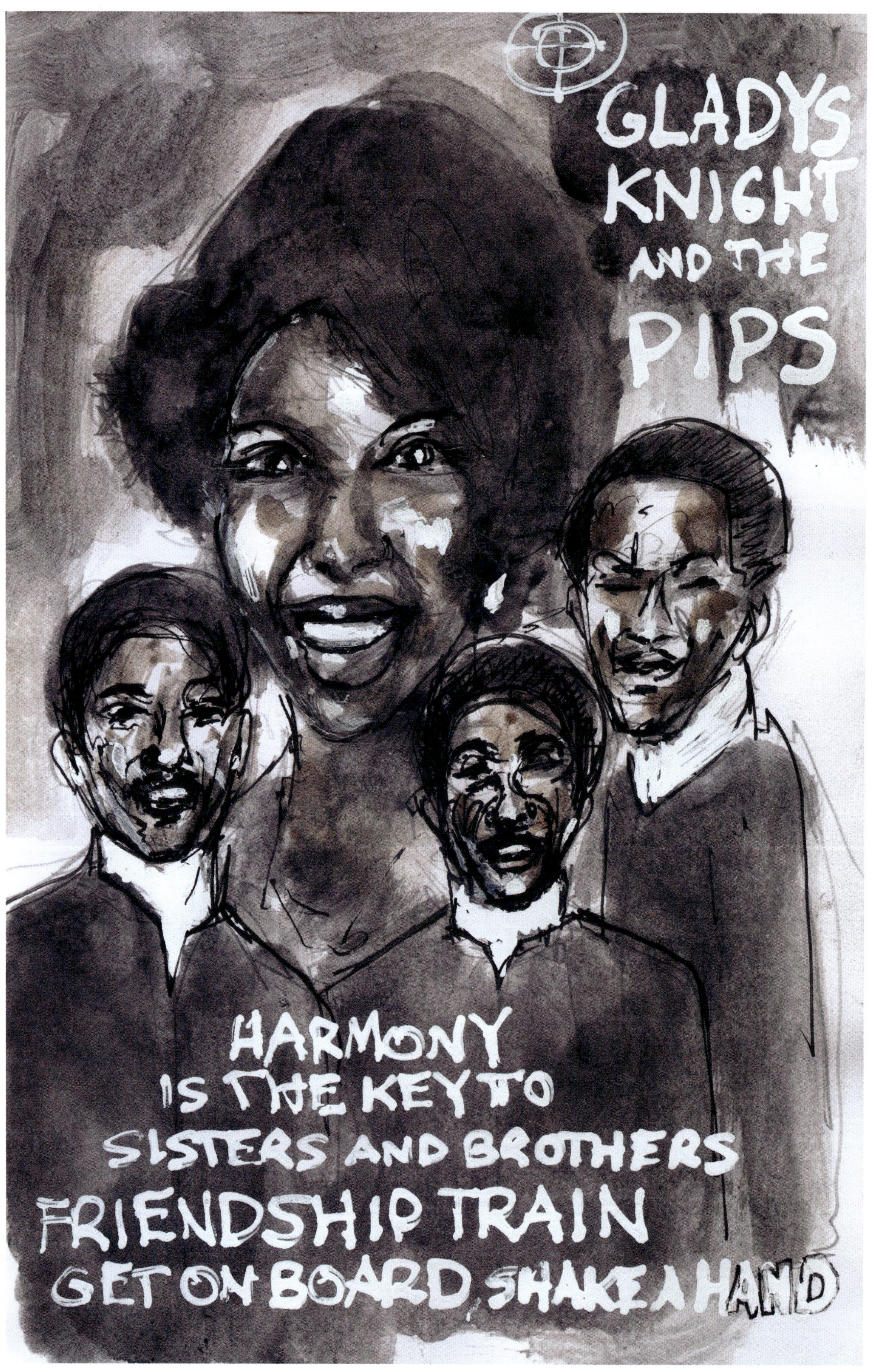
GLADYS KNIGHT AND THE PIPS
HARMONY IS THE KEY TO SISTERS AND BROTHERS
FRIENDSHIP TRAIN
GET ON BOARD, SHAKE A HAND

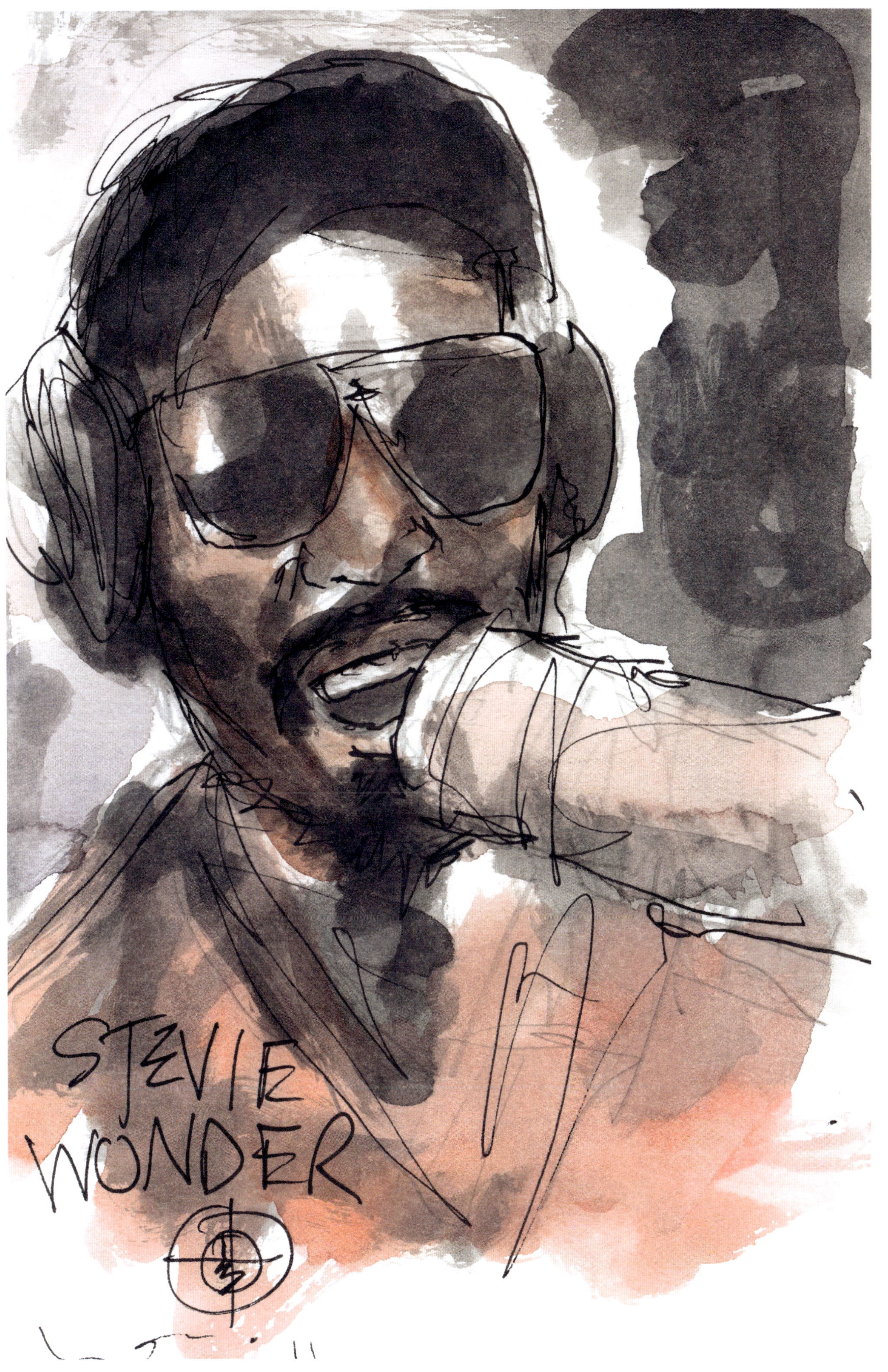
STEVIE
WONDER

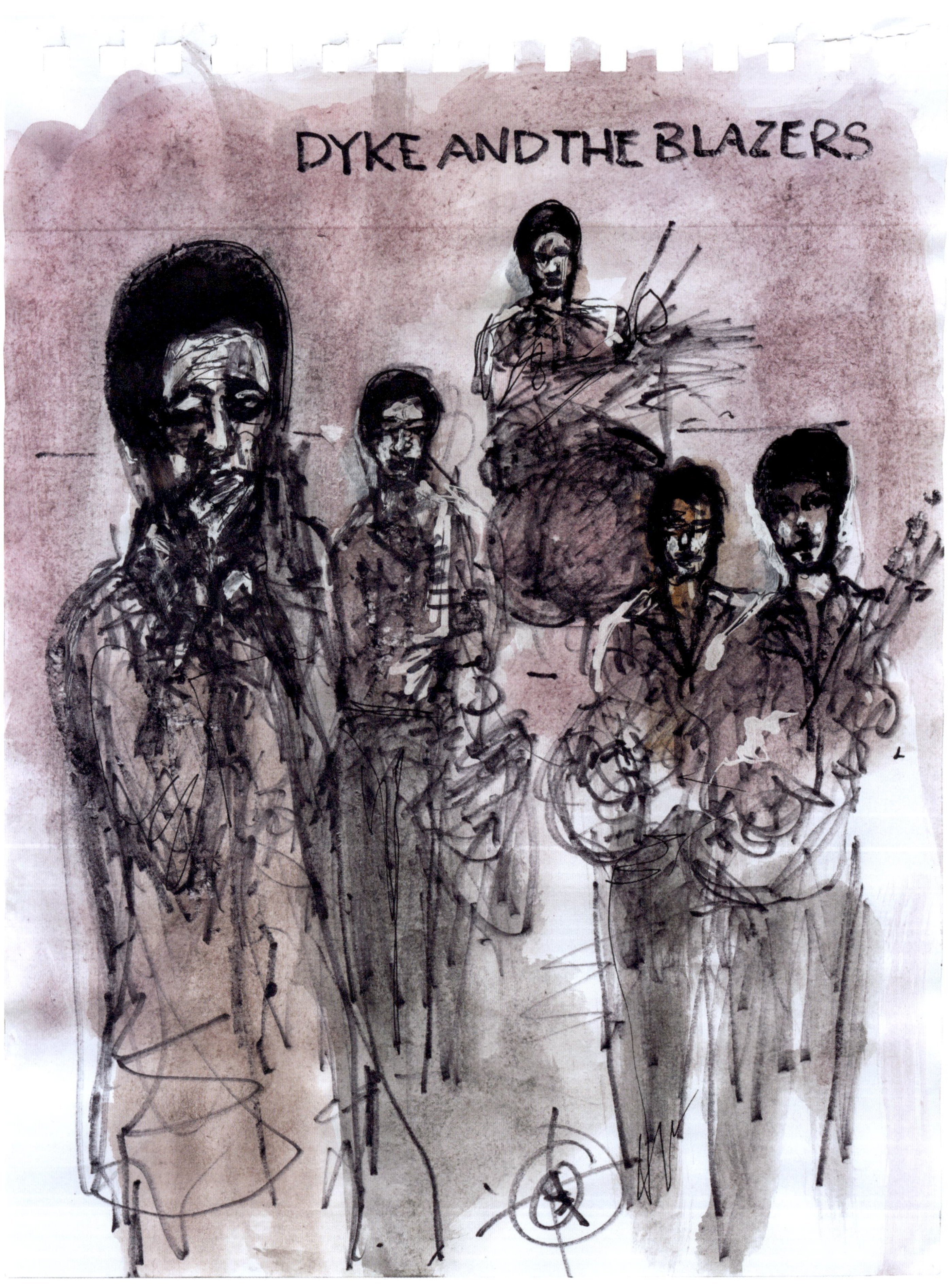
DYKE AND THE BLAZERS

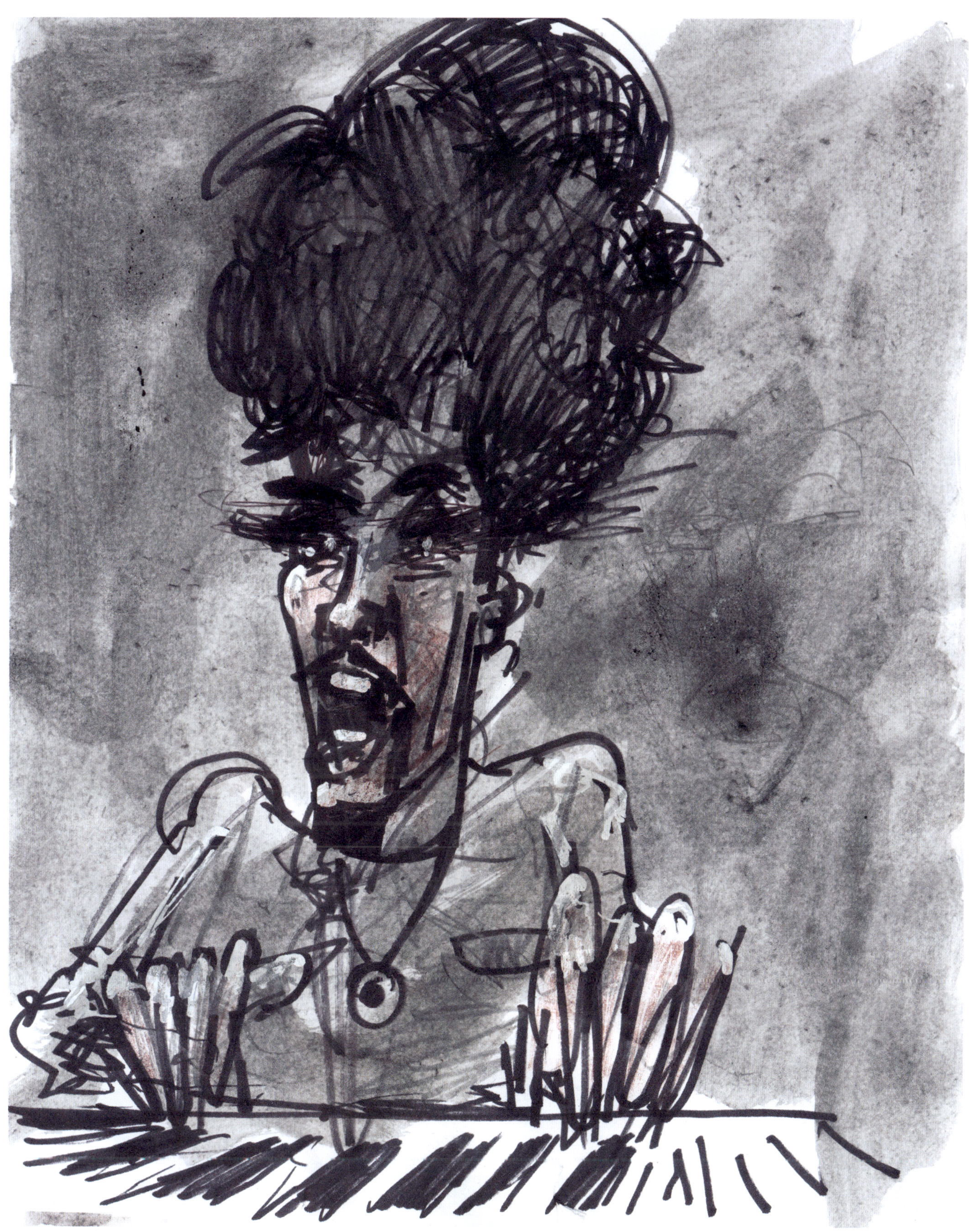

Some years ago, I interviewed Little Richard and he was awesome. There hasn't been anything close to his volcanic explosion of talent. Few singers have ever been able to hit those notes as loudly and powerfully. Elvis was a gamechanger, but so were Little Richard, Bo Diddley, Fats Domino, Chuck Berry and Jerry Lee Lewis. The King crown should have been shared.

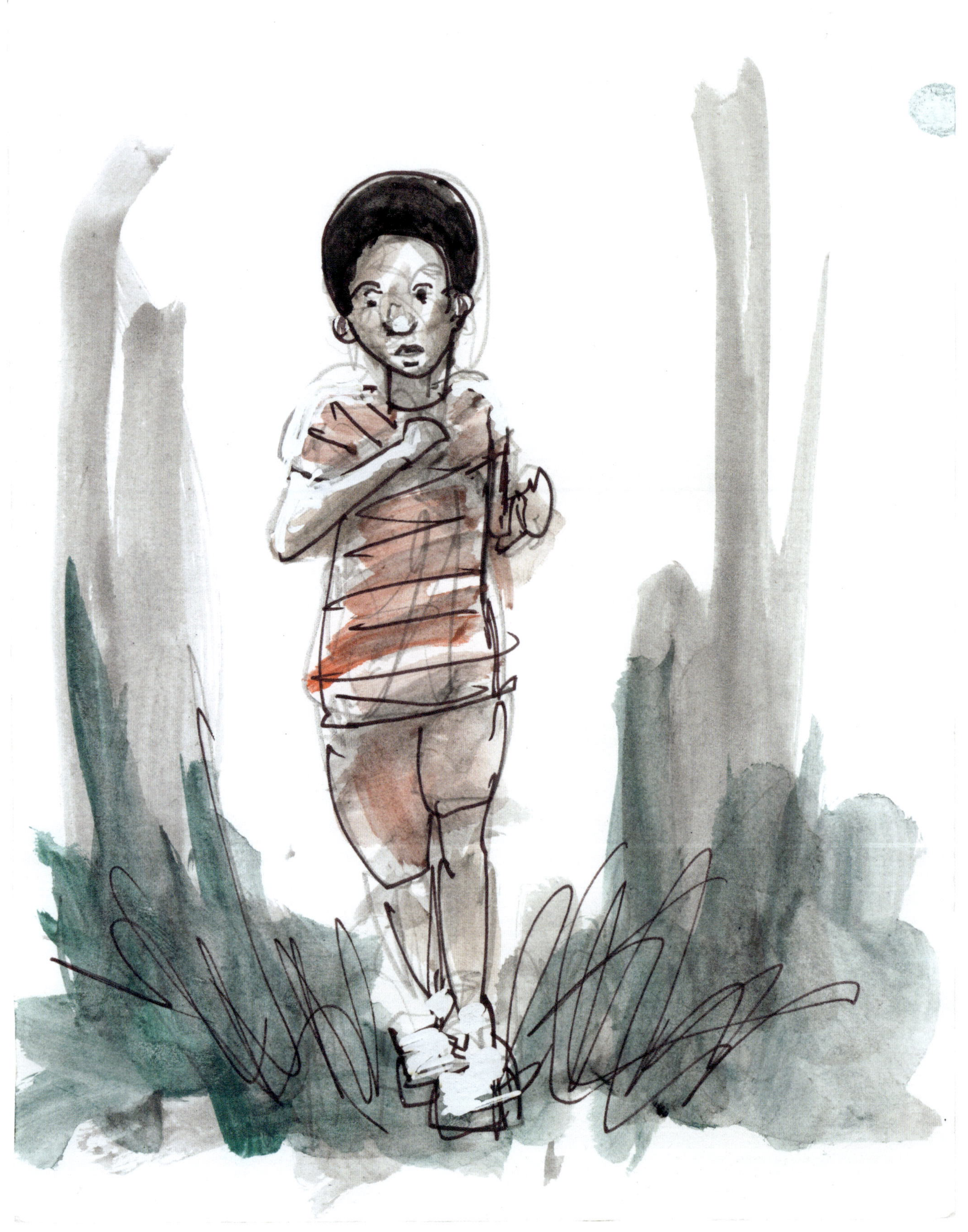

Running from the last century into the Terrordome.

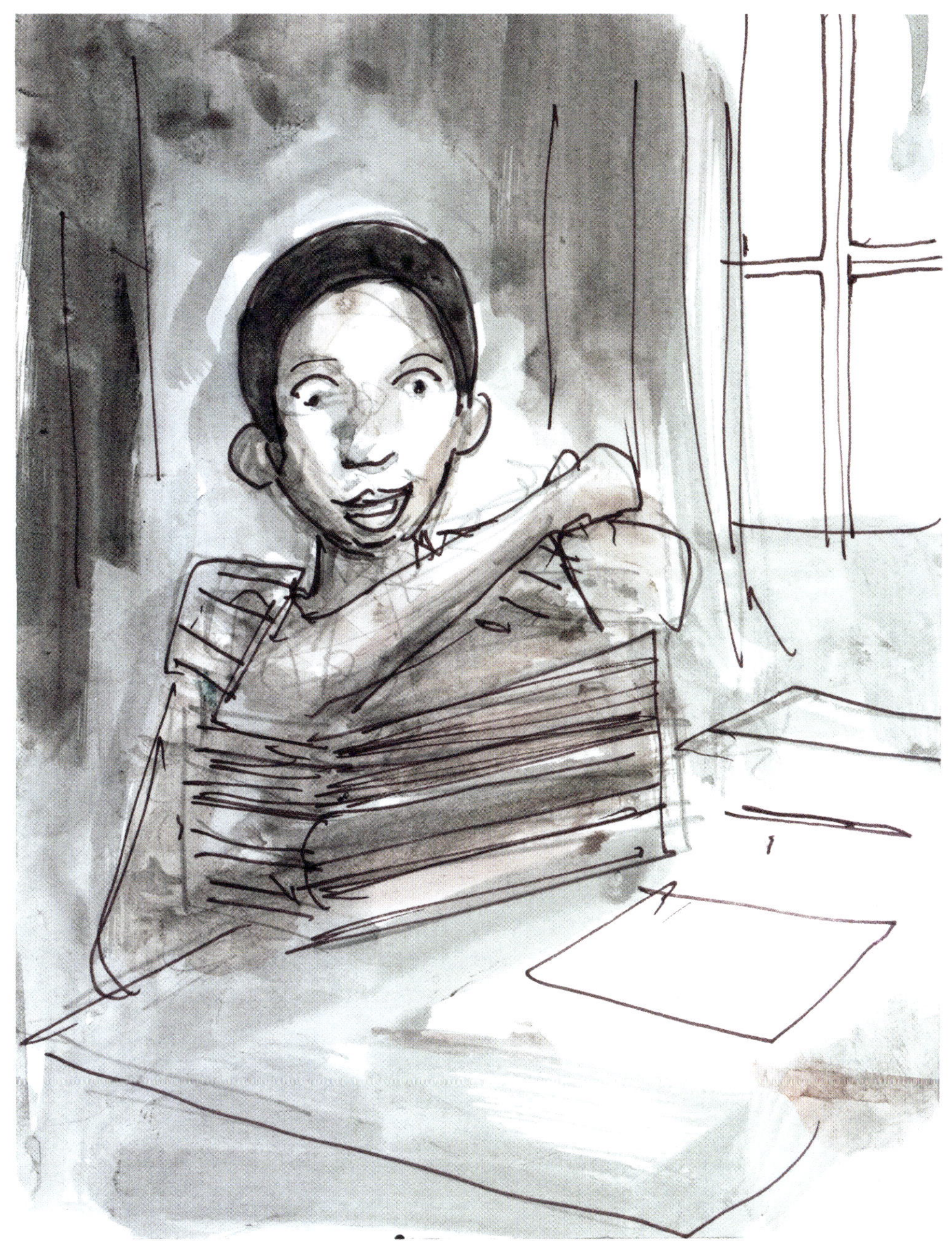

My family moved to Queens when I was an infant. That's something I have in common with Mobb Deep, Nas and the whole Queensbridge crew. Queens was affordable for a young black family. We moved to about eight or nine different places before we settled in one spot.

We moved from the Southside in Queens, which was black as hell, to Roosevelt in Long Island, which was even blacker. I was 11 years old and I remember thinking, 'Oh, we about to move to the country,' and then after a 15-minute drive we were in Roosevelt. The only major difference was a border. I was in fourth or fifth grade and I just thought it was incredible that we were coming to a town with a house that we could call our own.

Roosevelt in the Seventies was a community. Black fathers were not just fathers to their own children, but they contributed to the lives of everyone else's children too – running the boys club, coaching the peewee football and baseball teams and the junior basketball leagues. Youngsters who didn't have fathers in their homes had their coaches.

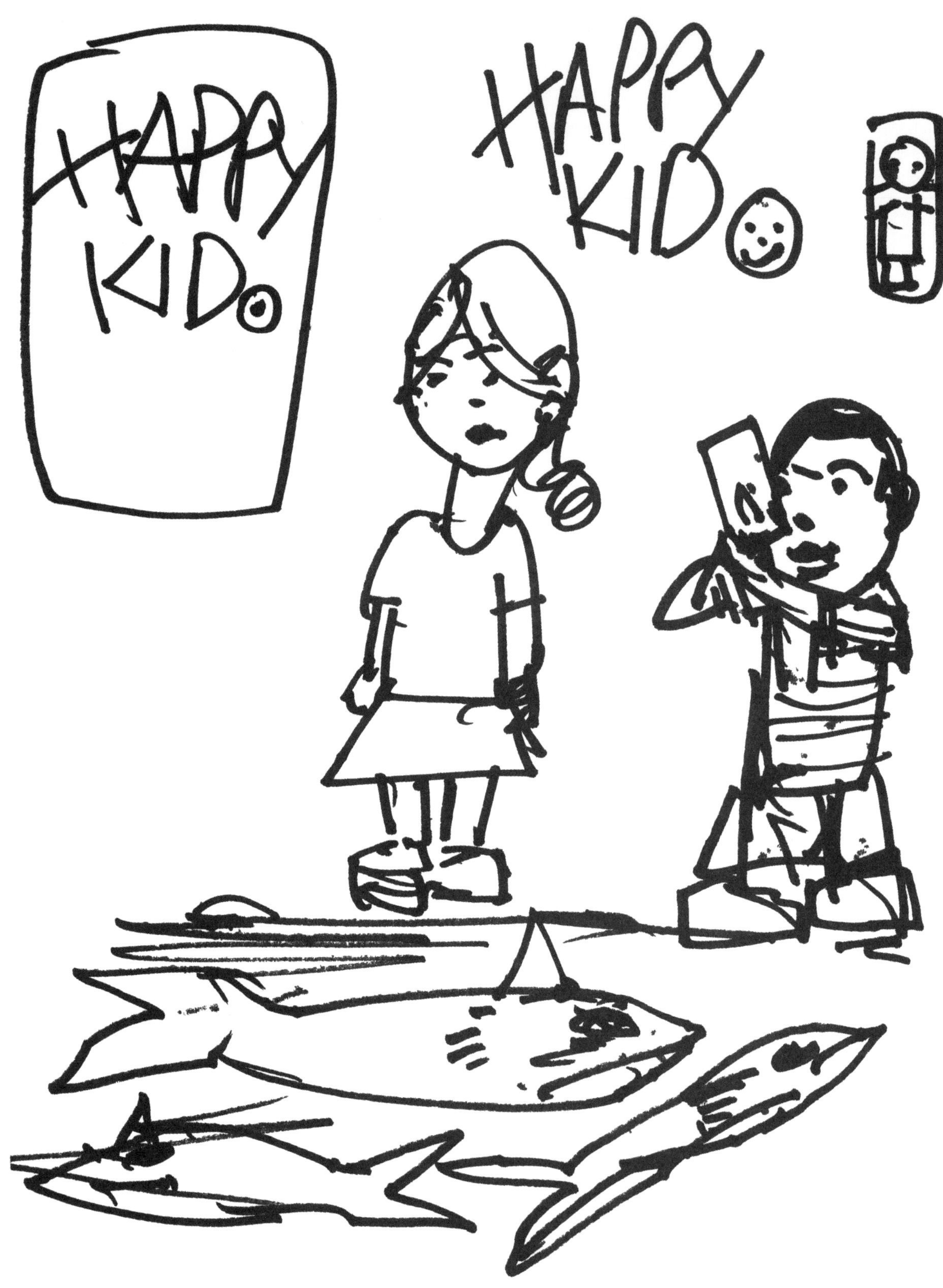

My mom, sis and brother.

My mom started the Roosevelt Community Theatre and ran it for 10 years. I was in plays and later became a stage manager. People like Eddie Murphy were in it – everyone in the town at least toyed with it. I hated it at the time because I thought of it as another chore that was keeping me from going to the park. But now I thank her because the work I did there was a serious training ground for me.

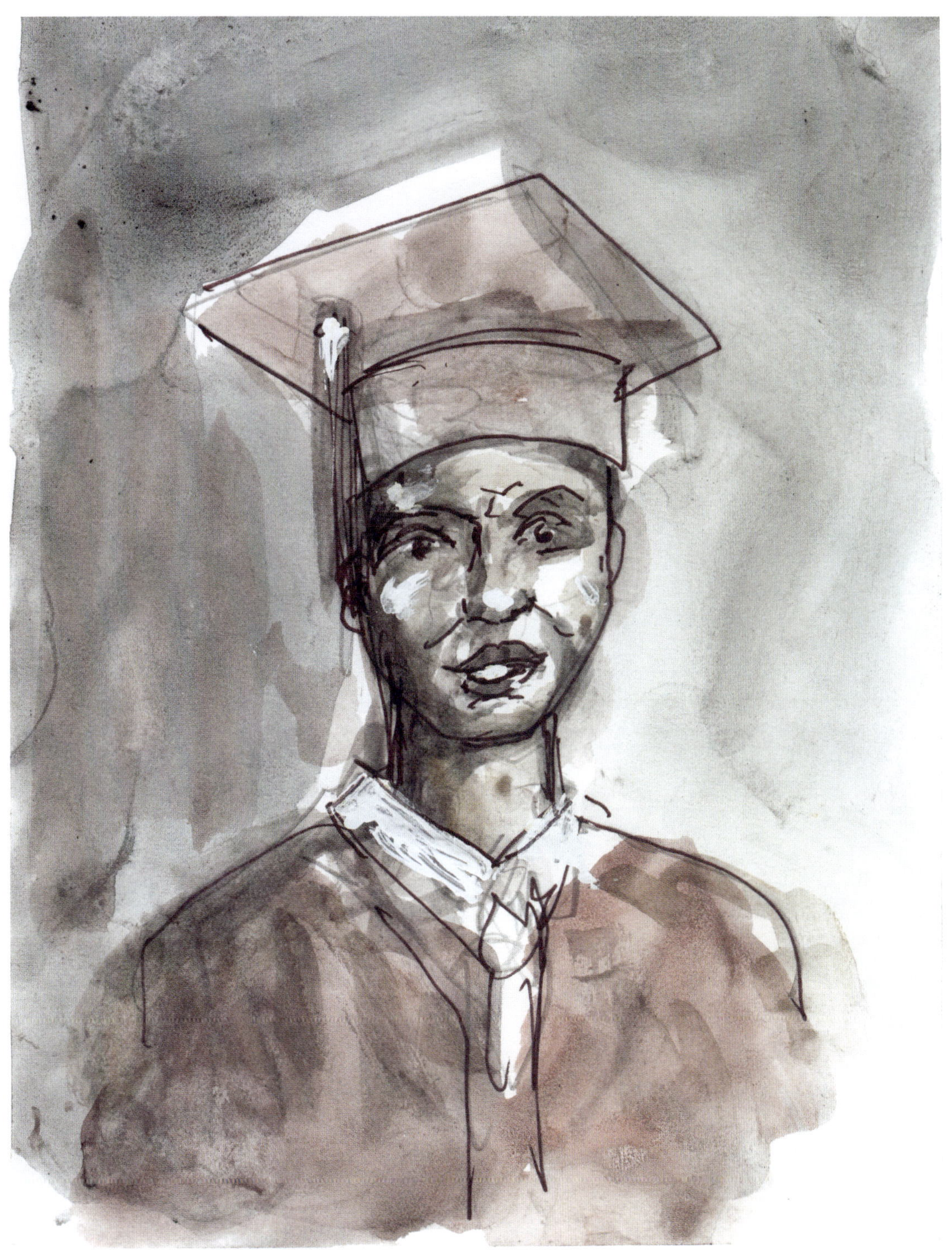

Growing up in Roosevelt, you lived in a black town surrounded by white towns. People didn't go to the other towns. It was like they were the end of the earth. I never had that. I was raised by my parents to think the whole country, and even the whole planet, was ours to travel in. But I knew there was a general thought of, 'Stay safe, stay in your own zone and don't cross the line.' As a kid, I would take long walks in territories I shouldn't have been in, but I didn't care. I was just walking. In Long Island you could get stopped for just walking in the wrong place – county cops were good at that.

I remember one time walking to college carrying a large portfolio. The police stopped me and asked where I was going. I wanted to say, 'I'm not going anywhere with this flat machine gun, sir.' But you knew not to give the police a wise-ass answer.

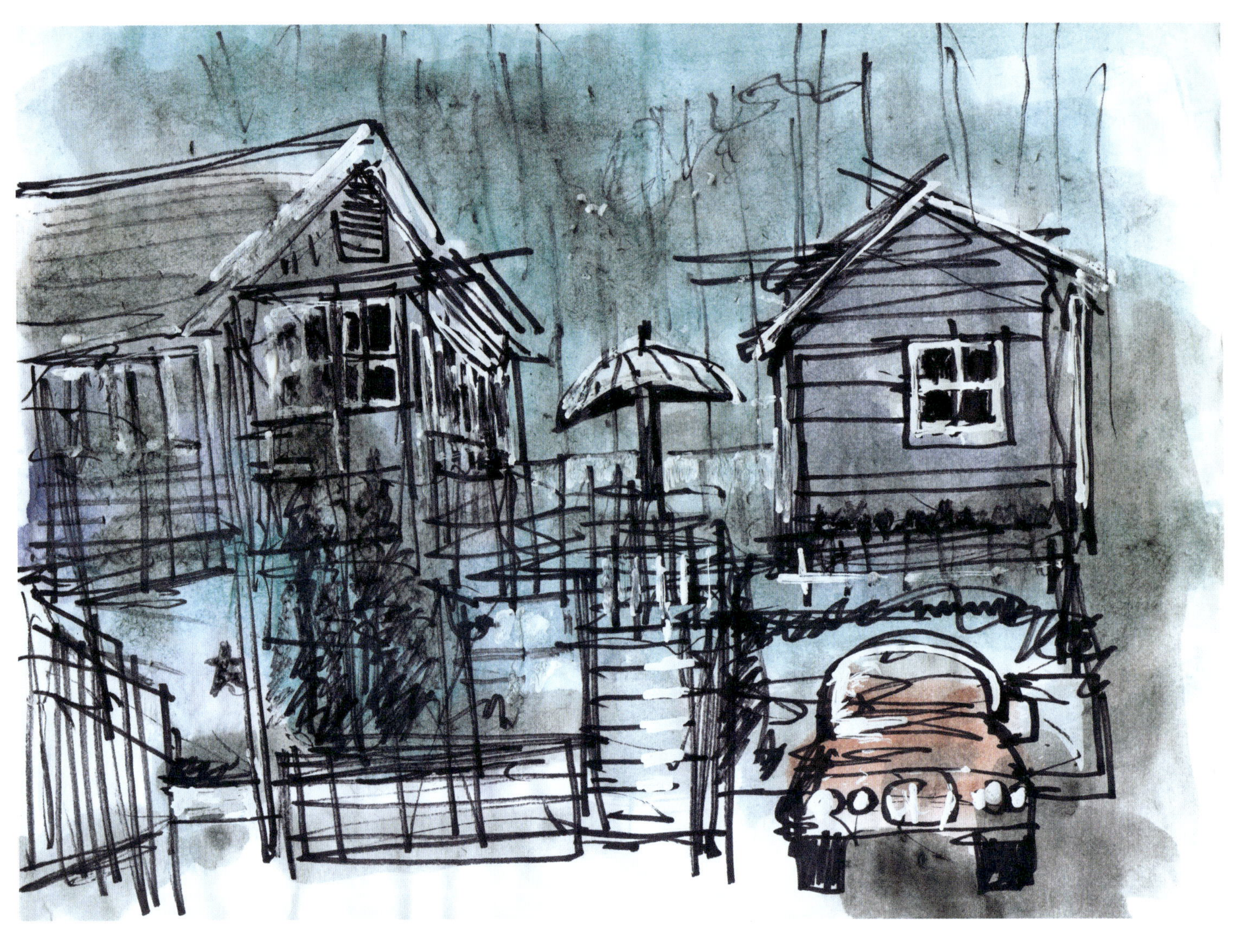

I came out a drawing and designing fool. I don't believe things travel in the blood, but my mother's grandfather George Washington Foster was the first licensed black architect in New Jersey and the second licensed black architect in New York. He worked on the Flatiron Building.

ILLUSTRATION

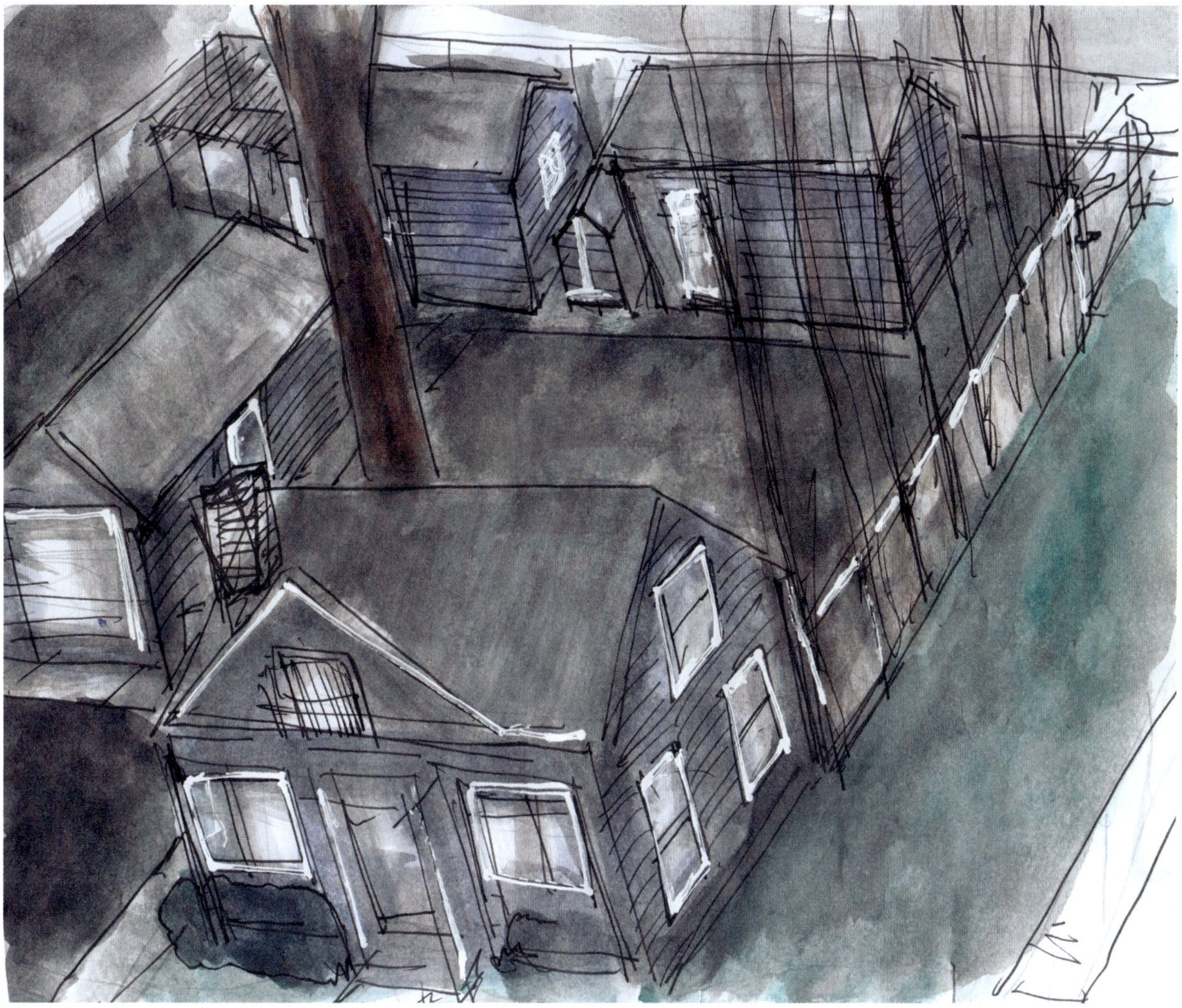

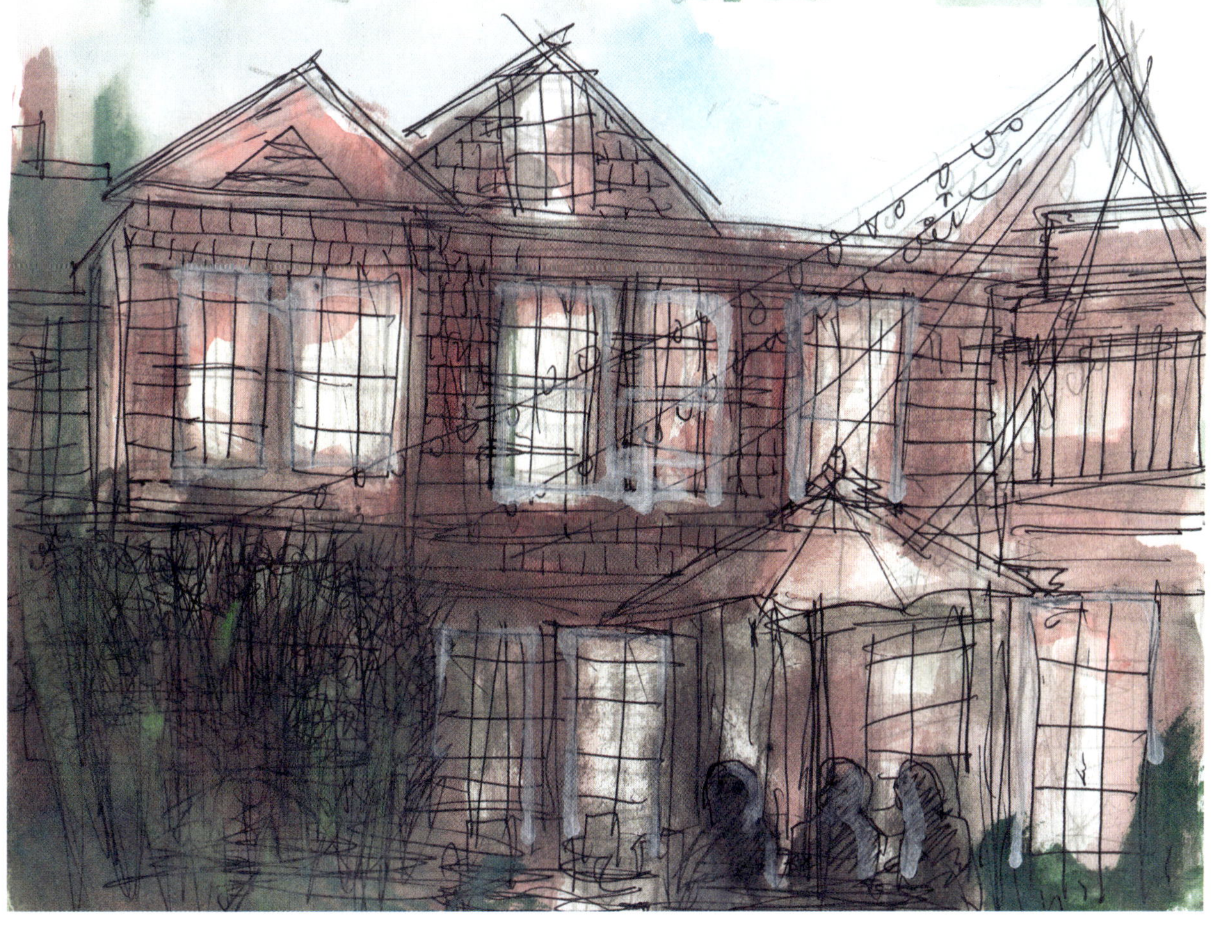

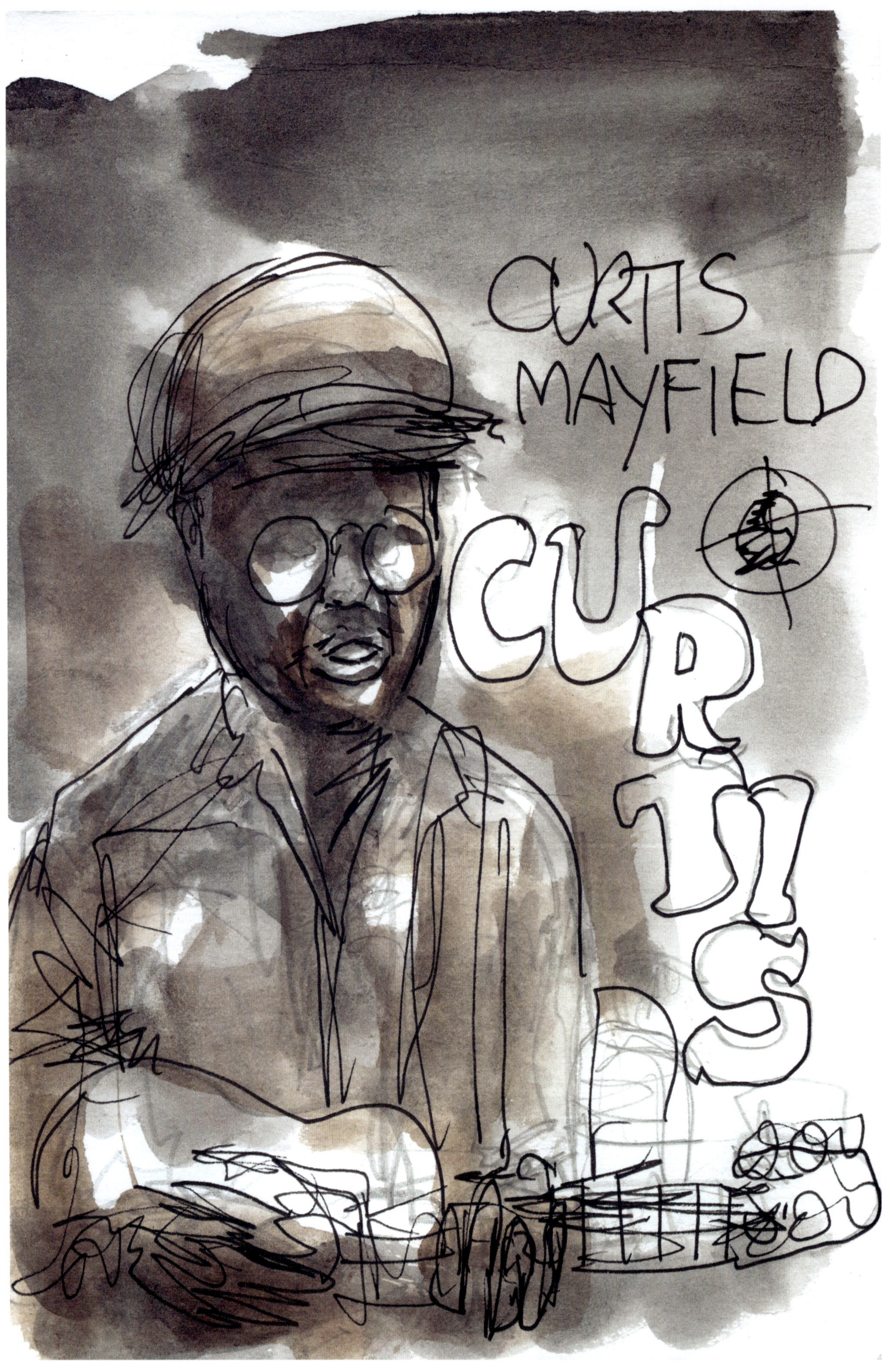
CURTIS
MAYFIELD
CURTIS

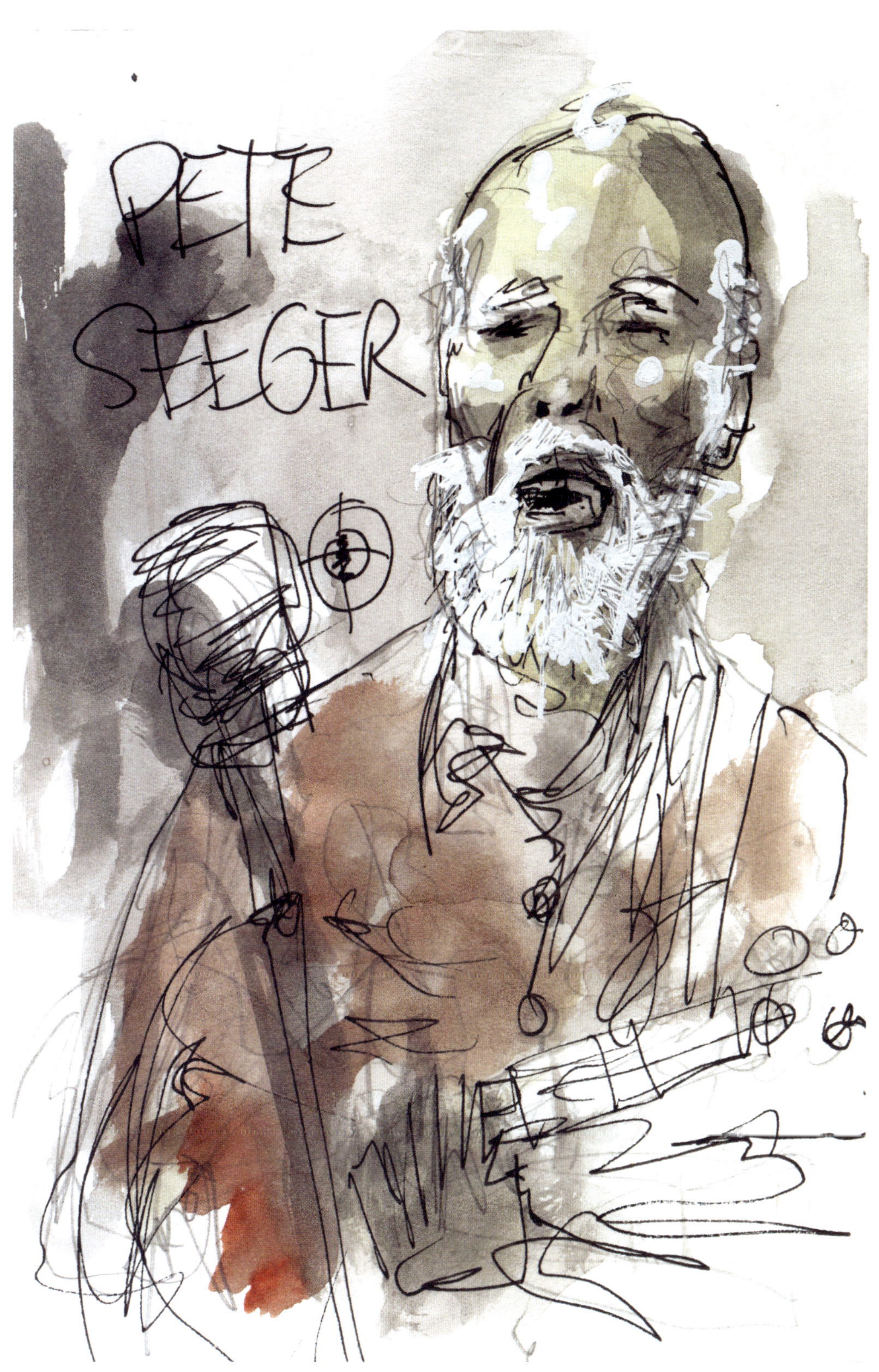

'Whatever you do, don't go to war for this country. Be a conscientious objector.' My mother's stern warning to me as a young boy in the mid-Sixties is one of my clearest memories of that chaotic period. For many young people who are a part of the hip-hop nation today, the Vietnam War is something they read about in history books. Not for me. I lived through that. I was personally affected and shaped as a child by the pervasive anti-war, civil rights and black power sentiments of the time.

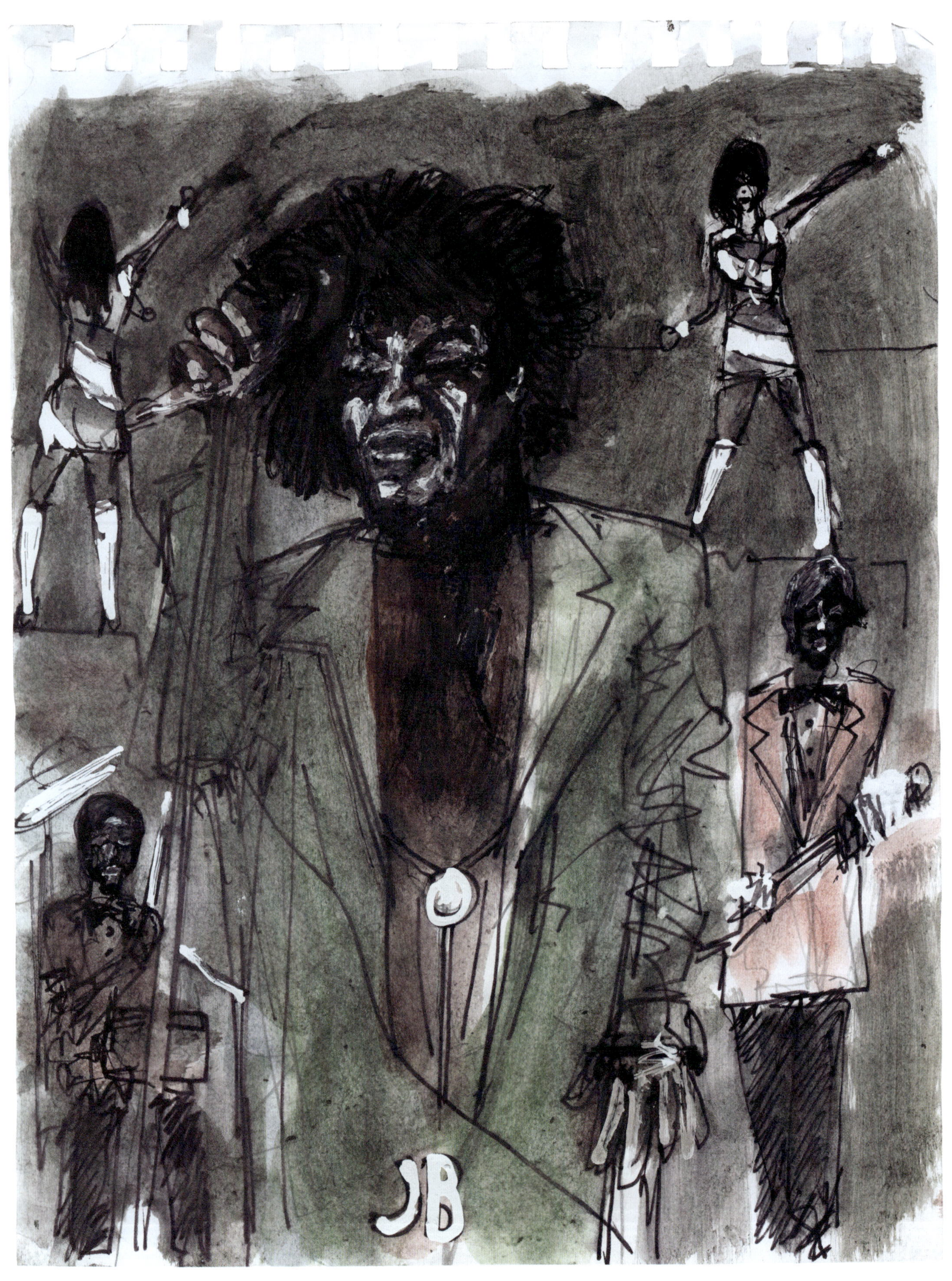

James Brown singlehandedly took a lost and confused nation of people and bonded them with a fix of words, music and attitude.

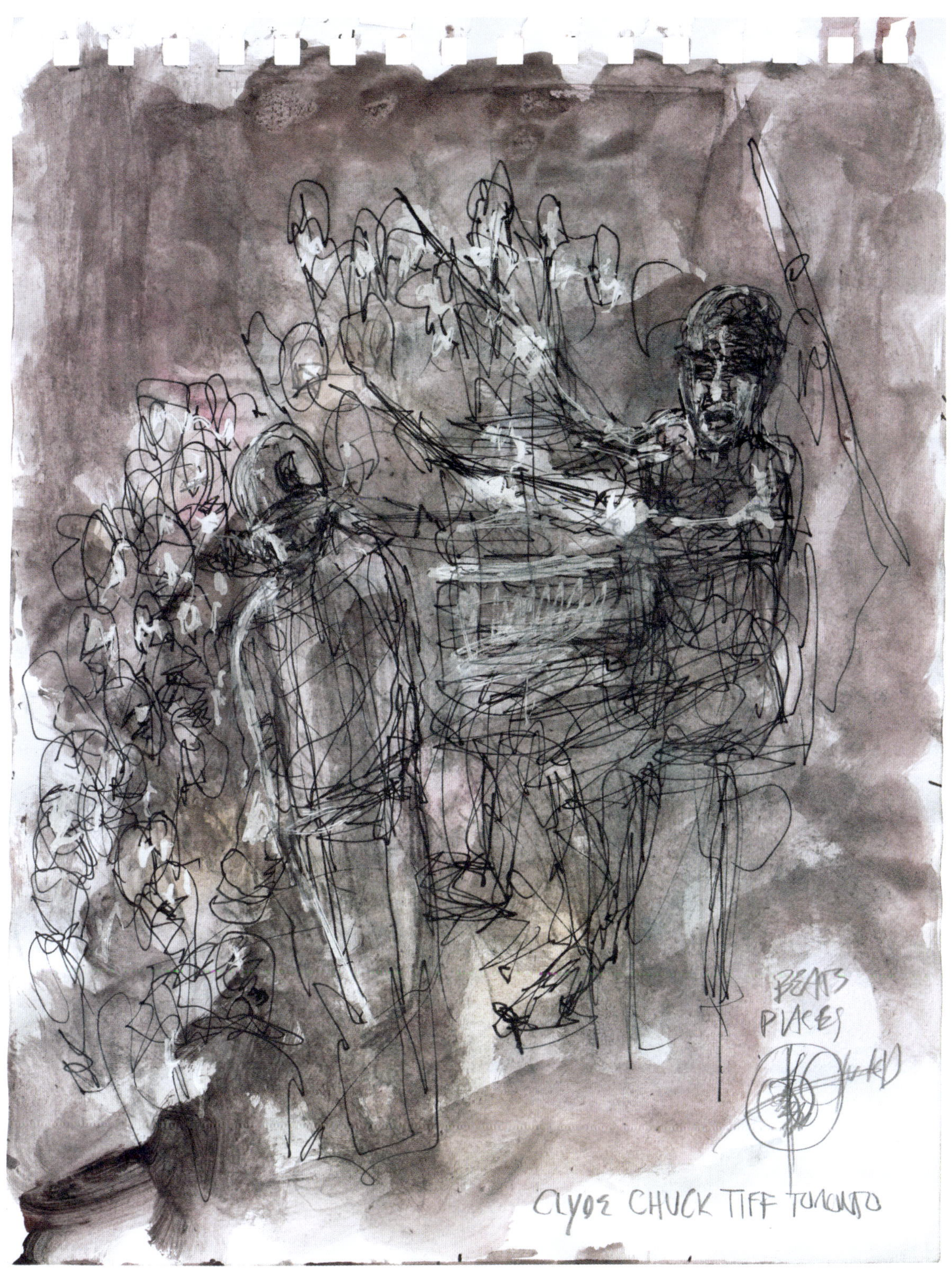

James Brown understood that Clyde Stubblefield was the one who took him to the next level, and he expressed that in his songs clearly. He let the world know that Clyde was the funk in his bones. I'm very honoured to have had conversations and performed with the man.

'Say It Loud – I'm Black and I'm Proud' was the phrase that prepared me for the third grade in 1969, and for the rest of my life. Black now signified where we was at, a new discovery of our bad self. As an adult, I was always fascinated by James Brown. He was the musician who took us from negro, to coloured, to black in one swoop. We'd say it loud: 'I'm black and I'm proud.'

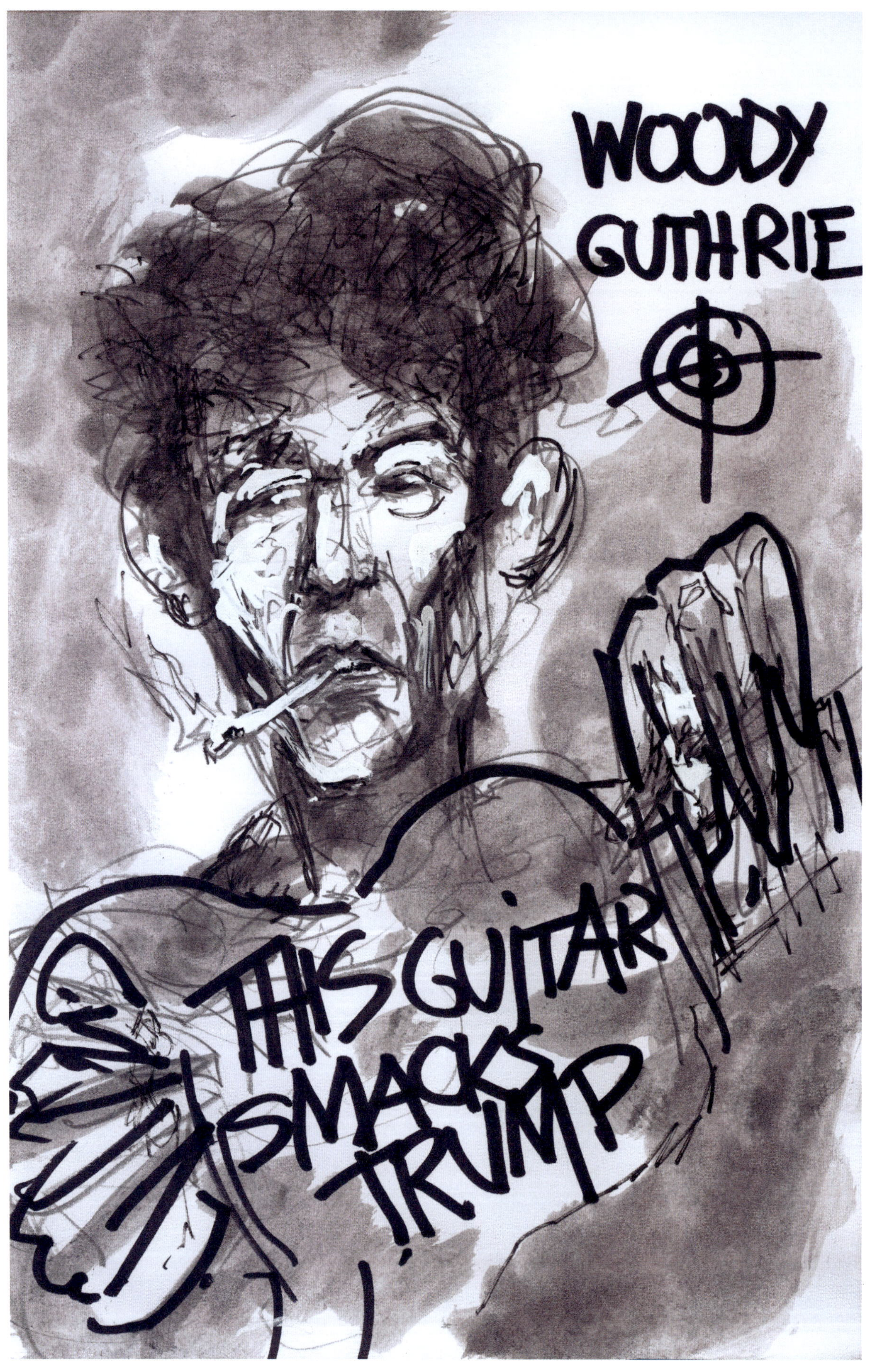

Woody Guthrie is the original rapper. Today is a Dust Bowl of a different sort. You have a political climate that is akin to a Dust Bowl, and it's swirling in the minds of confused Americans.

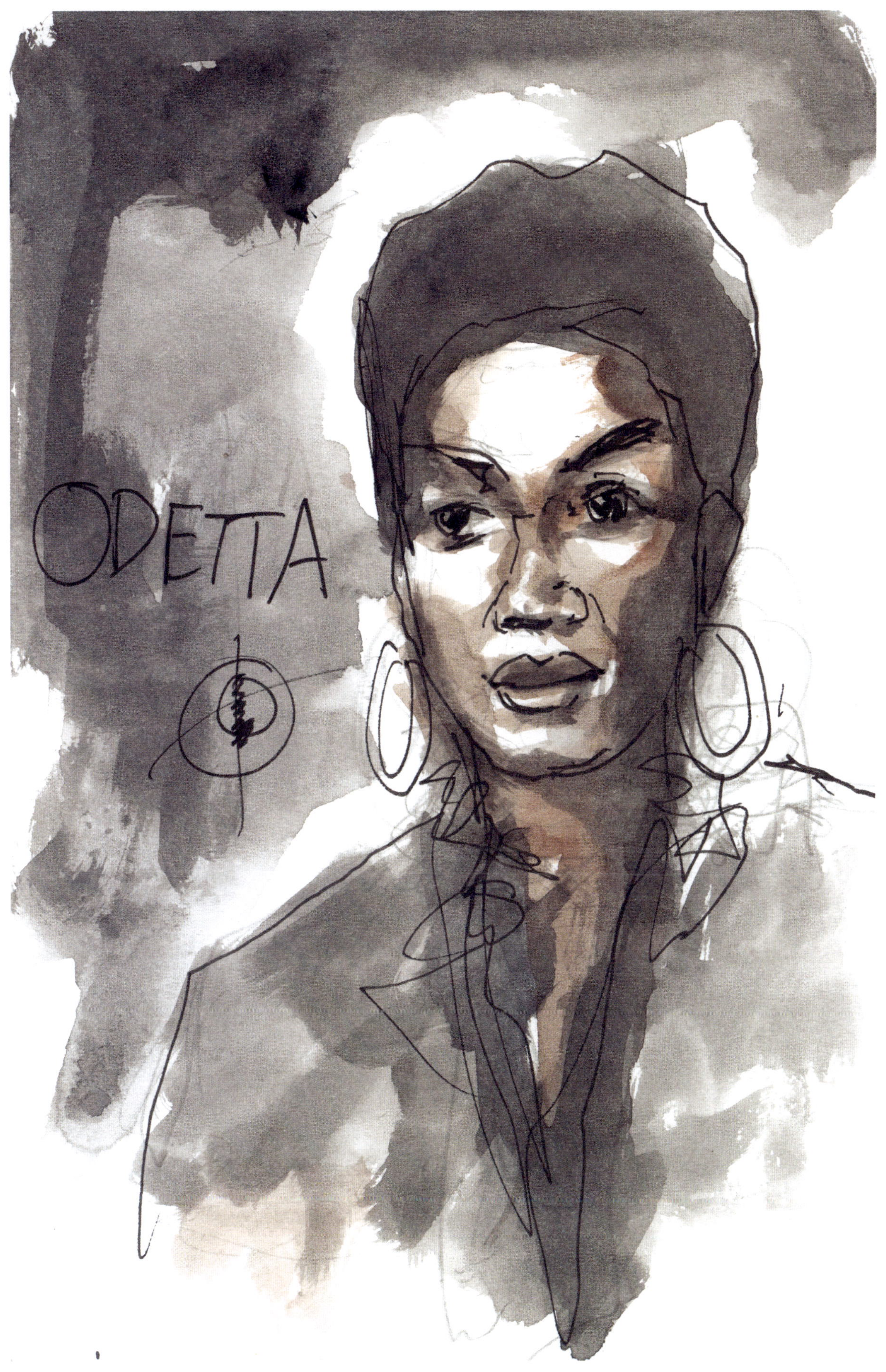

The Sixties is my favourite musical era. It was the best collision of musicians, engineers and experimentation. They made the most out of what little they had – it was sheer innovation.

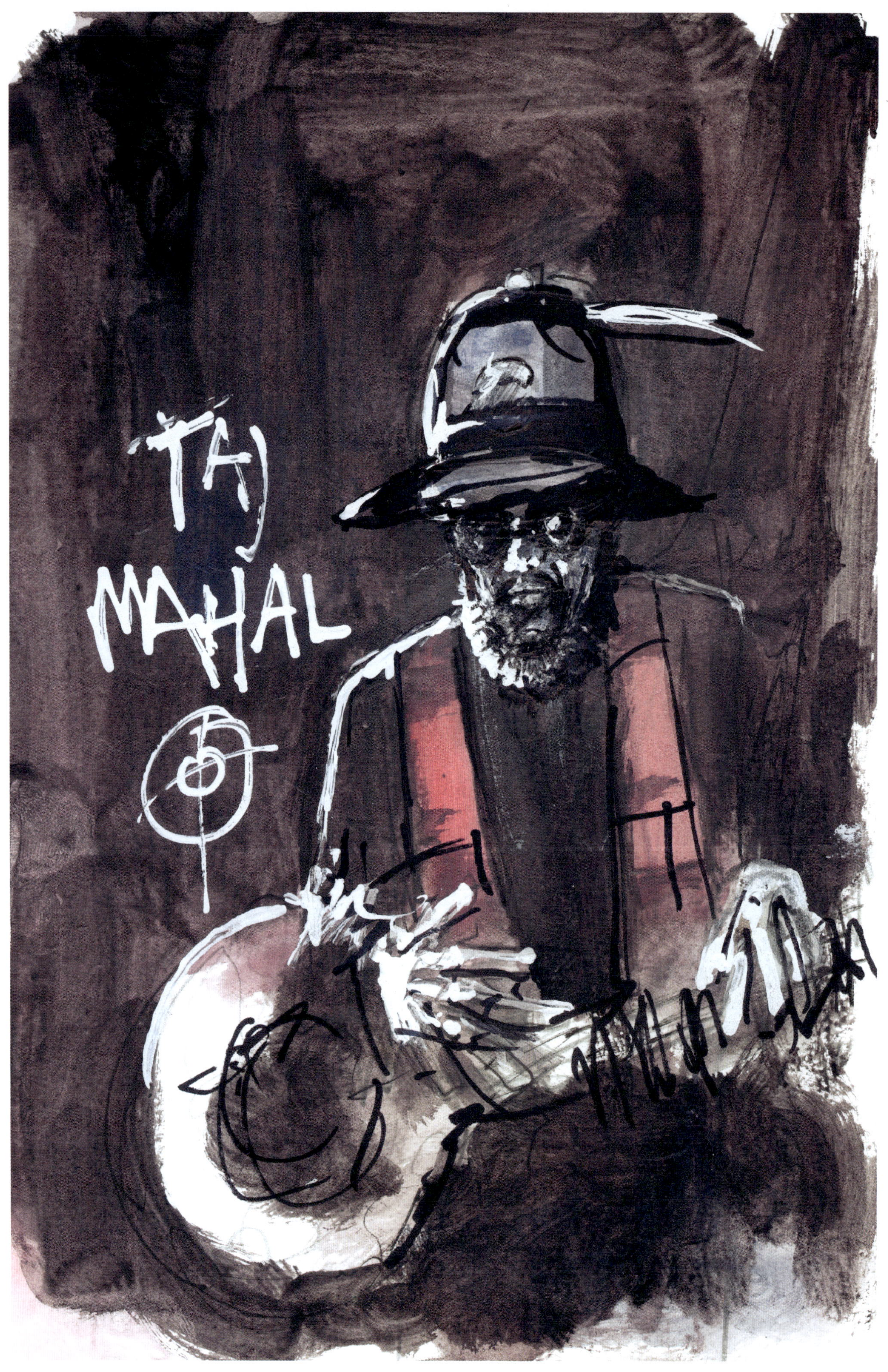
TAJ
MAHAL

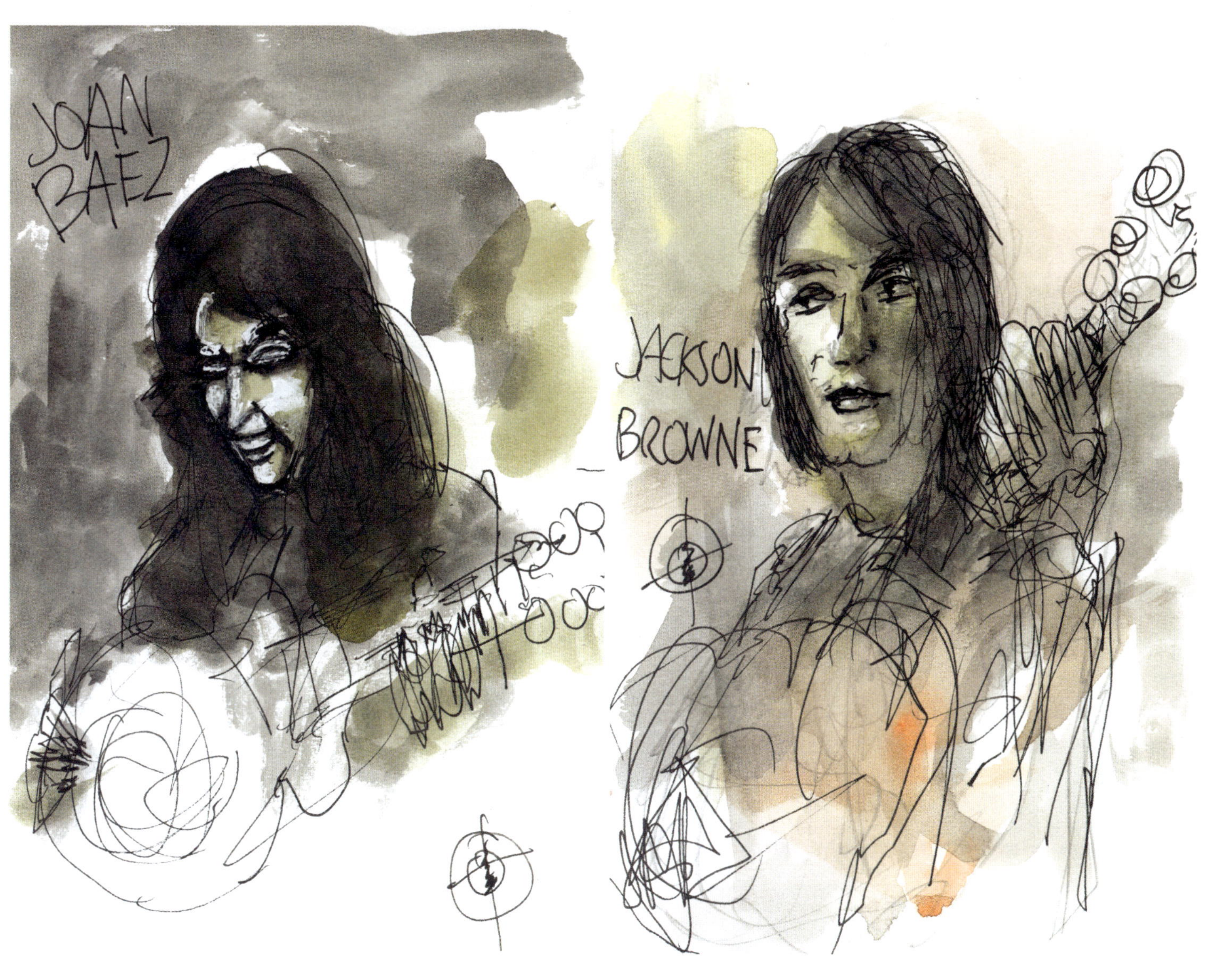

The soundtrack to my high school senior year was the great Jackson Browne.
I have listened to 'These Days' a thousand times.

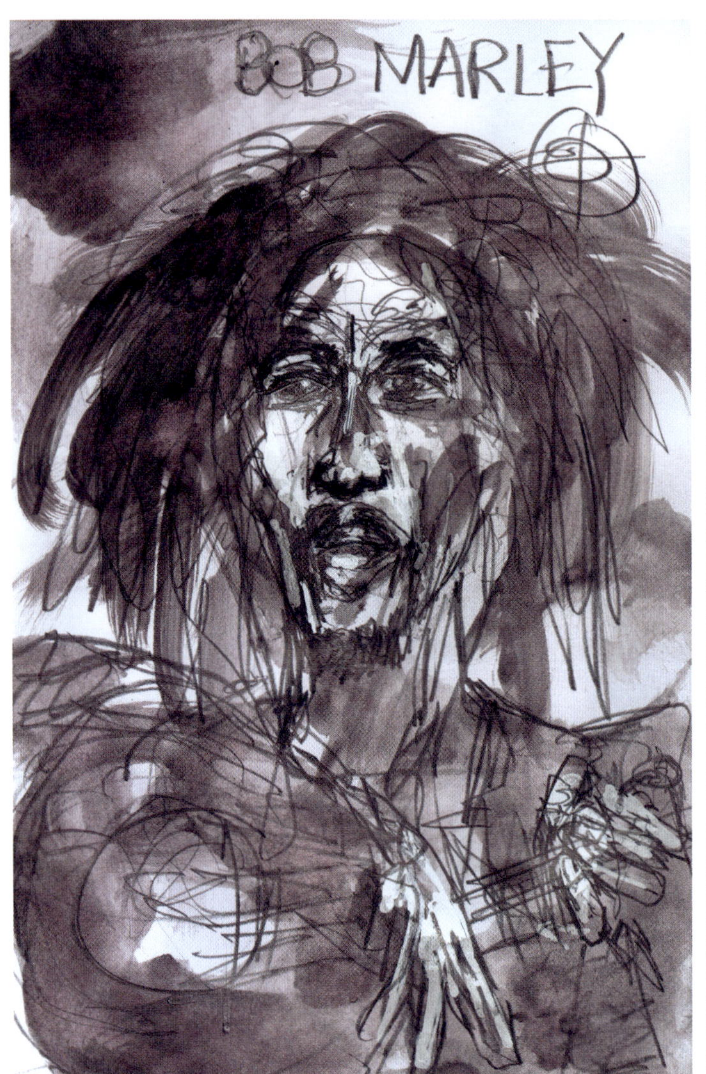

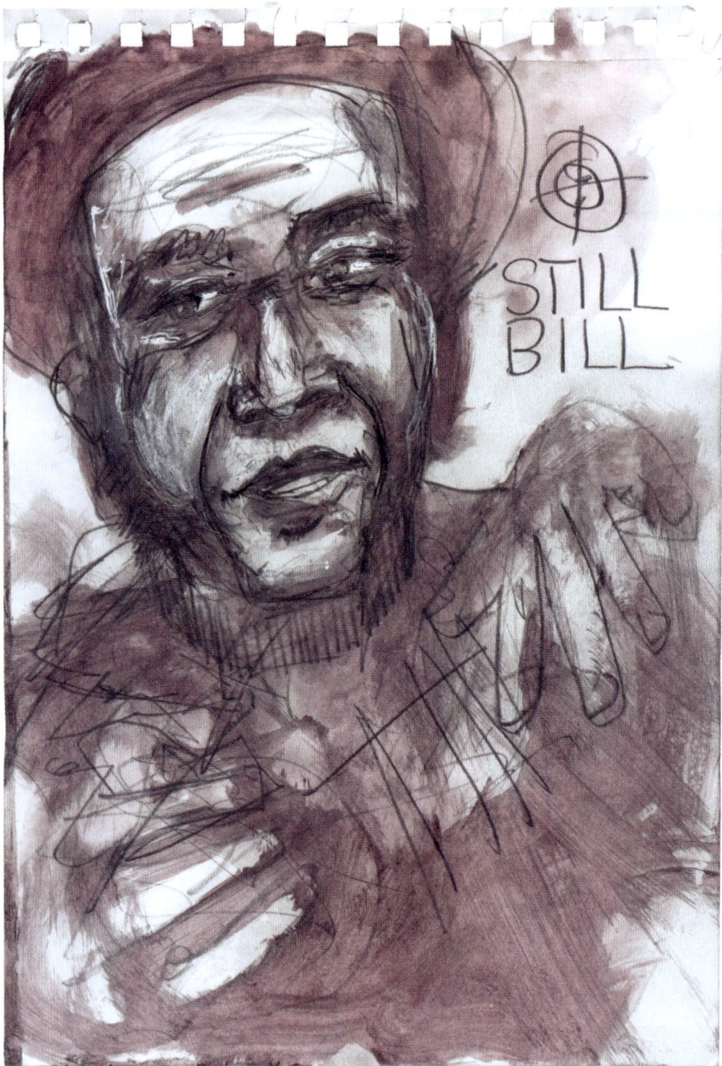

A lot of people respect Bob Marley. He was a giant in music around the world. I'm still just hoping to work up to that level someday.

I never set out to be another Bob Marley or another anyone in music. What Public Enemy does have in common with artists like the Clash and Bob Marley is that you can play the music today and think, 'Damn, what they're saying is as important today as it was back then.' It becomes a powerful historical document of a particular time of struggle and resistance. But this is the purpose of artists like Public Enemy – to speak truth to power.

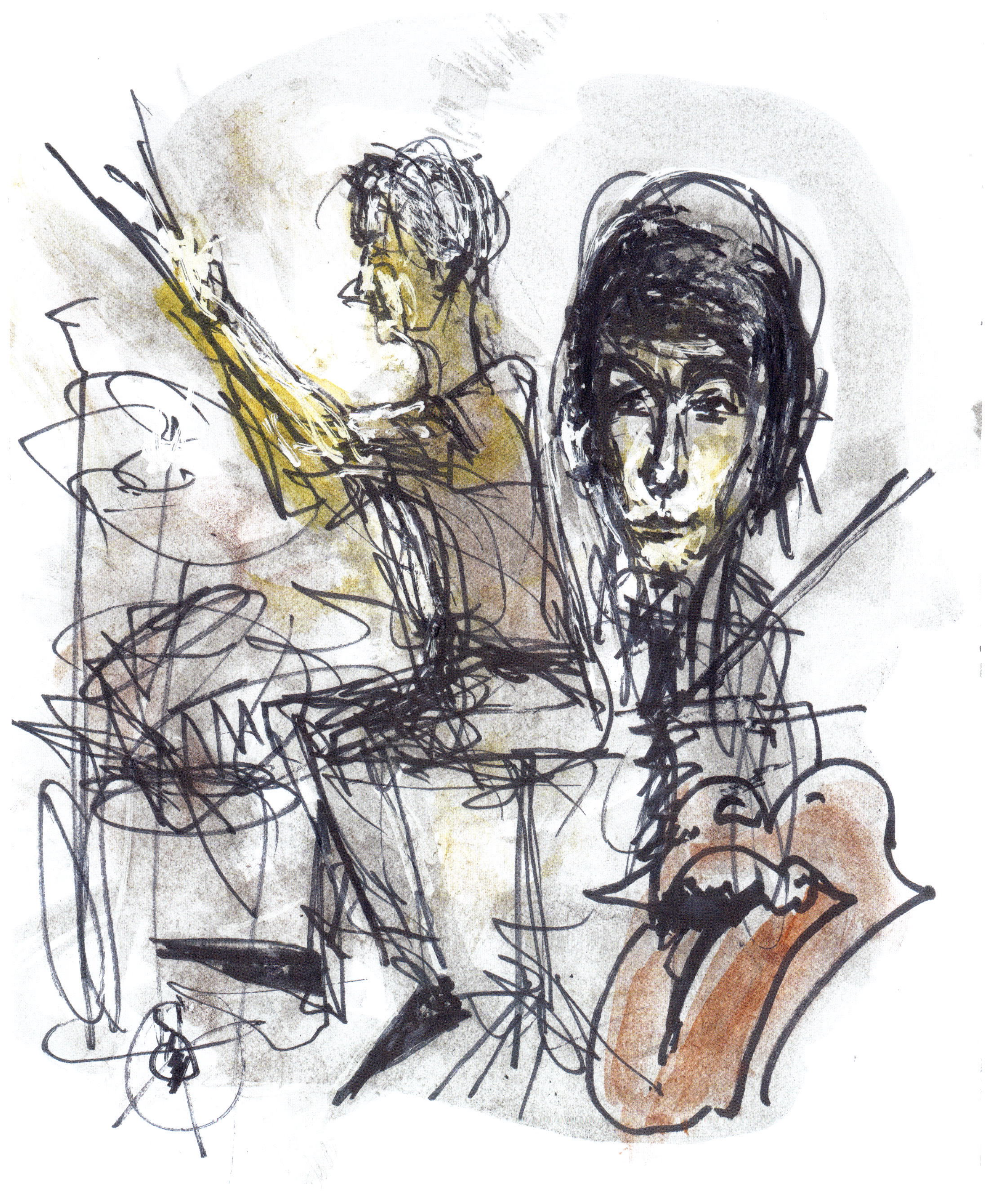

Here's an homage to the great Charlie Watts.

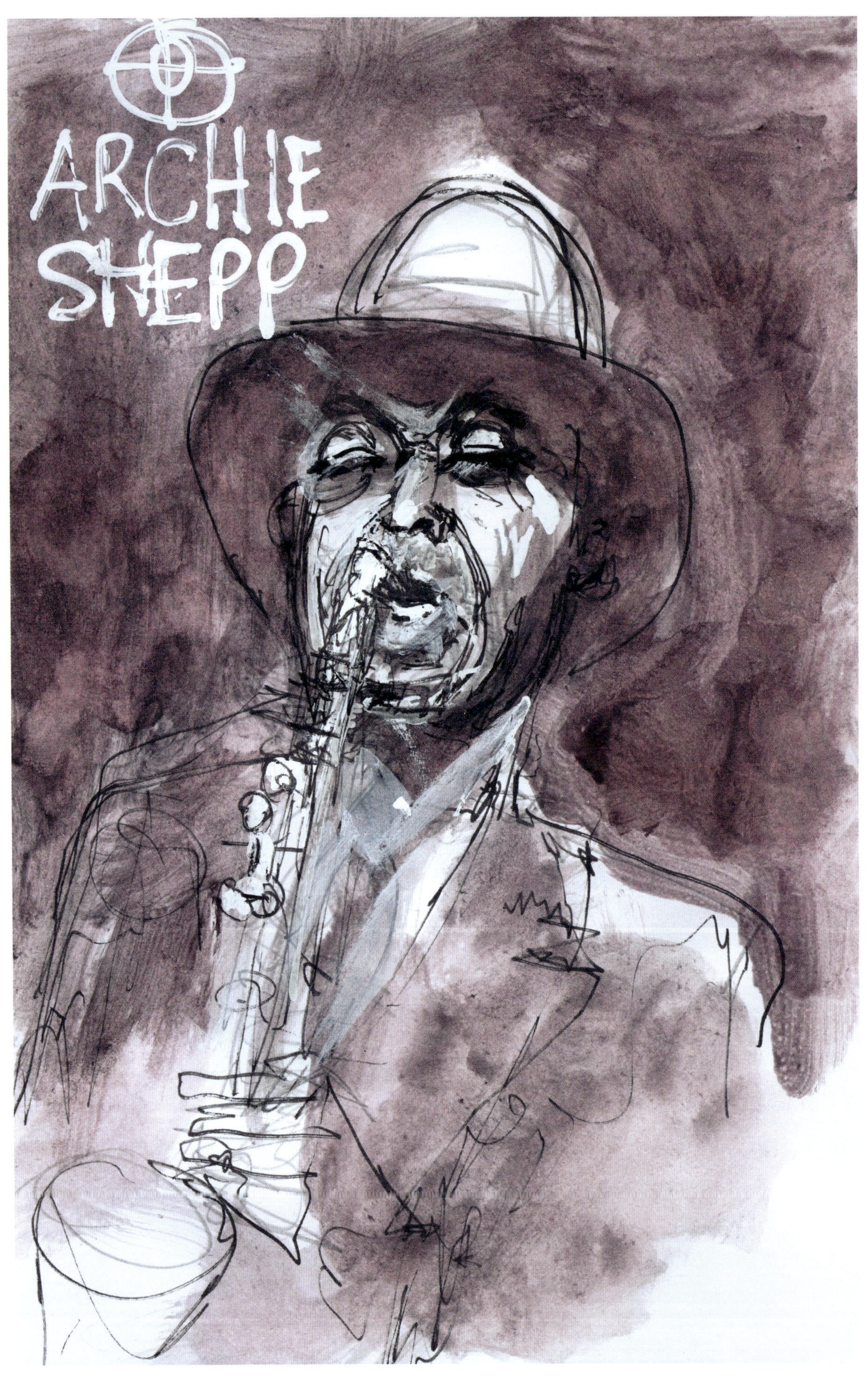

The great jazz artist Mr Archie Shepp, whom
I had pleasure of working with in Paris.

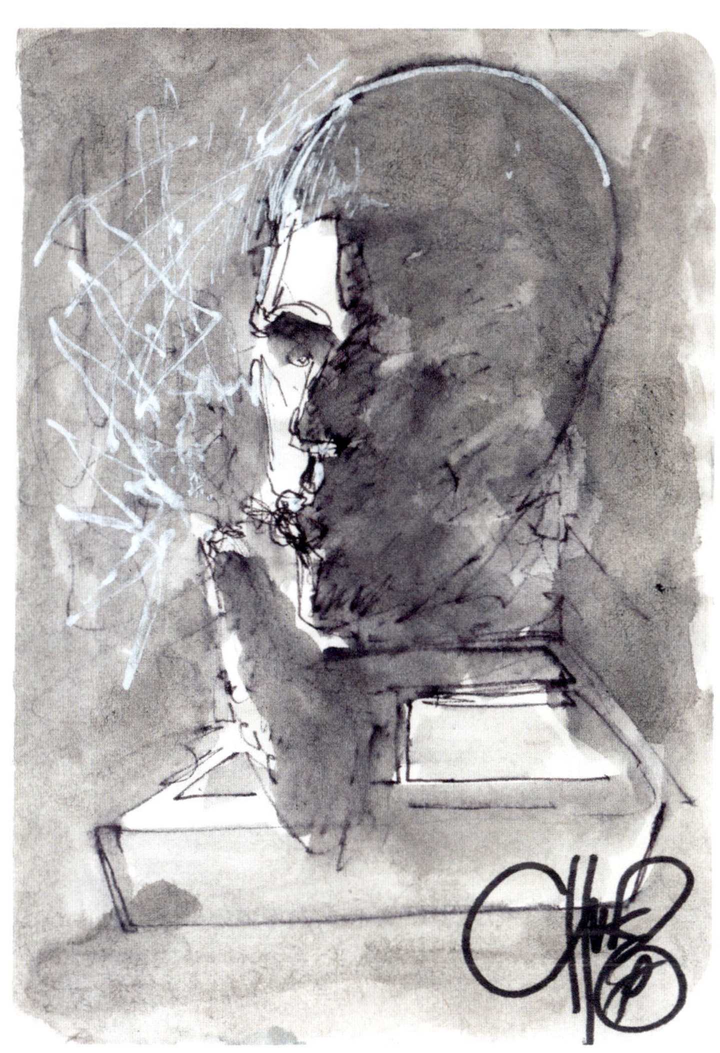

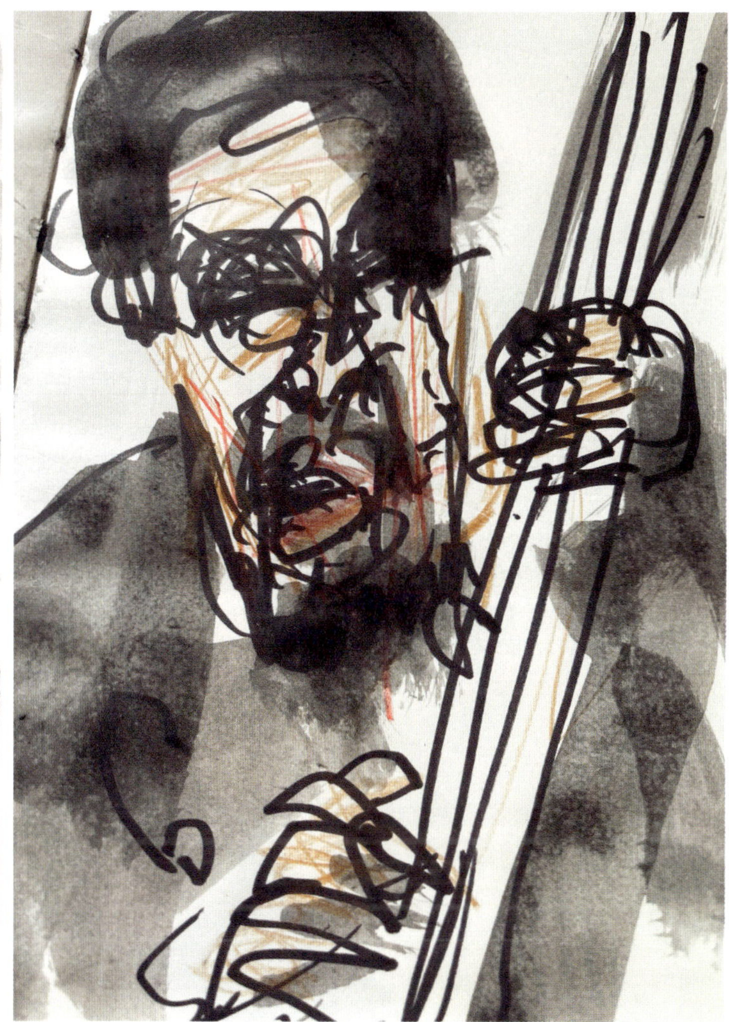

I always liked the Blue Note aesthetic more than the music.
The music is OK – it's jazz, it's cool – but I love the cover art. I'm hit by different tangents of what I love in art. The piece on the left was inspired by Dexter Gordon's Blue Note style.

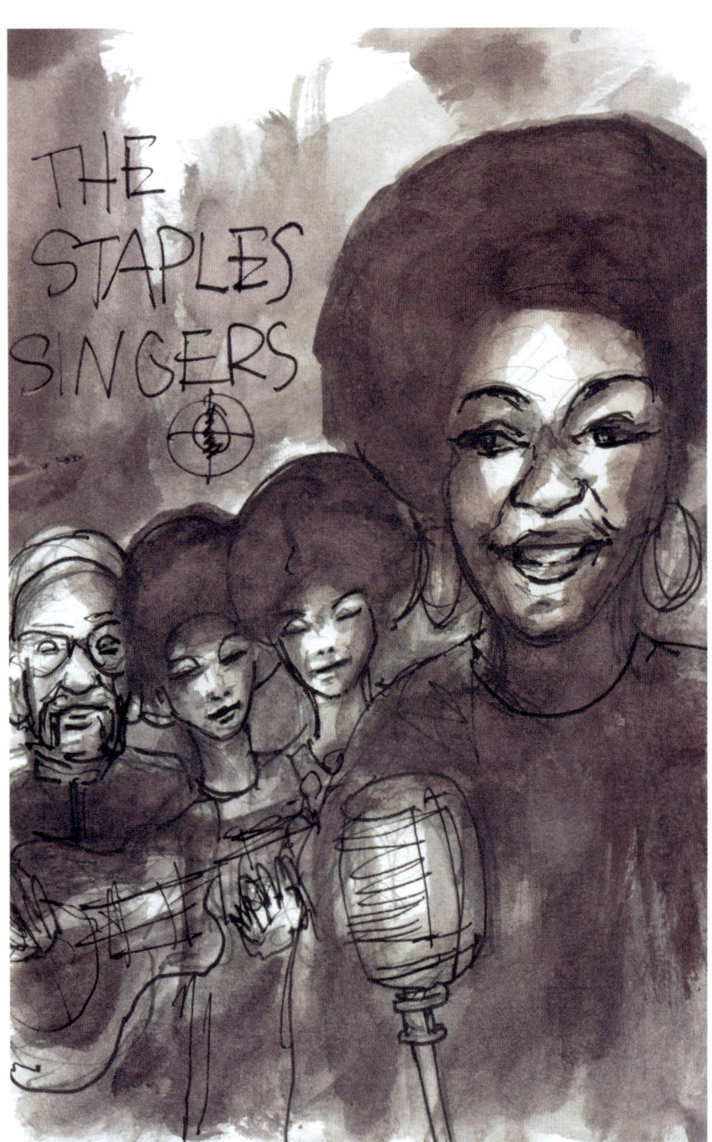

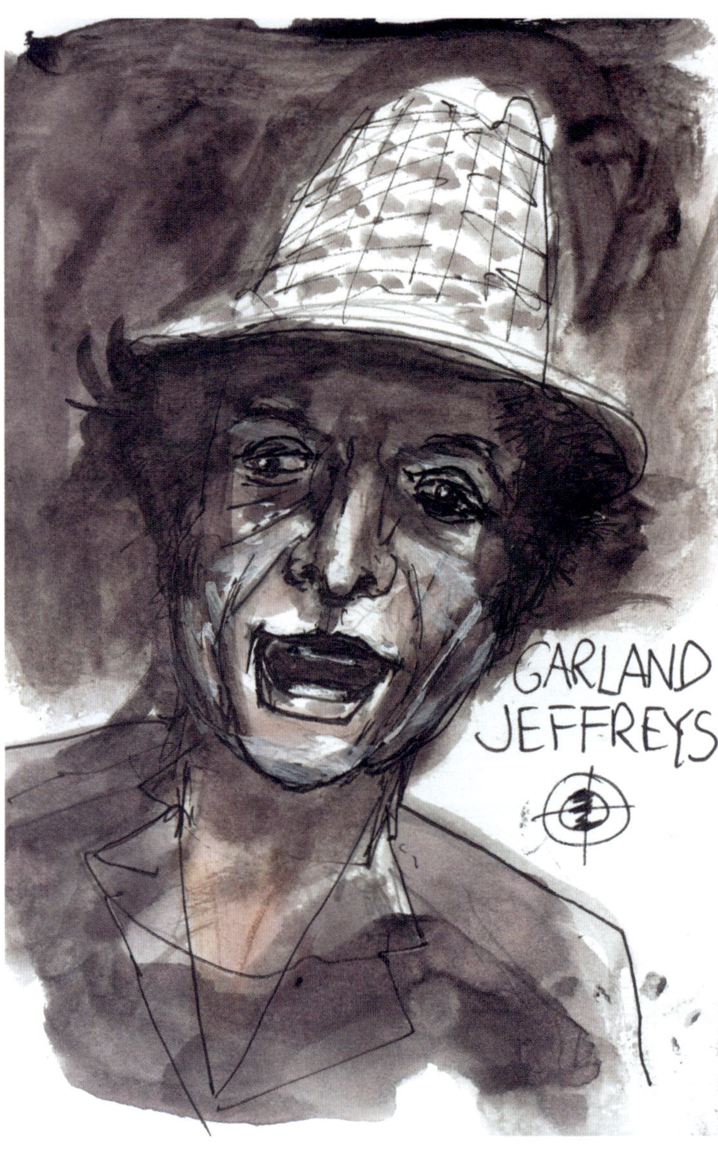

Know your history.

The history of music is very inviting to me. I listen to so much music out of the Forties and Fifties now. I like blues – Howlin' Wolf. I like rock 'n' roll from its very beginnings – Little Richard, Chuck Berry, Elvis, Bo Diddley – all the way up to what rock is today. And you have areas of funk such as James Brown and George Clinton. I love Aretha Franklin, Ike and Tina Turner, Nina Simone. To be the best hip-hop DJ, you must have a full knowledge of the records you're playing, the artists, the labels, where and when they came from. That's key if you want to get into hip-hop. Thoroughly be about it.

When people say they like hip-hop it's almost meaningless, because all music is embodied in hip-hop. So, when you like hip-hop you like all music.

BLUES

FOLK

COUNTRY

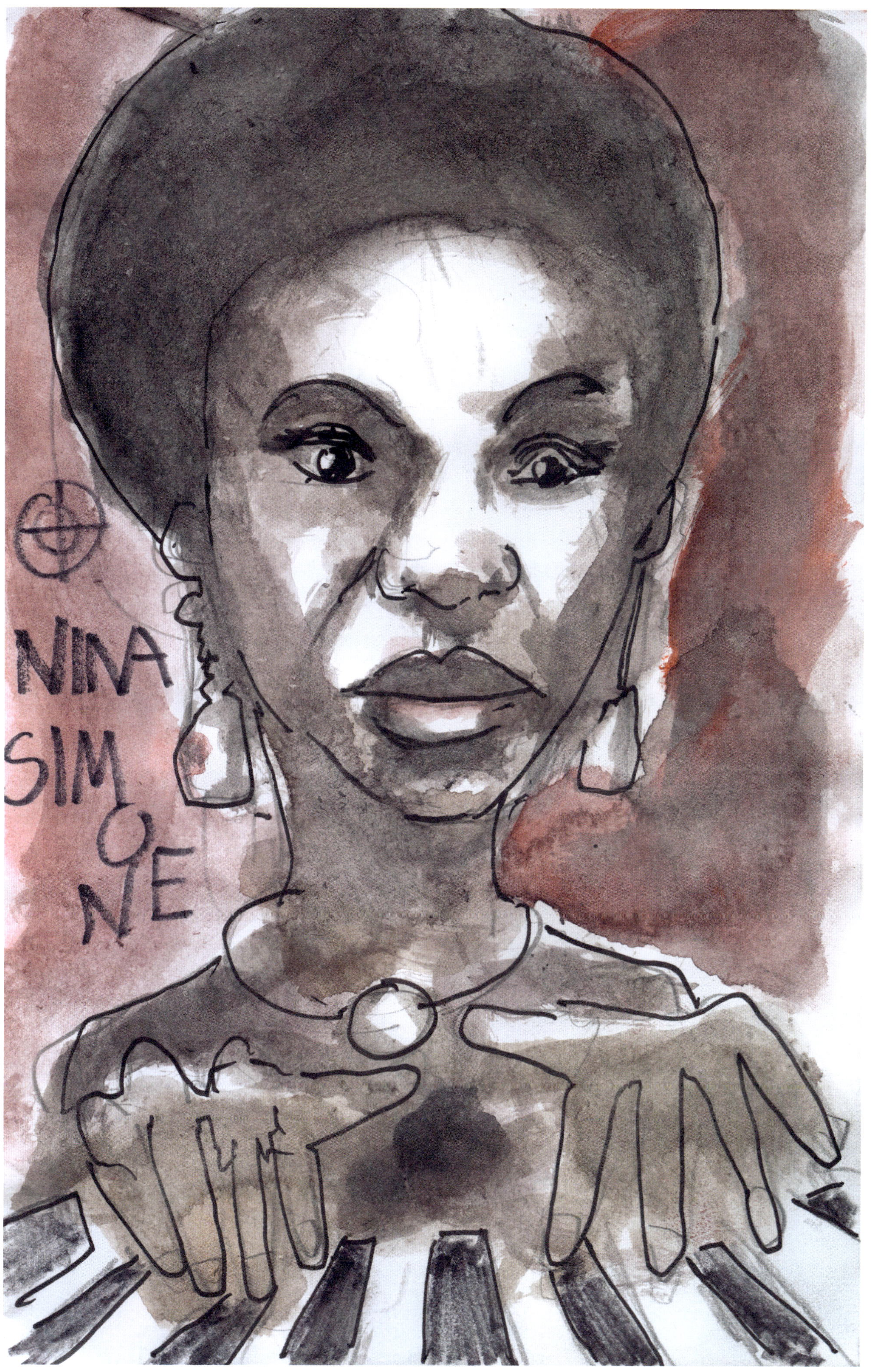
NINA
SIM
O
NE

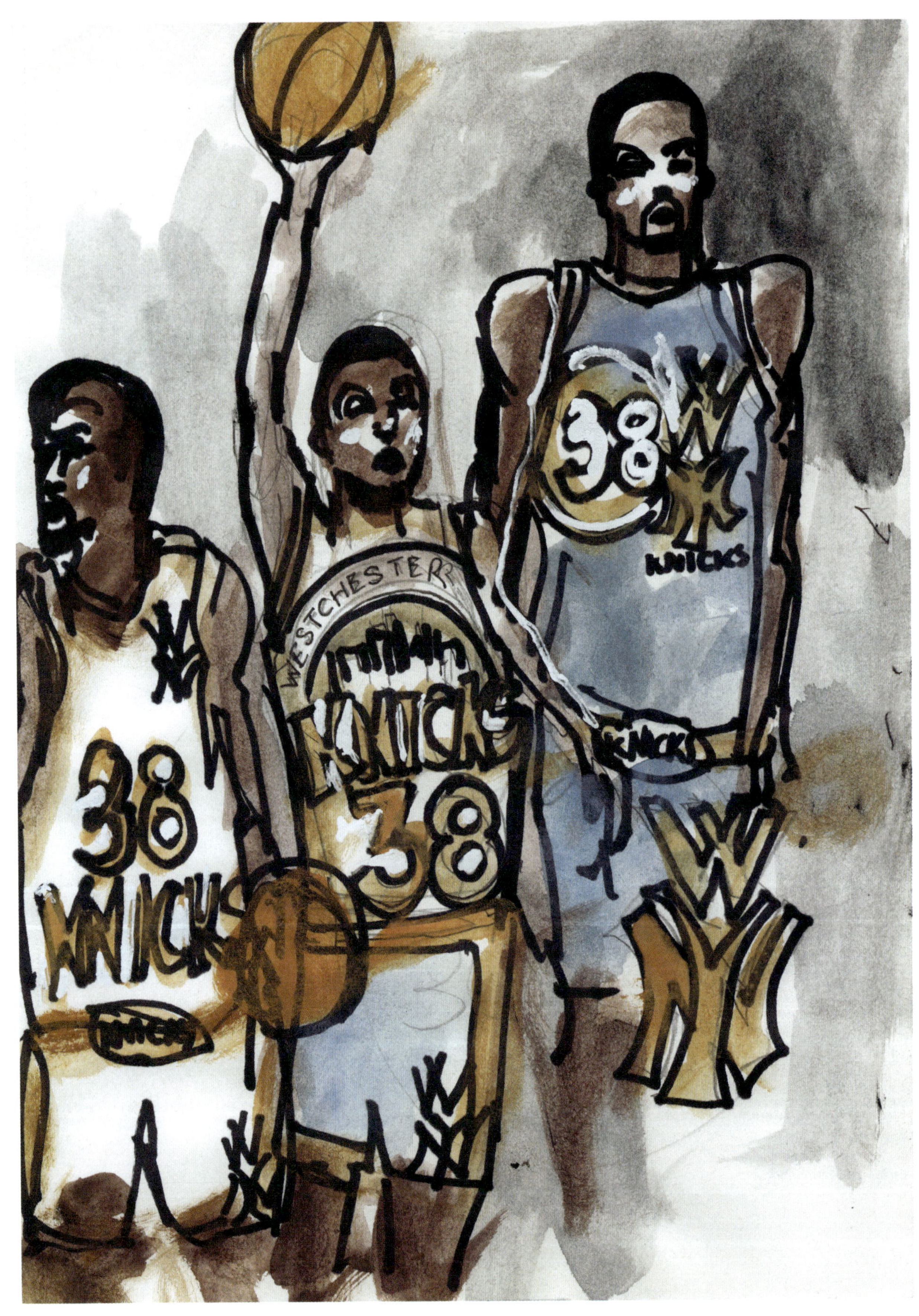

I've been a Knicks fan since 1967. They are heroes and spoke through culture, music, entertainment and sports.

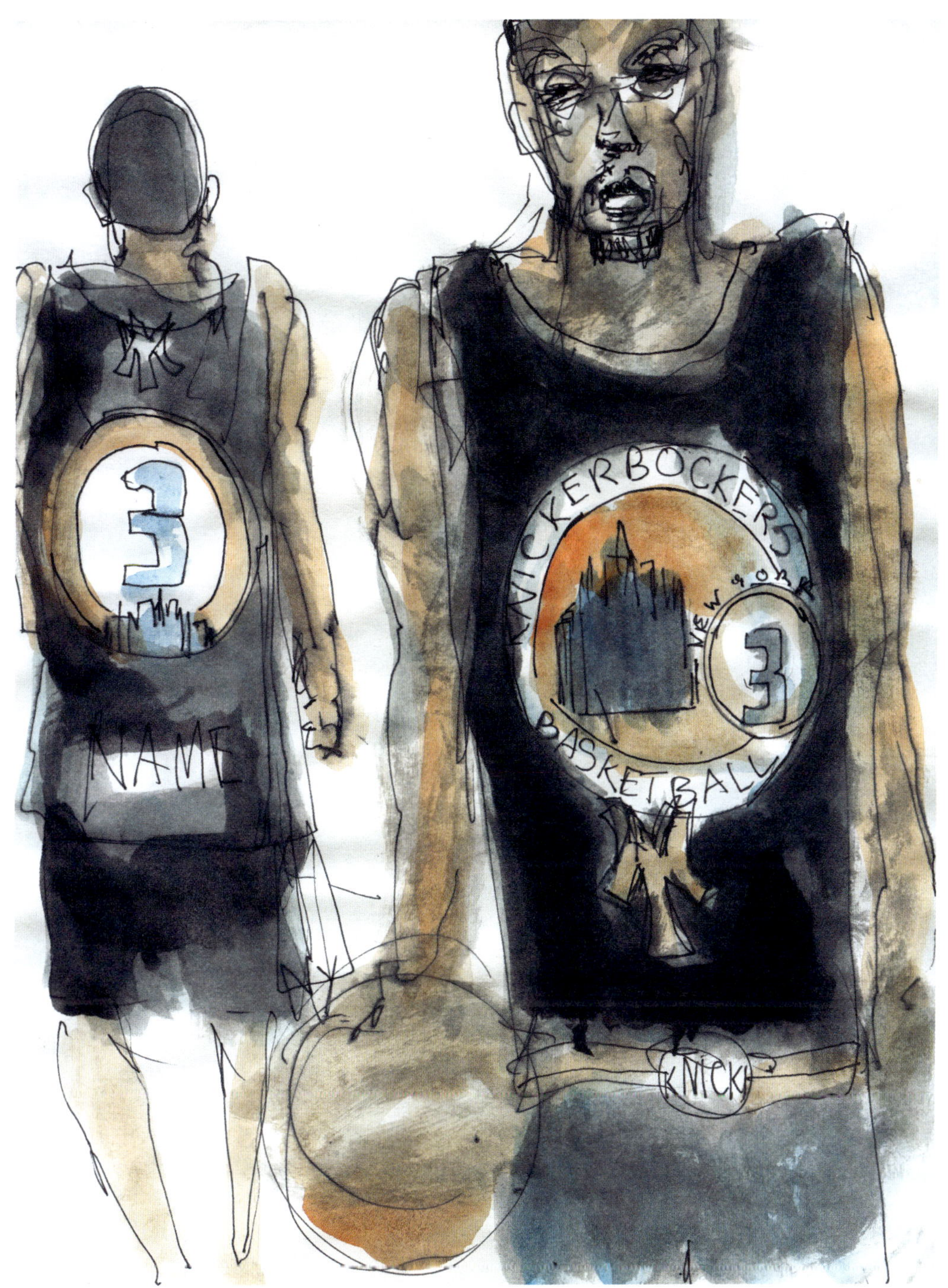

When I was a kid, I was such a sports idiot that the only person I ever wanted to be like was Julius Erving, Dr J. Later, I wanted to be the Dr J of rap. He came from Roosevelt and was the unprecedented hero of our square mile town, as well as a super-humble man.

In the Seventies, getting out of the hood to do music or comedy was inconceivable, but the basketball dream was alive and well, with Dr J being the absolute proof. There were a lot of people who chose basketball over books and lost sight of realities. One cat from Long Island went from being one of the state's best high school players to cracked out, drunken and homeless within eight years.

I've been befriended by heroes such as Kareem Abdul-Jabbar, Dr J, Earl the Pearl and George Gervin. These are all guys that rappers named themselves after. Ice Cube named himself after George Gervin, aka the Iceman; Dr Dre and Doctor Dré both named themselves after Dr J. In the late Seventies, Earl the Pearl was in everybody's rhymes. The interplay was ridiculous.

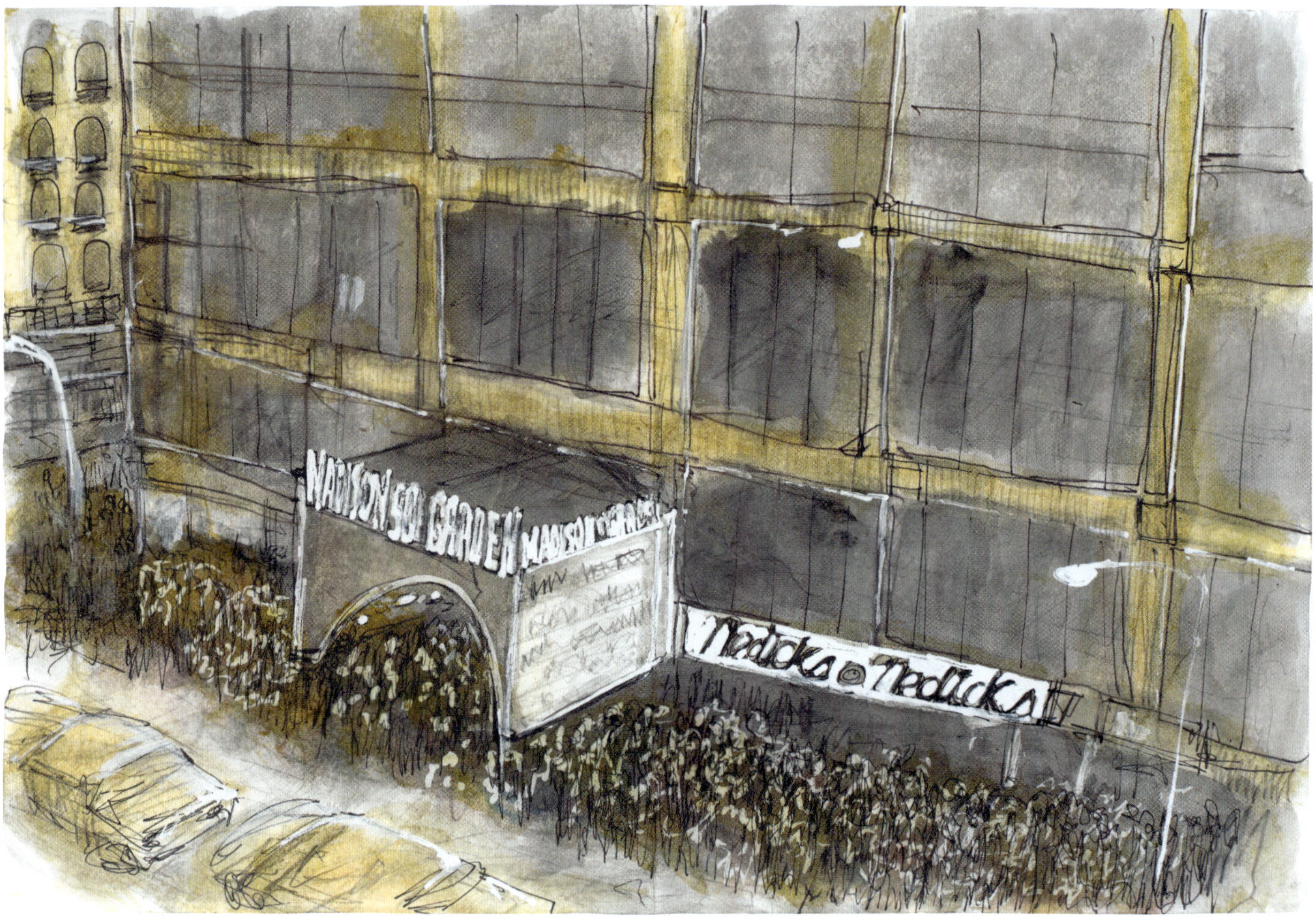

The old Madison Square Garden on 50th and 8th in New York City. I heard many stories about it from my parents. The Knicks played there in 1968, just before it was torn down, but I don't remember going there. I went to the present Garden later when the circus hit town.

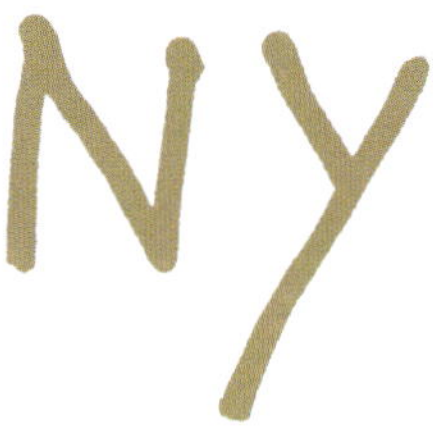

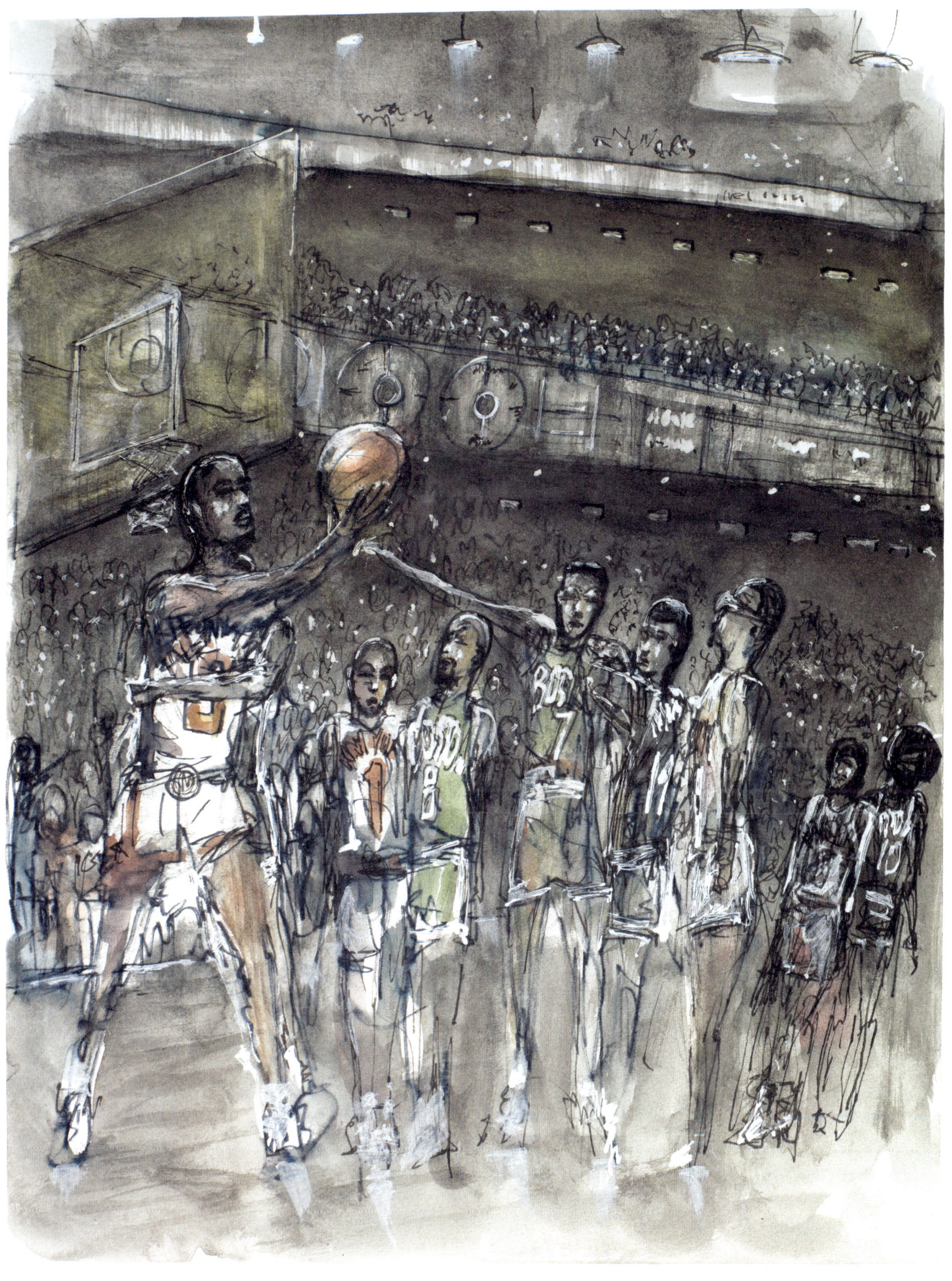

This is a Knicks versus Celtics battle at the old Madison Square Garden.
I based it on a combination of photos and imagination.

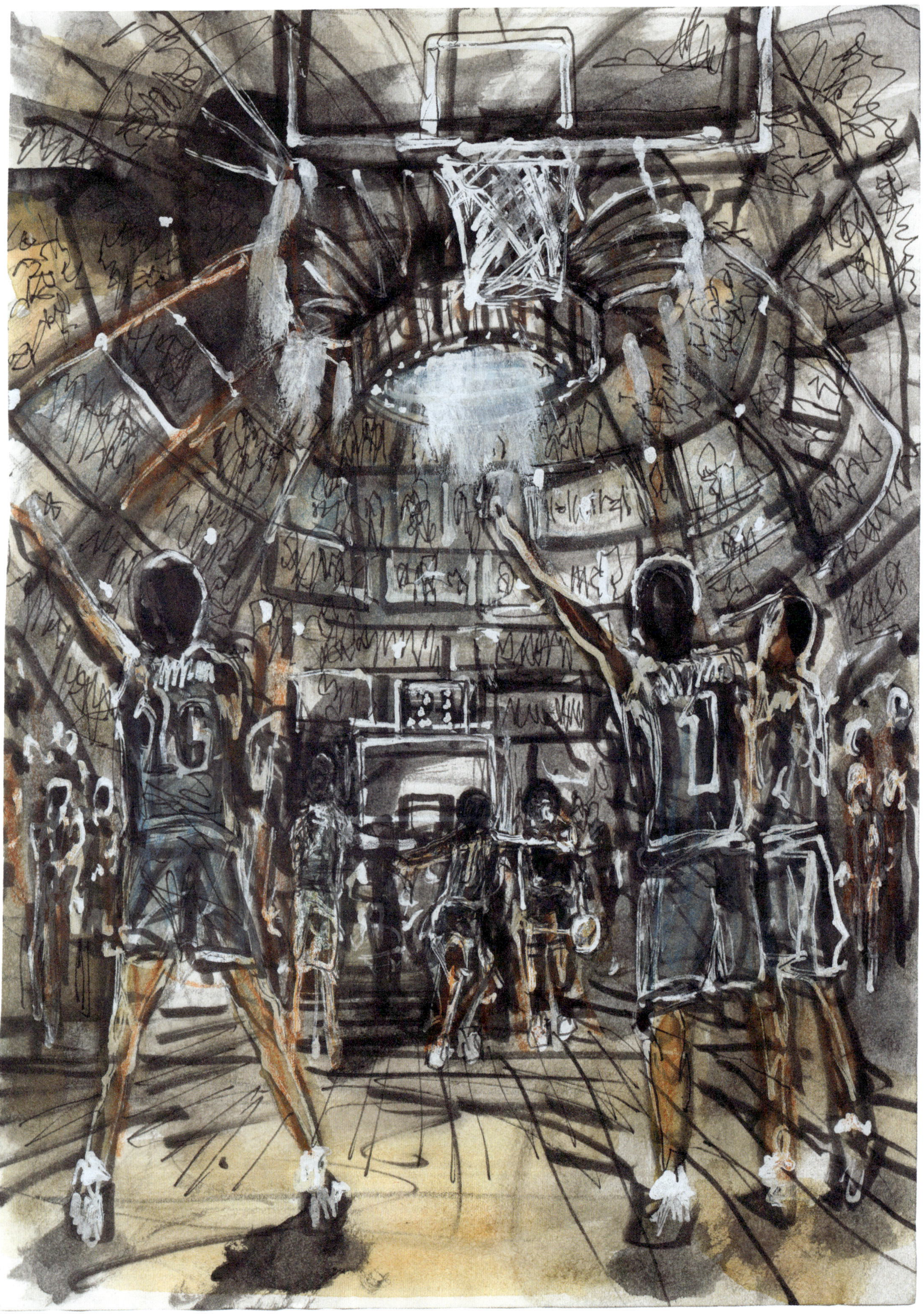

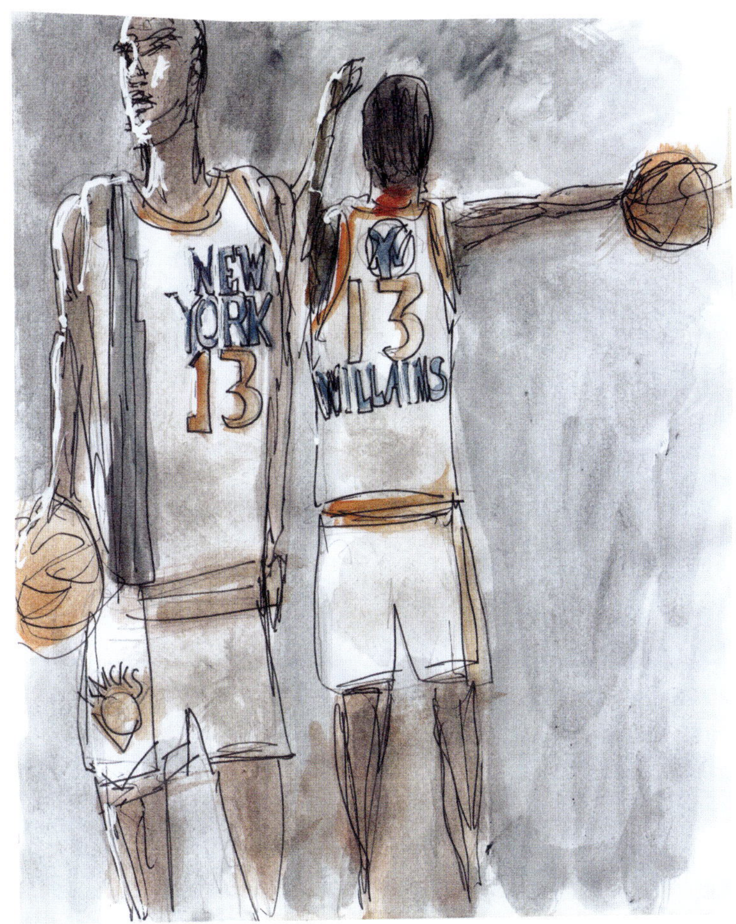

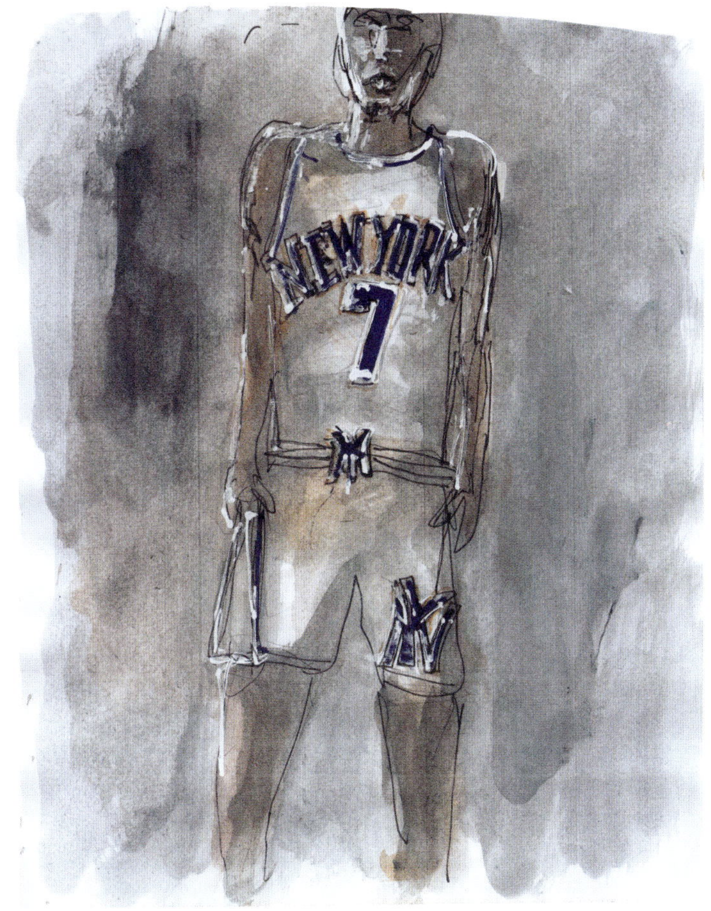

I still haven't seen many shooters like Carmelo Anthony. He's been through it. He mentors young players all over from both his own team and the opposition. When he talks, they listen. I've been saying for a long time that Anthony can play until 40 and it's good to see him as an OG in the league, especially in today's NBA.

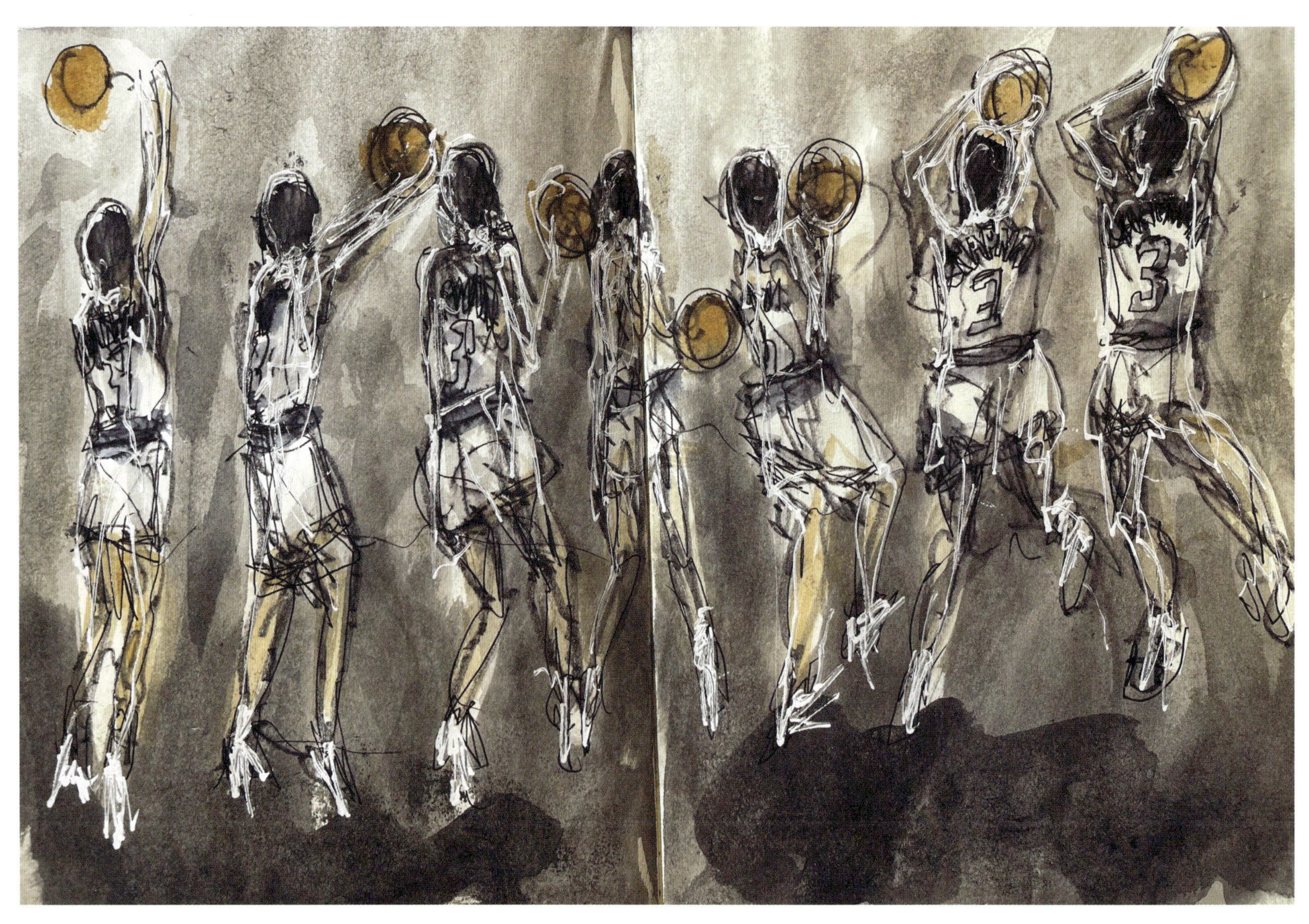

An abstract piece portraying Rex Chapman taking 'the shot' during the 1997 playoffs.

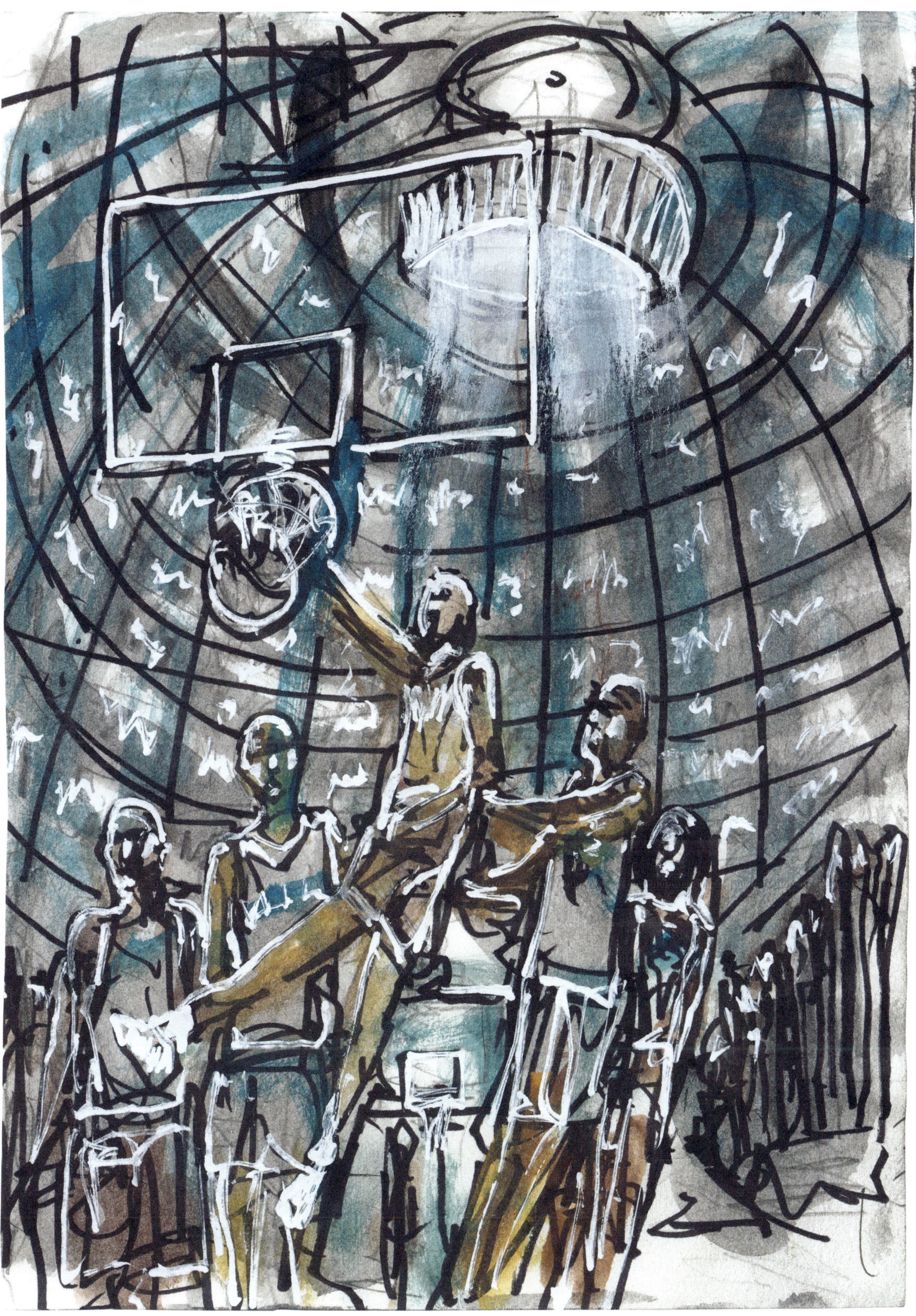

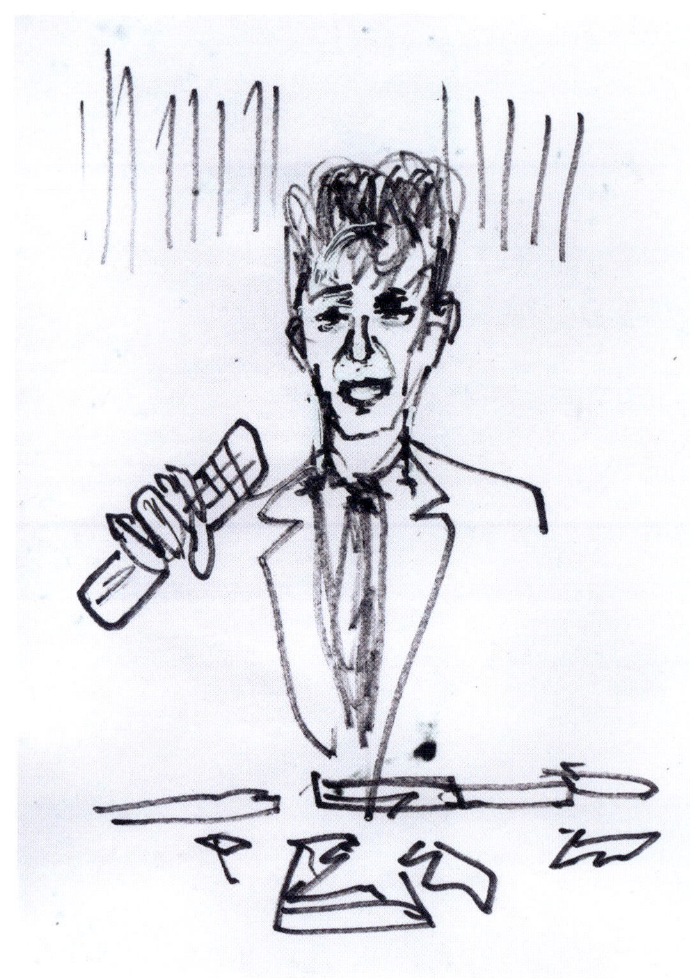

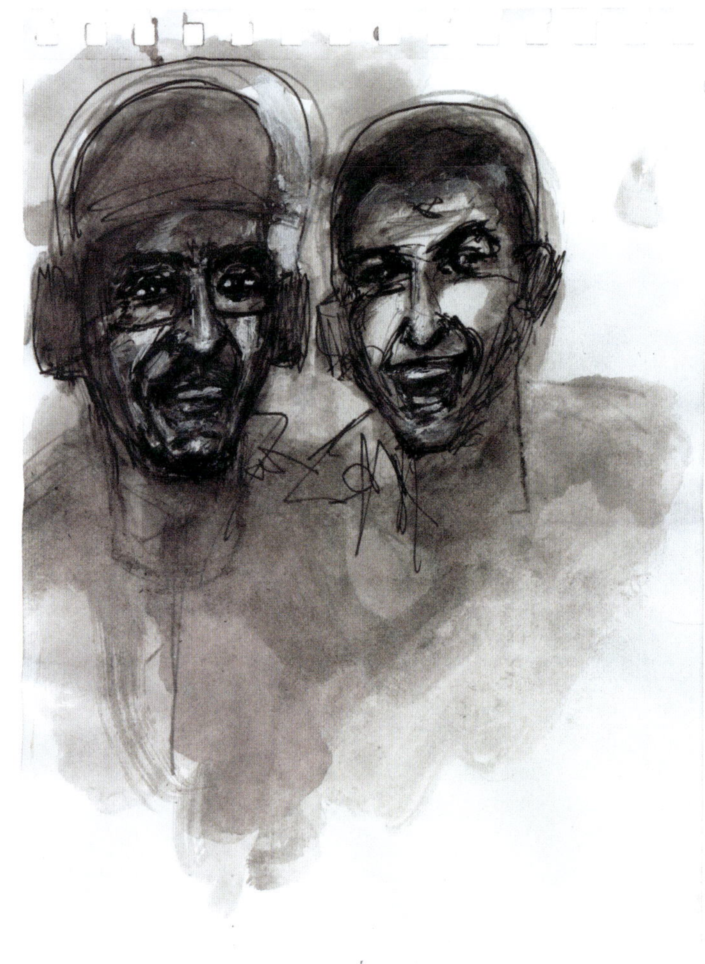

I grew up wanting to be a sportscaster or a baseball player and I ended up being a baseball nerd for many years before I moved into the record business. I took on being a musician the same way I took on being a baseball fan.

I'm a fan of *NBA Today* on SiriusXM, the flagship show that basketball great Eddie Johnson hosts daily with Justin Termine (shown together, above right). Music and sports have always been there, but with sports you have to engage yourself in front of a radio or a television, whereas music can be going on in the background.

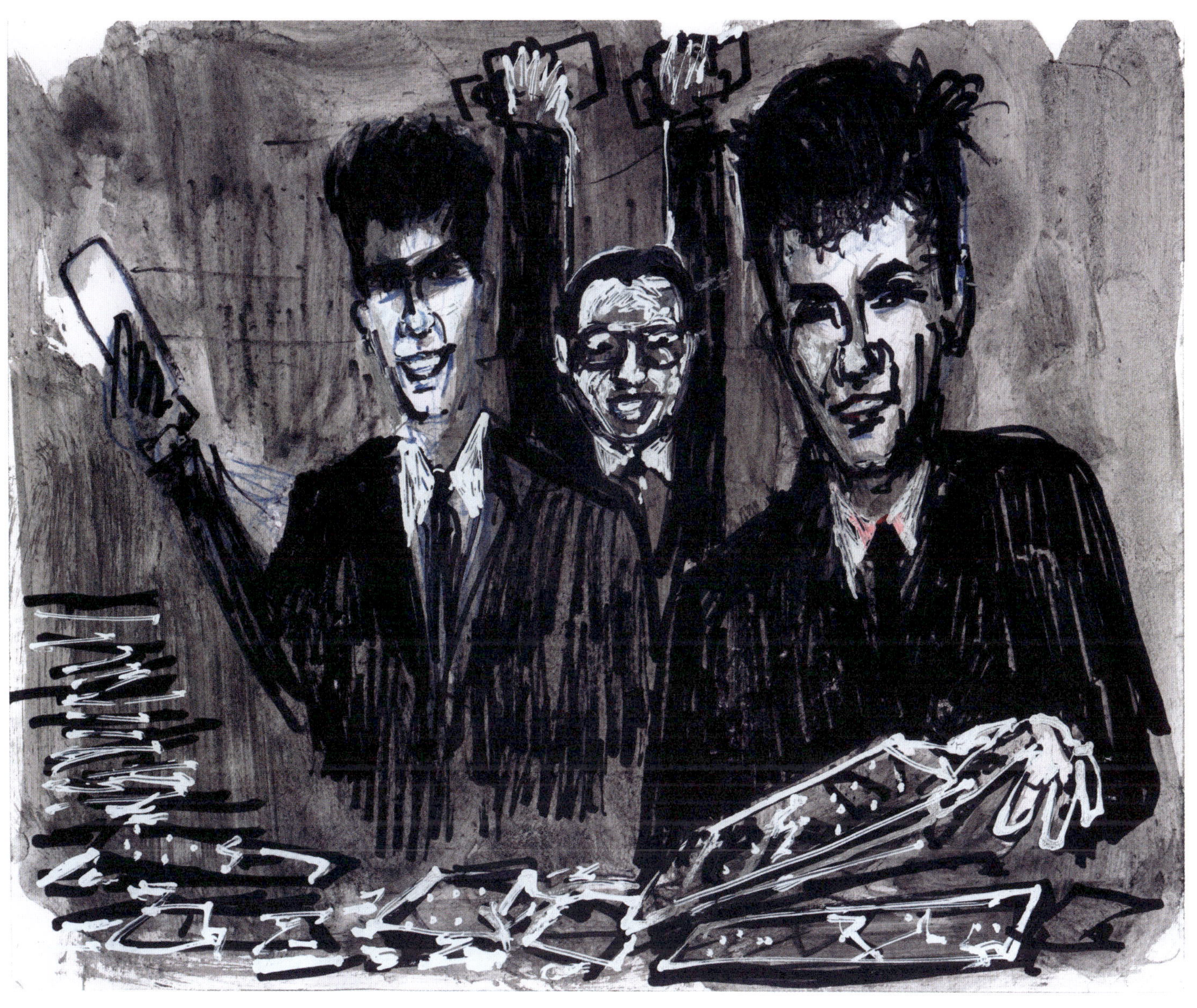

The thing that attracted me to hip-hop in 1976 was the technical aspect. The DJs – Frankie Crocker, Hank Spann – they all had their own style, like the great sportscasters. When hip-hop came around I saw it as a combination of the worlds of music and sport.

Way before doing the *He Got Game* soundtrack in 1998, I'd slip sports metaphors into my lyrics. I would practise my sportscaster voice and intonations either in my room at home playing some dice sports game or down at Roosevelt Park where the summer league basketball legends dwelled. I could get any of those voices down.

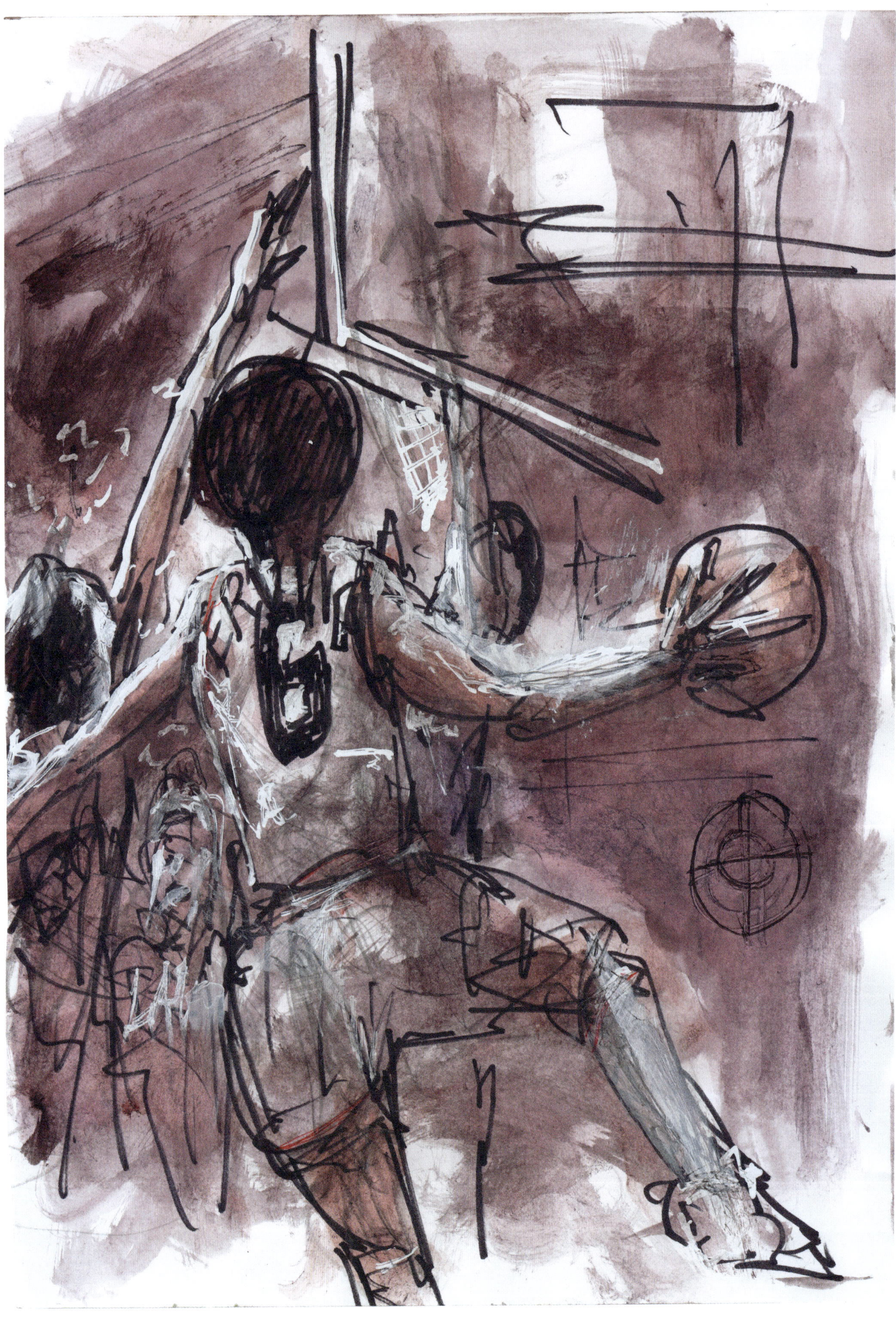

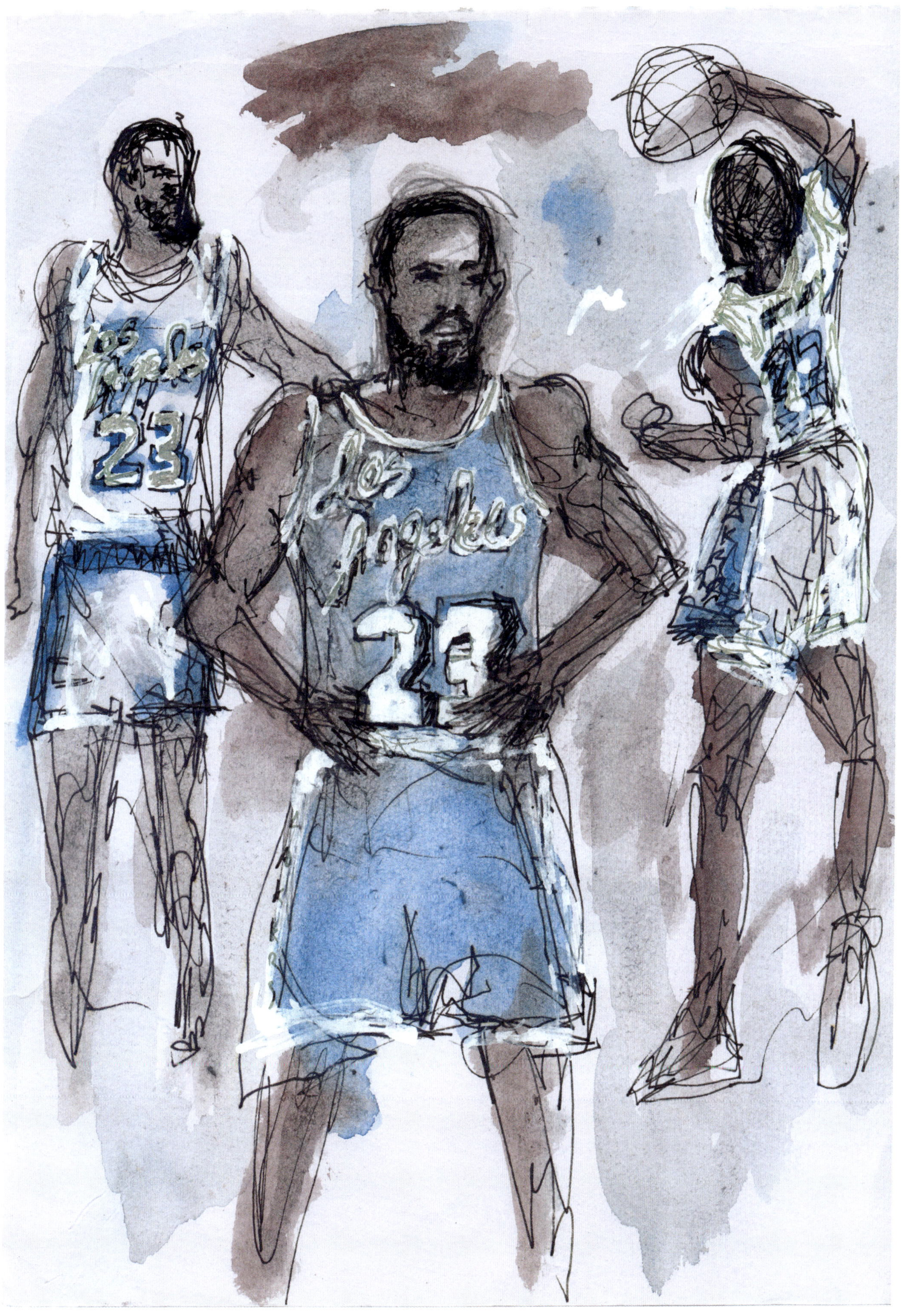
Los Angeles
23
Los Angeles
23

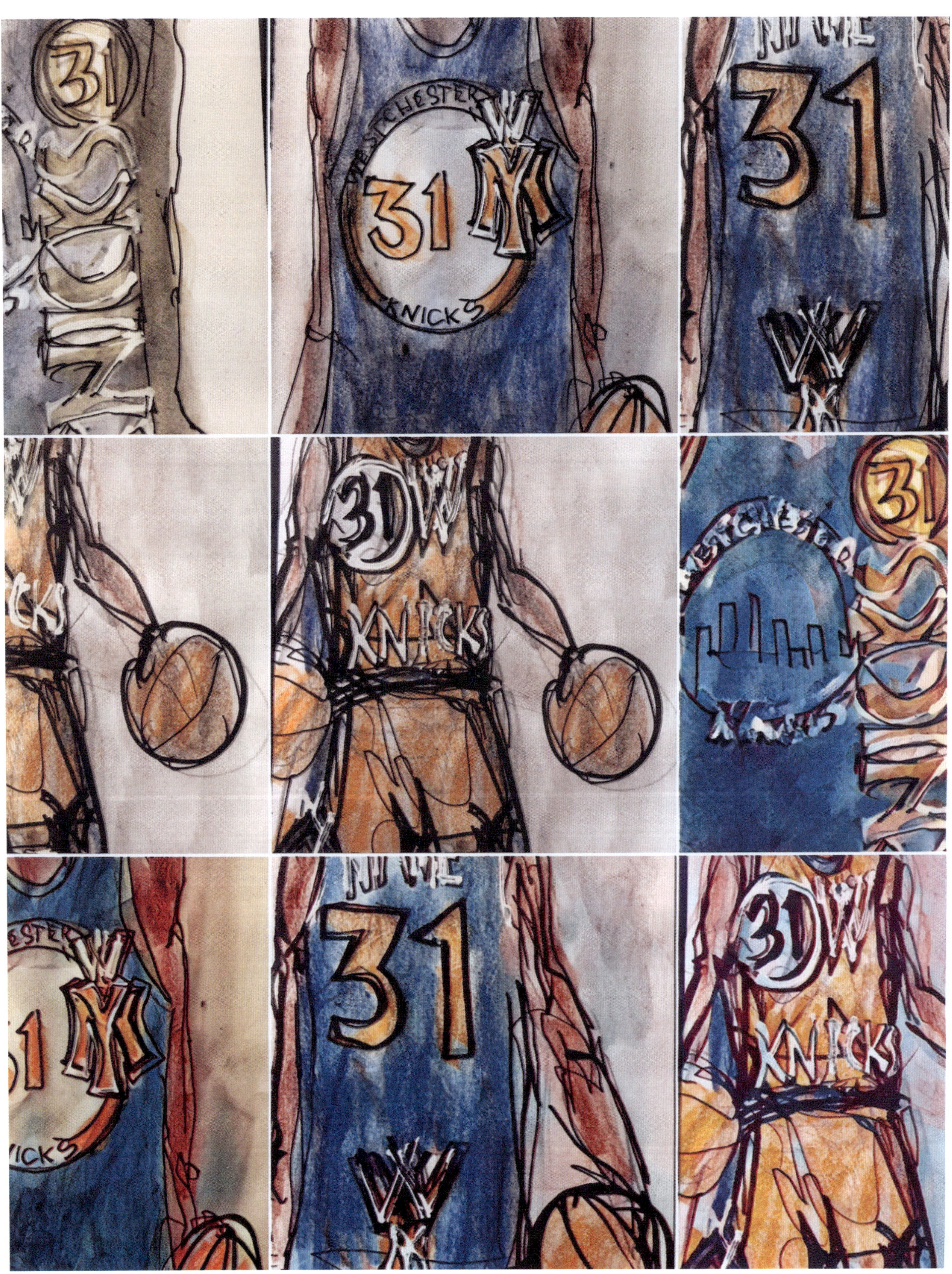
31
WESTCHESTER
31
KNICKS
31
31
KNICKS
31
31
31
KNICKS

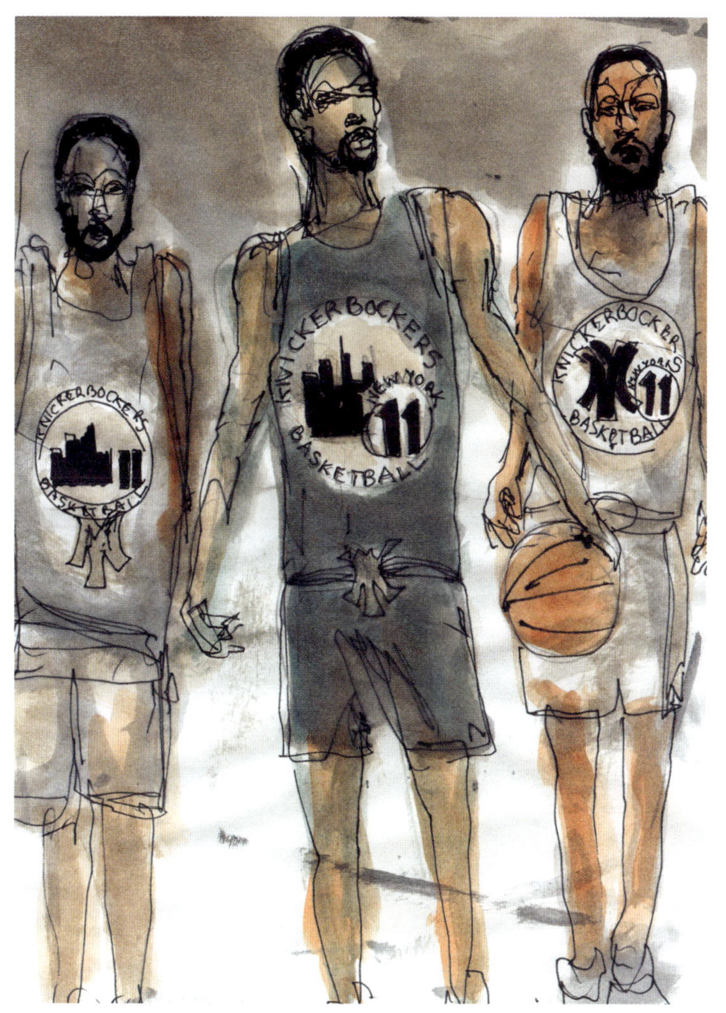

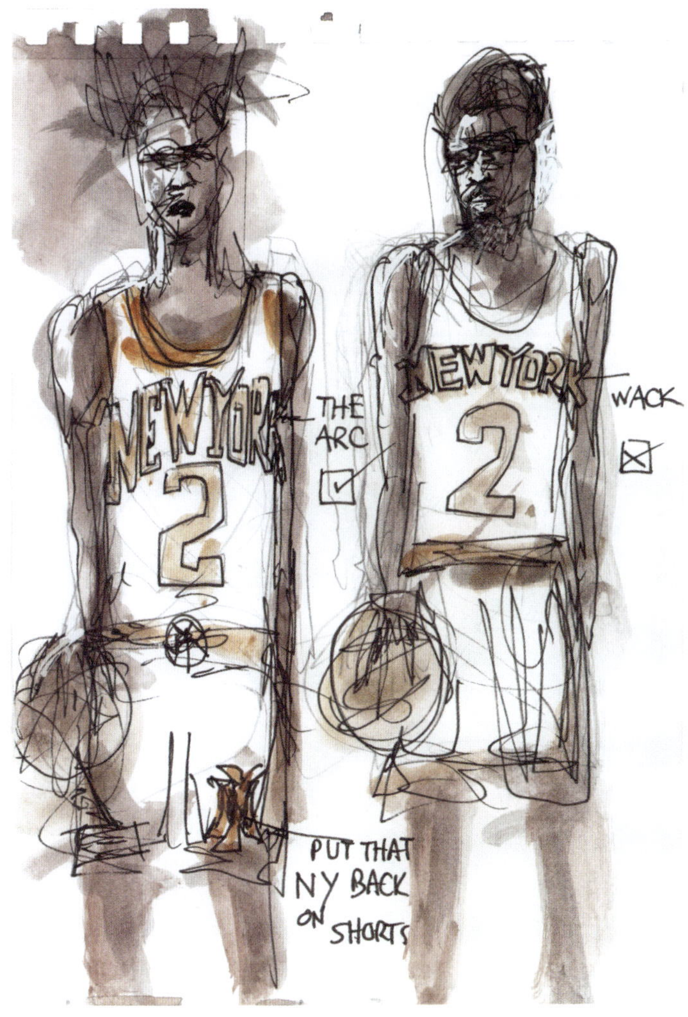

I remain a cheerleader for the arts, especially in the midst of the blizzard of big business sports. In a sports-driven society, the facts and the figures – not to mention the games behind the game – take up gigantic amounts of space in our lives.

I don't like the Dollar Tree font on the Knicks jerseys. They went and got some press-up letters and tacked them on the uniform. Listen, if you're dealing with 6 foot 5 guys, there's enough space for a font that arches. It's a fashion statement.

One of my ideas was to spell out 'Knickerbockers Basketball' in the circle, and bring back the 'NY' logo.

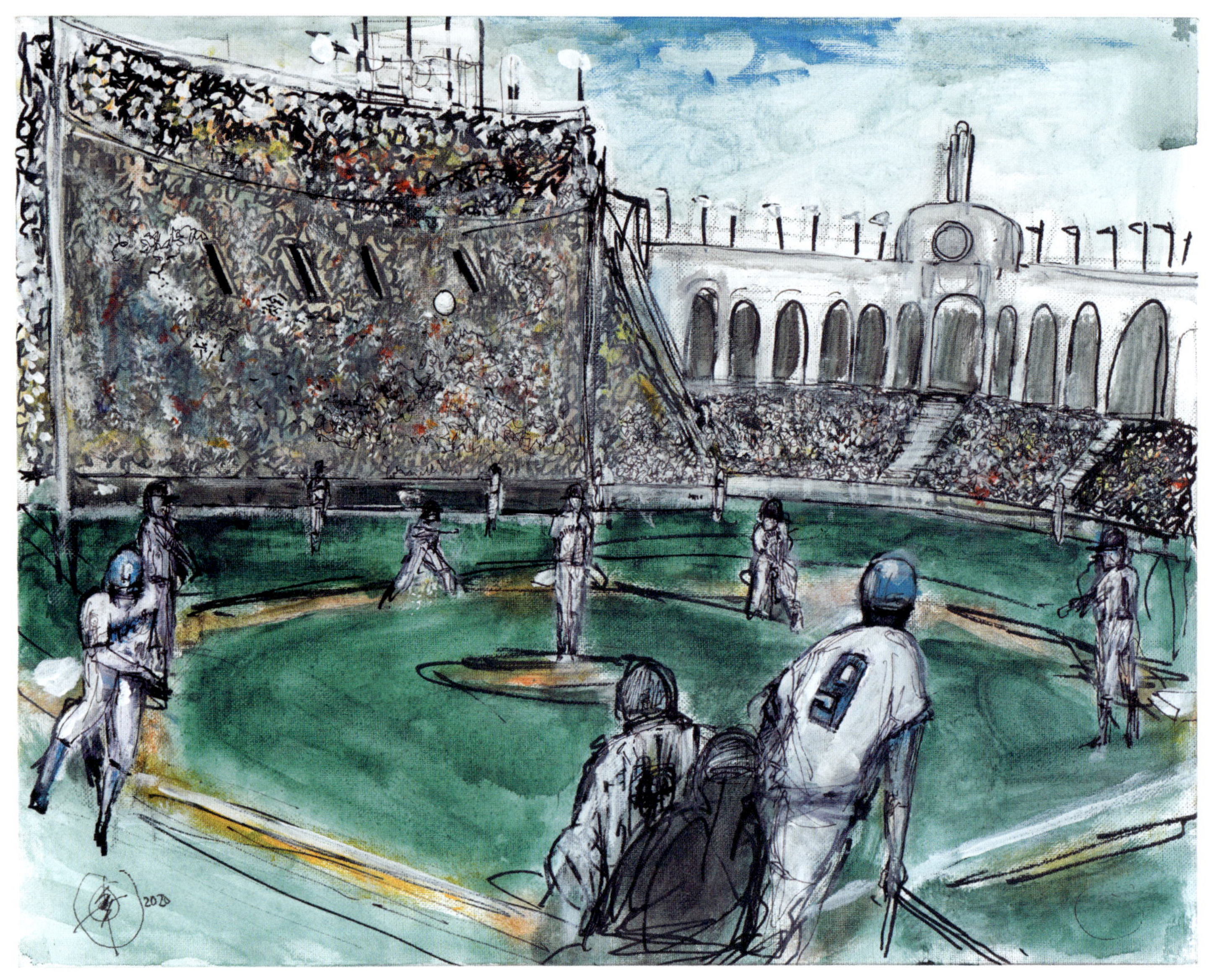

I had a great childhood.

I was the eldest child, so I was in charge of things. Maybe that's where that elder statesman title started. I was sporty as a kid, but when I turned 20 I started to get more into music. I found out I wasn't that good at sports. As you get older, the standard gets higher. Still, I was a fanatic – football, baseball, basketball, I liked them all.

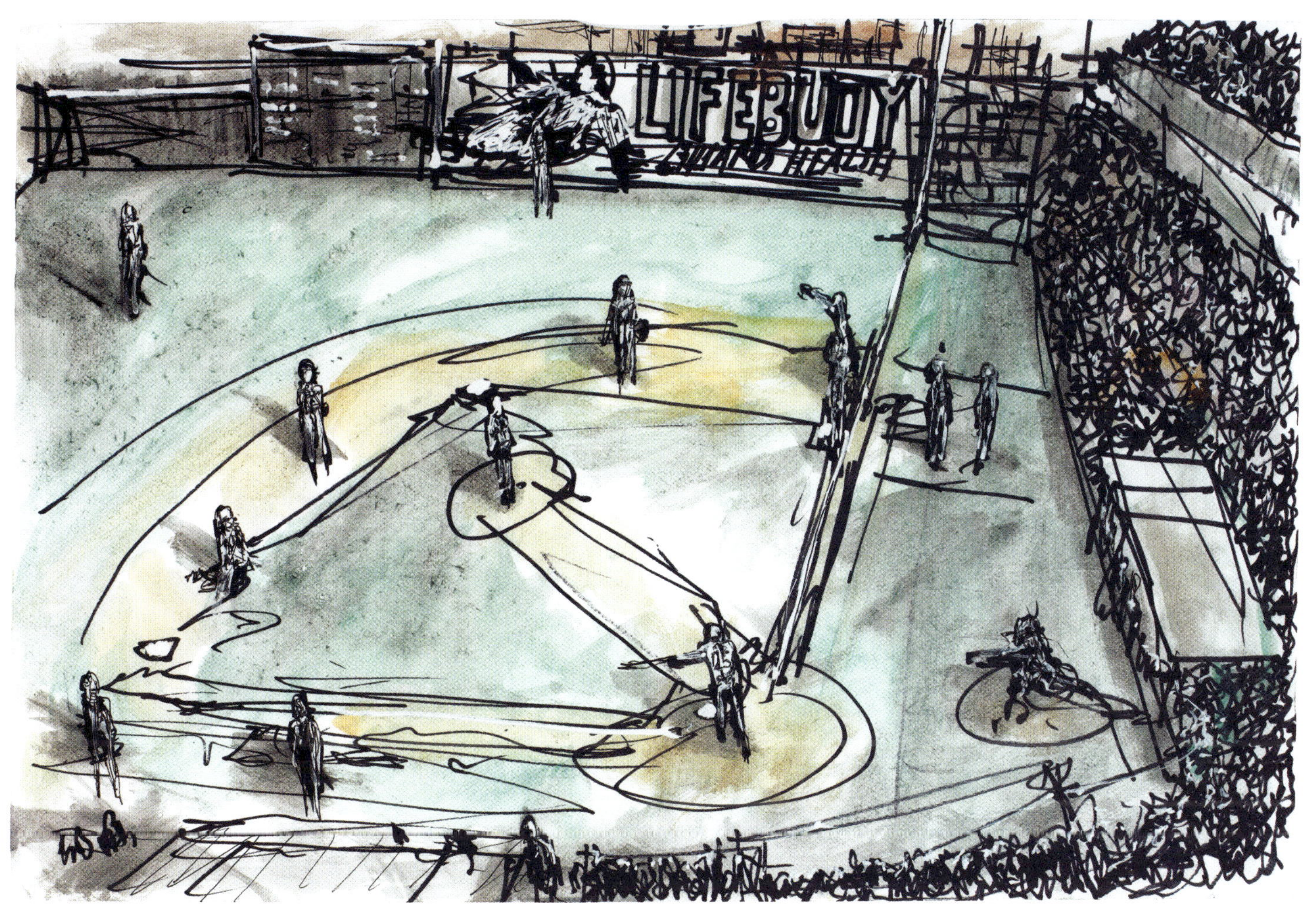

A lot of people in the hood say that baseball does not reach them. But it's got to be a concentrated effort on both sides. People have to find out what's there and what the opportunities are. You play, you learn all the nuances, and you fall in love with the game. But baseball's got to put in the effort too.

You can say anything about the sport, but players play with and among each other. That's very important. The fans might not always be on the same page, but usually the players are.

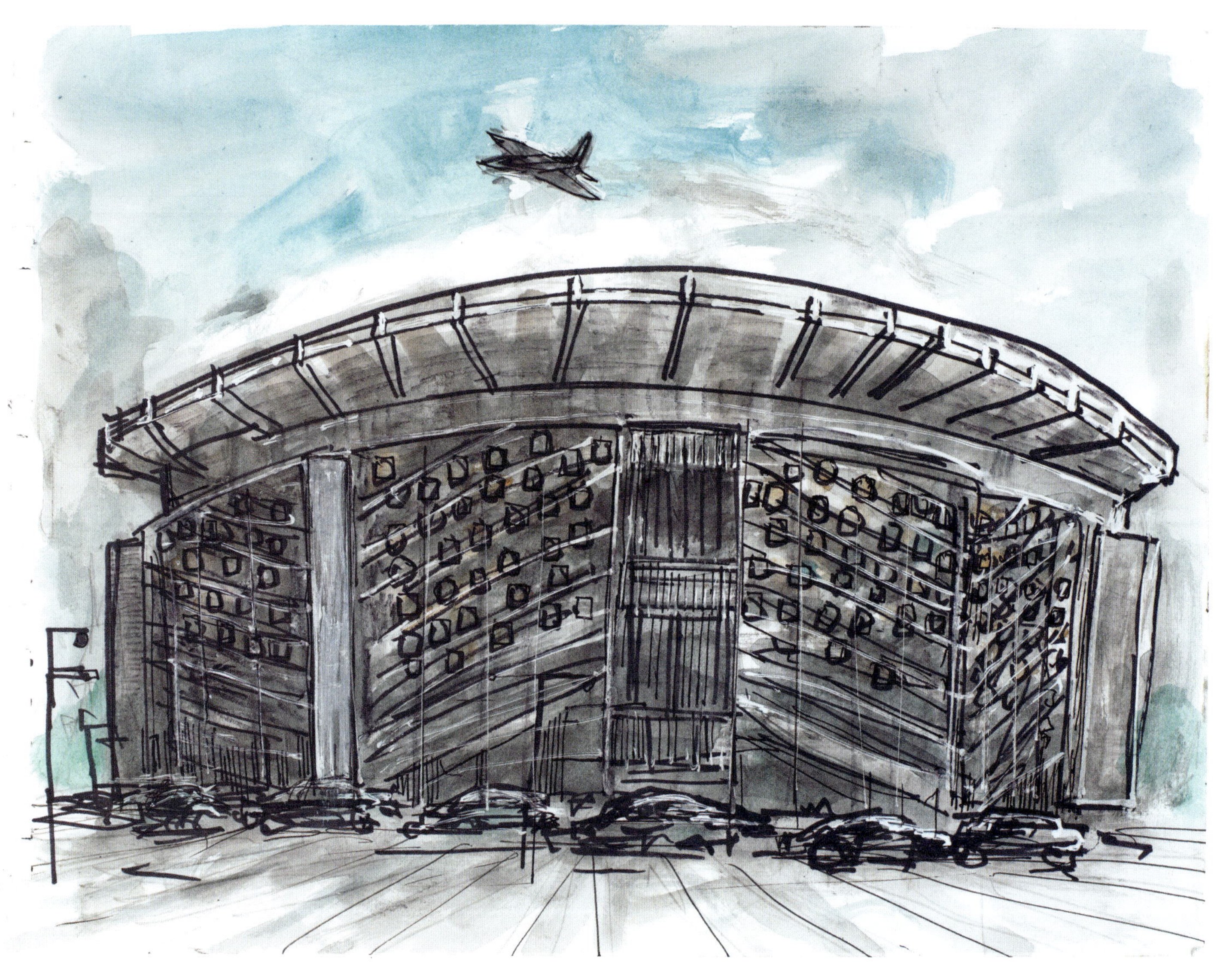

Shea Stadium. I was born within minutes of here... Home of the Mets, Jets and The Beatles in New York City. A municipal city-owned building, torn down and replaced.

BASEBALL

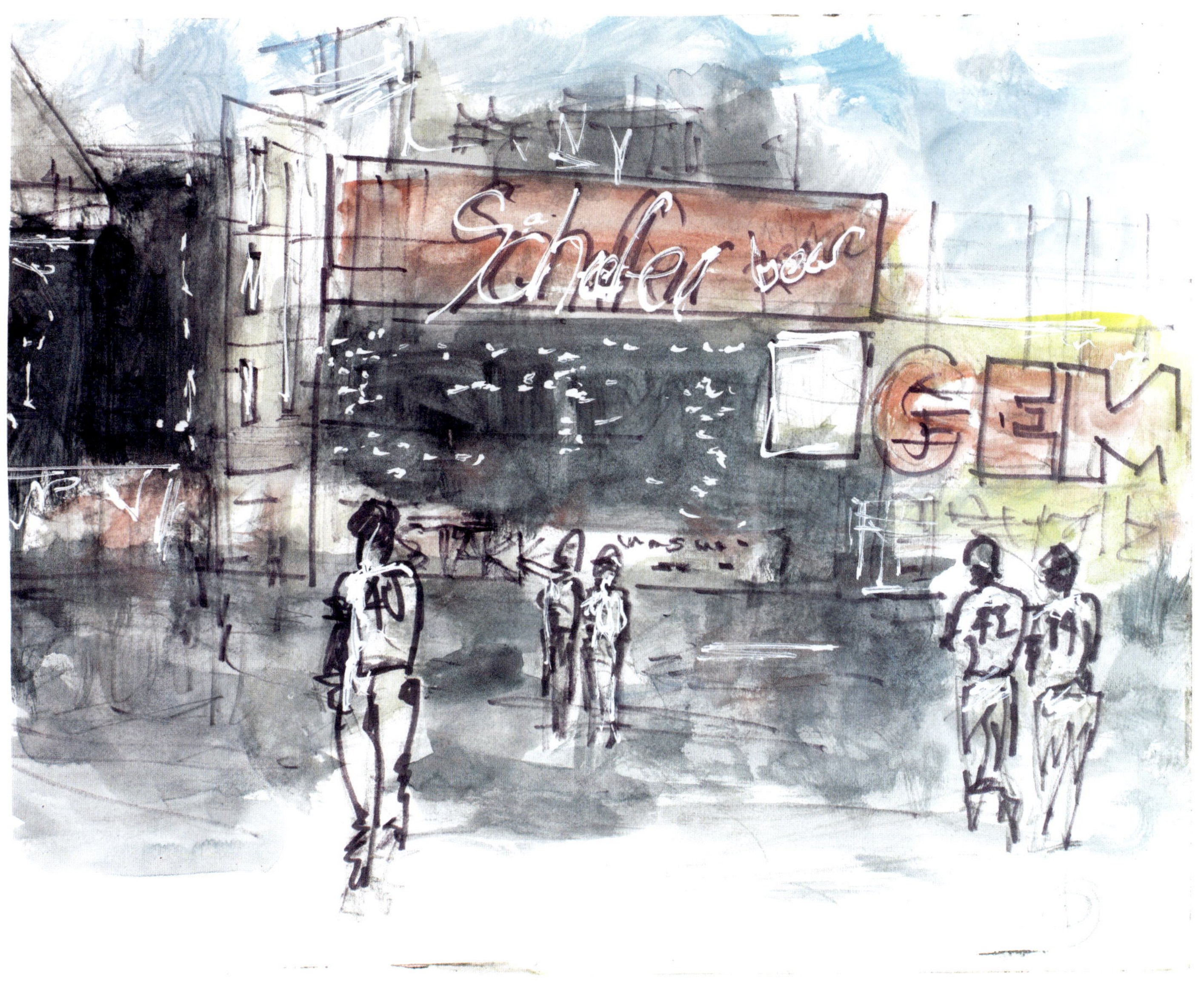

I'm drawing my childhood. I'm also inspired by two artists that are in my realm. One is Andy Katz, who does hip-hop rhymes as well as illustrations of great musicians and baseball players. The other is Graig Kreindler, who is probably the greatest baseball painter I've ever seen. They were inspirational to me when I was looking for a style. I decided to stay in the illustrator pocket more than in the painting pocket.

This is a quick sketch and watercolour of Ebbets Field in Brooklyn, home of the Dodgers. It's not based on any one photo but compiled in my mind. I never saw it in real life, as it was torn down months before I was born.

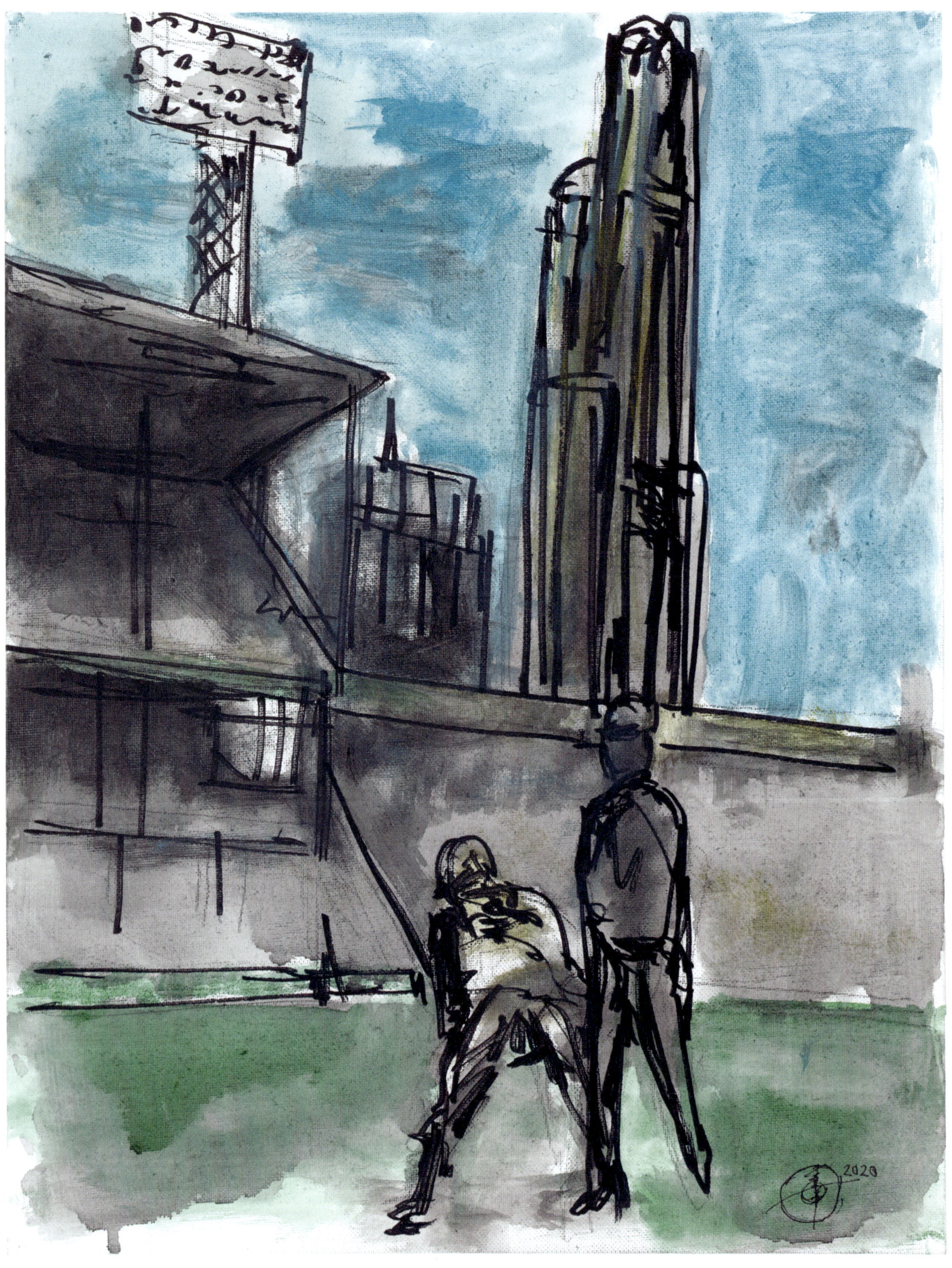
2020

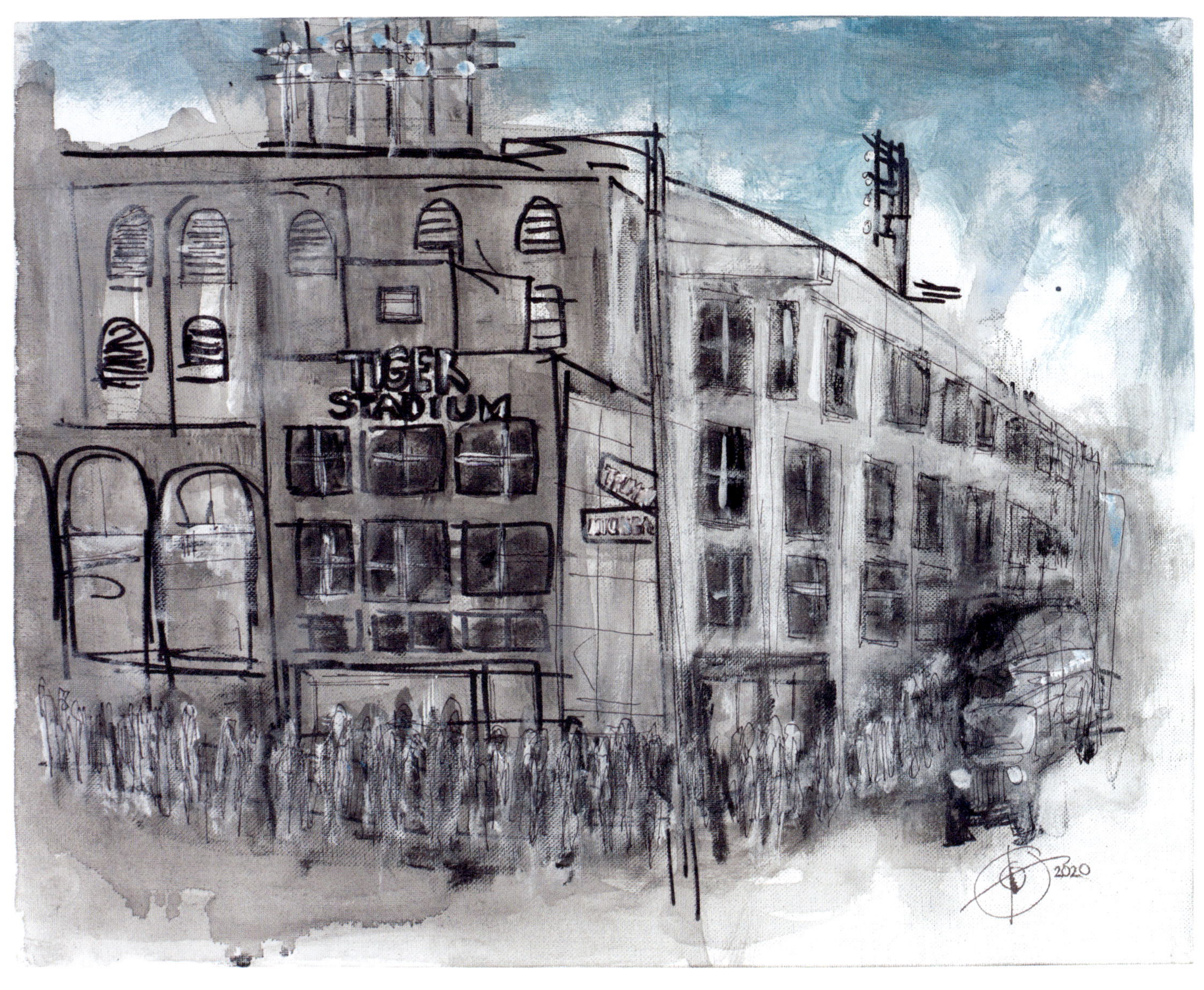

It's always the same story throughout the years. During Jackie Robinson's time, they were saying black players and black lives didn't matter. The black players had to fight collectively in a righteous way. They were saying, 'Look, treat us equal, just like everybody else.'

Baseball was a sport that seriously epitomised these gracious, dignified movements. People were saying, 'Give us a shot in this and we'll show we're just as good and, in many cases, better. We want to make everybody finally recognise that this game is something that brings people together for the best of us.' It's about maintaining awareness.

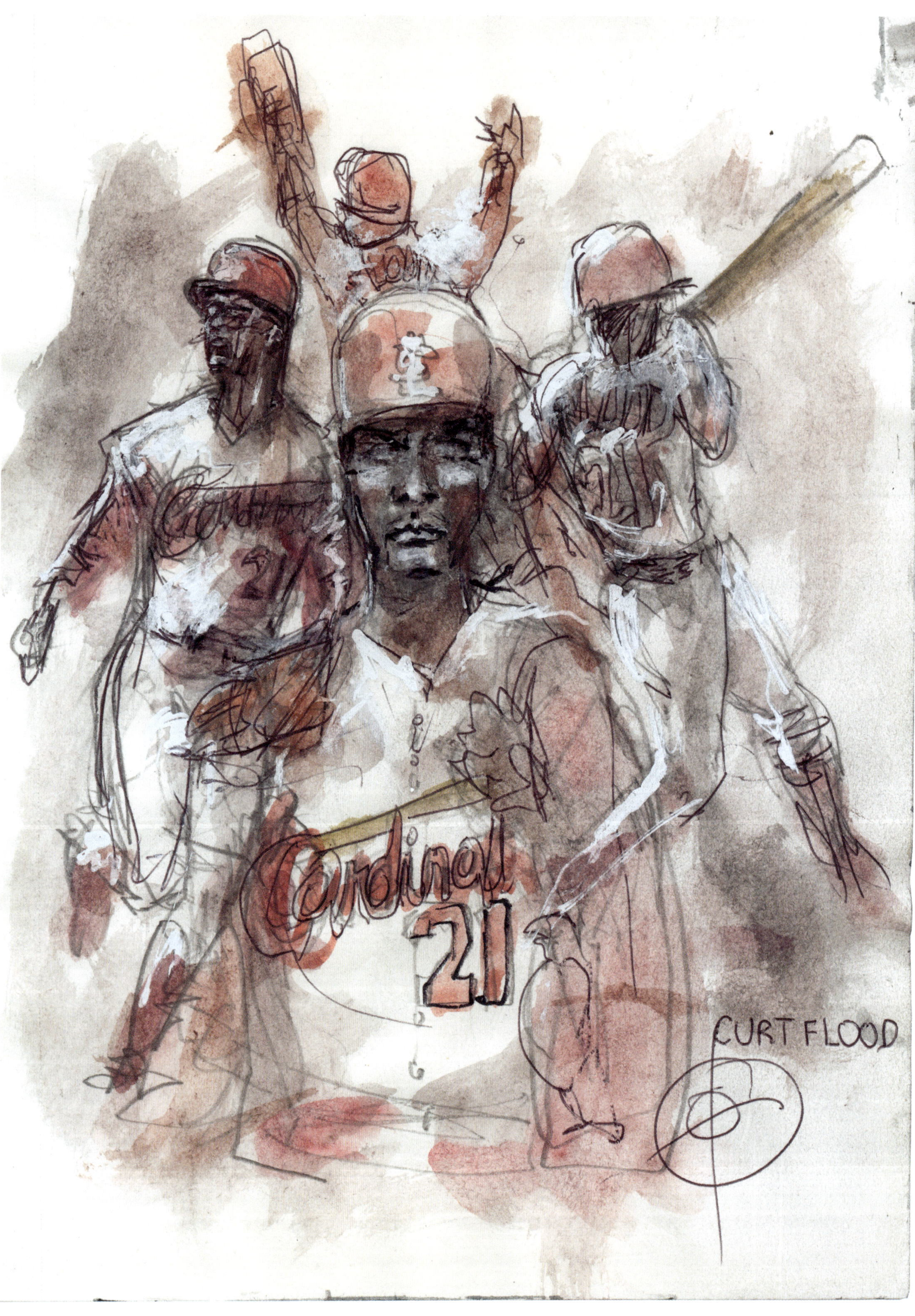
Cardinal
21
CURT FLOOD

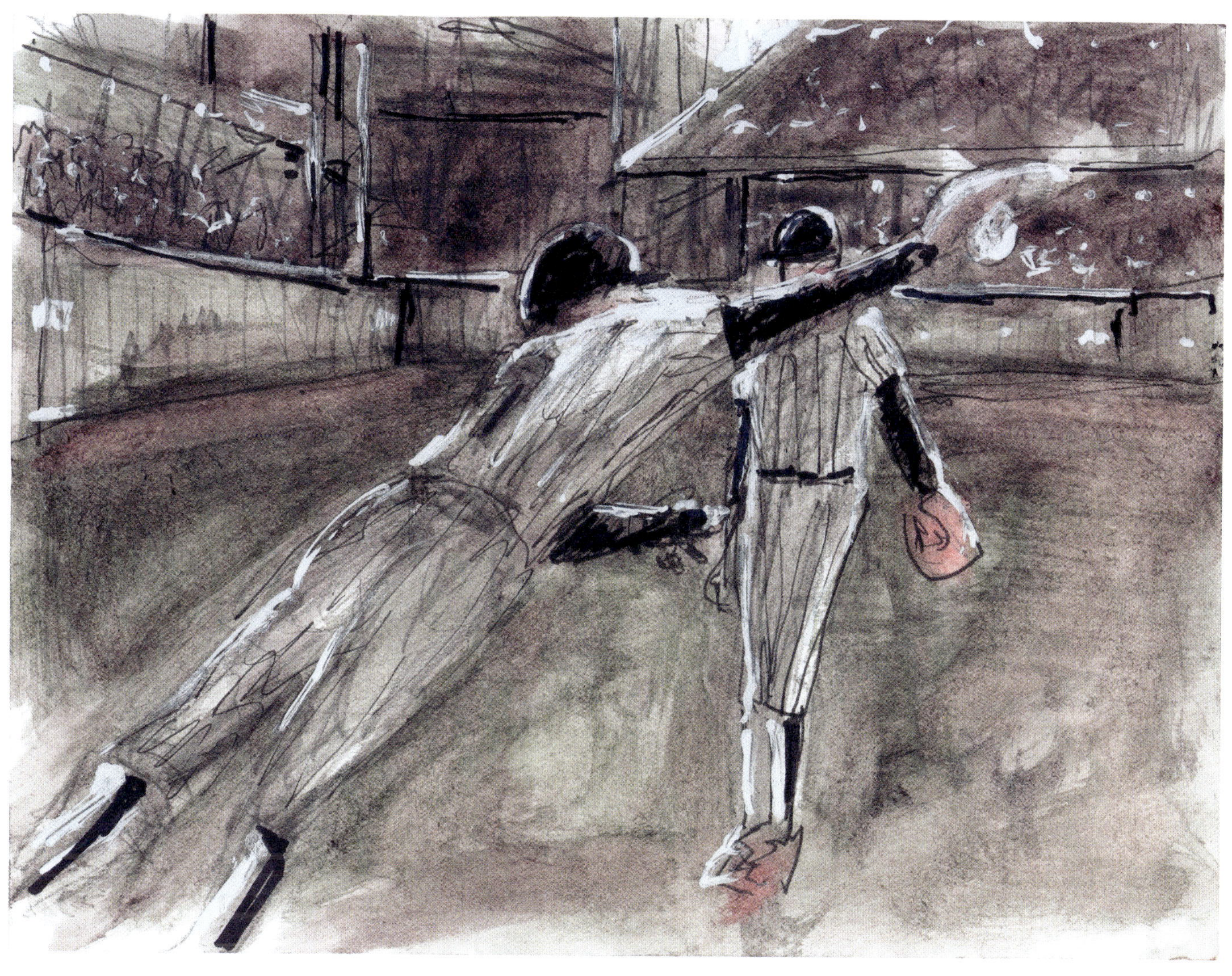

Today's athletes are pacified by what they're paid. An unfortunate reality is most athletes don't have a historical understanding and appreciation of those who paved the way for them.

Curt Flood was a National League All-Star baseball player in the Sixties. His opposition to the reserve clause in major league contracts is a big reason athletes of today get millions of dollars on the free agent market. The reserve clause meant that a ballplayer was completely tied to the team he had signed for until he got traded or sold. It was the sports equivalent of slavery. What Curt Flood sacrificed his career to achieve was a player's right to sign a contract with any team after his existing contract expired.

Athletes of today don't even know Curt Flood's name.

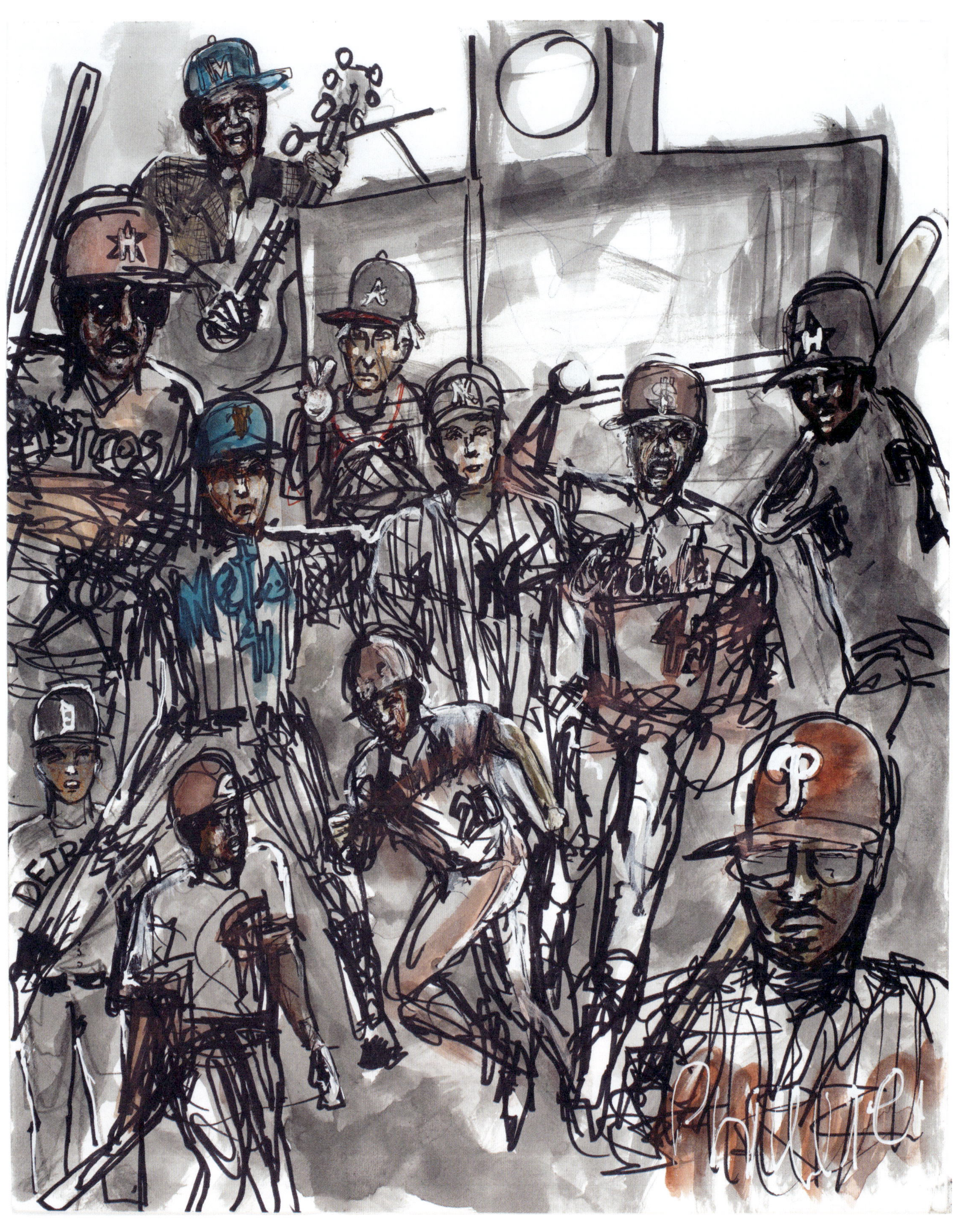

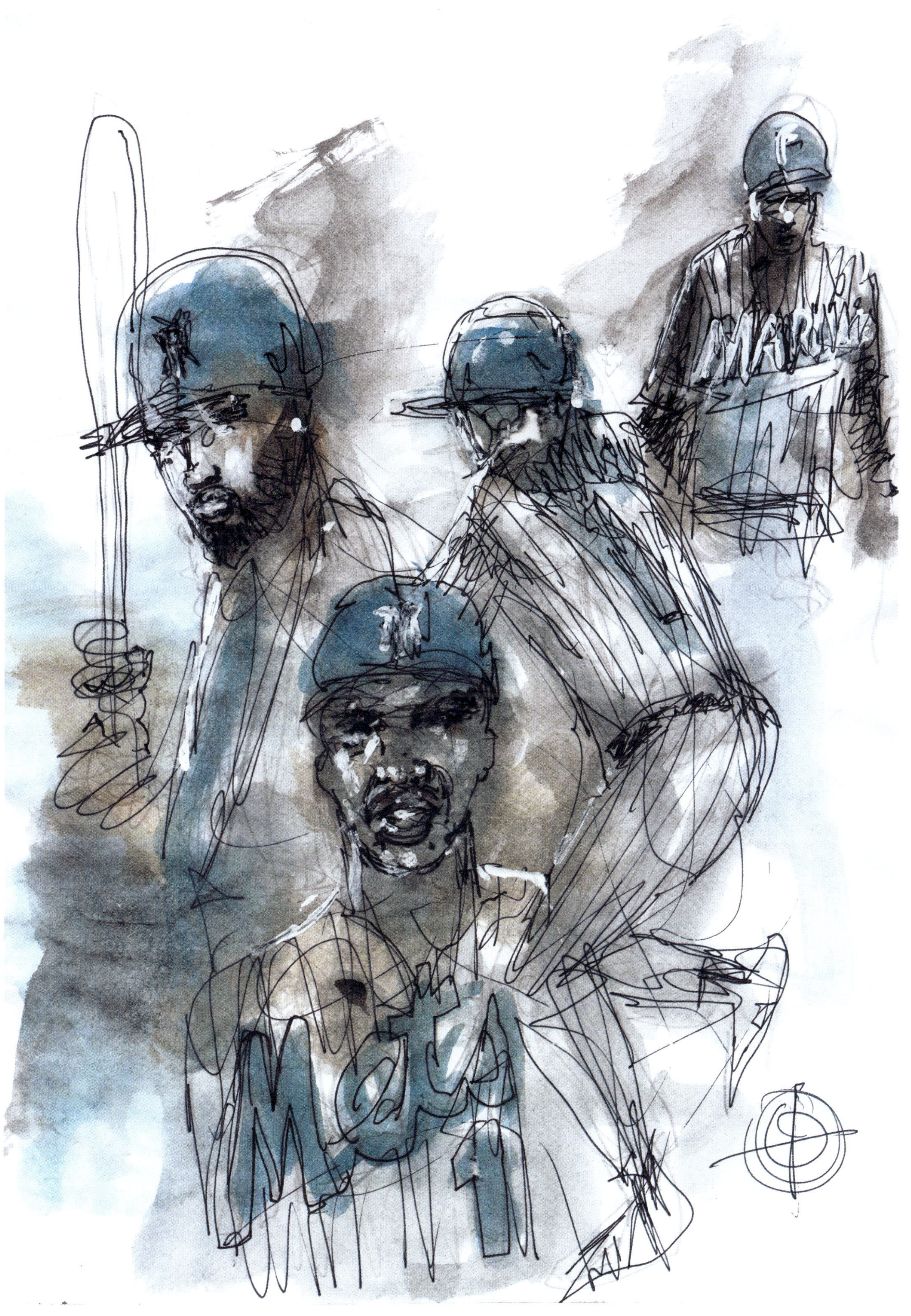
Mets

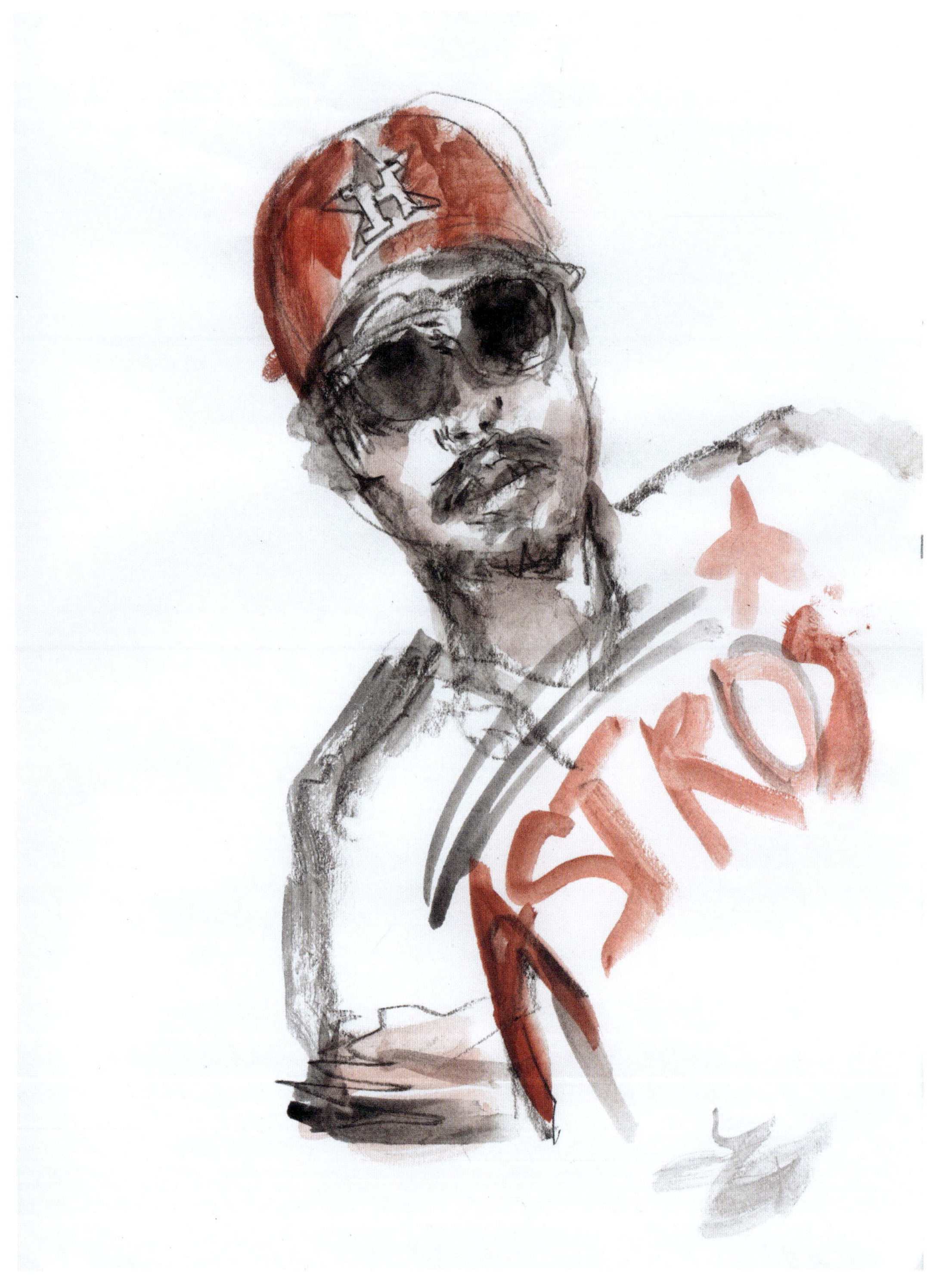

I did the illustration of Bob Watson and sent it to his son, Keith. Bob, it turned out, was on his last days. He really enjoyed the illustration I did of him.

When these players pass, it's almost like a chapter of your life comes to an end too. They're greatly reflected by the baseball cards that, when I became grown, my dad kept in the garage. My dad died in 2015 and when I reached out to Keith he was comforting to me as I spoke about the great times my dad and I had watching his father and peers play the game together. This illustration was the best way I could express myself, and the song 'It's So Hard to See My Baseball Cards Move On' came out of that.

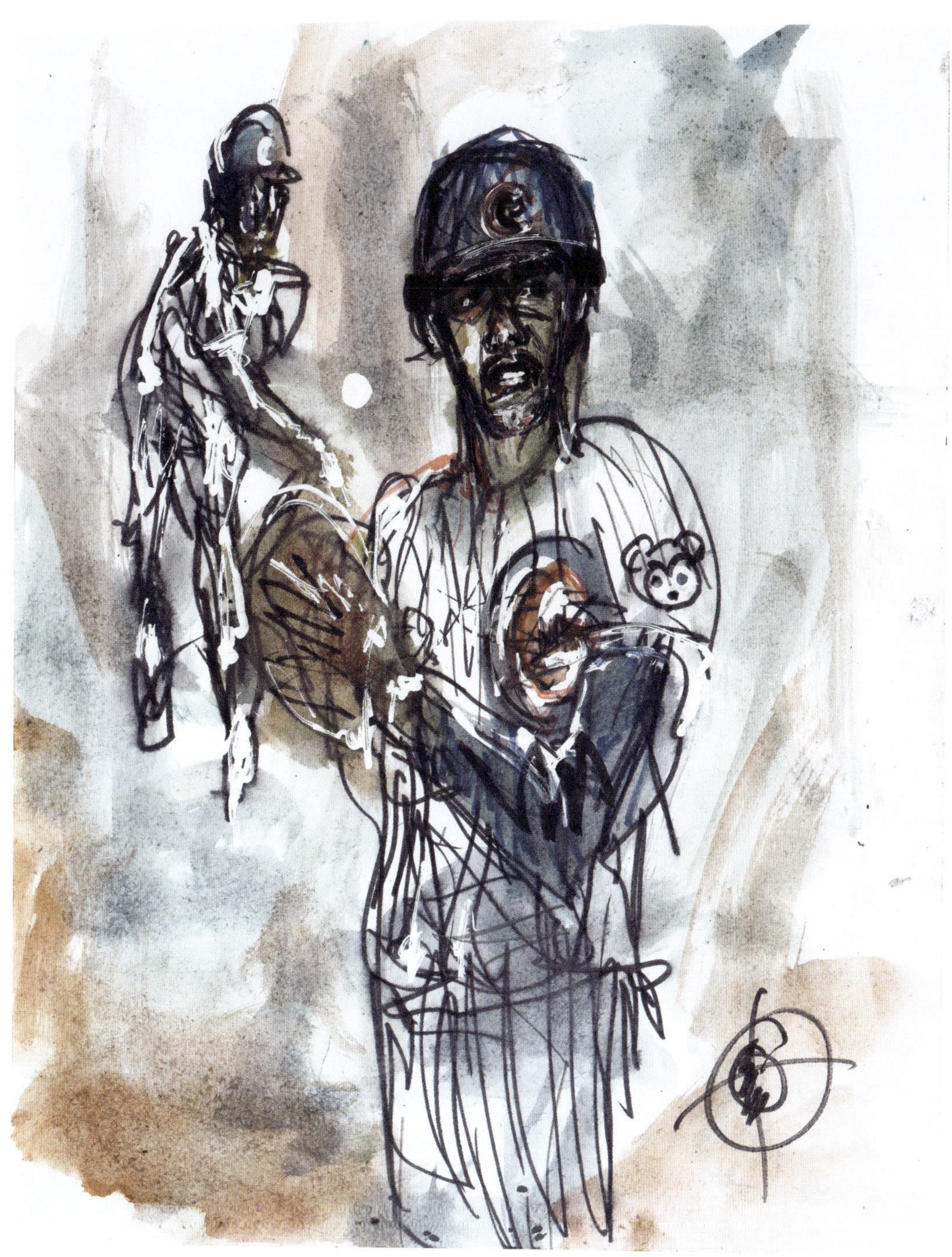

It's a father and son connection. That love of baseball, that was our time together. Anything that happens in the game of baseball, especially for those recognisable names... man, it strikes a chord in me.

I'm fortunate to be skilled in the arts and music, where I can do something that touches people. People think rap is limited but it's really vast, a bit like country and western. My dad also loved country music, especially Charley Pride, the black country artist who also played baseball within the Mets' minor league system.

He was a great musician and we both looked up to him. It shows the commonality in all of us. This is rap, that's country. Johnny Cash is the 'Man in Black', but I call myself the 'Black in Man'.

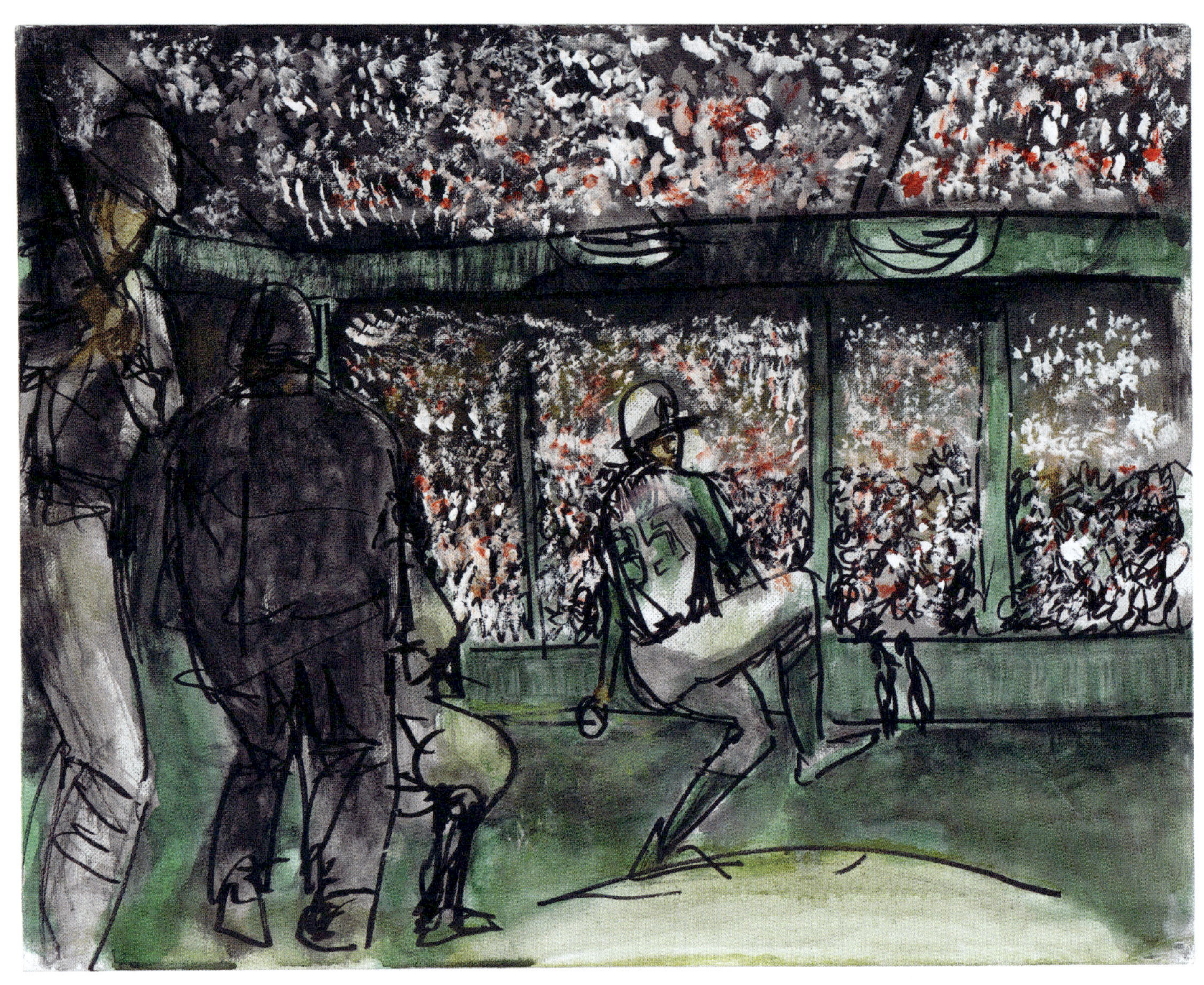

This is a series commemorating the 1971 Major League Baseball All-Star game, which is the game that really made me fall in love with baseball.

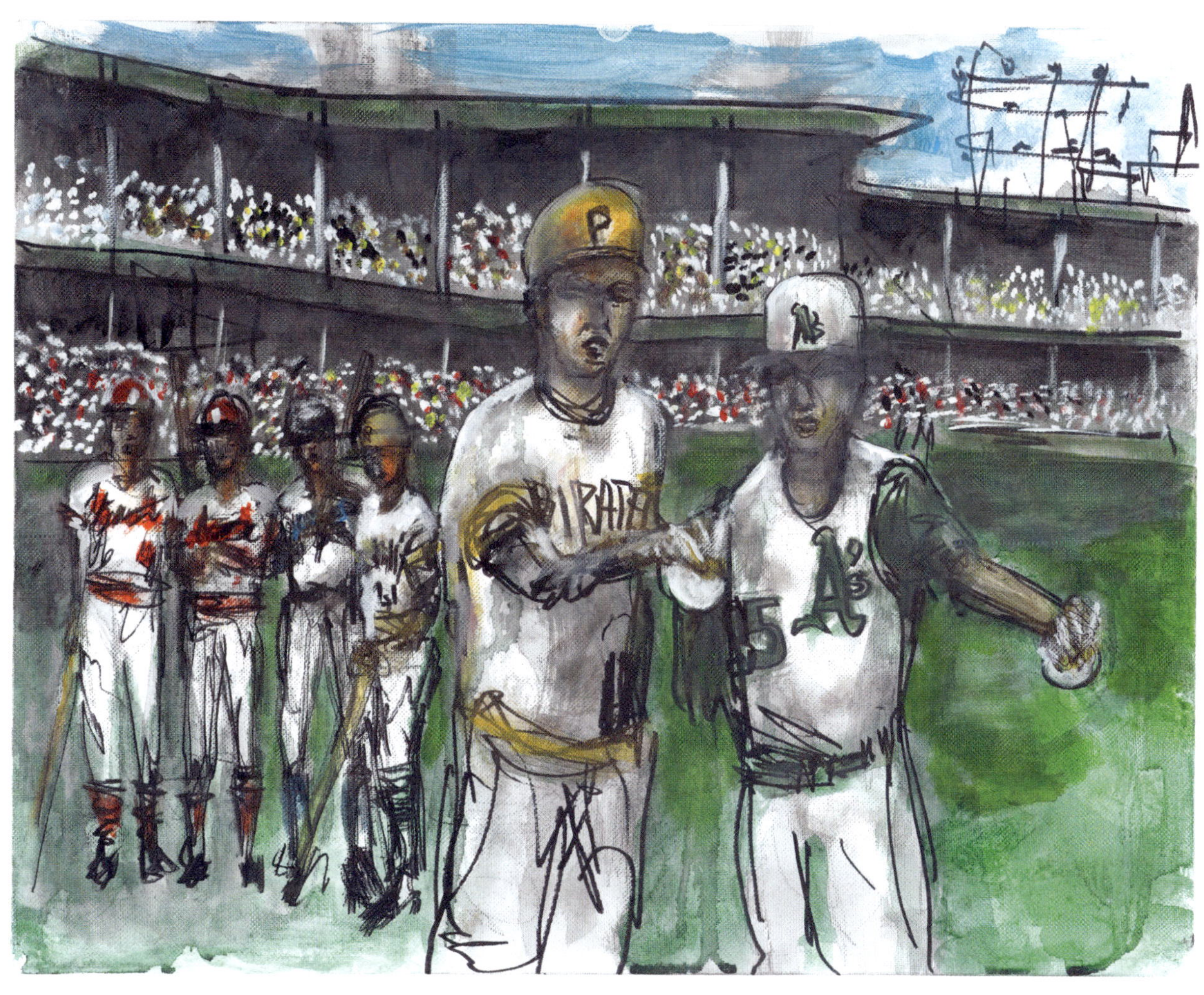

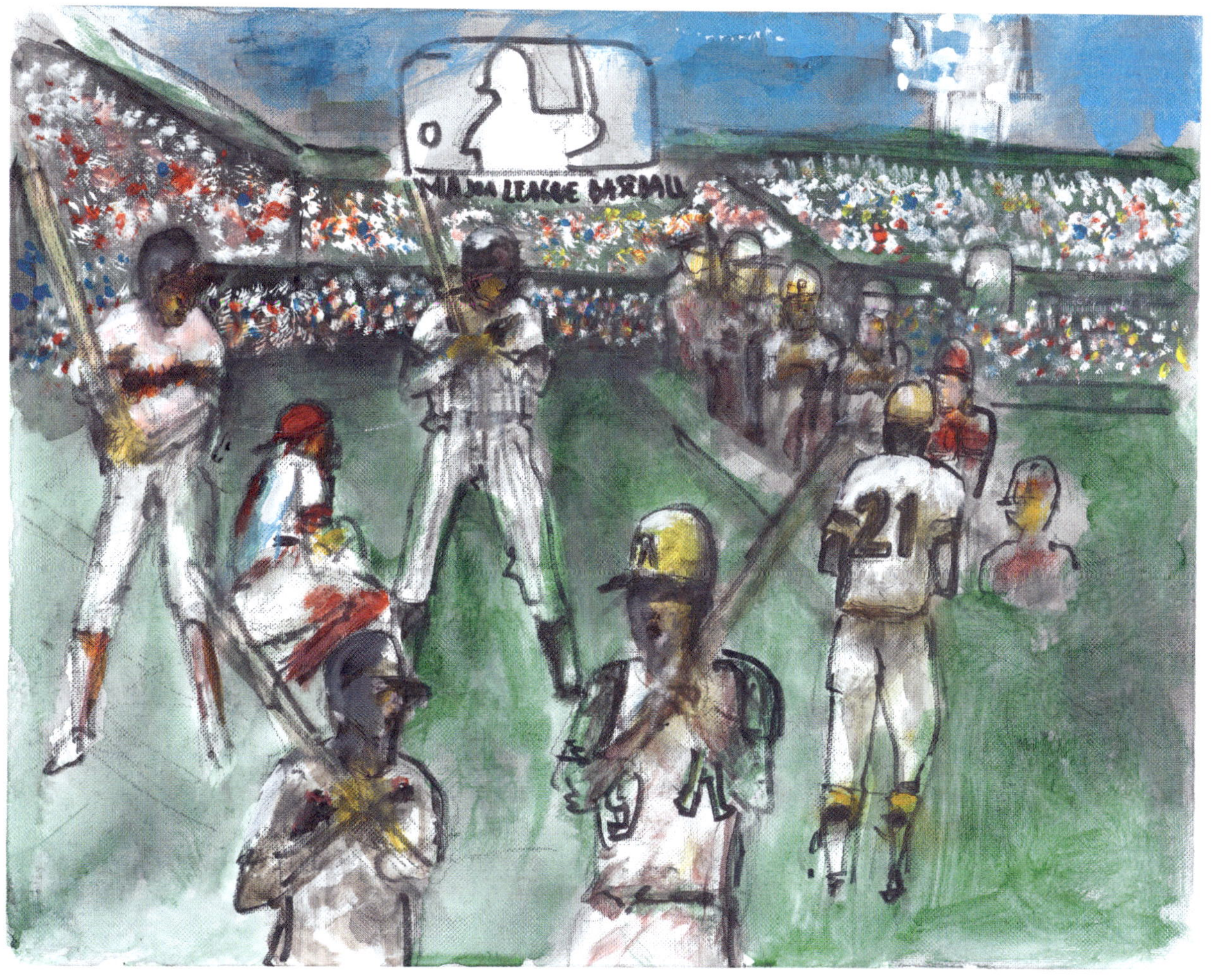
MAJOR LEAGUE BASEBALL

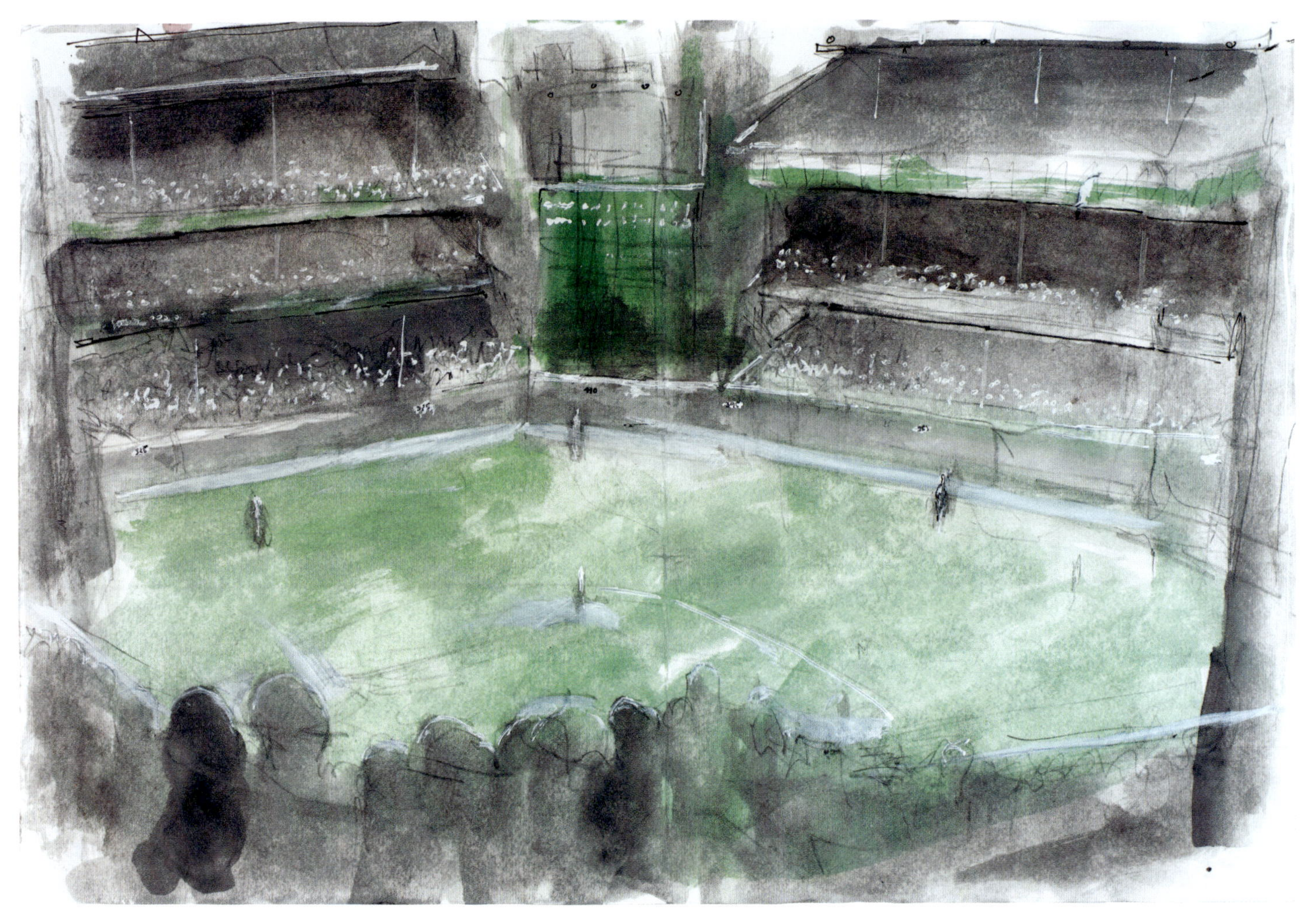

Because I grew up in Dr J's hometown, basketball was number one, but baseball and football ranked almost as high. Each game's beauty depends on the beholder of the game and not the popularity.

Like boxing, football is an unforgiving sport. Guys are raised to intimidate and scramble the opposition's body and brains, if need be. The fans are nuts. In football, ageing is sudden death.

I boycotted the NFL. No fantasy leagues, no hats, nothing. I'm a Jets fan and I like the game, but I turned my back on it because of the way they mistreated Colin Kaepernick. I wore my comrade's jersey in protest. However, there are plenty creating their own reasons to keep watching the NFL while pretending to protest against it, thus the confusion. In stereotypical fashion the NFL is a room full of older, super-rich white men who are socially out of touch and deem the black community leaderless.

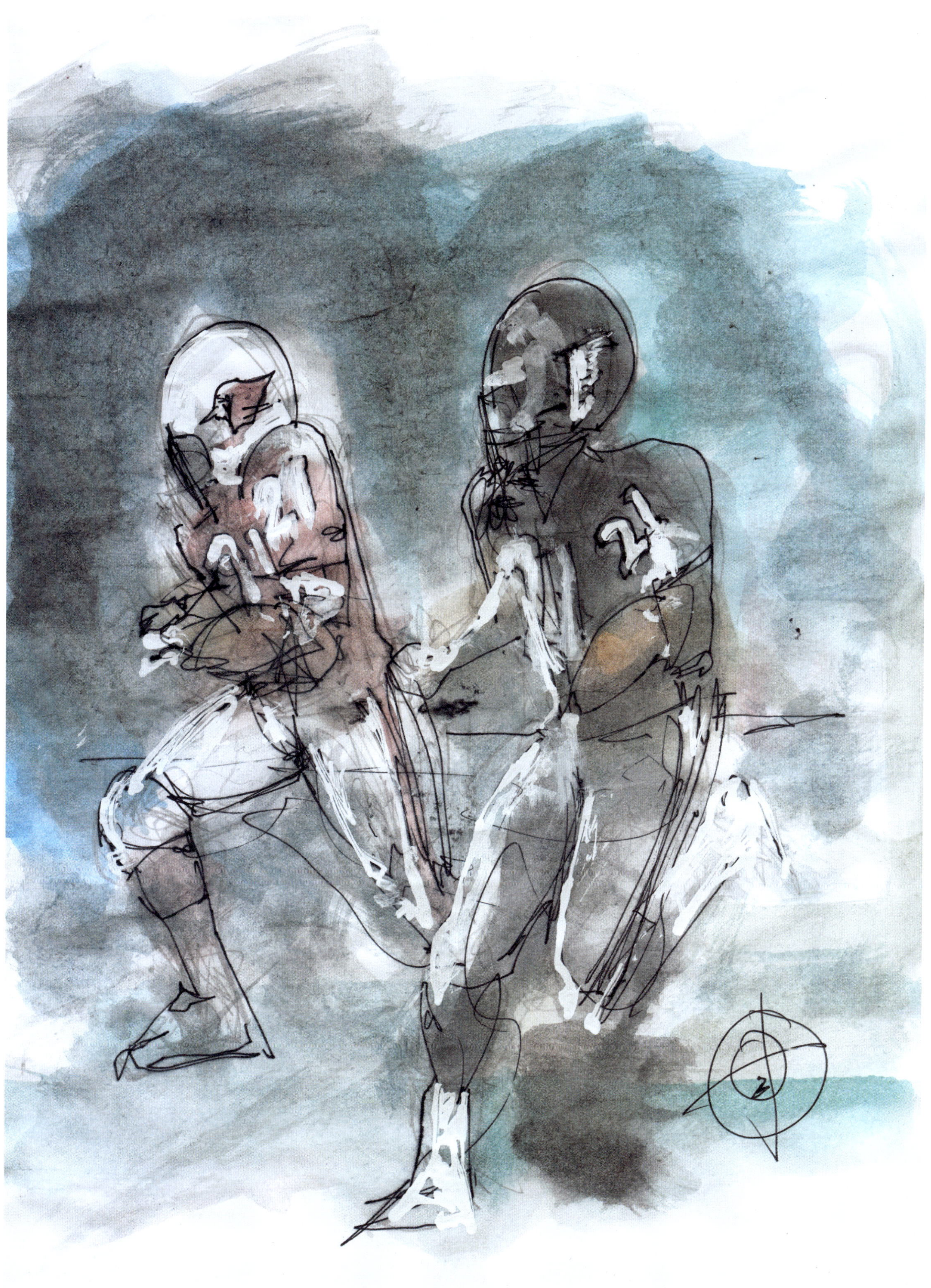

KOOL HERC

Hip-hop as we know it began in the Bronx in 1973 with Kool Herc and a party he held for his little sister.

His turntable experimentalism and how he made something out of nothing was the epitome of hip-hop as an art form.

Cultural groups like the Black Panthers and Nation of Islam were reference points. Our parents introduced us to the work of these groups, which was both educational and inspiring. My mom and dad were radicals, but more than anything they were young parents who understood the need for change.

At 26 I was considered too old when I cut my first recording, but while my age may have appeared as a disadvantage for some, I saw it as an advantage because of the knowledge I had gained.

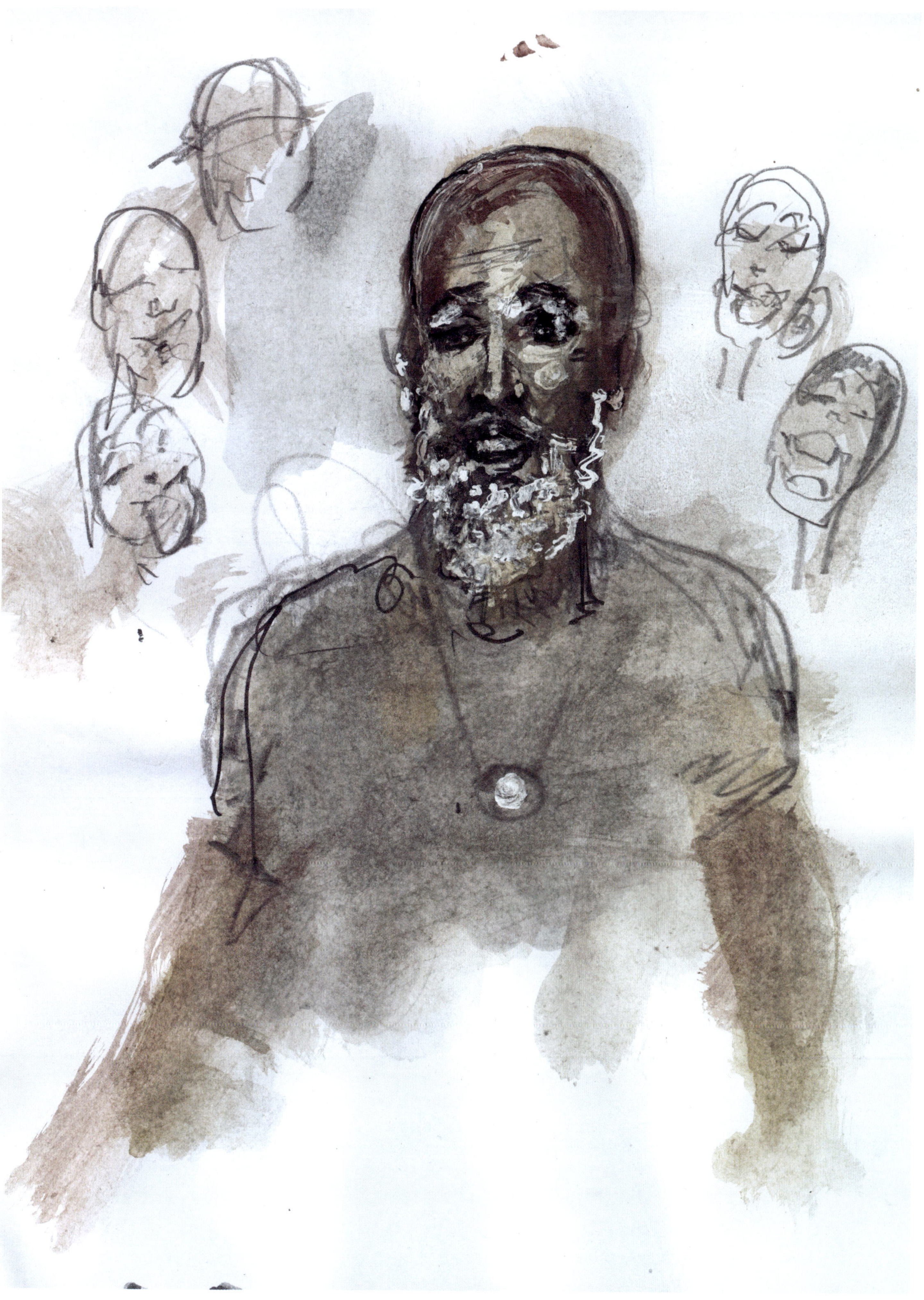

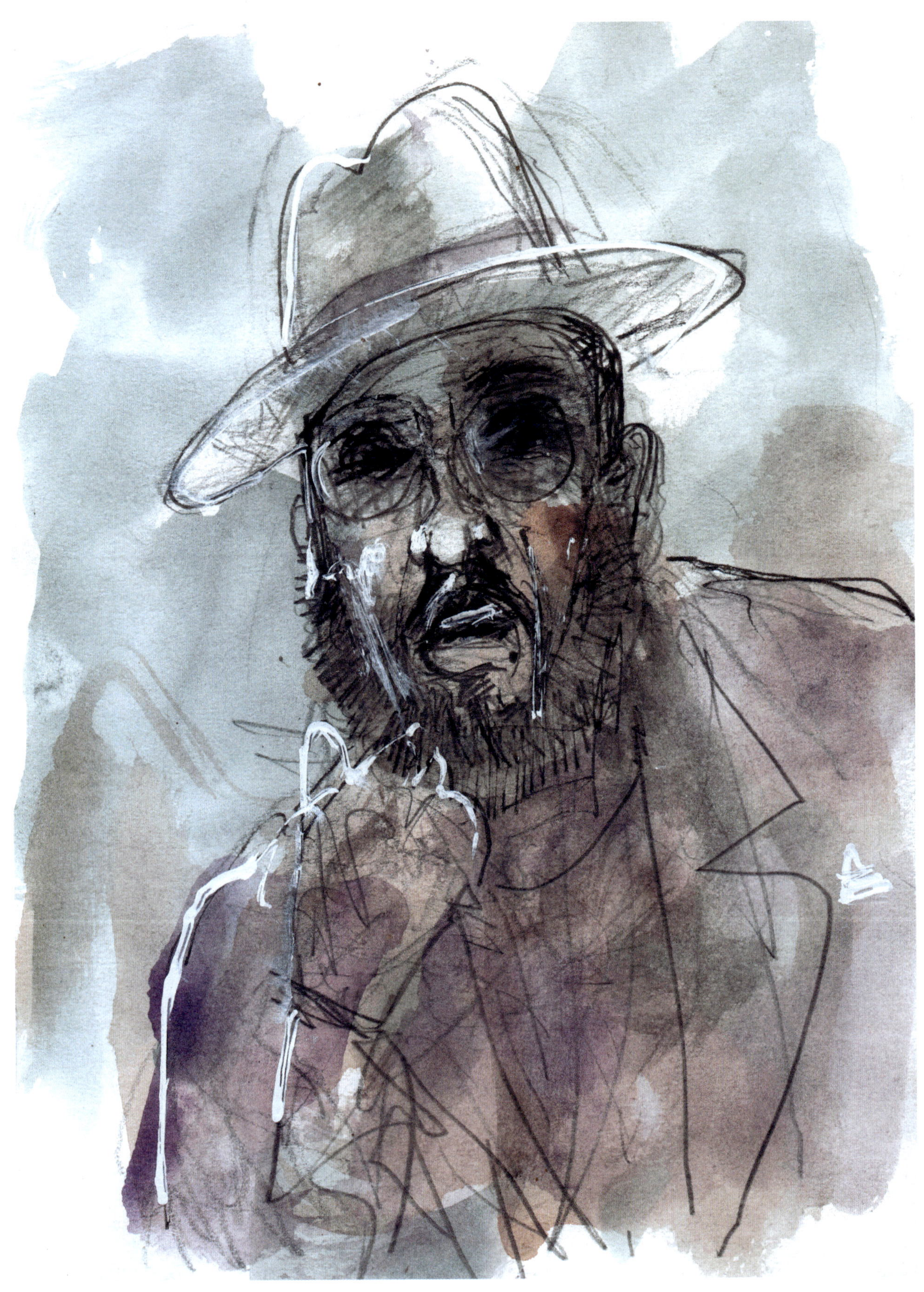

When I was a teenager, I heard the record *Funkentelechy vs. the Placebo Syndrome* by Parliament for the first time. I hated it; I couldn't understand it. But after a month and a half, I couldn't get it out of my system and I ended up loving it. That album is what dragged me into the Parliament and Funkadelic system.

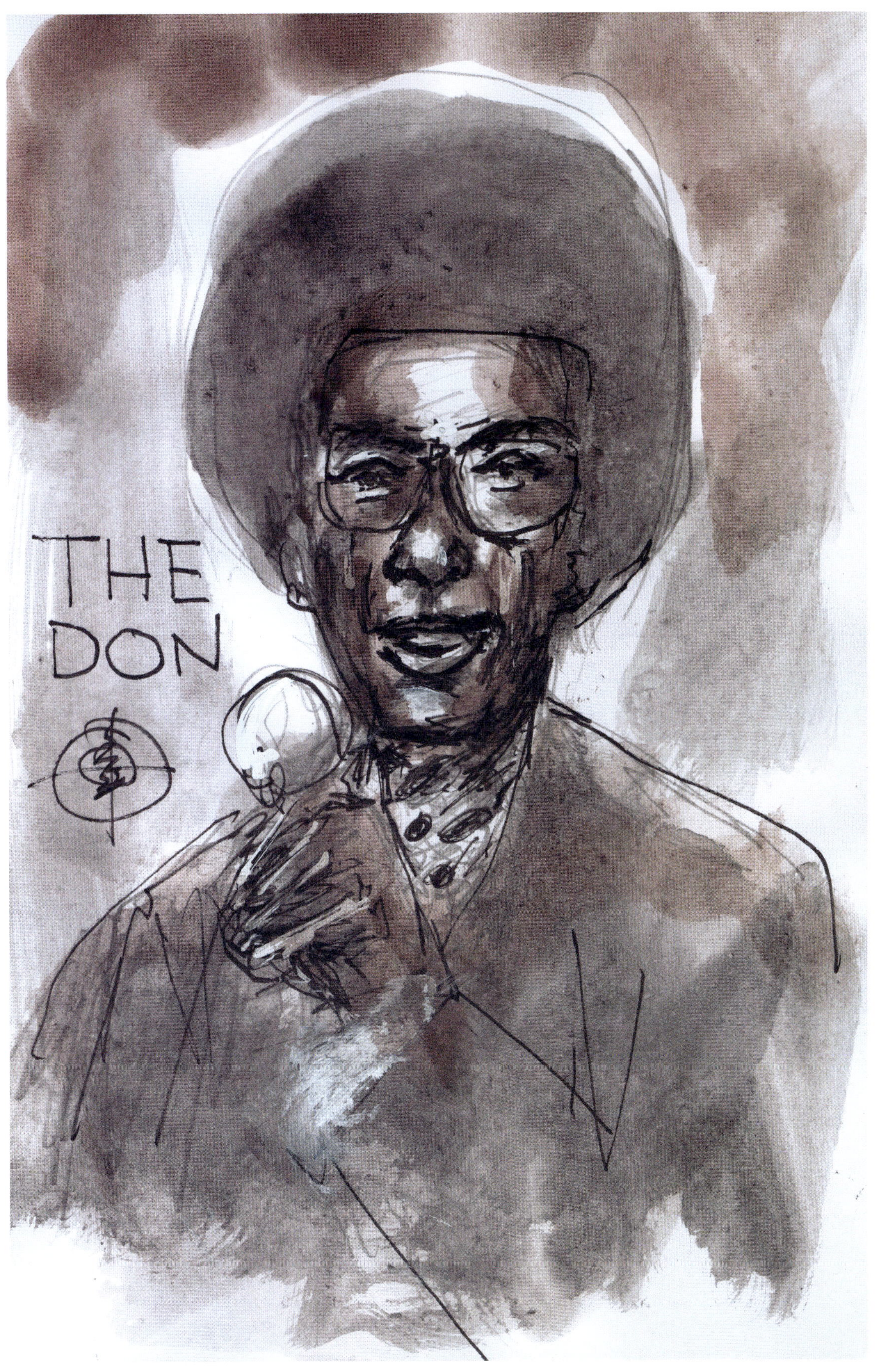

One of the most tragic episodes in black music was what happened to Don Cornelius, the creator of *Soul Train*. I felt that the industry turned its back on him. He made it possible for black music to breathe in a certain way. He was overlooked and bypassed by people who felt that they had better control over the culture than he had.

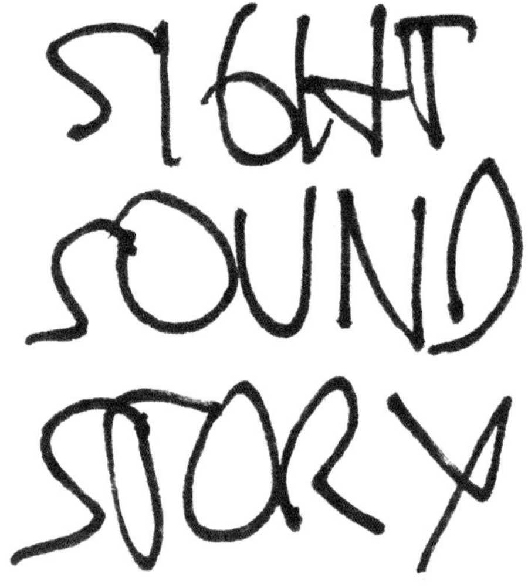

I think a lot of wit and word play left music for the sake of a quick, easy route to a youth audience.

When you're rapping, you can play with vocabulary to be creative. On 'The Long and Whining Road' I just wanted to tell the story of Public Enemy by referencing Dylan titles, almost like an 'Easter egg' type of thing. Dylan was a spokesperson for his generation and some people have said that I was for mine, so I thought it would be interesting. Somebody later pointed out that 'The Long and Winding Road' was a Beatles record. Well, maybe the Beatles stepped up their music after they got weeded up with Dylan.

I think a lot of the songs that are written today don't have a story beyond the lyrics. As a fan of music, I'm just as interested in the story behind a song as the song itself.

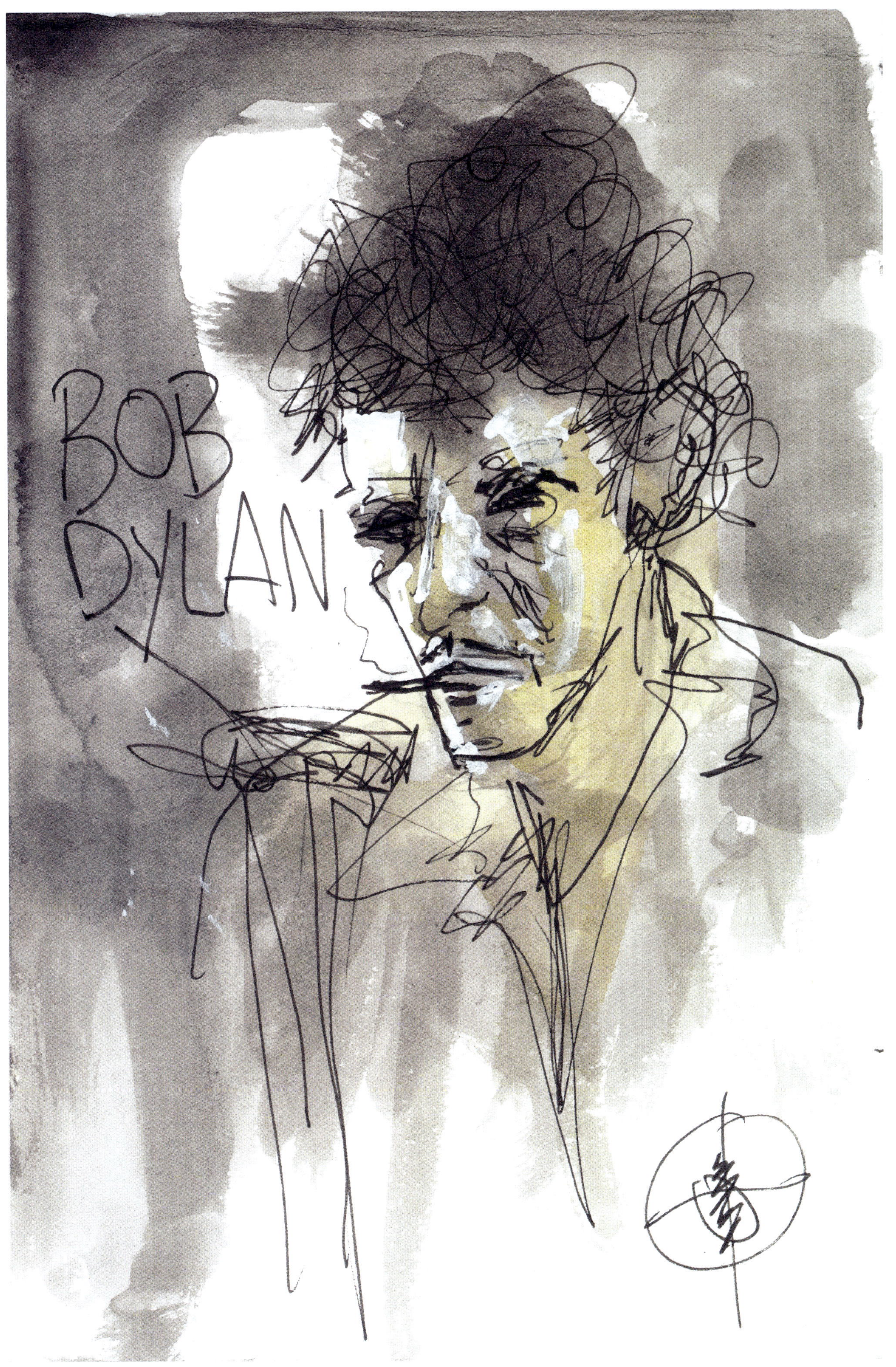
BOB
DYLAN

Myself, Hank and others would put Malcolm X on flyers to promote gigs. A cat rolled up to us and said, 'Who's this Malcolm the Tenth?' That's when we realised we needed to make music that meant something.

My involvement in hip-hop began with flyers and graphic design, which was my major in college. I was always artistic, so the left side of my brain was kicking. In 1979 I got involved with Spectrum City, which was one of Long Island's biggest mobile DJ operations. I was a big fan of theirs so after one function I approached their founders, Hank and Keith Shocklee, to offer to do flyers for them, but they were on some 'yeah OK… go away' type shit.

Coincidentally, the first hip-hop records came out that year. The hip-hop bug had bit me but I couldn't conceive of such a thing as a hip-hop or rap record, because I only knew hip-hop as a party thing that lasted three hours. The Sugarhill Gang's 'Rapper's Delight' – the second ever hip-hop single – was 15 minutes long.

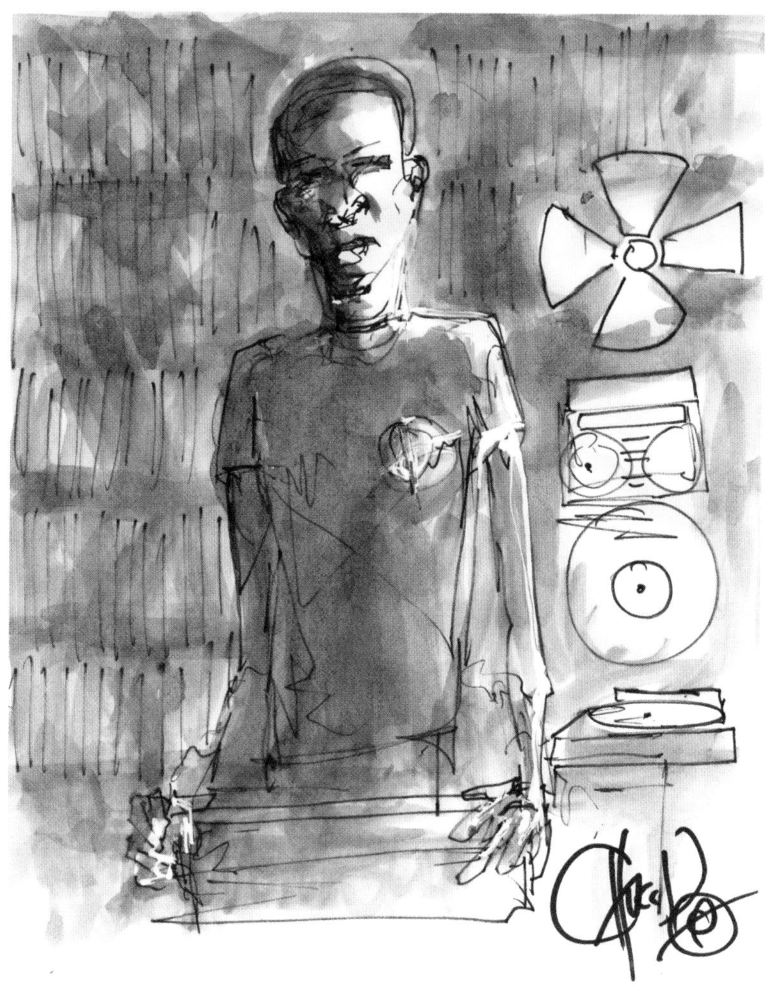

HANK SHOCKLEE

The summer of 1979 was berserk. Long Island was hip-hop crazy – everybody was rhyming. It was a summer of rap fanaticism, and it began reaching the black mainstream. I went to a lot of parties back then. You had these whack-ass cats getting on the mic, and everybody swore they had rhymes for the music. Sometimes you'd be trying to get your dance on with a chick and some cat would get on the mic and disturb the groove. I said to my fellas, 'I'm gonna get on the mic just to get these motherfuckers off!'

Hank Shocklee happened to be at the Thursday Night Throwdown and heard me rapping. He was surprised to see that it was the same dude who came to him about the flyers. He approached me and said he wanted an MC for his group but it had to be a special kind of MC. I was flattered. I was just a fan. I asked him to give me the weekend to think about it.

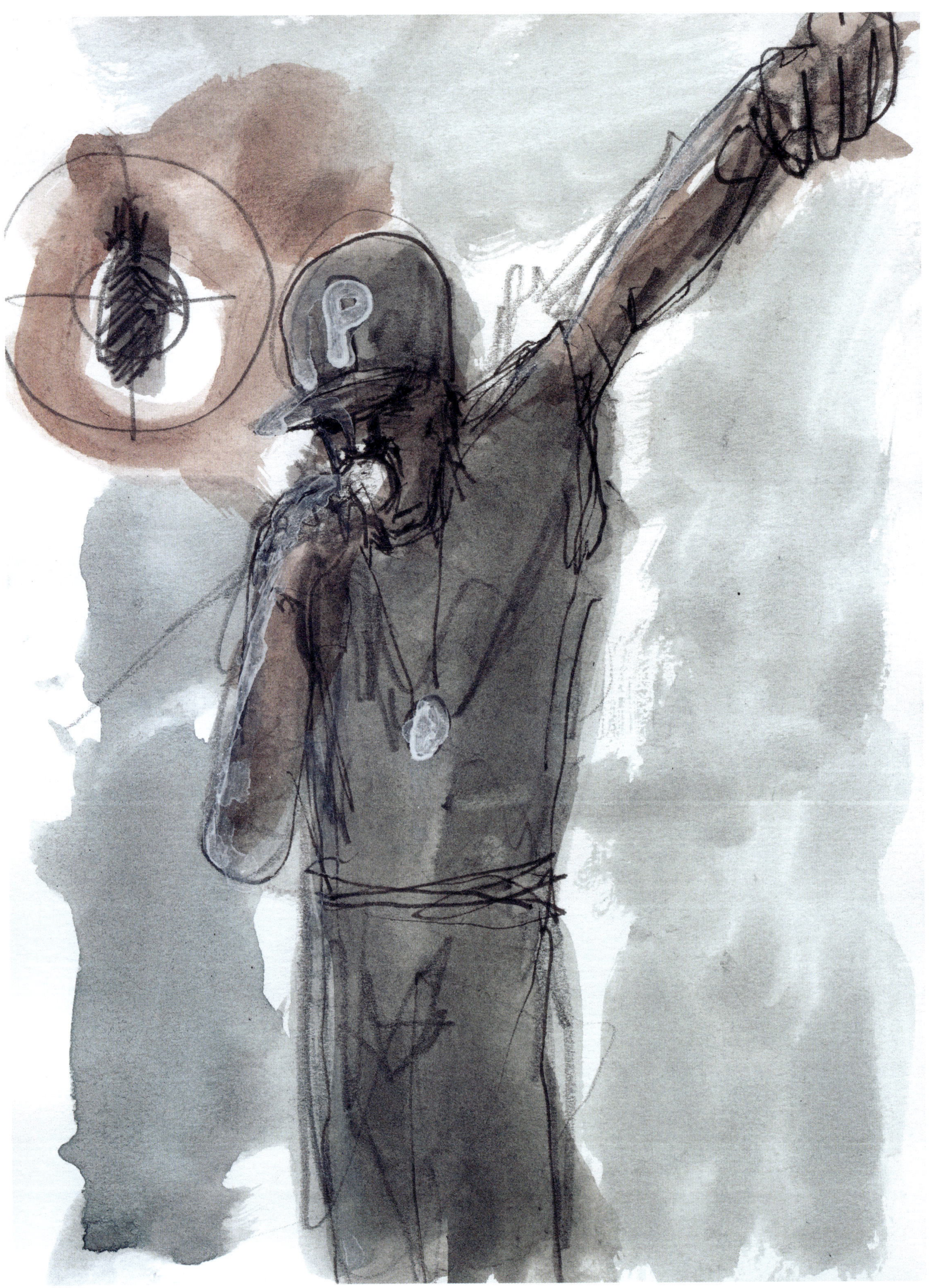

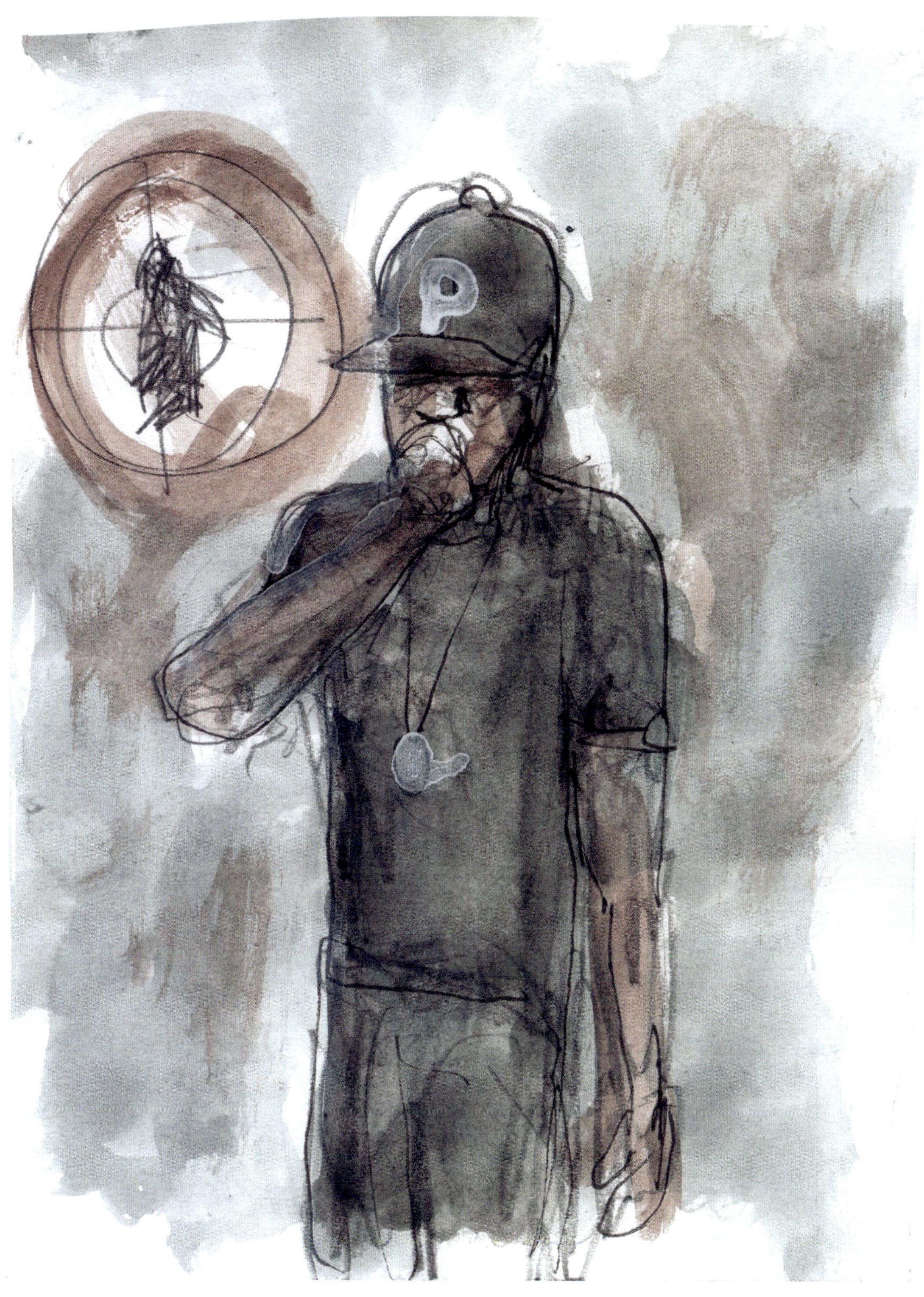

THINGS JUST HAPPEN

I inherited my voice from my father. When he yelled at us, it was heard. If I could say I'm the best at anything as an MC, it wouldn't be the rhymes, the flow or the lyrics. It would be the volume. I know that I'm louder than anybody. When I was young, I would show off... I've blown speakers and mics out before. I was the MC that would make a Radio Shack system sound like a trillion dollars. Hank and Keith could do that too, so I was the perfect MC for them. It's not the stuff you buy it's what you do with it, and you're never going to get it if you've not got it.

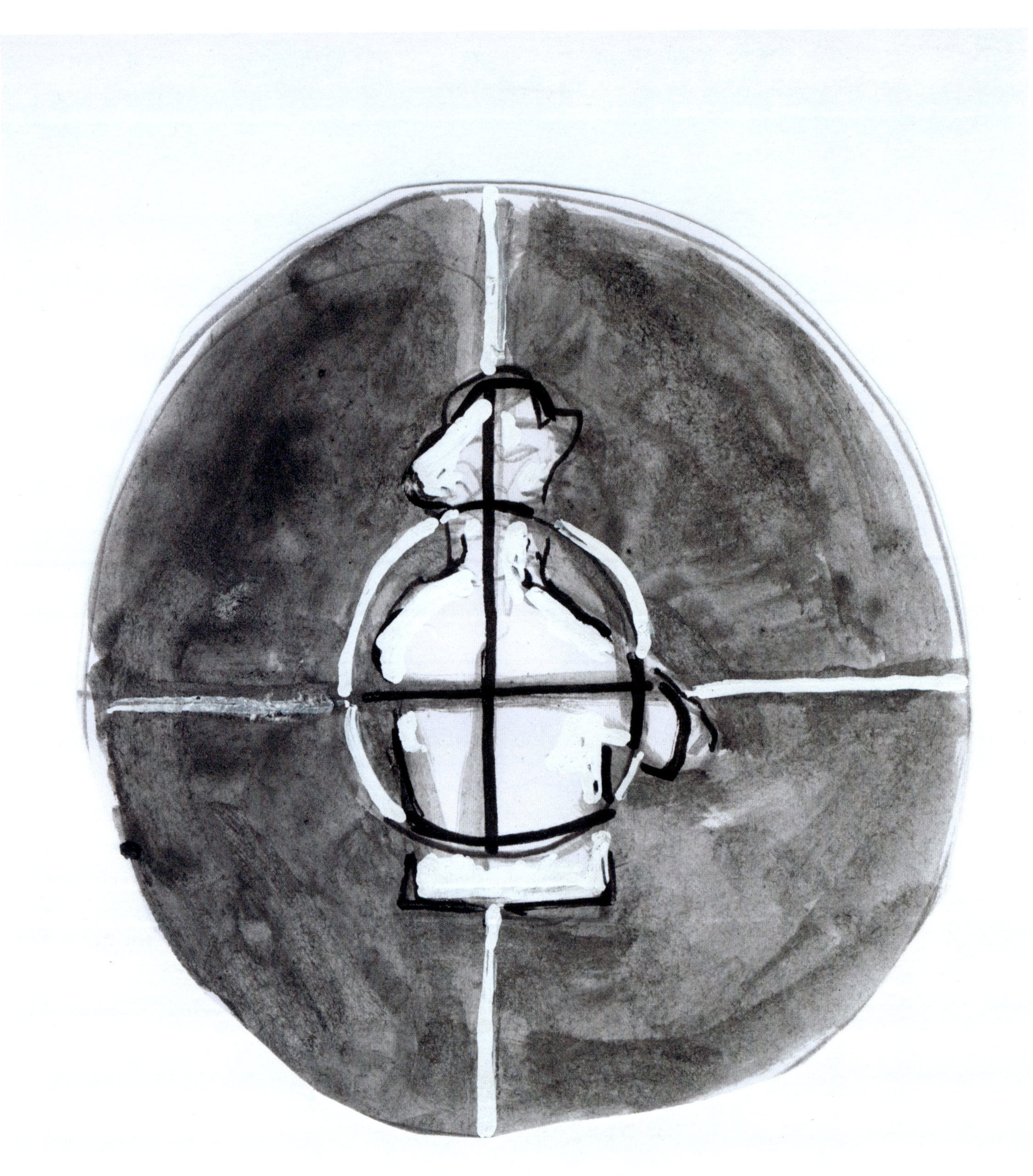

Public Enemy is the antithesis of what the music business is about. We've always taken the unpopular route.

Being the underdog is a feeling I revel in. I came in against the grain. Sometimes I feel that everyone's playing into the scene I set anyway. On the first album, I said, 'I'm the uncool.' Whatever was cool, I was the opposite. With Public Enemy, the whole key was to rebel against the status quo, even when we became the status quo. I've never done two albums alike, never said the same thing twice – that's just me and my perverse mind.

We knew what people were not doing, which allowed us to be daring. *Yo! Bum Rush the Show* said if you can't get what you deserve, kick that door down by any means. *It Takes a Nation of Millions to Hold Us Back* was about how there's millions of motherfuckers stopping us from getting what we need to get. And, from a black nationalist point of view, there's millions of us holding *ourselves* back.

I designed the Public Enemy logo because I believed that hip-hop should have logos, just like the Rockettes. My influence was what Iron Maiden were doing, what the Rolling Stones were doing with their tongue.

I used to work as a DJ at WBAU, the student radio station at Adelphi. One time I invited Tony Allen from the Townhouse 3 over to do a tape, and he brought a guest. Initially, I was a little pissed because I couldn't understand why he would bring somebody. But his guest was none other than the world-famous Flavor Flav. And that was the first day I saw him. He was wearing a black hat, black jacket, black pants, black shades, a black Jheri curl, and he had bought some Player cigarettes the first day they came out and scraped off the front to make it look like he had his own brand of black cigarettes. Then he kept fucking with my black keyboard. So here was this cat with this black Jheri curl, black clothes, a black pack of cigarettes, fucking with my black keyboard. At least we knew he was black.

My first words to Flavor were, 'You can't smoke up here. You have to go outside.' Eventually, he started hanging out up at the station and people would crack on him all the time. Flavor would be the target of many snaps.

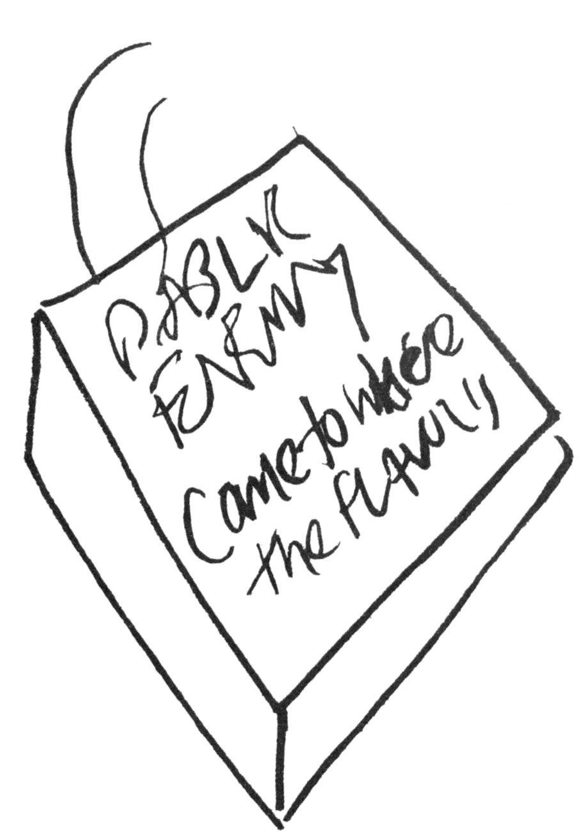

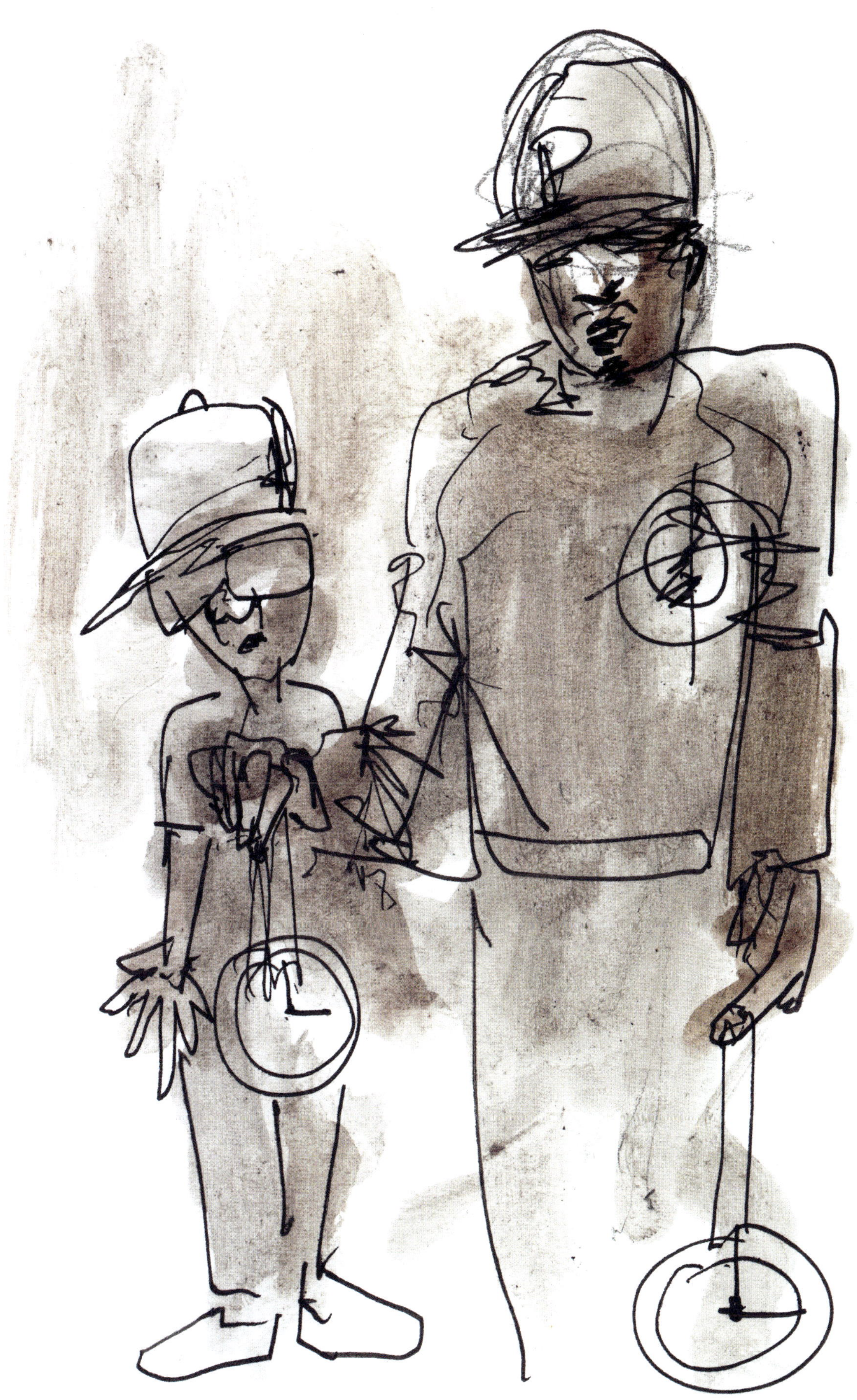

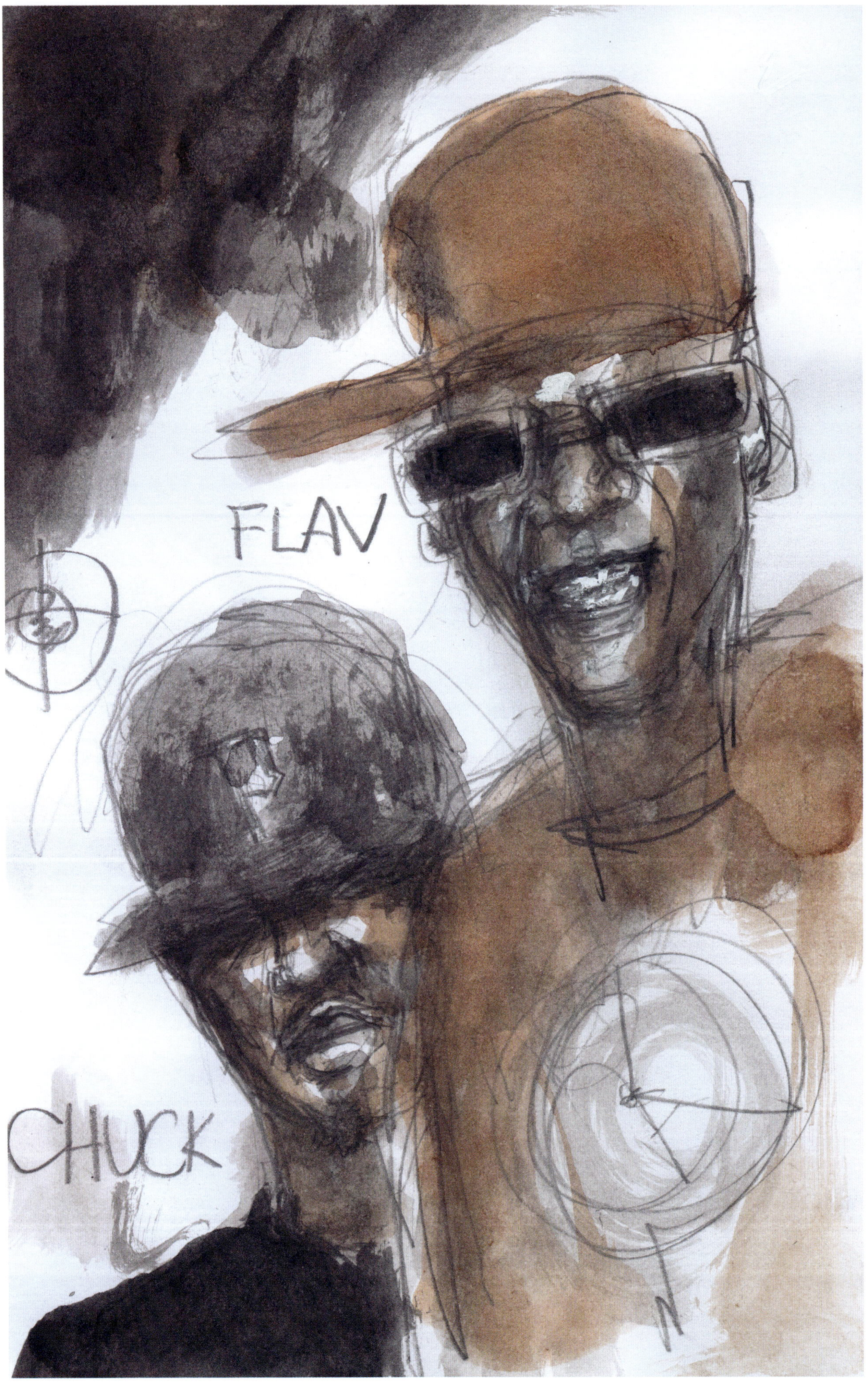
FLAV
CHUCK

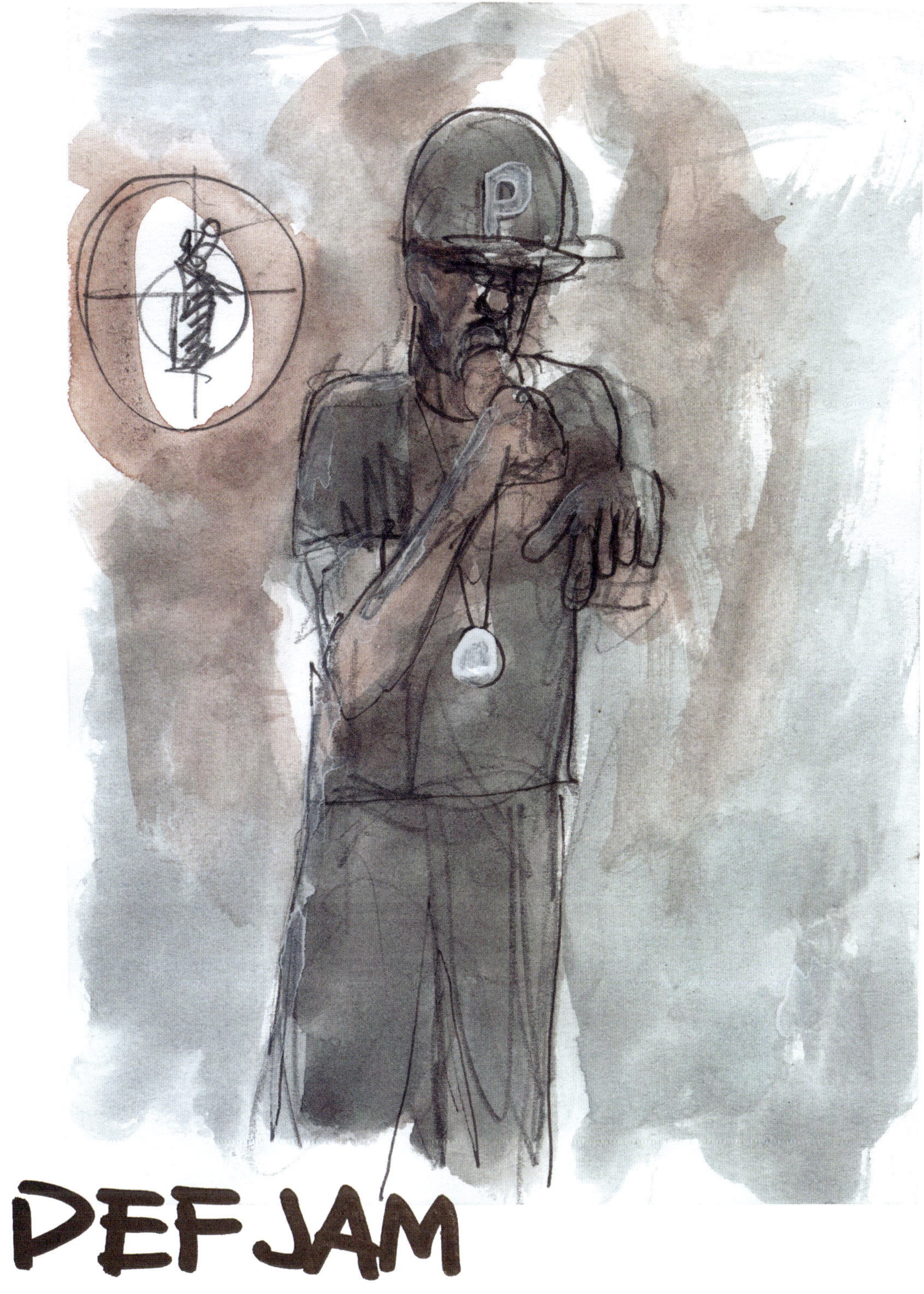

DEF JAM

We signed with Def Jam in June of 1986. I said, 'You can't have me unless you bring Flavor.' Rick Rubin's big question was, 'What does Flavor do? I'm not going to sign anybody that's not a vocalist.' We really couldn't explain what Flavor did – he had his own unique thing.

All I knew was that I didn't want to do it alone and, secondly, I wanted to do something similar to James Brown and Bobby Byrd. I needed someone that I could bounce off and Flavor was perfect for that. It was something we pushed hard for. We said he would be a vocalist. On the first album, he had very limited vocals, but he was there just enough to justify a contract.

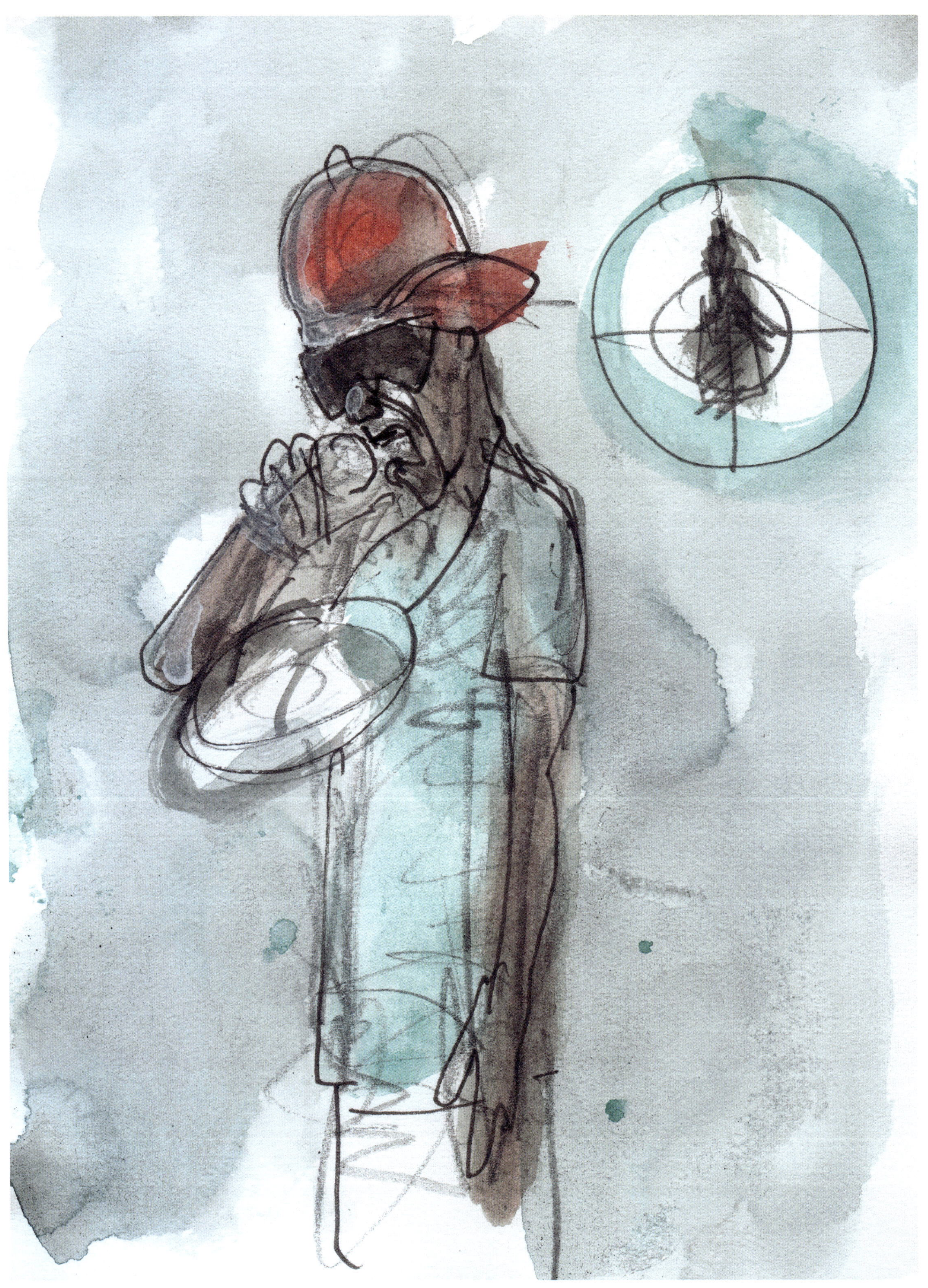

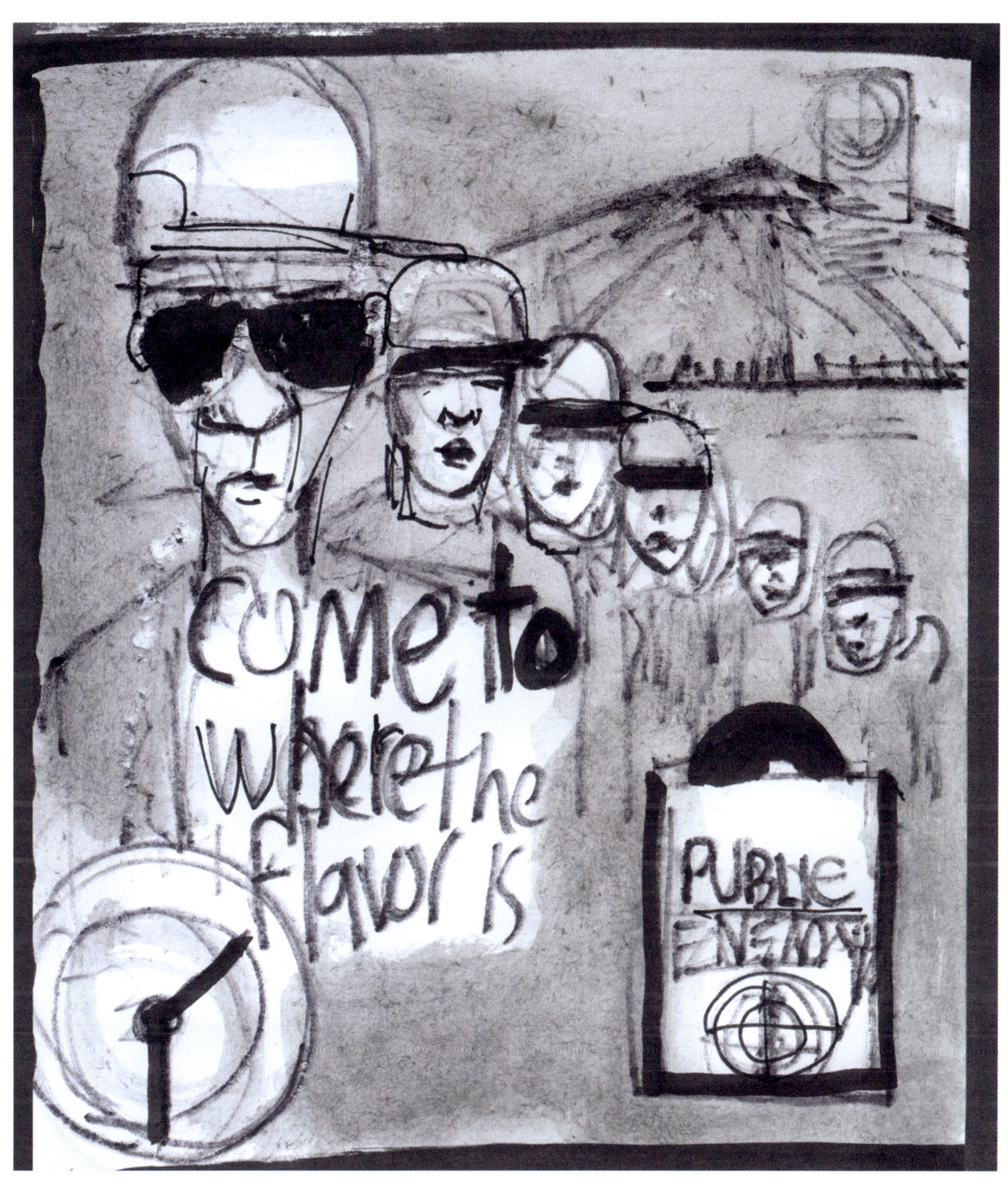

Flavor's job is to step into the room and suck the stardom out of it. There has never been anybody better at that. Comedians, actors and other rappers make millions by imitating him, but they can never duplicate him. They take a piece of Flavor and use it for whatever they do.

I told Def Jam that if I was going to do a record they had to take what I gave them and that's why the album's called *Yo! Bum Rush the Show.* It ain't *Chuck D Gets a Record Deal*. I brought all these guys I knew with me. Hank came in, Bill Stephney became an executive, Harry Allen became the first hip-hop journalist, and then you've got Flavor who became a hypeman. There's Professor Griff and the Security of the First World, the S1Ws – what were they? Teminator X too. 'Bum rushing the show' is when you're trying to get into a spot but they won't let you in and you can't afford the door charge. All you've got to do is get a toe in that door at the side and you're all in. That was our invasion of the record industry on our own terms. We said that we were going to give ourselves two years to change the game.

We made a demo called 'Public Enemy No. 1', which was about being able to speak for yourself despite the outside world stereotyping you. 'Public Enemy No. 1' brought us to the name Public Enemy. We were all interested in music as well as trying to give the town and surrounding areas something positive to do, because we felt that there was an absence of opportunities for young people around that time. All of a sudden there was a plethora of guns and drugs coming into the black communities. We tried to dispel that from people's minds and focus their attention on the music. In the lyrics we would drop in some points of reference and good vibes about us as a people.

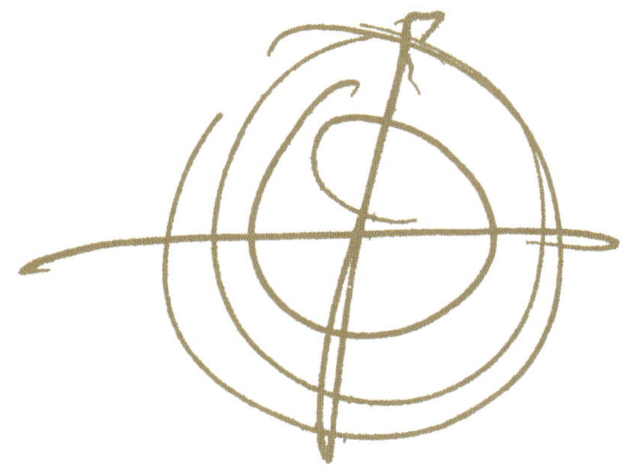

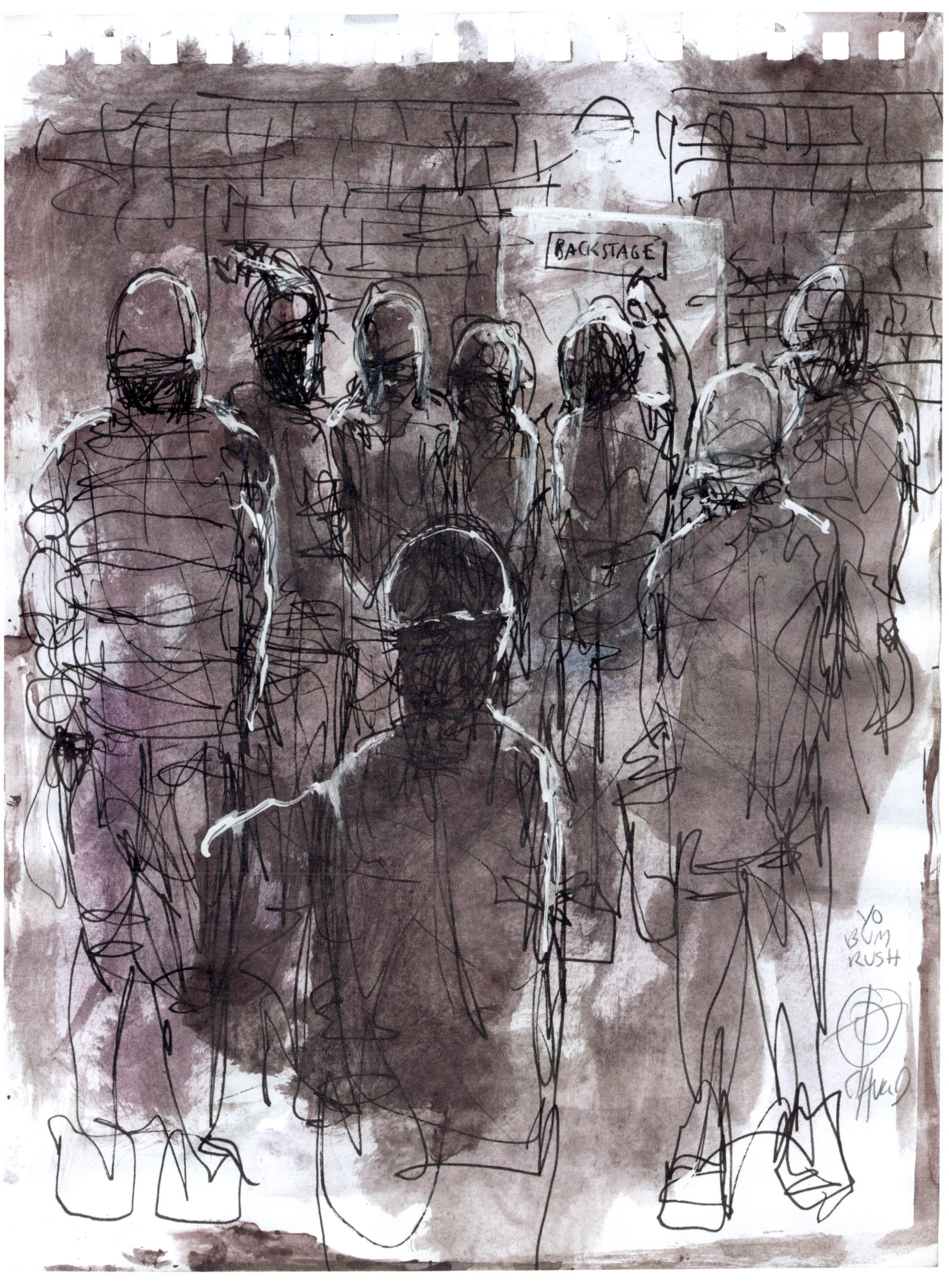
BACKSTAGE
YO
BUM
RUSH

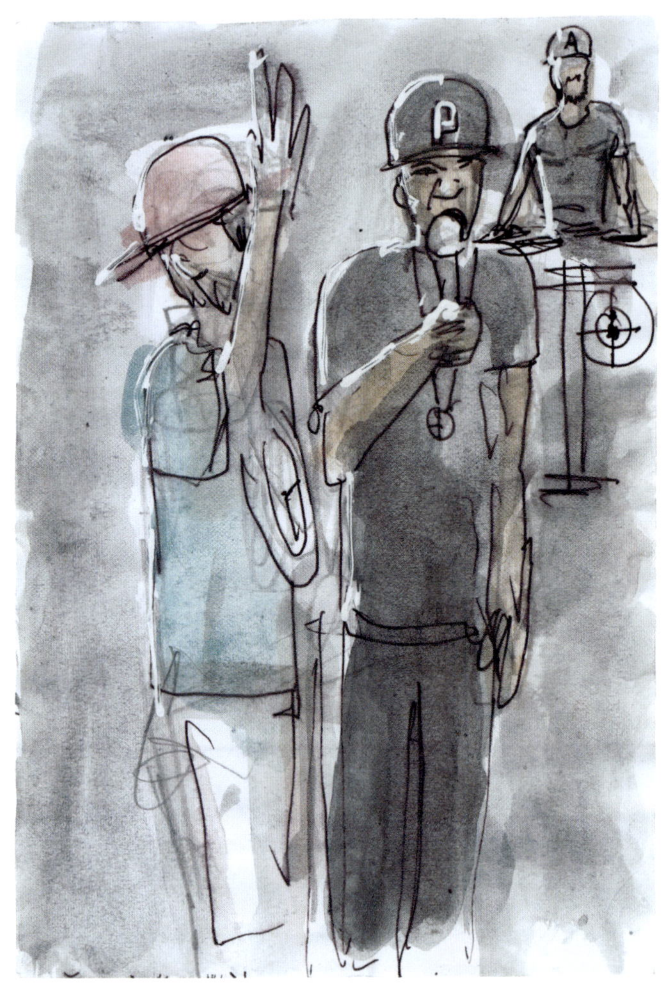

21ST CENTURY RHYMES

In the early days my father had a furniture shop in Queens and he would move furniture for fabric companies in Manhattan. Flavor and I would do this for a little income. Most of the time I would drive because I wasn't going to sit in the passenger seat with that crazy motherfucker at the wheel. While in the truck we would practise routines; I would be the rapper and Flavor would do what he does. We would ride around town in my father's U-Haul truck when it was crazy cold, putting up flyers on the poles to promote our next gig until our hands froze.

People would drive by looking at us, splashing slush on us, but when the gigs rolled around they wanted to get in. There would be times after we'd finished where I would be driving the truck and Flavor and Keith were in the back and I'd turn the corners real fast to make them fly around with the refrigerators, desks and chairs that were back there. Those were the days. We had the most fun.

At the beginning of 'Public Enemy No. 1', Flavor says, 'Now remember that line you was kicking to me on the way out to LA Laurelton Queens while we was in the car on our way to the shop?' That came from when Flavor and I were working for my pops.

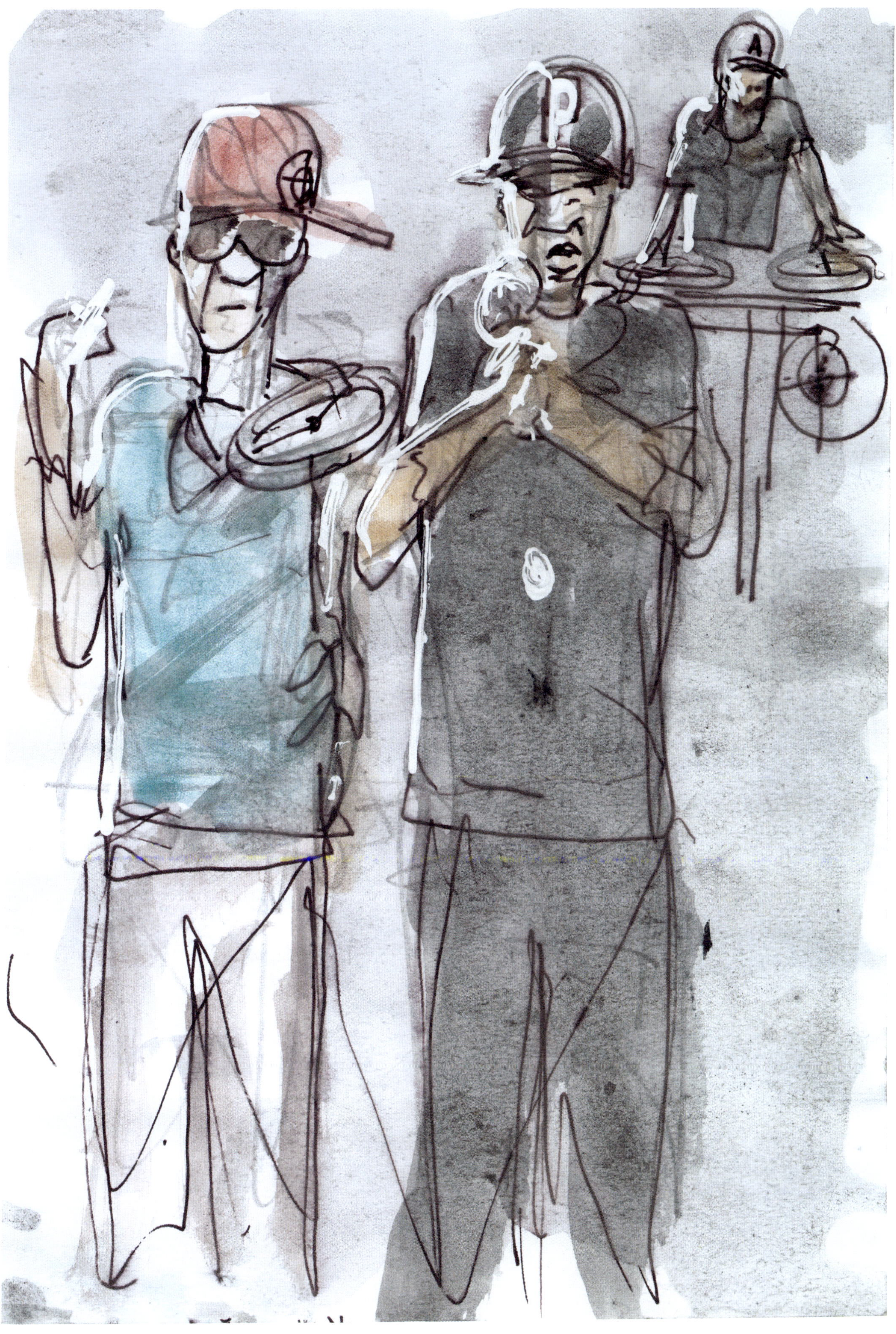

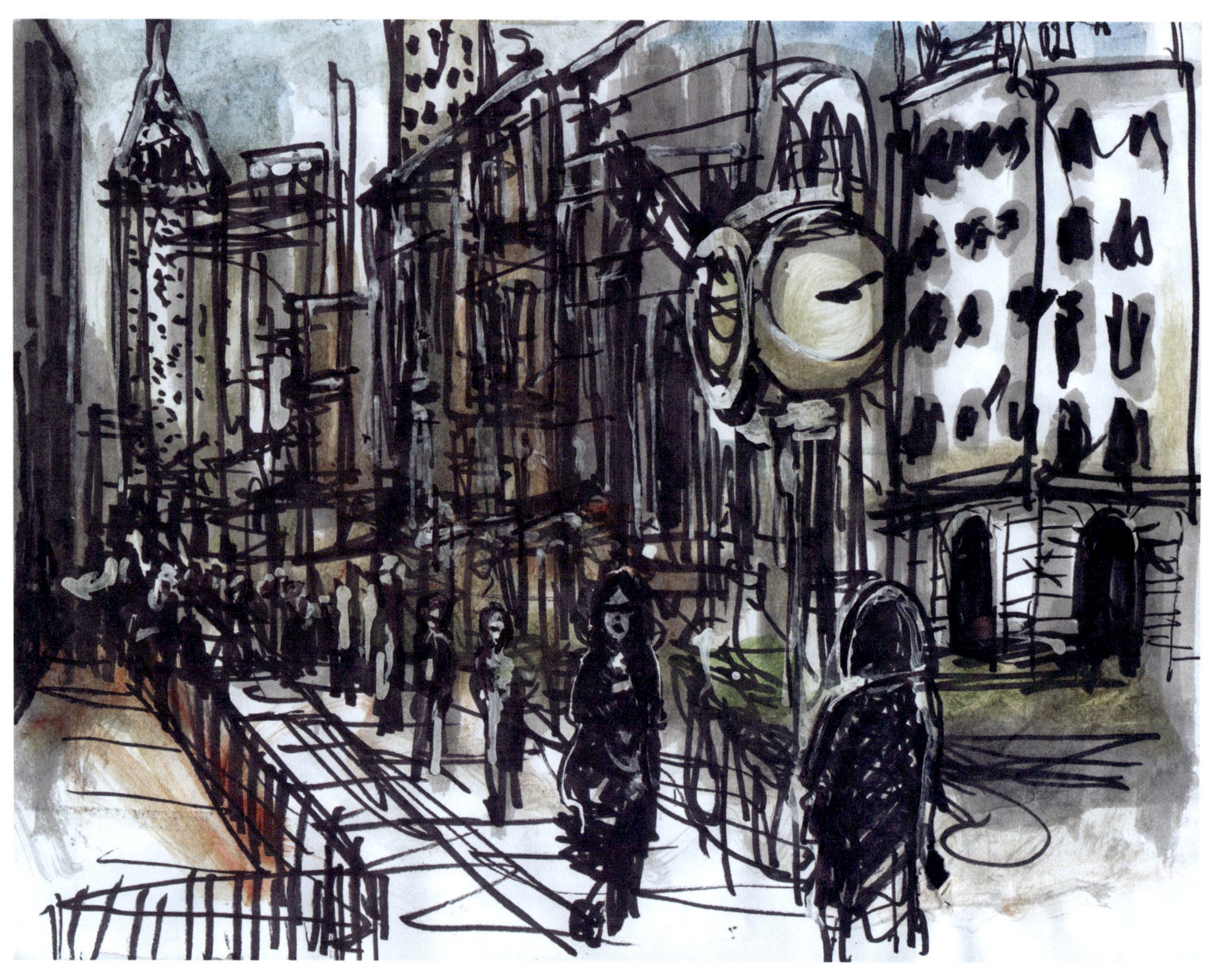

Public Enemy's first gig in New York City took place at a popular club called Latin Quarter. I had my father's van, which was a rickety yellow and white Chevy that smoked a lot, and it was questionable if it would make it from Long Island to the city. But it did and we pulled up right out front, opened the door and about 20 of us got out and rolled up in there.

Melle Mel, who was part of Grandmaster Flash and the Furious Five, was quite bitter about what was going on in the industry at the time and started lashing out while we were doing our first show. I could hear him shouting, 'Y'all suck, get the fuck off the stage.' I just had to keep going forward. It was part of the breaking-in process.

I didn't take it personally. New York City has never been a place that gives up props to another place, that's just the personality of the city. As a matter of fact, it was the best thing that could have happened to us because it showed us that we had to earn our respect. All that we'd done in Long Island was known, but if we wanted to conquer other places we would have to go there and perform. Melle Mel let us have it that night.

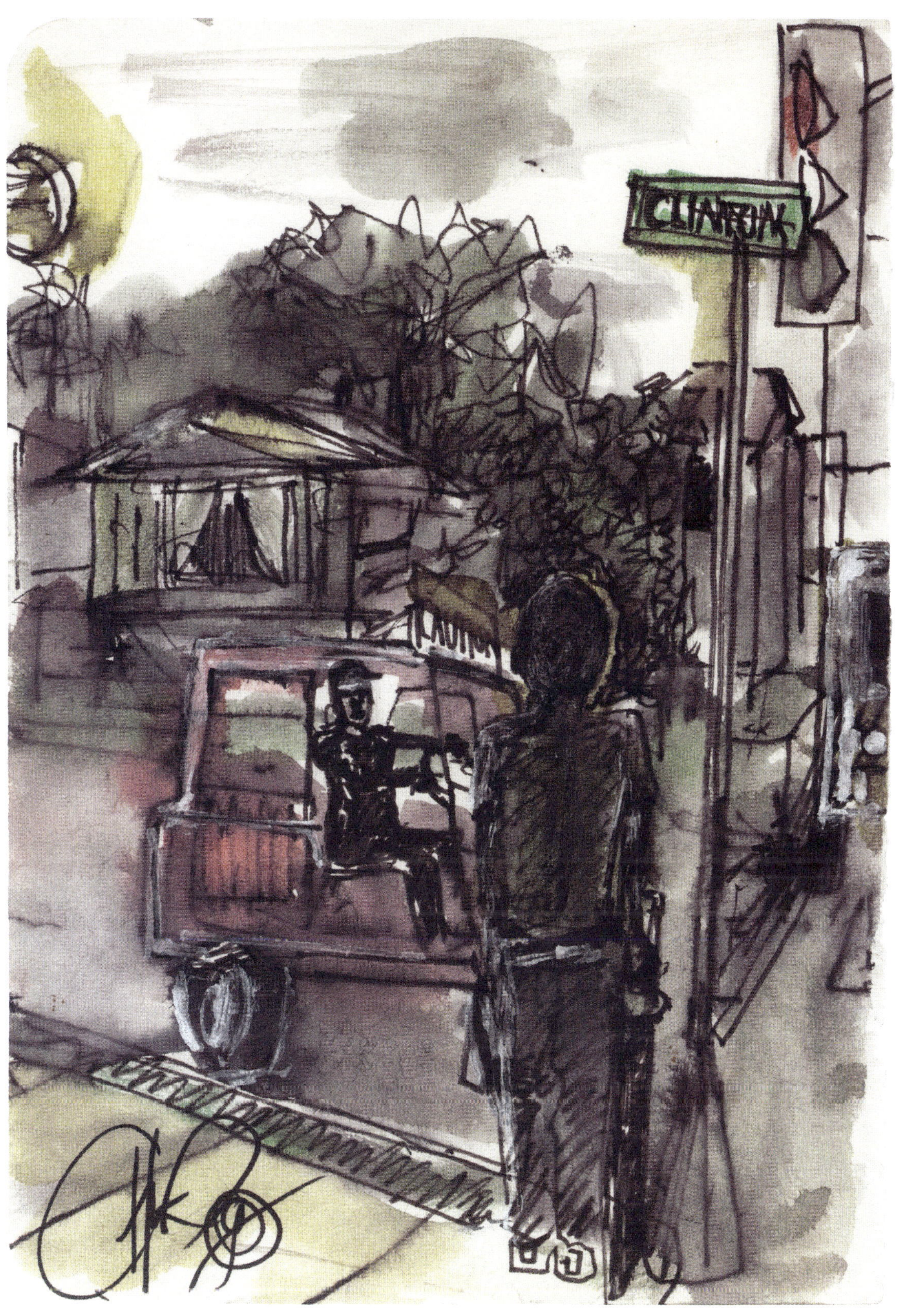

I've been to 107 countries and I have different favourites at different times, but I'm forever amazed by New York. It's always shaping into something else. New York has been romanticised, but there was nothing to romanticise about a ripped-up, torn-down, burnt-out Bronx. There was nothing to romanticise about a disenfranchised Harlem, a dirty Lower East Side. The beauty of New York is the people. The New York that's shined up and expensive now is a beautiful thing, but they forgot the people in the process.

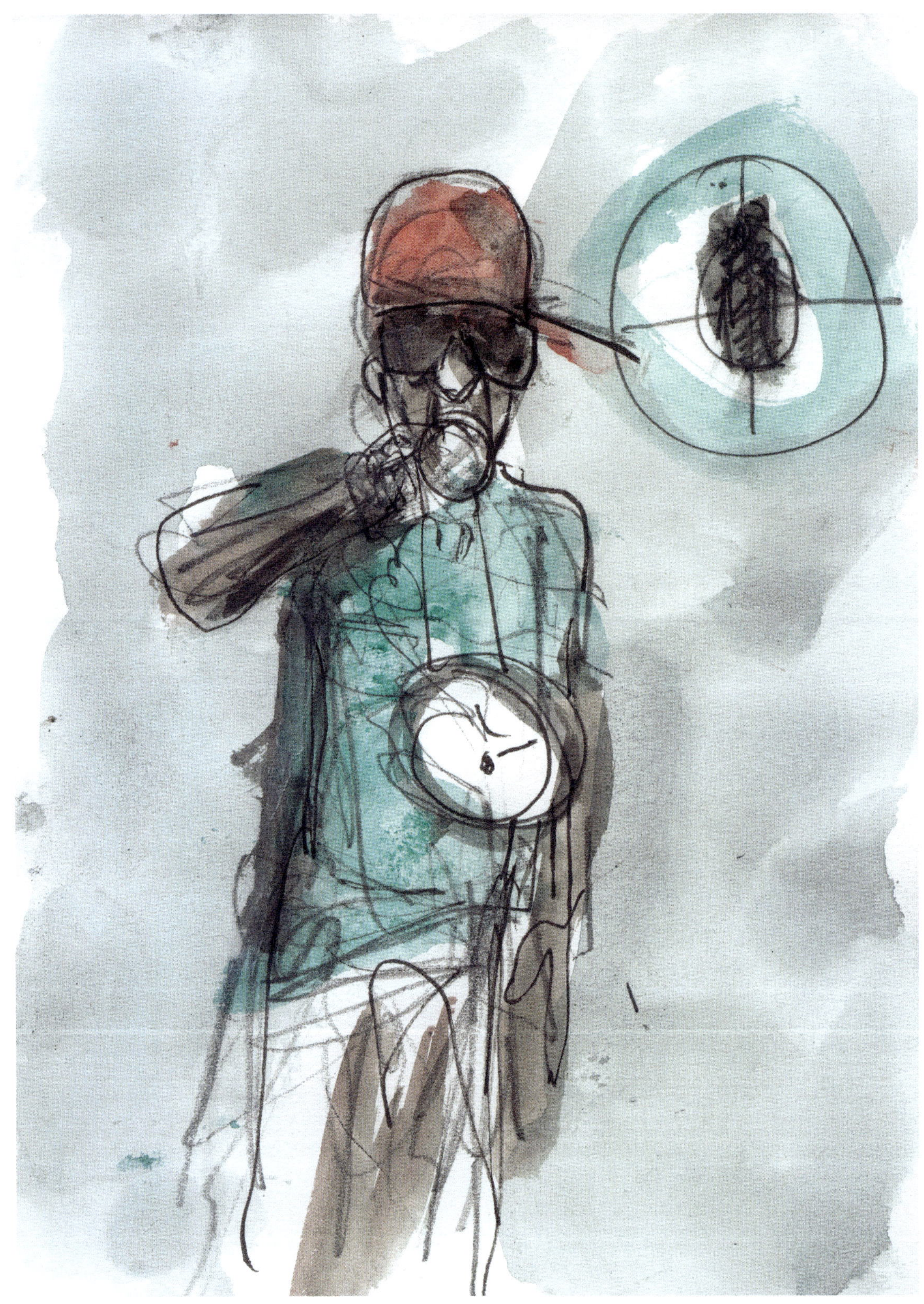

Flavor would do crazy shit. At the beginning of his WBAU show he would play a tape of the actual sounds of Penn Station. He recorded the guy making the announcements, put that on the radio and people bugged out.

Everywhere he went he took his big boombox and recorded everything. He would go around town taping people. He just wanted to do something different. He was always one of those out-of-the-ordinary type of brothers, so the shit that he played on the radio was original.

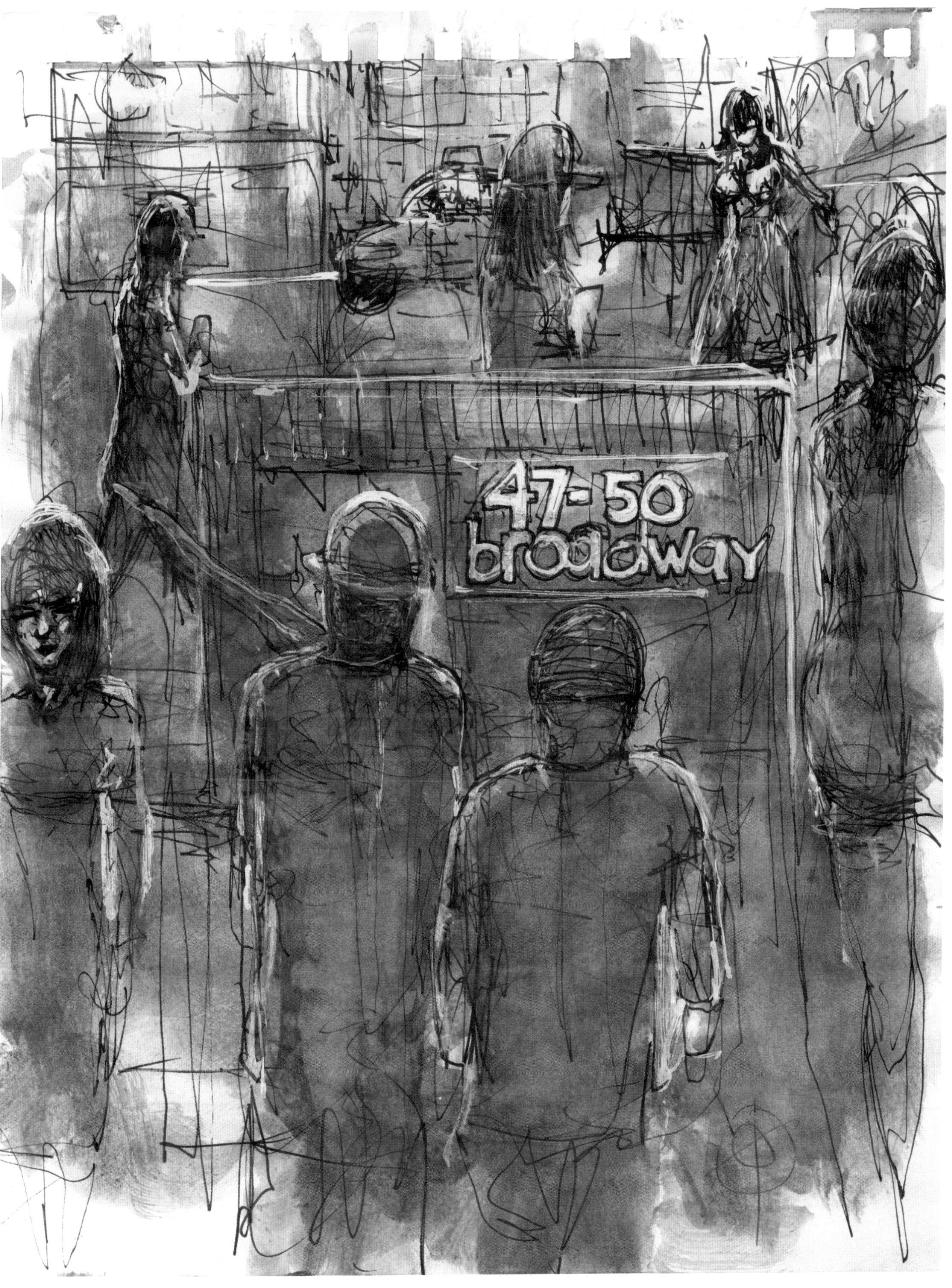
47-50
broadway

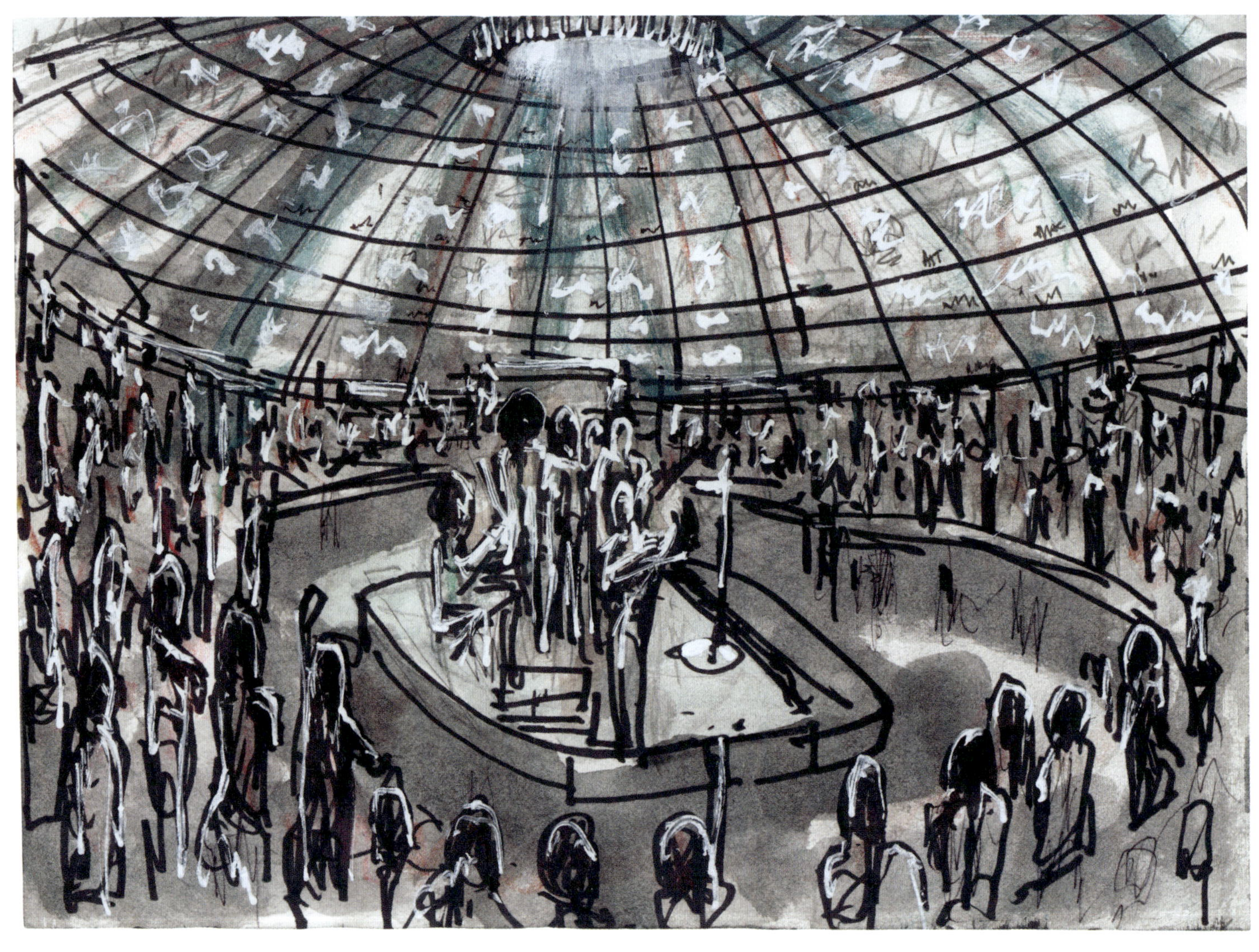

I still remember when Run-DMC did a concert at Madison Square Garden. That's the concert where Run said to the audience, 'Put all the Adidas in the air,' and over half the audience held up their Adidas shoes.

I was invited to the concert by Russell Simmons and his Rush Productions people, who were trying to sign me to Def Jam, and I was very impressed with the warmth of the whole family. Run-DMC were always very humble. When they came up to WBAU for their first interview they were humble, then when they came back to WBAU they were humble, and after they had just finished rocking thousands of people at Madison Square Garden, they were still humble as ever. I was very impressed, and it made me think, 'Damn, and they want me to get down with them?' That was one of the things that helped me make the decision to go for it.

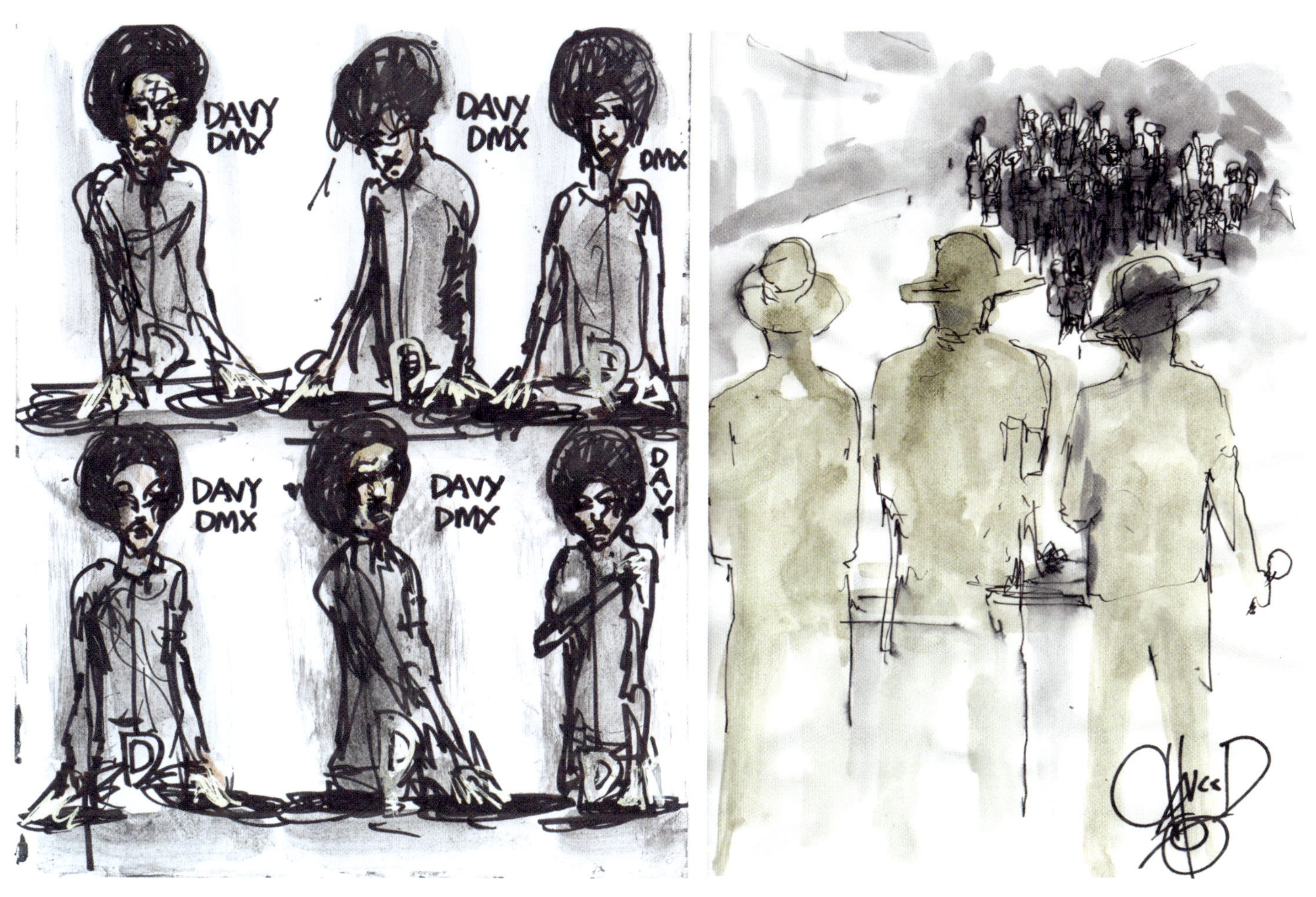

I was convinced that rap was big-time based on Run-DMC's success. When they debuted *Raising Hell* (produced by Davy DMX) in 1986 I was stunned. I saw it in Record World at the Green Acres Mall in Valley Stream and noticed that in one picture they wore the New York Mets colours. Run looked like he was counting money, DMC was in the room and Jam Master Jay was sneaking out of the back. I stared at that album for about half an hour. I kept turning it to the back and then to the front. That album looked big-time. It looked like something you would see in the rock world. I said to myself, 'This shit is incredible.'

Run-DMC changed the rap and rock worlds with 'Walk This Way'. The story of Rick Rubin rubbing his Long Beach, Long Island rock roots into Run-DMC and Jam Master Jay's hip-hop and rap is a legend. The video broke across the US via MTV, but the song set off many alarms familiar to fanatics of both genres.

As early as 1982, I thought that hip-hop and rap music could rival what the rock guys were doing in Long Island.

If you know anything about Long Island in the Eighties, rock music had a strong presence at the local level, the mid-level and the gigantic level. The Good Guys were a local group that made a living in the tri-state area and didn't care about going anywhere else. They would do sold-out shows in Long Island for 5,000 people every weekend, so they didn't have to go anywhere. Then you had Anthrax, which was the next level up. They had a record contract where they ventured out with Twisted Sister. And then you had KISS, who were gigantic.

What Rick Rubin and Russell Simmons did with Run-DMC was make rap rival rock. So, when I came along with Public Enemy, it was a great situation to mimic.

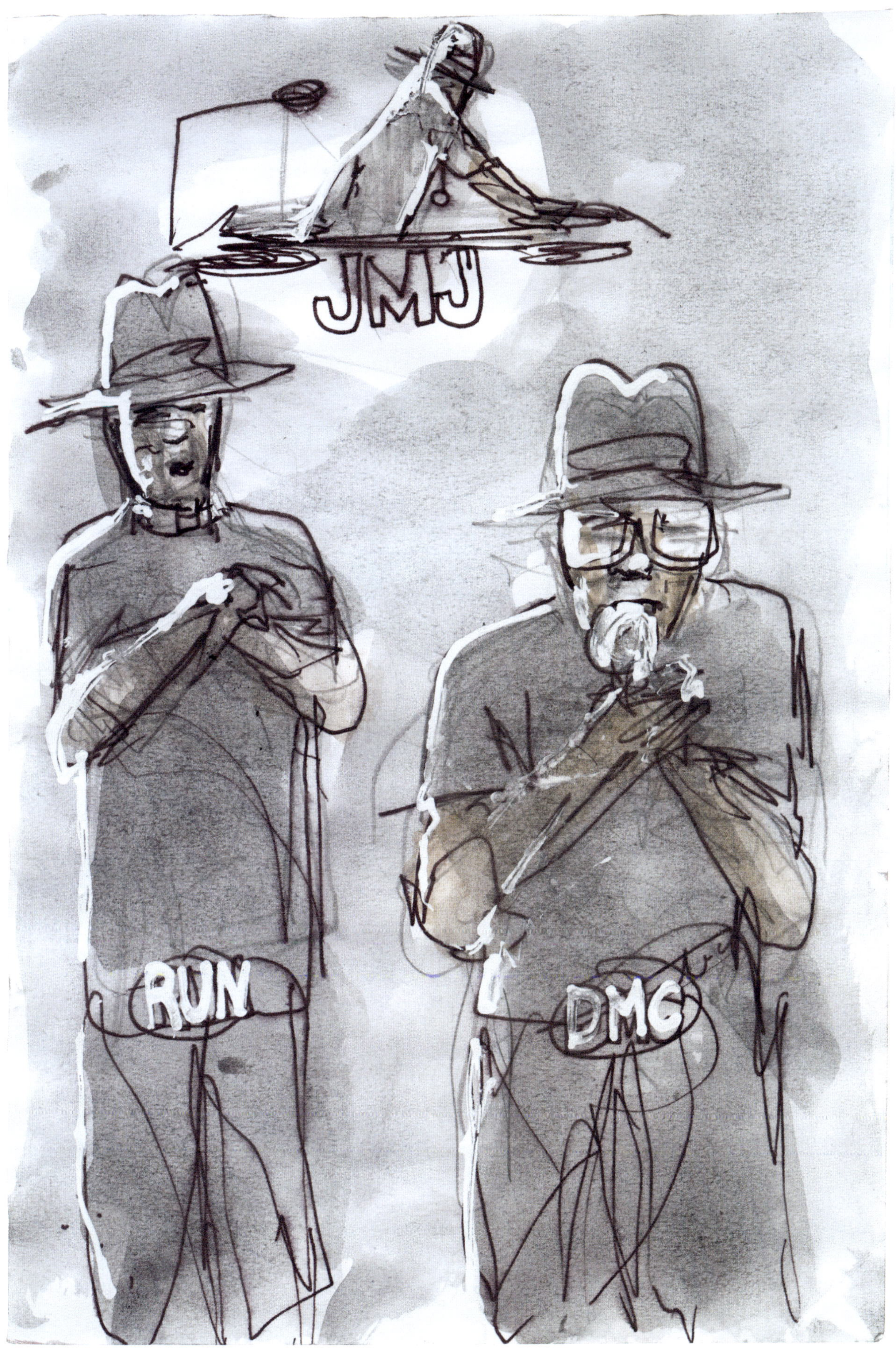
JMJ
RUN
DMC

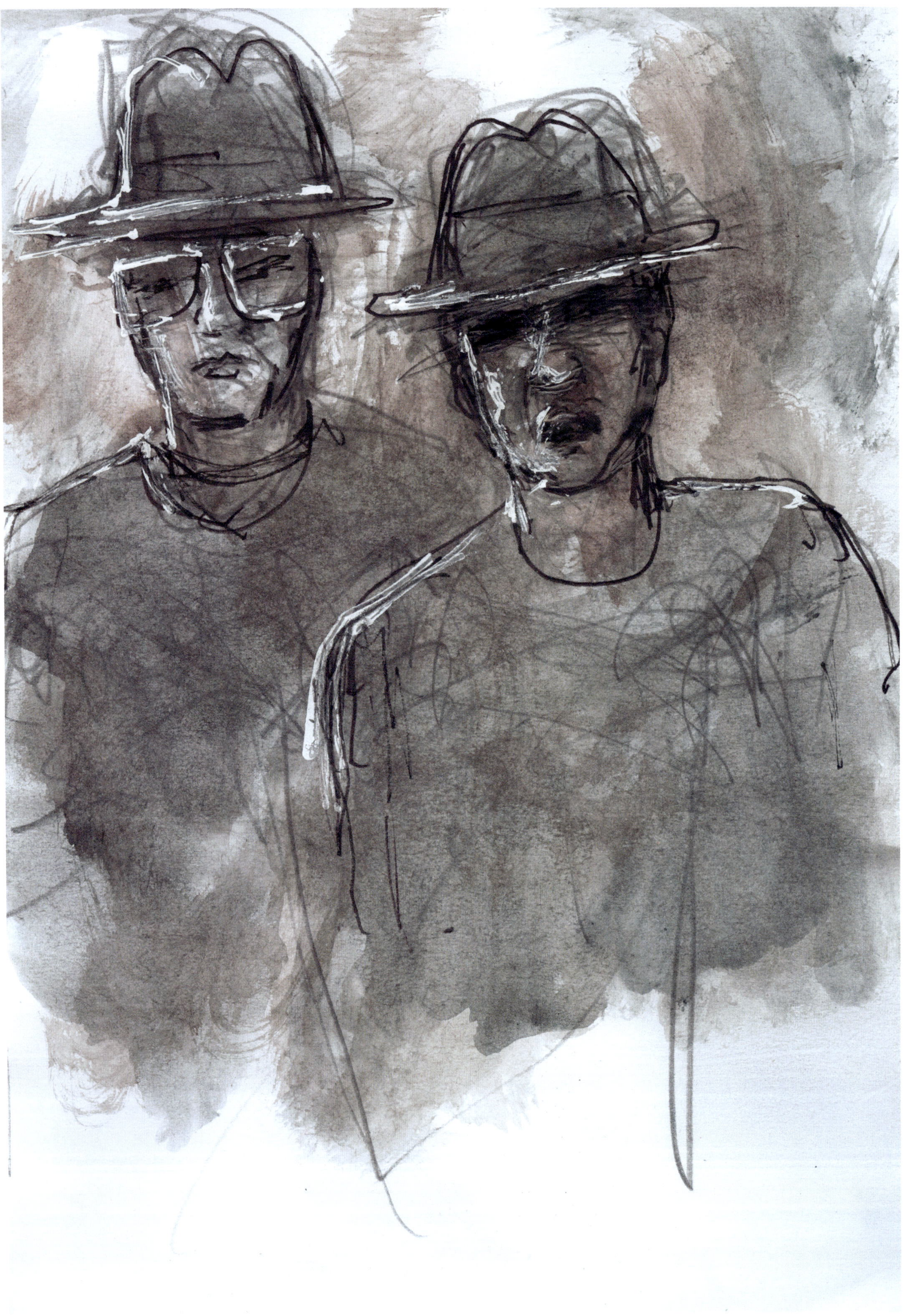

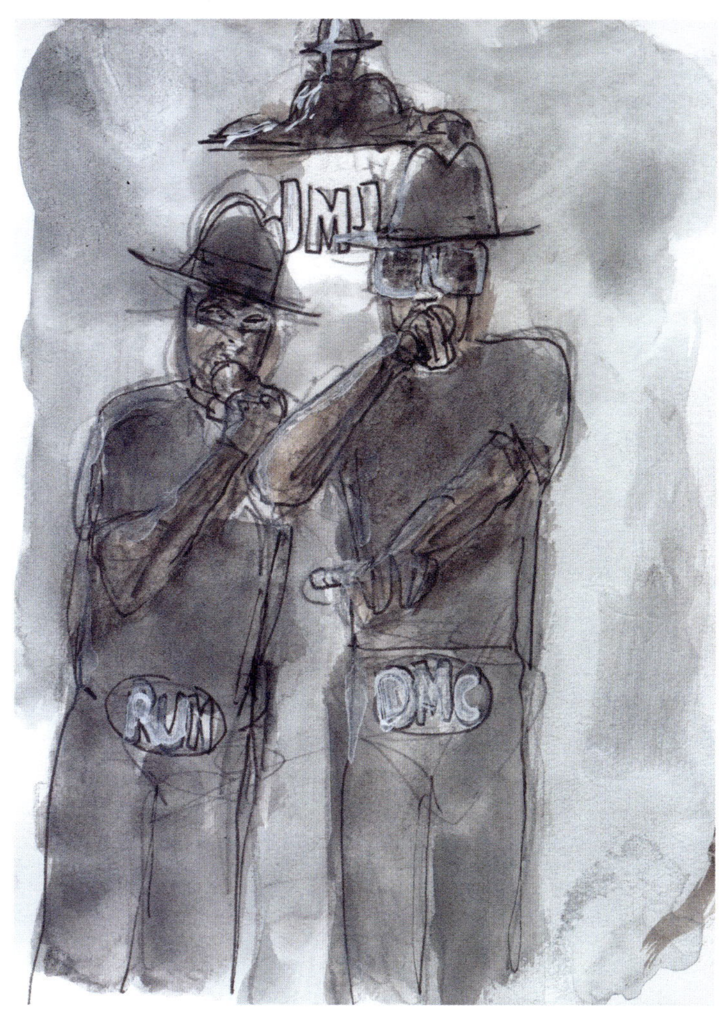

RUN DMC

Run-DMC used to bring their WBAU tapes on tour and play them, which was flattering.

WBAU helped inspire Run-DMC to do their music, and their music helped inspire us to do better radio. They would go around the world and come back to WBAU with tapes, and then take the tapes from the station out to wherever they went to, so we became like their home base.

Later, their album-making process was an influence on Public Enemy. Although there had been hip-hop and rap albums before, Run-DMC was the template we used for *Yo! Bum Rush the Show*. It was the invasion of the group concept into an area where there seemed to be a lot of threes and soloists. We wanted Public Enemy to come across like one too many. It was convenient for me because I'd rather be tucked in the back and heard not seen, so being part of a unit cloaked me.

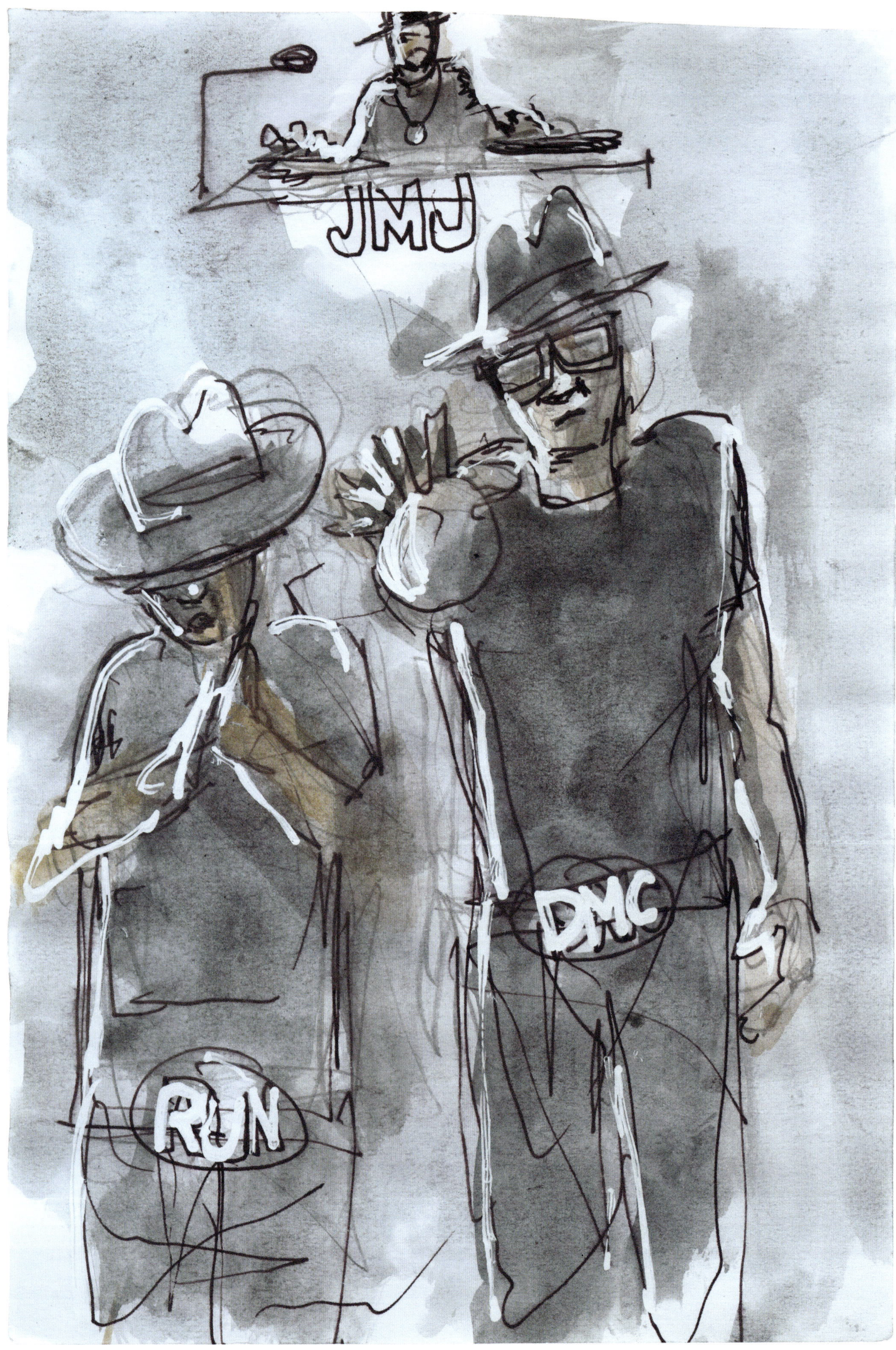
JMJ
RUN
DMC

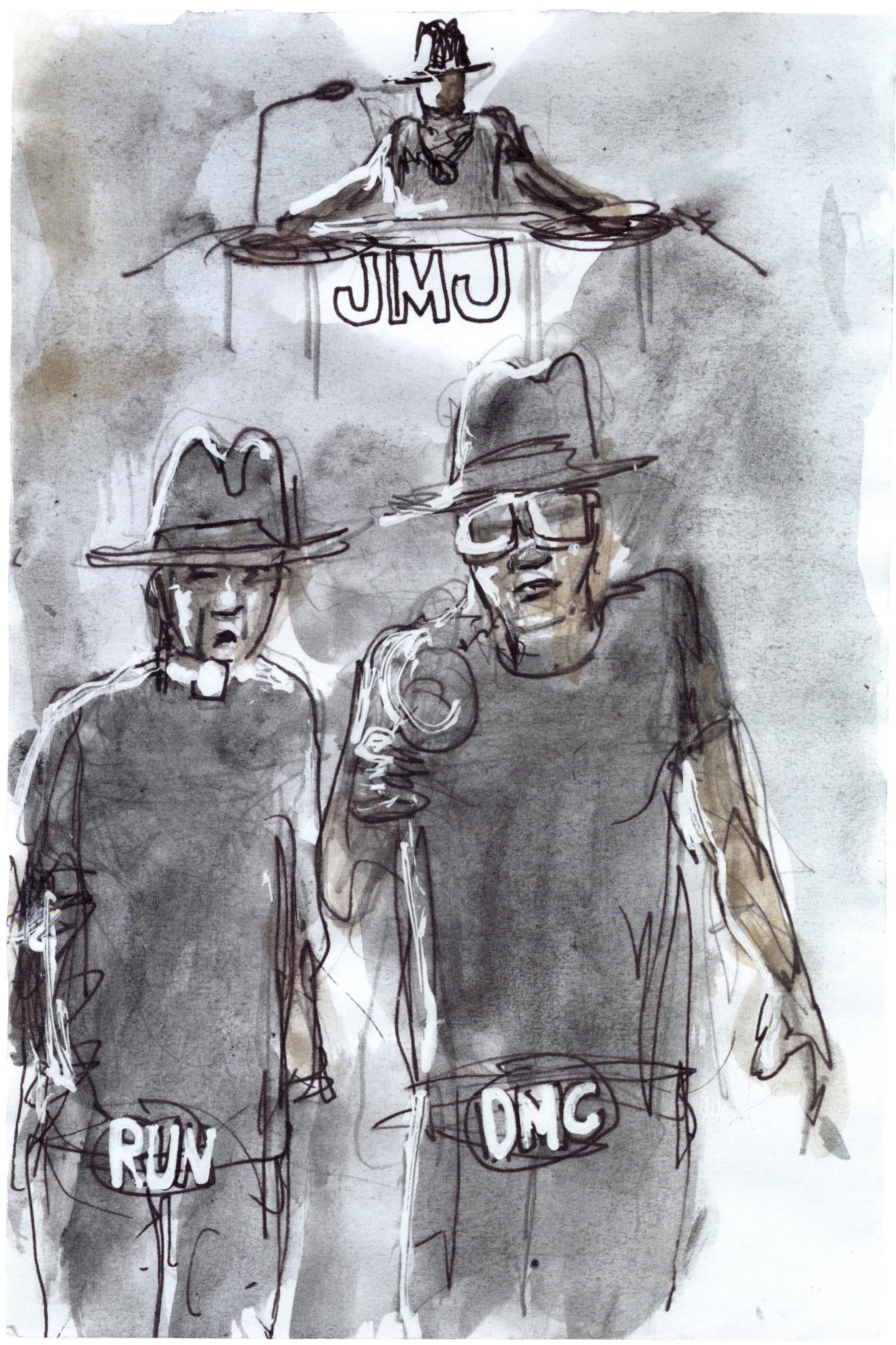
JMJ
RUN
DMC

Time and time again, in word and in practice, the Beastie Boys honoured pop's founding principles. As true musicians they moved beyond drum machines and repetitive samples and picked up their own instruments. It was their way of paying tribute to the musicians who preceded them, who built the foundations of hip-hop. In particular, Adam Yauch belongs with the greatest.

He was the one who committed the Beastie Boys to their lengthy campaign for Freedom for Tibet, which not only helped to shine a light on Tibet's struggle for independence but allowed them to move from fighting for their right to party to fighting for their right to fight.

There's no adequate measure for the impact that they had on rap music and yours truly, Public Enemy, during our formative years. Artistically, they were our role models. They gave us some of our richest support, which is uncharacteristic of many advisers in this game. The very first time the Beastie Boys headlined their own tour in January of 1987, the Licensed to Ill tour, they invited us to join the bill in April. The line-up was the Beastie Boys, Murphy's Law and Public Enemy. Watching them tear the house up, we learned so much about the importance of a great stage show.

They made us rethink what we should do onstage and affirmed for us how important our own Beastie Boy, Flavor Flav, might be to our success. In that way, the Beastie Boys helped Public Enemy to get our act together by more than living up to their name night after night on the road. They are one of the greatest live acts in music.

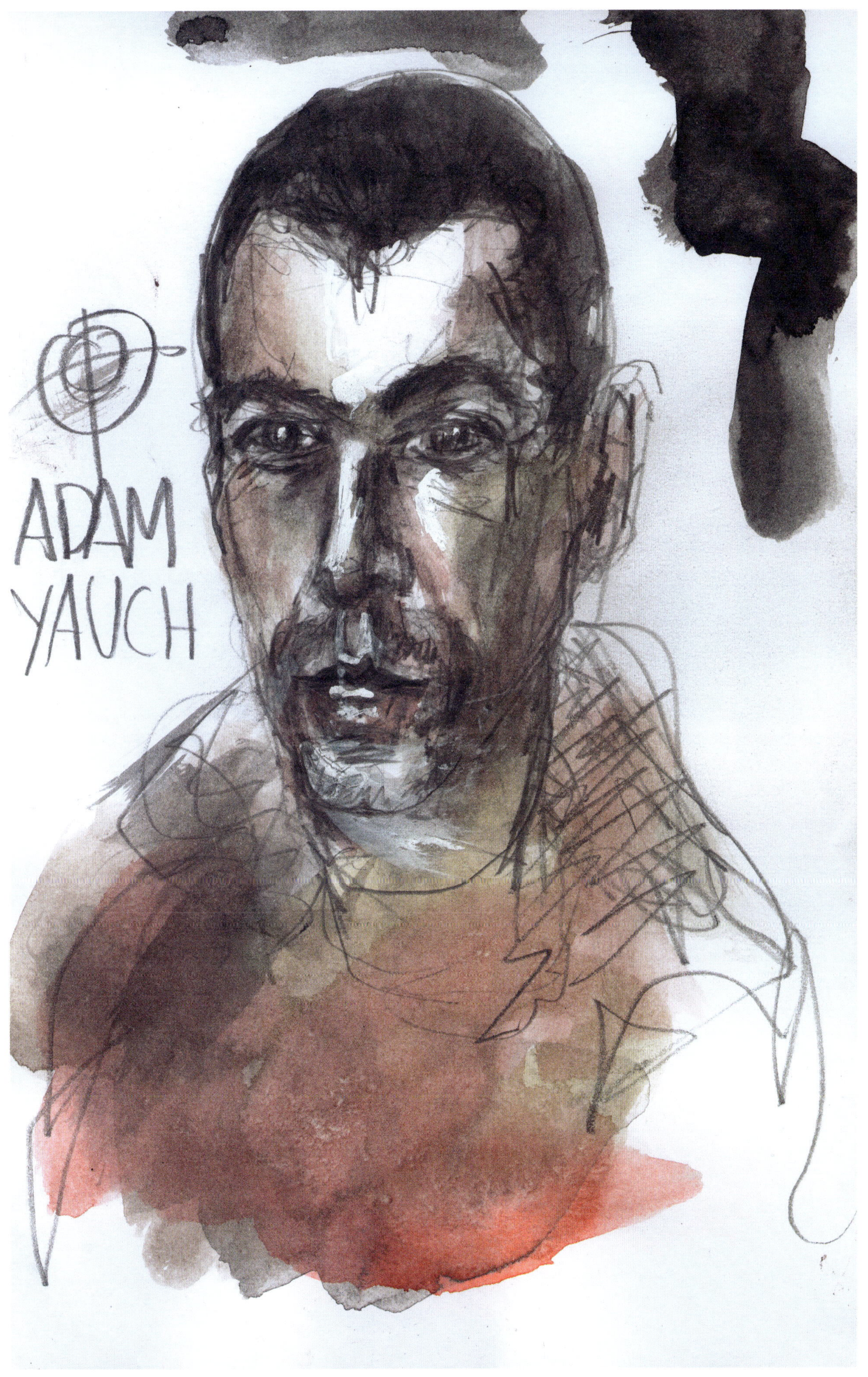
ADAM
YAUCH

HIP HOP

When the Beastie Boys emerged from their pop beginnings in 1983, I was working at WBAU. I was a DJ there under Mr Bill Adler and later Dr Andre Brown, aka Dr Dre. After WBAU, Dre became the DJ for the Beasties on their tour and never looked back.

Programme director for WBAU, Bill Stephney, had already played their punk tracks from as early as 1983 and continued with Def Jam label releases in 1984 and 1985. Then came the Def Jam purple-label indie days and the beginnings of the rap/rock mix. By the time *Licensed to Ill* was a national sensation, WBAU had already played the Beastie Boys for four years and they were regular mainstays.

People get me to talk about Jay-Z or Eminem, but it's impossible to talk about those dudes without mentioning guys of the magnitude of LL Cool J and the Beastie Boys, who made it possible for them. Jay-Z and Eminem are evolutionary MCs, but LL Cool J and the Beastie Boys were revolutionary MCs. They created the standard.

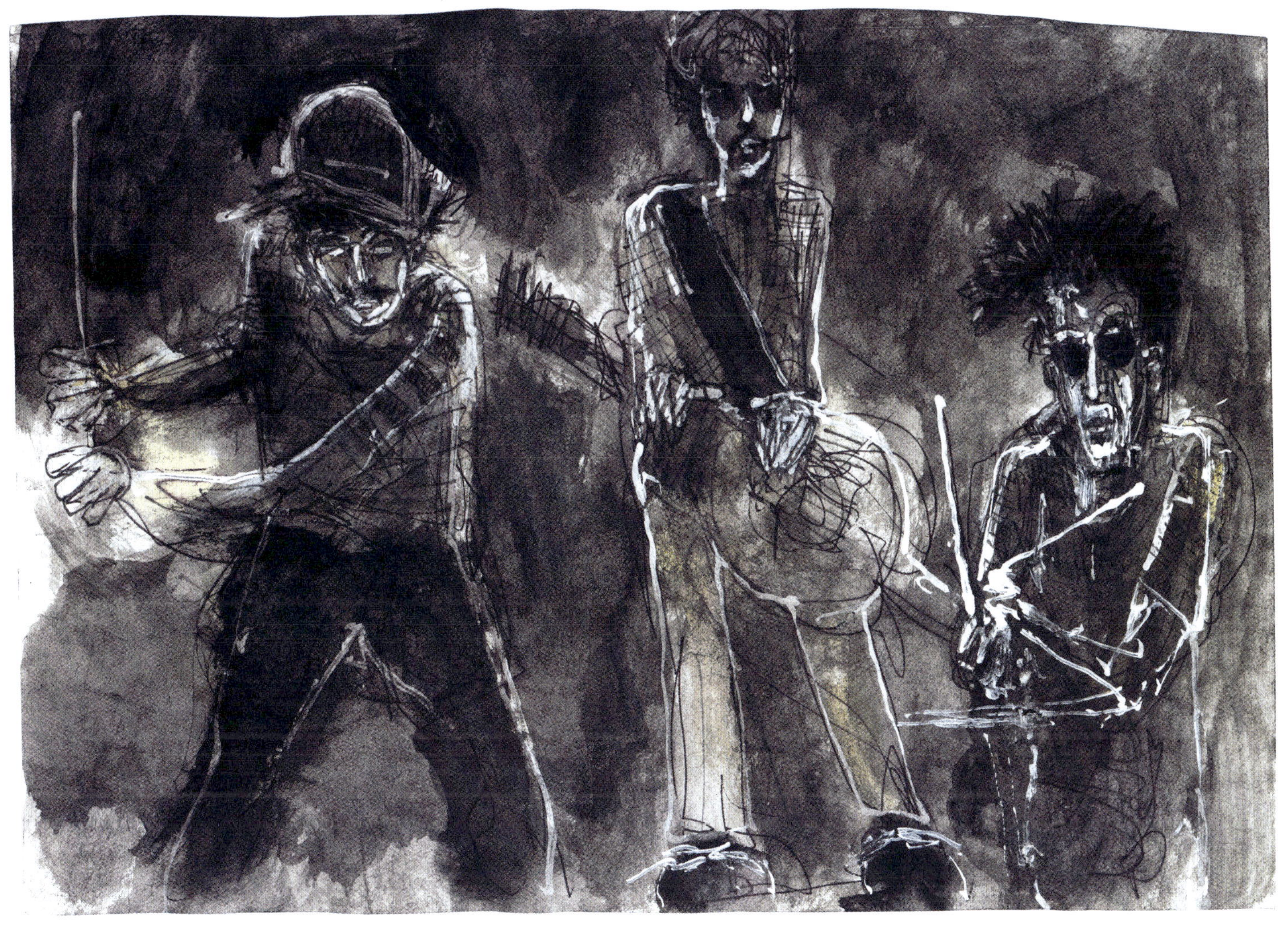

BEASTIE BOYS

One of the most admirable qualities about the Beastie Boys was that they stayed so true to the game over the years, no matter what was going on with hip-hop culture in general. As far as I'm concerned, the trend towards individualism in hip-hop has crippled the art form. Yet through it all, they remained a team of MCs in the style of the groups that inspired them.

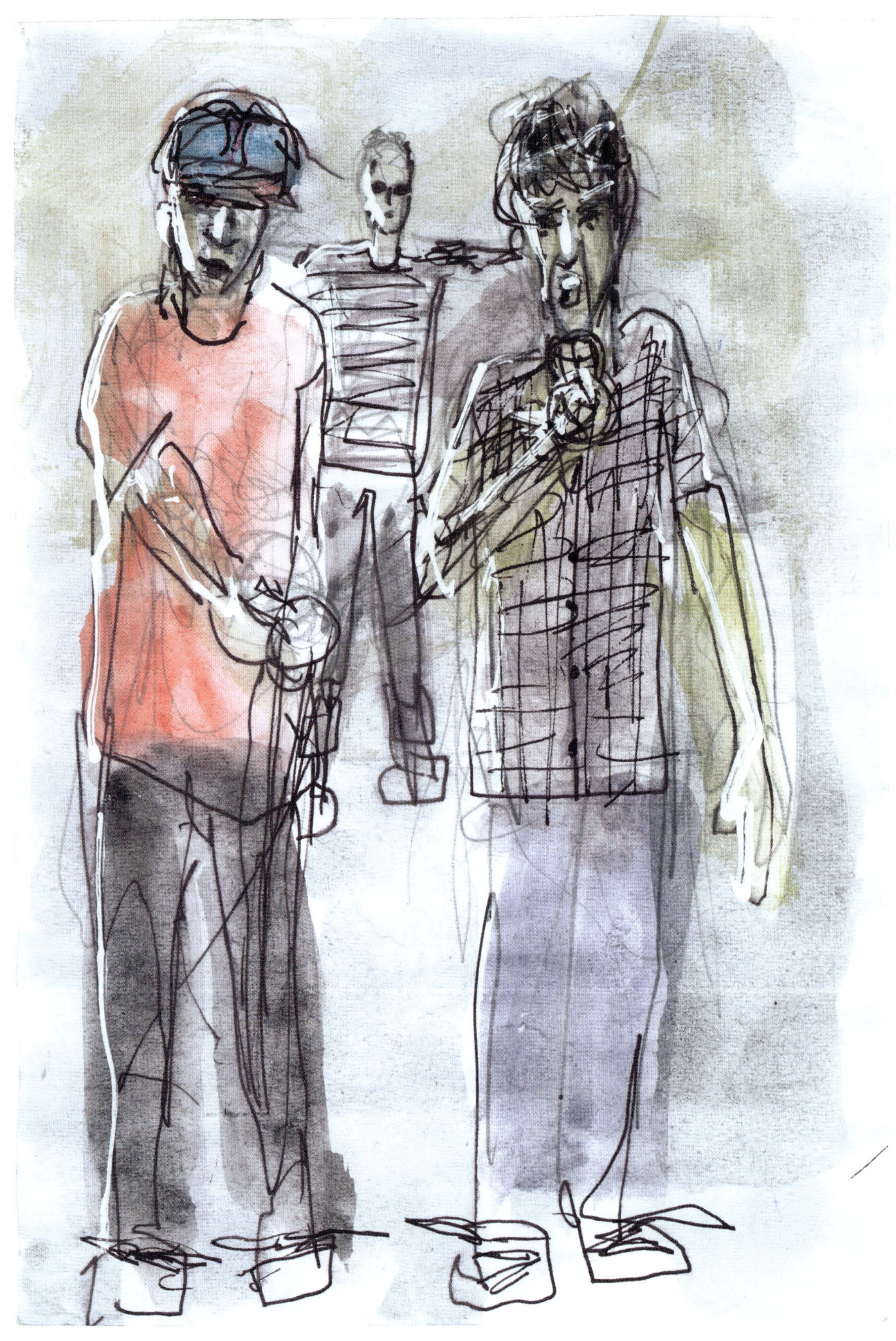

No matter what their lyrical subjects are, the Beastie Boys remind us that this is a craft not a hustle. They represent the best of the hip-hop idiom.

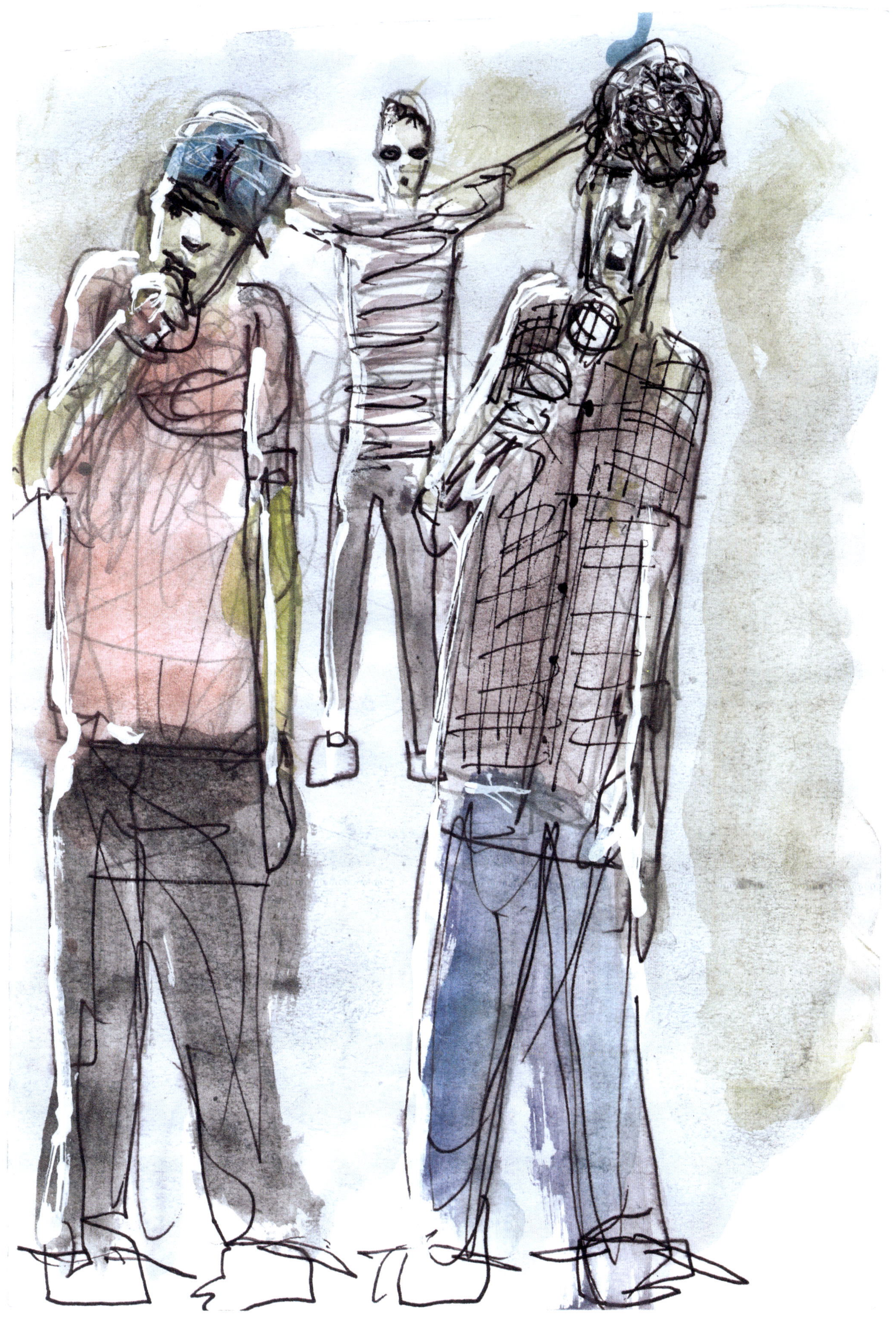

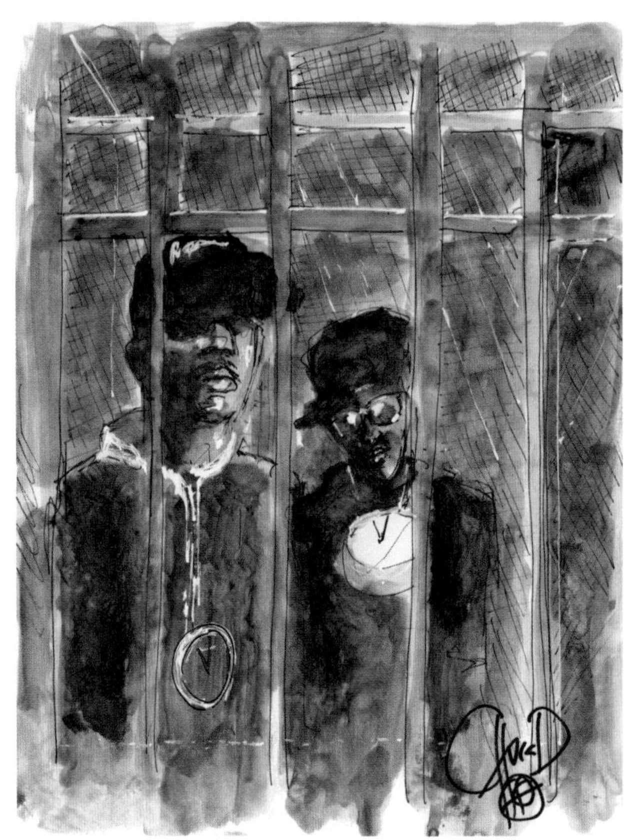

The minute you hear *It Takes a Nation of Millions to Hold Us Back*, you know goddamn well our base has never been the USA.

Our base has always been London. That's why we wanted to put the scream on there. We weren't number one in New York, we weren't number one in Philly (we had Philly for a couple of years, but you only get a US city for a little while), but we took London, man. And when you take London, you take the continent. So, we travelled there the first year.

It was an album that happened to cross the roads in the right place at the right time. Rap music, as recorded work, was just eight years in. The music was ready to break nationally in album form as opposed to what it had been, which was a singles genre. The album was released by a small, radical label called Def Jam, which was distributed by Columbia Records. We found that loophole: using a staunch, old-school distribution system to reach the people with a brand-new state of mind. We wanted to be a social critic, a community voice. We wanted everyone to know and truly understand that our music was from the people, not above the people.

IT TAKES A NATION OF MILLIONS....

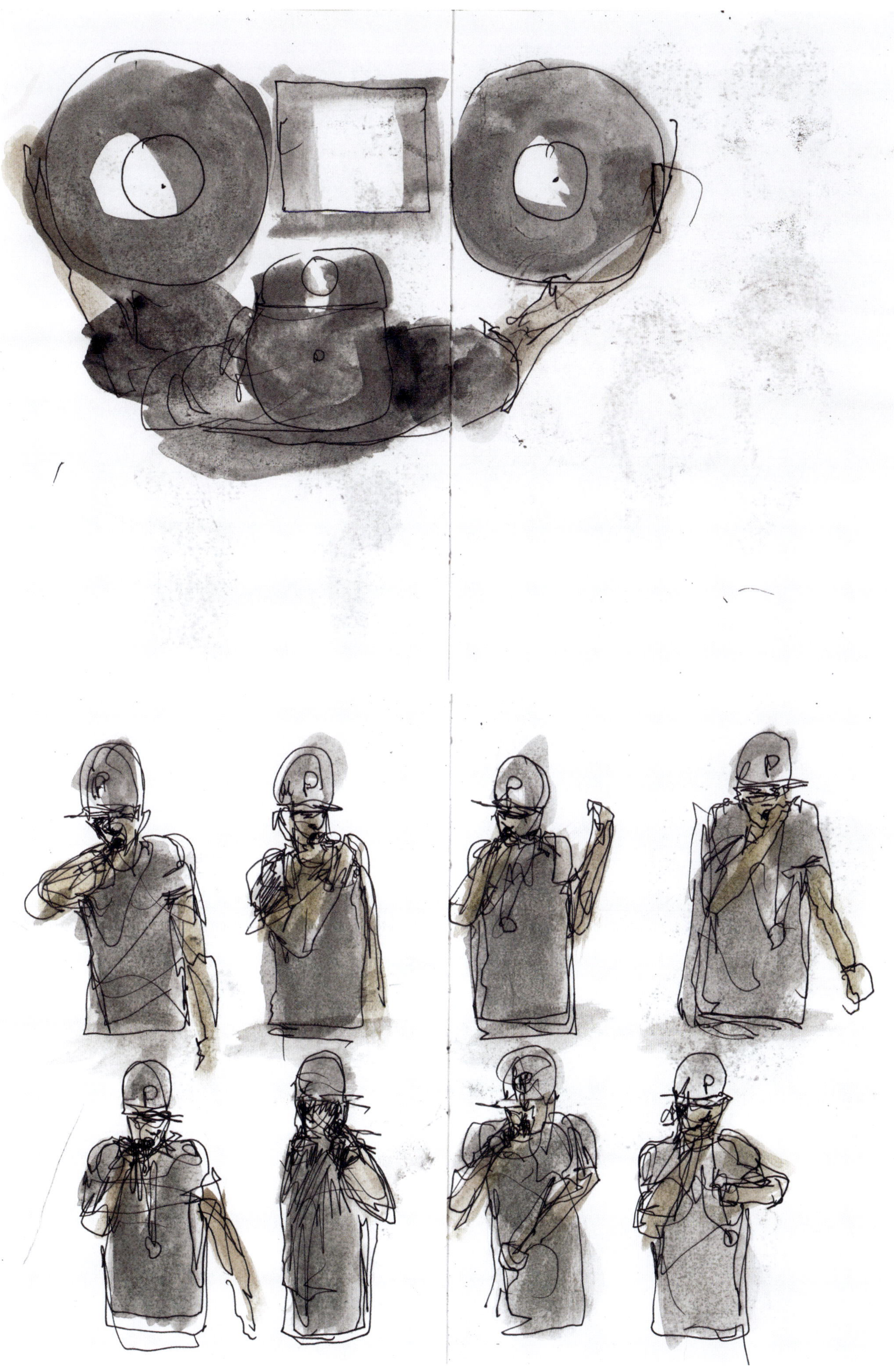

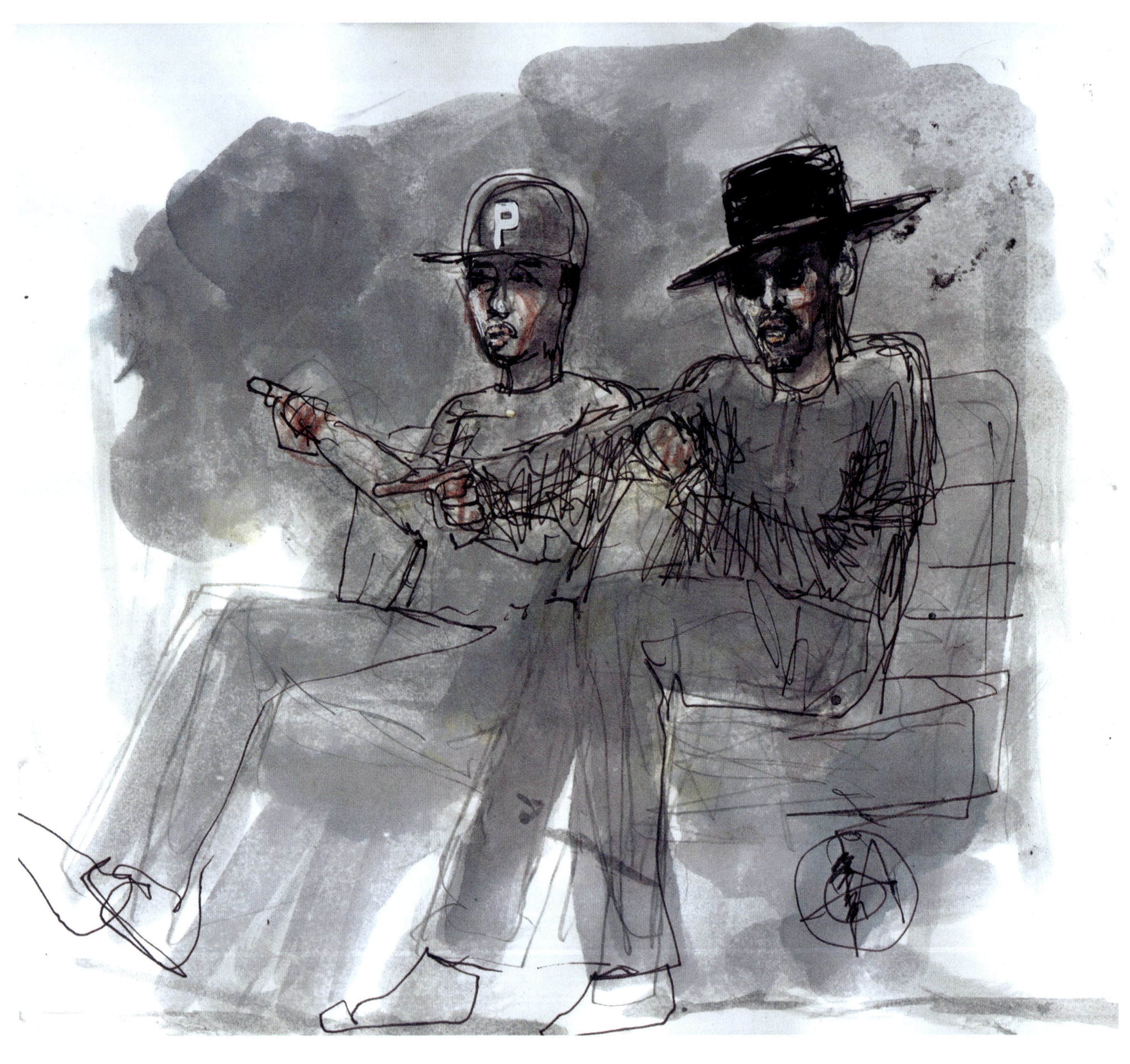

This is me and my good friend and mentor John 'Ecstasy' Fletcher, who passed away in December 2020.

I remember when I entered the Def Jam tour with Public Enemy in 1987 I tended to get nervous looking out at 15,000 fans in front of me each night. There were two MCs that directly mentored my calm that summer. The first was Doug E. Fresh and the other was Ecstasy. They were always there to reassure me with advice and tips.

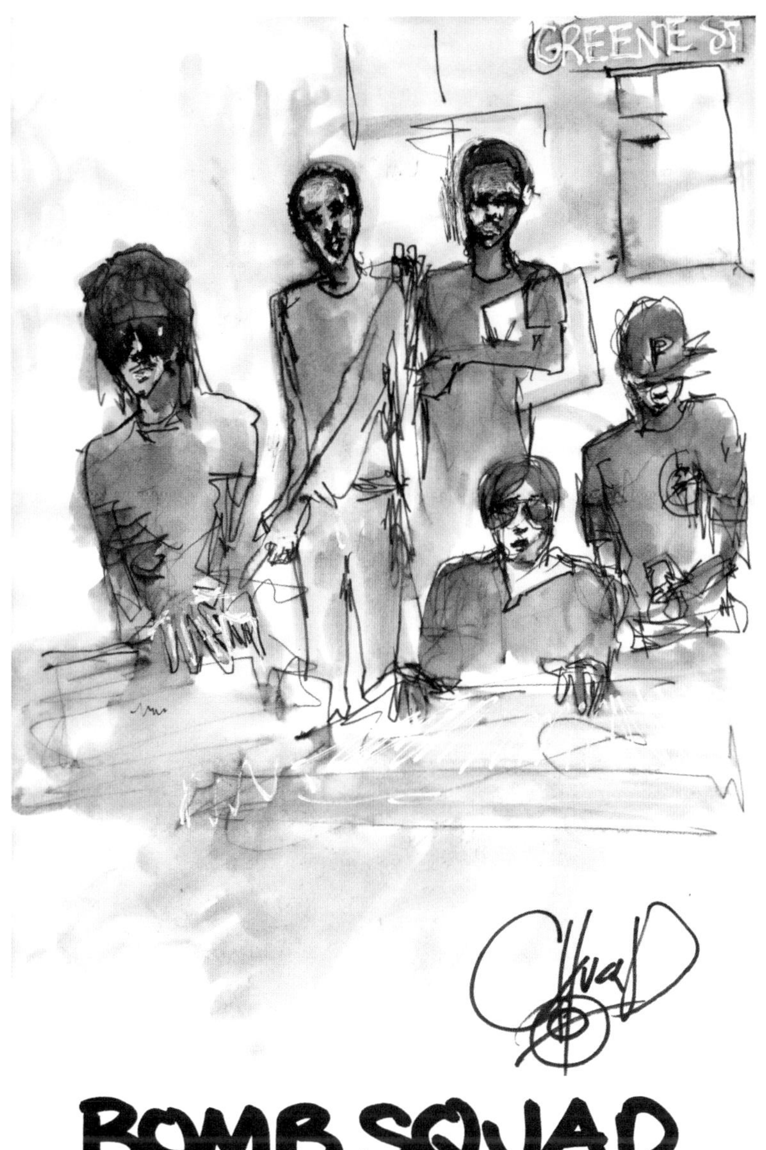

BOMB SQUAD

As the Bomb Squad, we'd developed a system that was similar to the Motown assembly line machine, where everybody had their role and responsibility to complete on a song. I would write the song, pick the samples that fit and arrange it, combined with Hank Shocklee, Keith Shocklee, Eric 'Vietnam' Sadler and later Gary G-Wiz. It was about putting a song together from different vantage points. We had strength in numbers.

The whole thing with the Bomb Squad was trying to do something that nobody else was doing. The Bomb Squad reached into certain sonic forays because we had the available time to dare to do anything – we had 12 tracks to try it and all of us knew music. Everybody had a great body of knowledge behind them, especially Hank, who is a sonic genius. Nobody came in saying, 'I'm a rap fan, and the only thing I know is rap music.' No. Everybody was a fan of music.

We got used to pioneering things. But then people jump on it and turns it into a cash cow, so it eventually becomes less interesting.

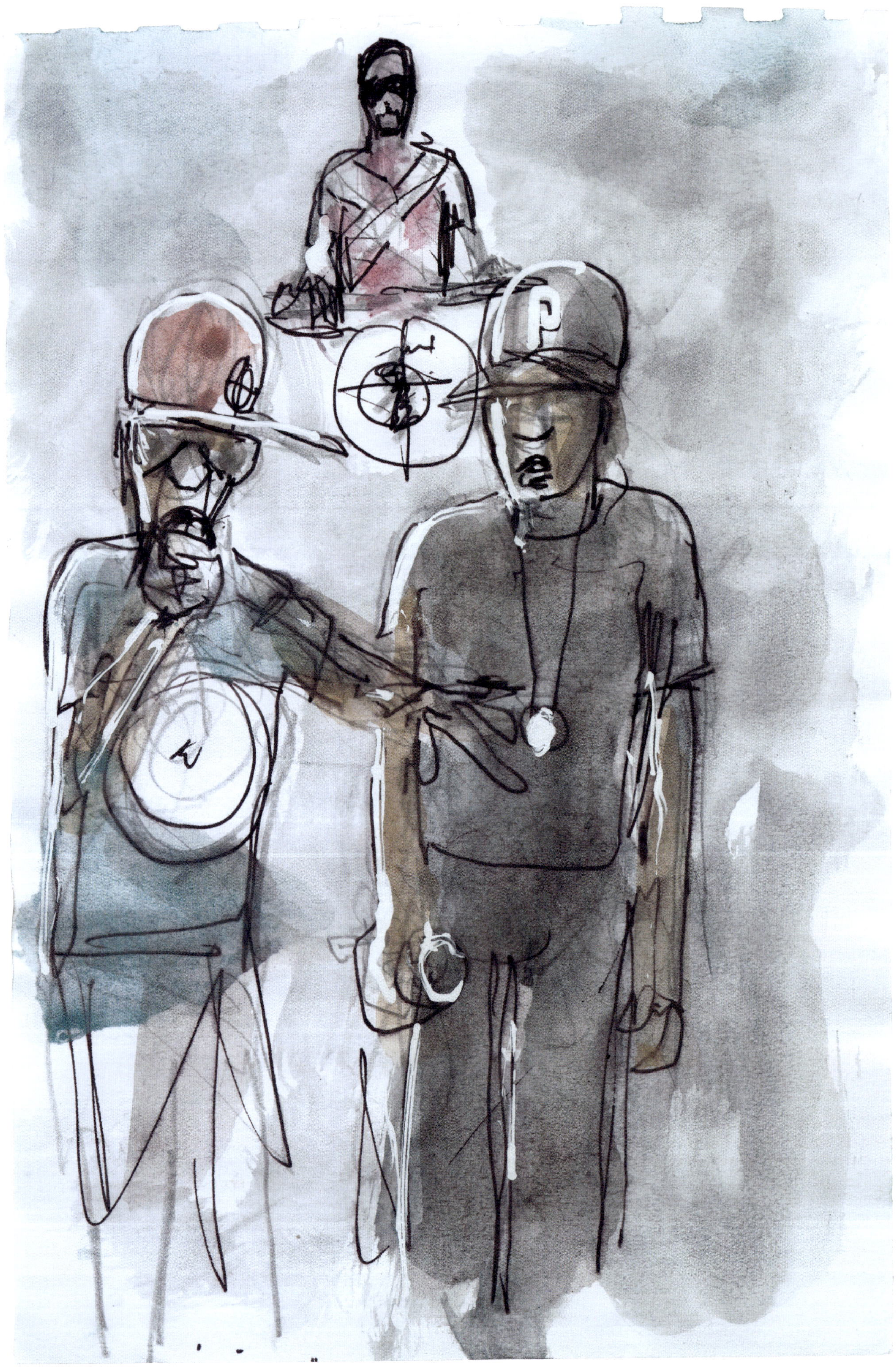

When we came out with the concept of being the Black Panthers of rap, we set ourselves apart from any other rap group, and that generated great interest in Europe.

Public Enemy were the first hip-hop group to go into Ireland, near the end of 1987. We visited Trinity College, which was very posh and British at the time. This was when there was a lot going on in Northern Ireland with the IRA. I mean, it was hardcore. We weren't comfortable playing for these British kids at Trinity, which was walled up and protected by the aristocracy, while everyone else in Dublin was bone-broke and mad at this aristocracy. So, we made sure that before we played at Trinity we went into some hard-knock clubs in the city.

We put legendary shows on that no one ever forgot. We showed the people of Dublin that you don't have to be from New York City or from London. We weren't from New York City, we were from Long Island. You've just got to be harder, swifter, better and keep coming with it. I saw that, the minute House of Pain did their thing.

We were coming out of the black community with this thing called rap music, which was basically black men yelling at the top of our lungs about what we liked and what we didn't. It really shook things up. Those in power didn't know what to make of us but they knew that we had to be silenced, stopped in any way from expressing our outrage.

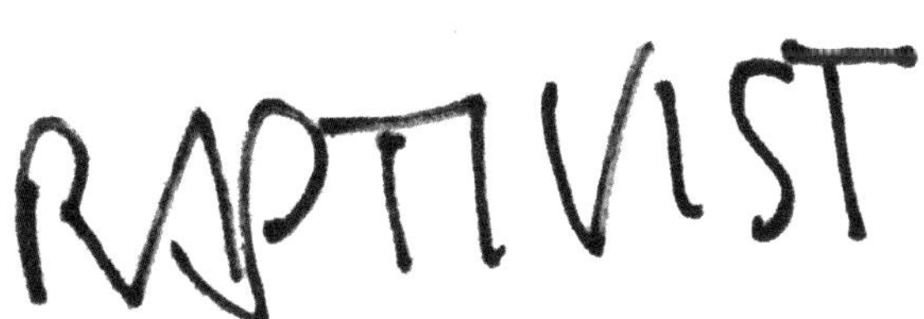

We cut 'Rebel Without a Pause' at the end of April 1987. Hank and I went to Def Jam and said, 'We have this jam that's the bomb and we have to go with it.' The slated single for us to release was 'You're Gonna Get Yours', which was from the first album, with 'Miuzi Weighs a Ton' on the B-side. We wanted to sneak 'Rebel' on the B-side. Russell Simmons immediately vetoed the idea. He didn't want us to waste new material by putting it out as a B-side, because he thought it would ruin the album sales.

Russell was going over to London with Run and DMC. We followed them all the way to JFK to try and get his approval. They were ready to leave and we said, 'Russell, let us get this jam on there.' He said he'd talk about it when he got back, turned and went to get on the plane. Then Run turned around, looked at us, and said, 'Go ahead and do it.'

That's all we needed, somebody to give us the go-ahead. We went to Columbia Records, filed all the information and rushed the process through the system.

The beautiful thing about music is that you can weave life teachings through it more easily, because it has a shake and a bounce. That's Public Enemy, there's a shake and a bounce.

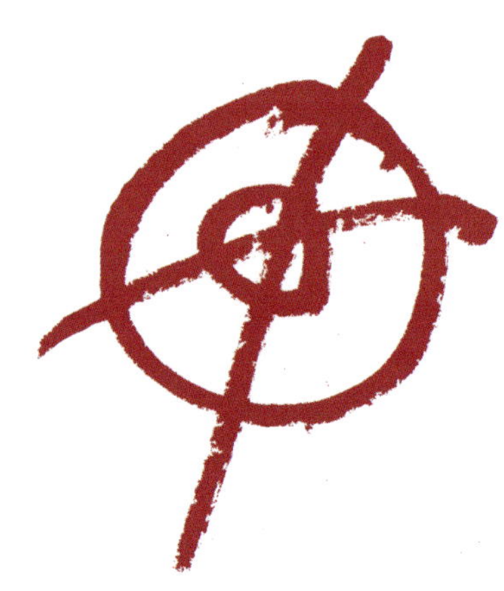

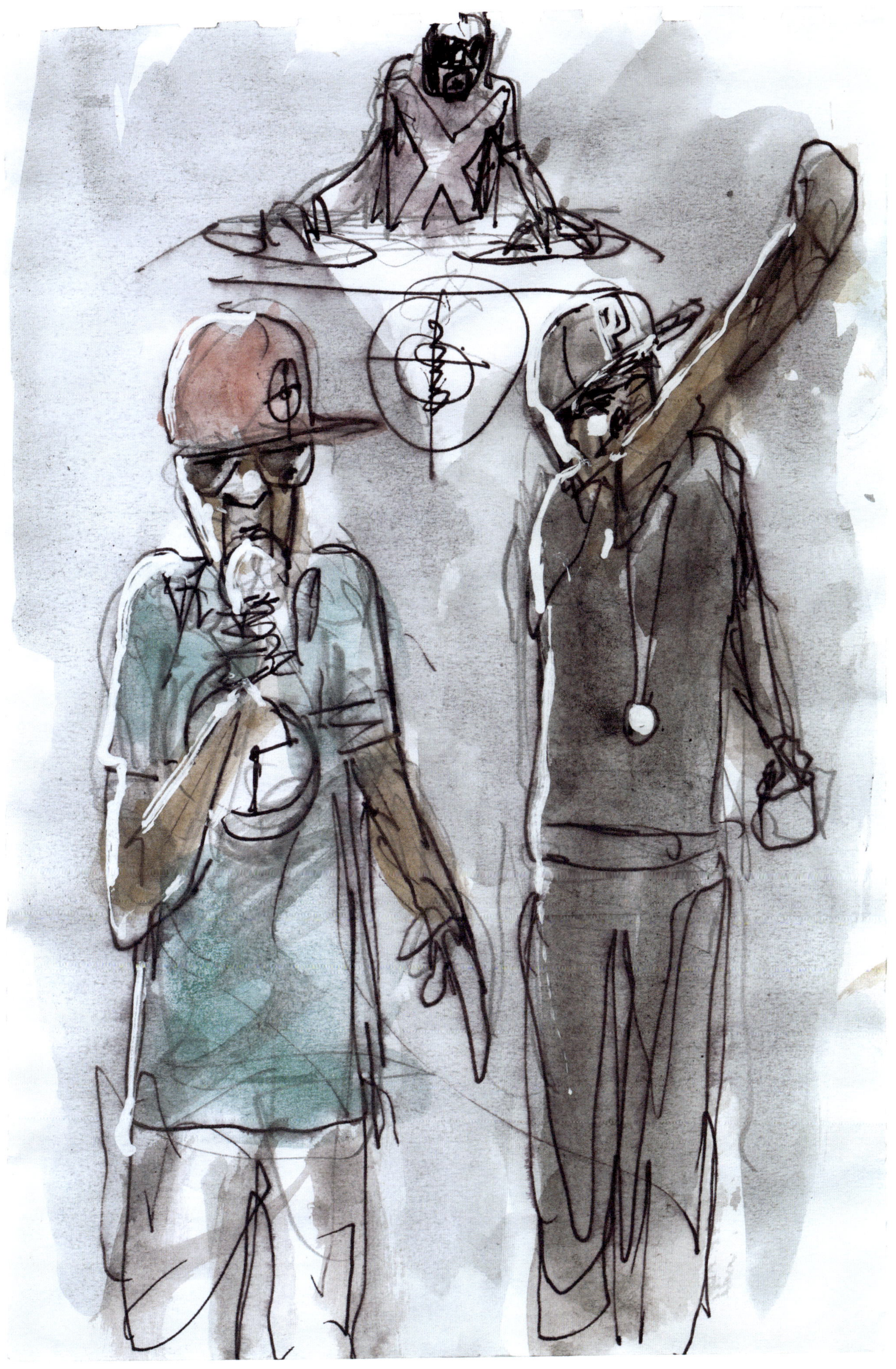

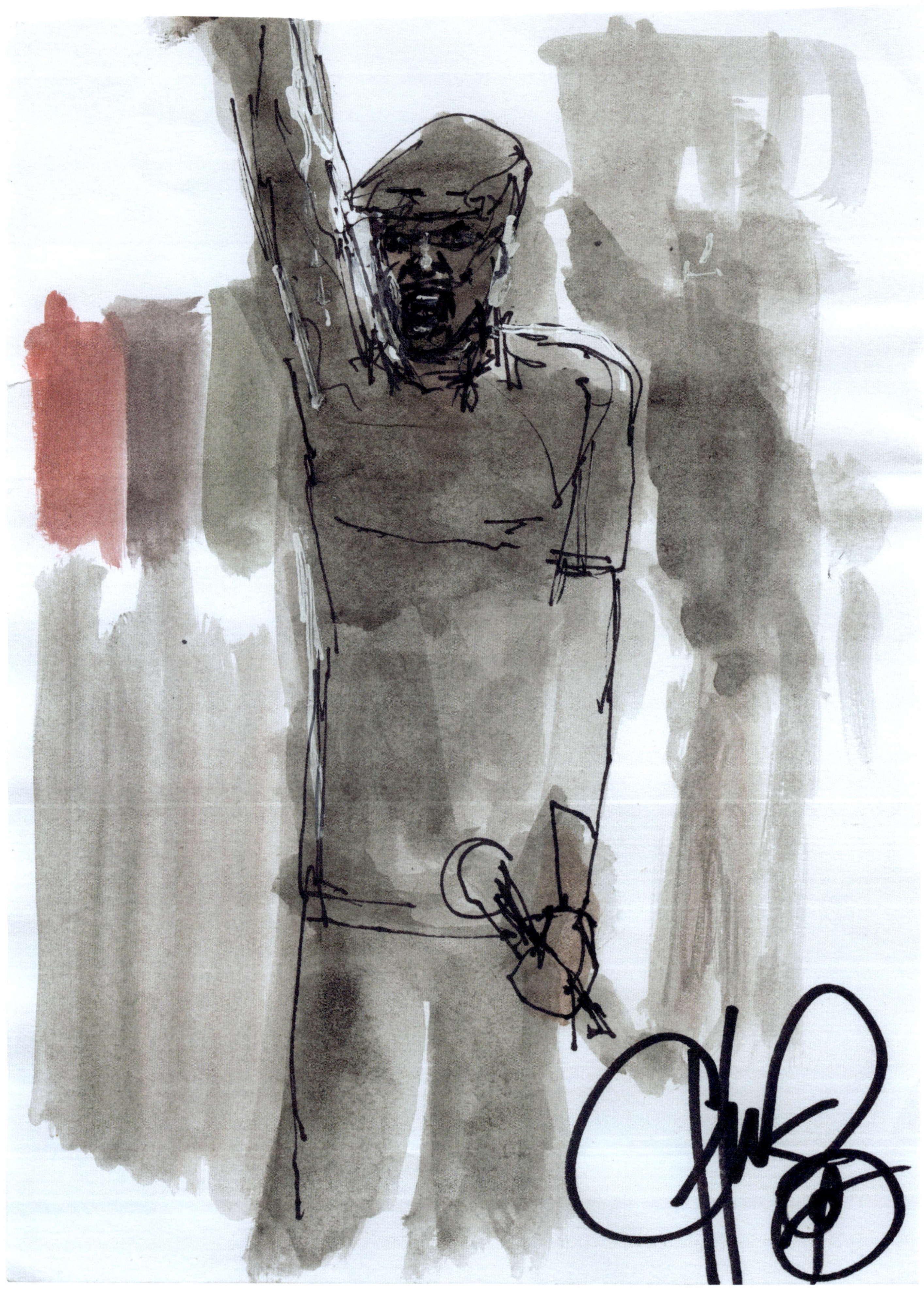

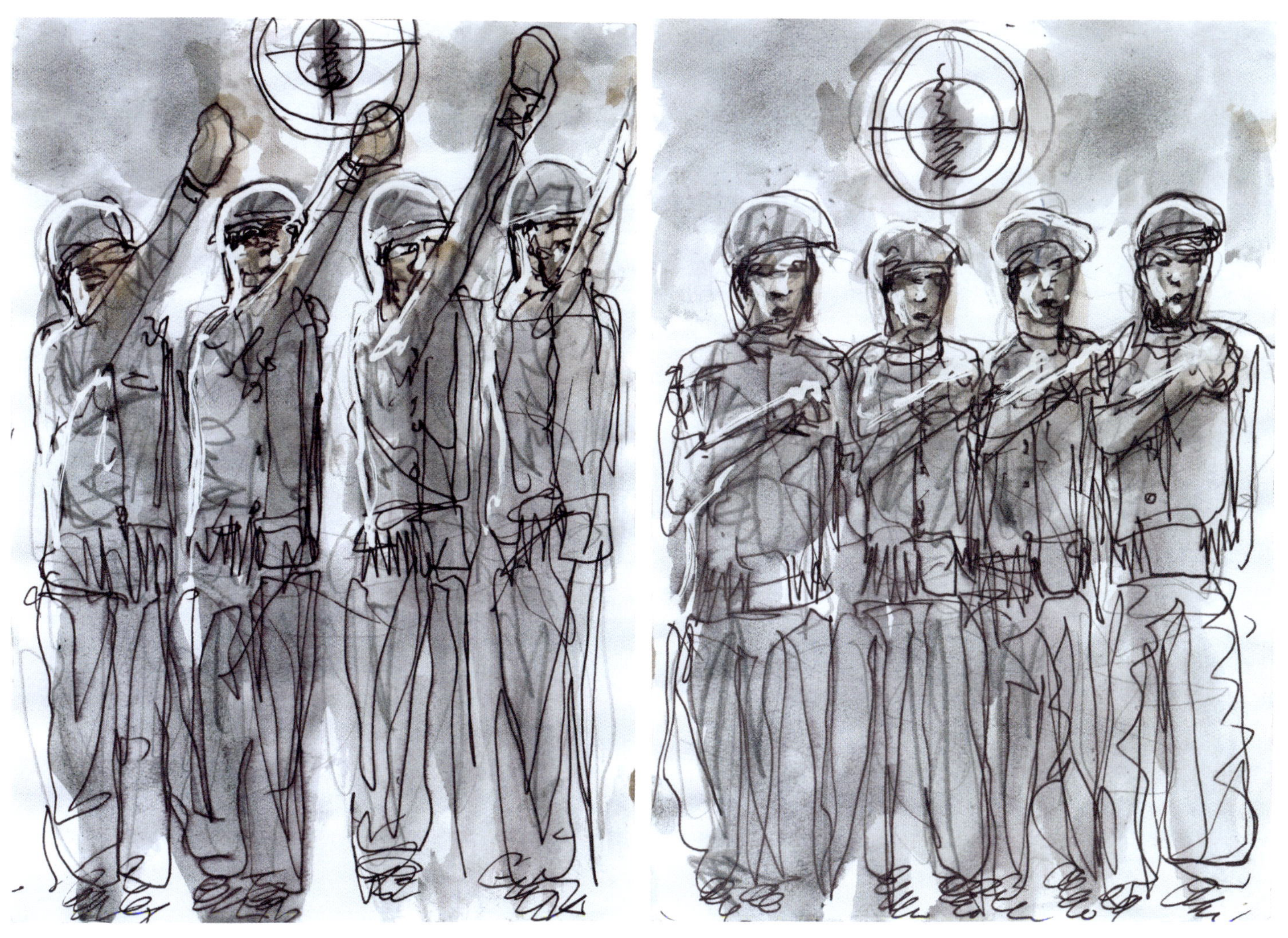

Public Enemy is a sum of many parts, many of which we introduced to hip-hop. Professor Griff and Security of the First World is just one of them. At the door of every fly party you've got to have security.

In the United States there's still a lot of segregation. We perform to vast crowds made up of different diversities and we want to be able to get our message across to all Americans. But we're not able to, because black people only get attention when we're at our worst. If you're making great music to enlighten people, that gets overlooked.

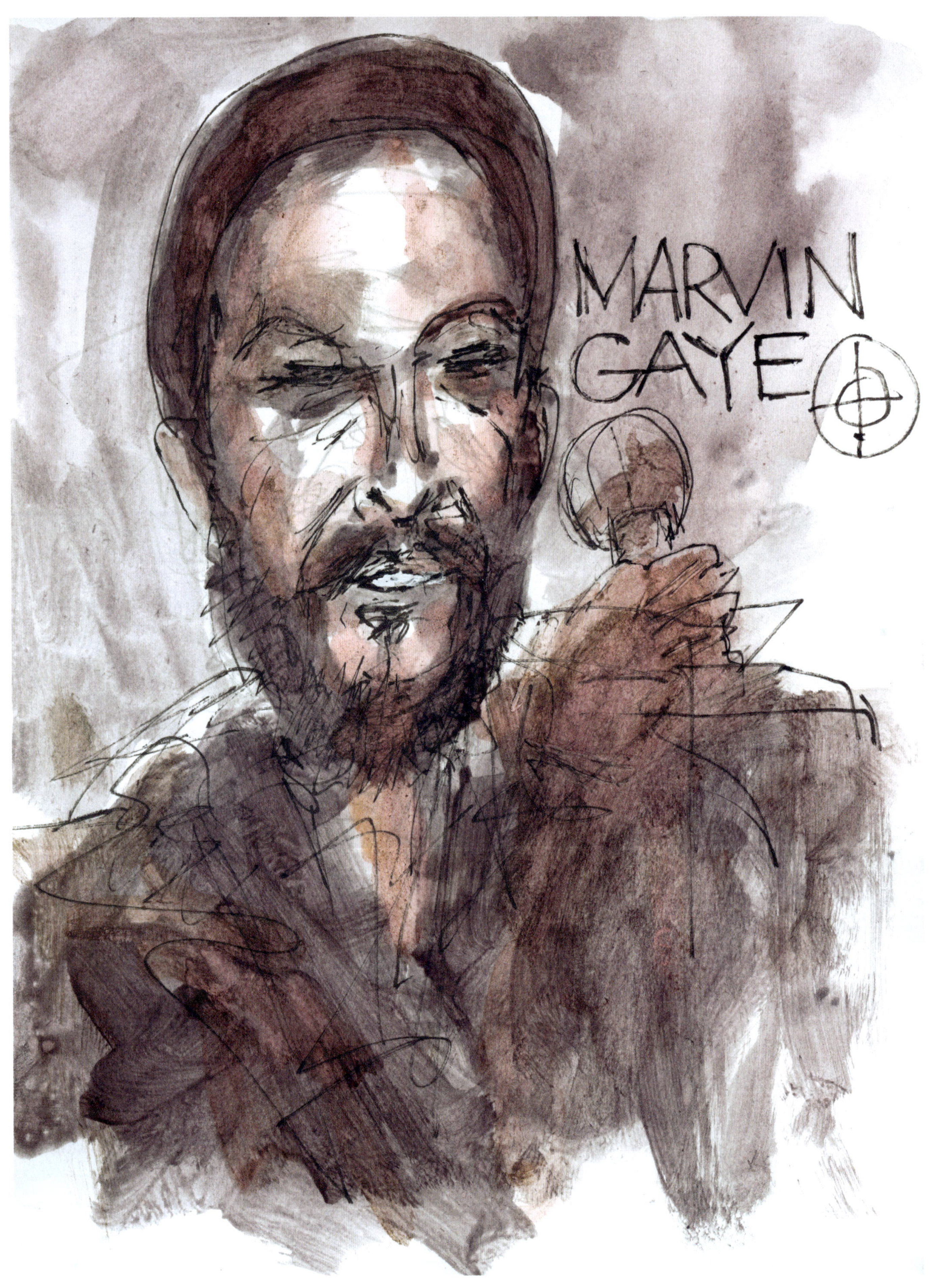

I wanted to make *It Takes a Nation of Millions to Hold Us Back* Public Enemy's version of *What's Going On* by Marvin Gaye.

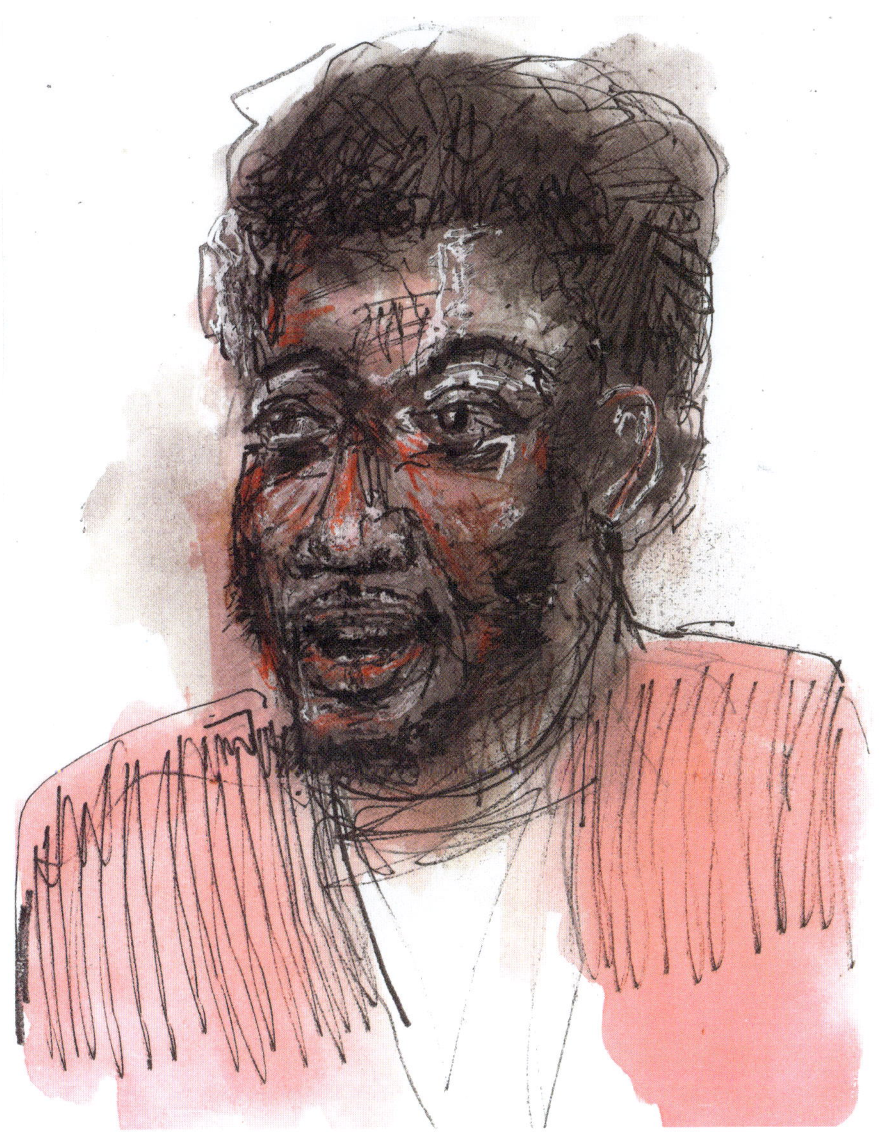

In 1967, my uncle had just got out of high school, and he was drafted by the Marines to go fight in Vietnam. That Sixties spirit culminated with *It Takes a Nation* in 1988. We were able to bring to hip-hop a lot of things that people didn't realise were already there.

The song 'Party for Your Right to Fight' was really a dedication to the Black Panther Party. The Party was an organisation that fought for the right to fight. On that record, I talk about the Black Panthers' founders Eldridge Cleaver, Huey Newton and Bobby Seale and mention the COINTELPRO (the FBI's Counter Intelligence Project).

I remember the solemn mood that permeated my grandparents' house that day in 1965 when the news of Malcolm X's assassination reached us. I was in the third grade when Dr Martin Luther King was gunned down three years later. My mother wore all black to work the next day. When she got back home that night, she said a lot of white people were paranoid and didn't know how to act because they had never experienced black people being so profoundly moved by one man's passing. I had been taught that Dr King was a man of peace who fought for black people's rights, and it hit me hard that he would get killed for that. All of it was big news, including the massacre of the Black Panthers' Fred Hampton (above) and Mark Clark in Chicago in 1969. It was not taken lightly in my home.

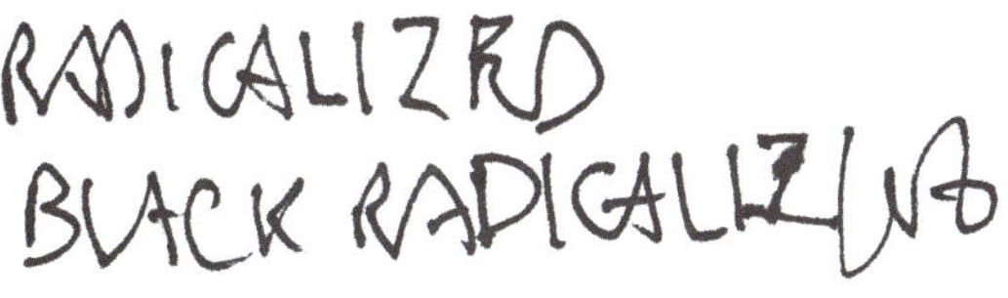

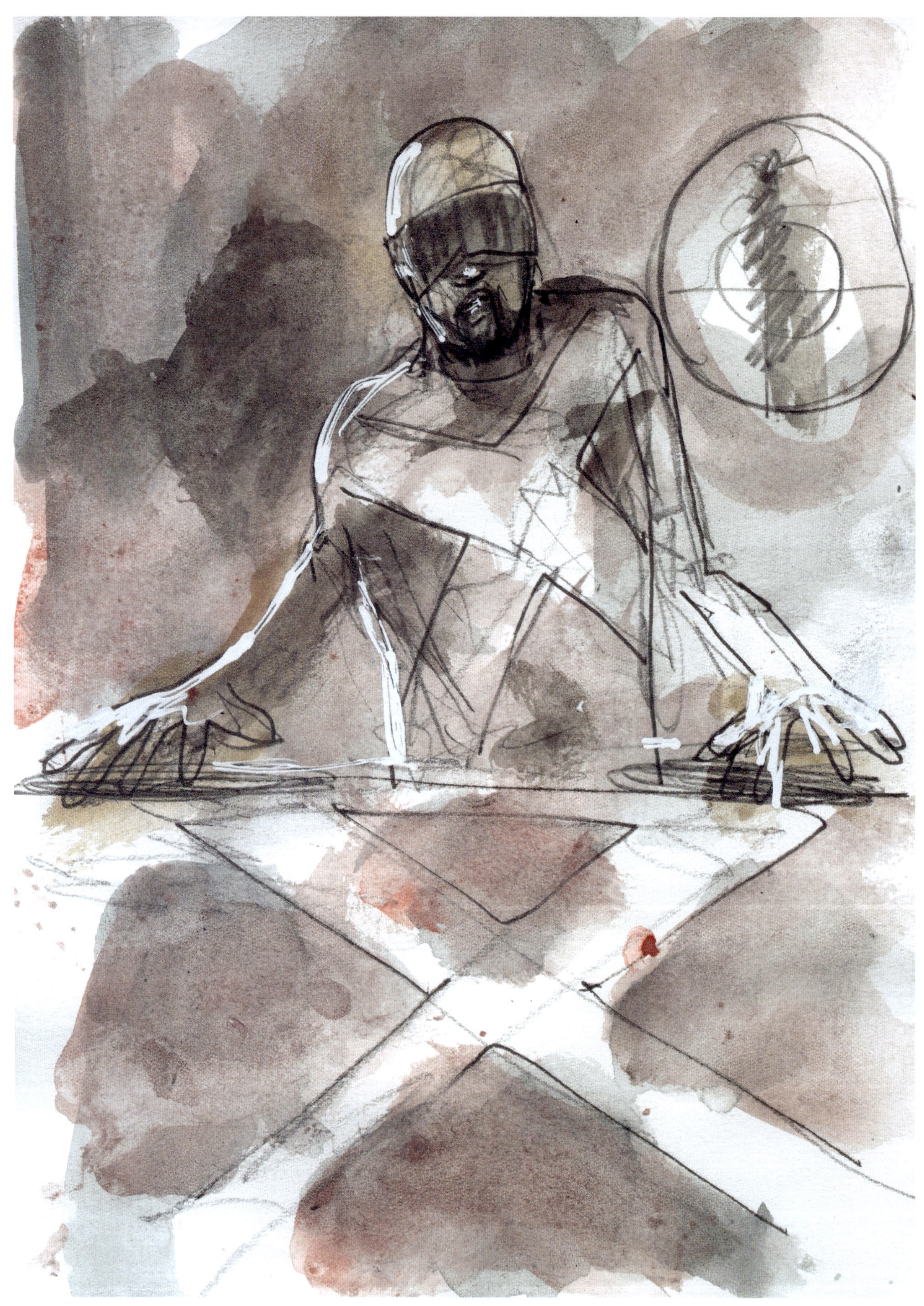

In hip-hop, the biggest difference between then and now is that it was a group effort in the Eighties. The elements were all in conference with each other. DJing – which was the ruler of the roost – MCing, breakdancing, art, expression and graffiti.

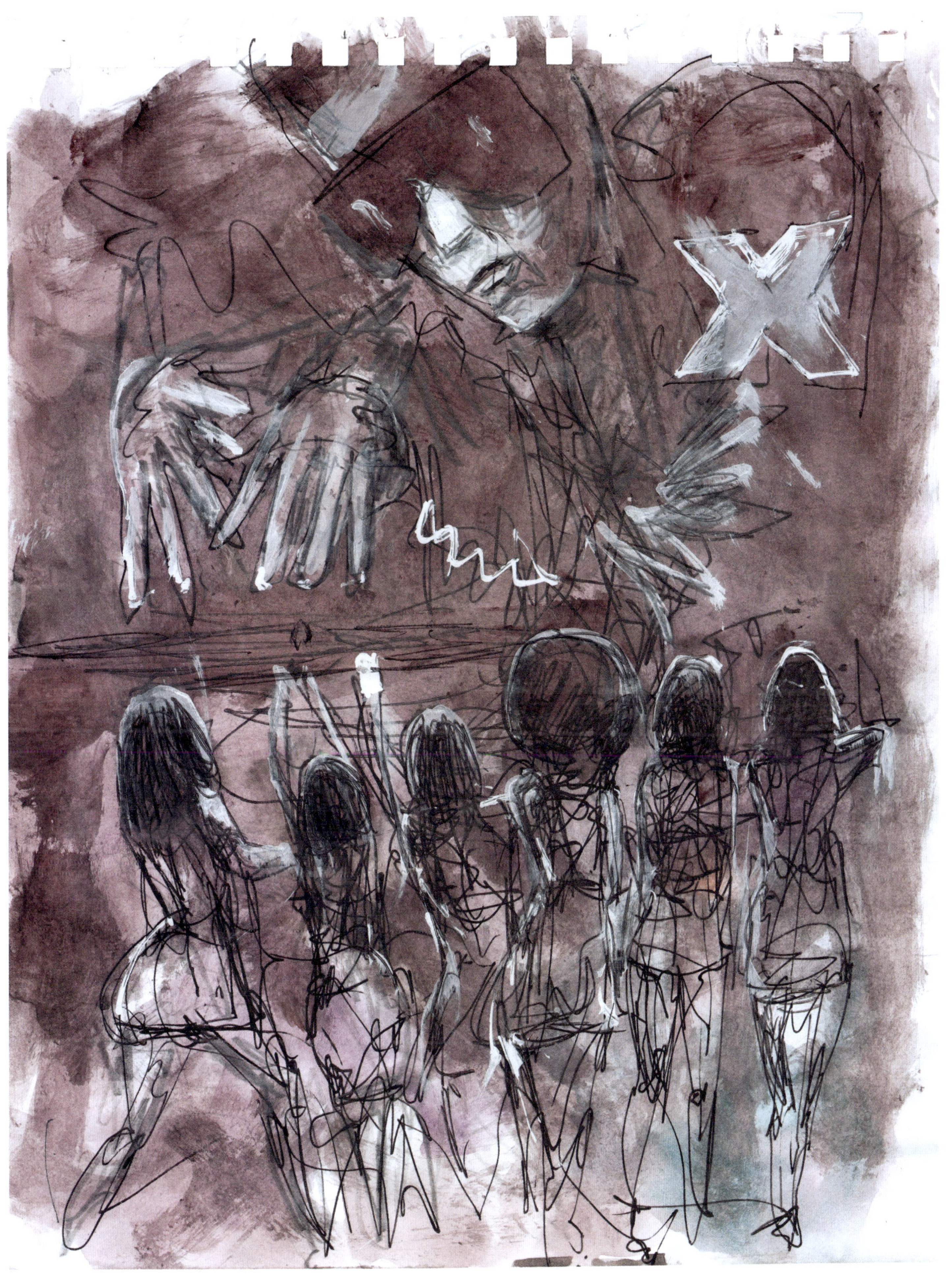

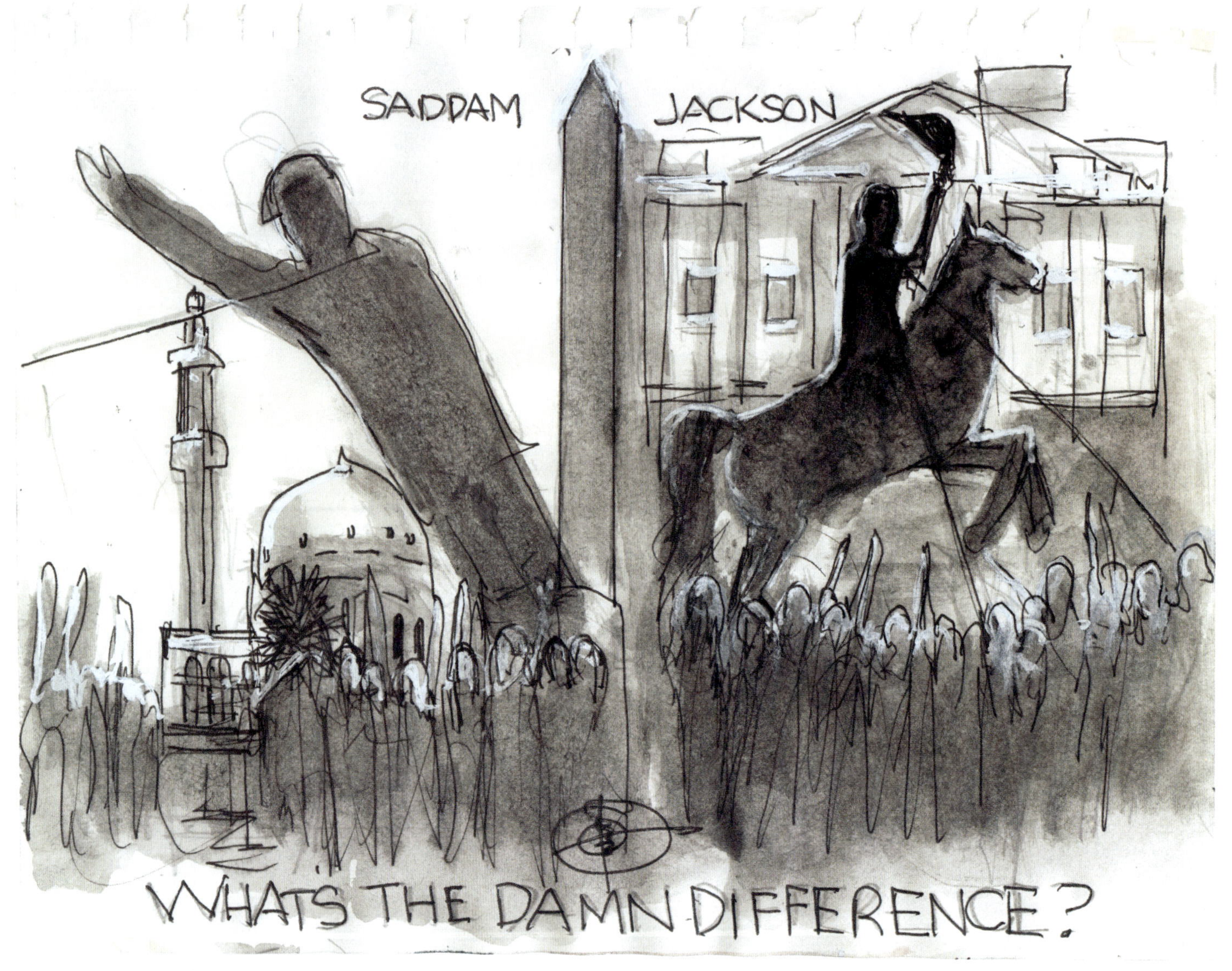

Public Enemy was a benchmark in rap music during the mid-Eighties. As we were older than the average rap artists, we felt a need to progress the music and say something meaningful. It was a time of heightened right-wing politics, and that climate dictated the direction of the group. The Berlin Wall was up, Nelson Mandela was in prison, Margaret Thatcher was running the UK, Reagan was out of control in the White House and Bush Sr. was soon to take over. You can say we were up against it.

Now, the world is in a similar situation. It's turned a full circle.

PUBLIC ENEMY

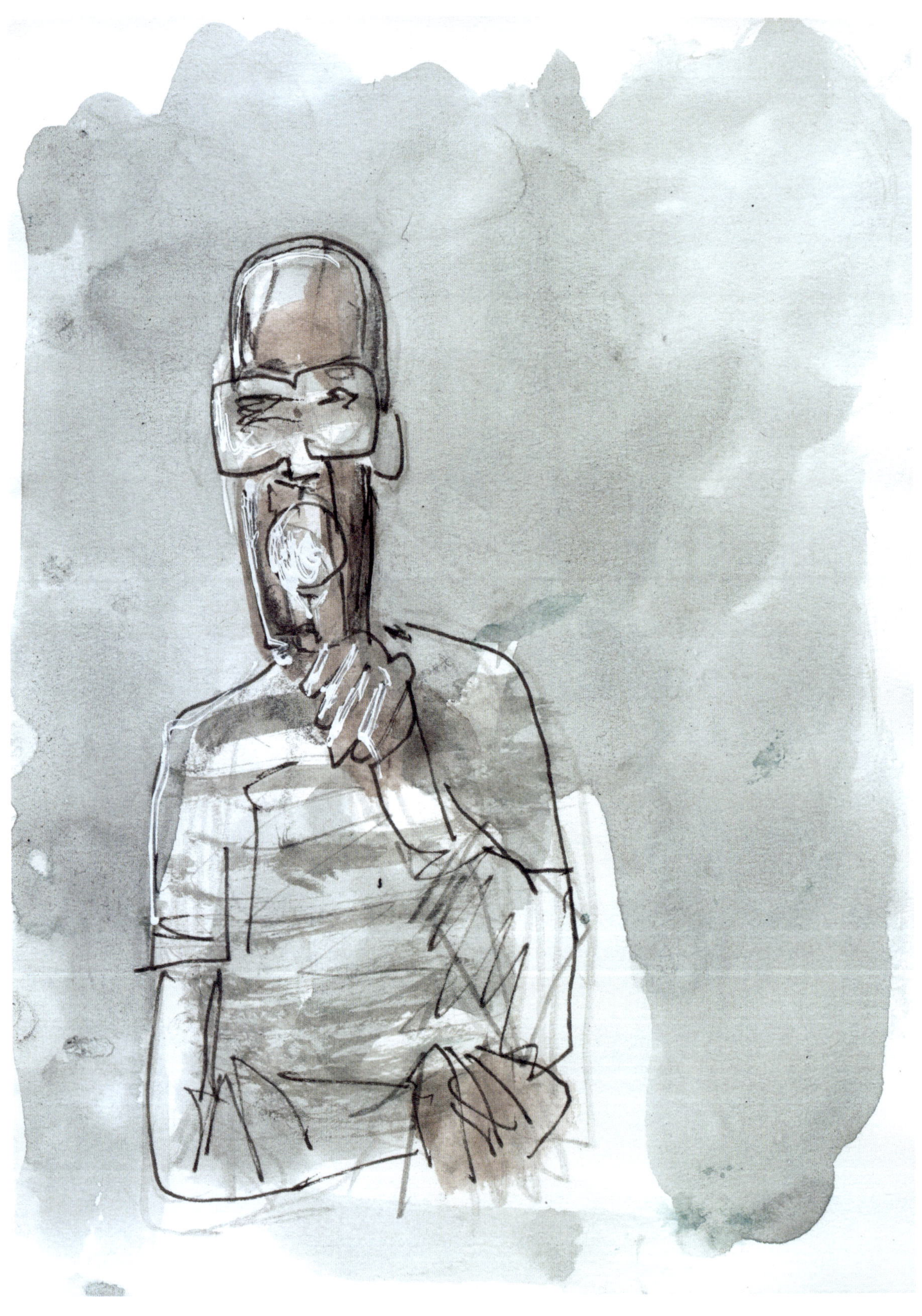

The great Daddy-O from Stetsasonic, who is a master teacher of hip-hop and rap music.

He's the Tom Petty of hip-hop. They say Petty never made a bad rock song; Daddy-O has never made a bad hip-hop record.

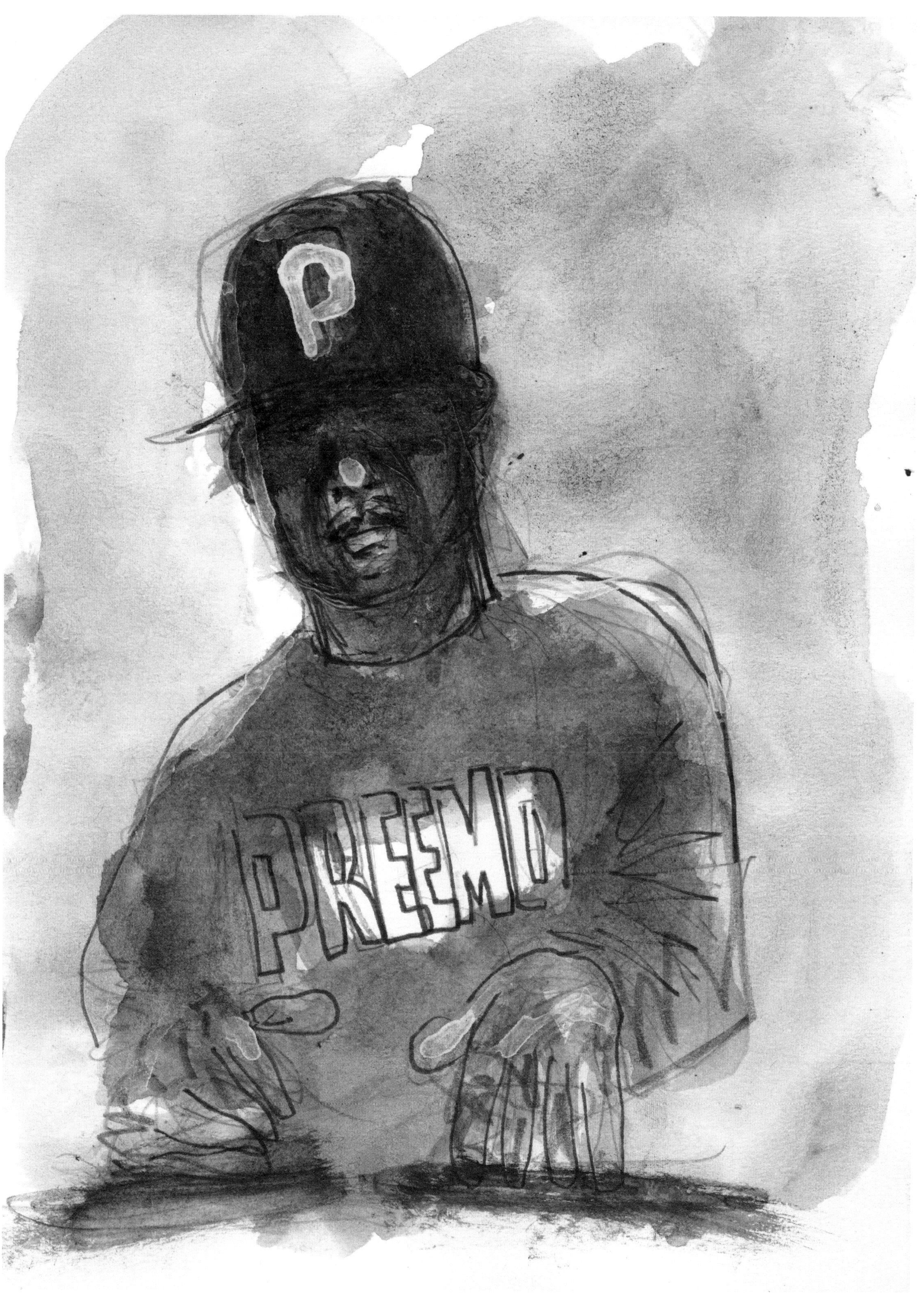
P
PREEMO

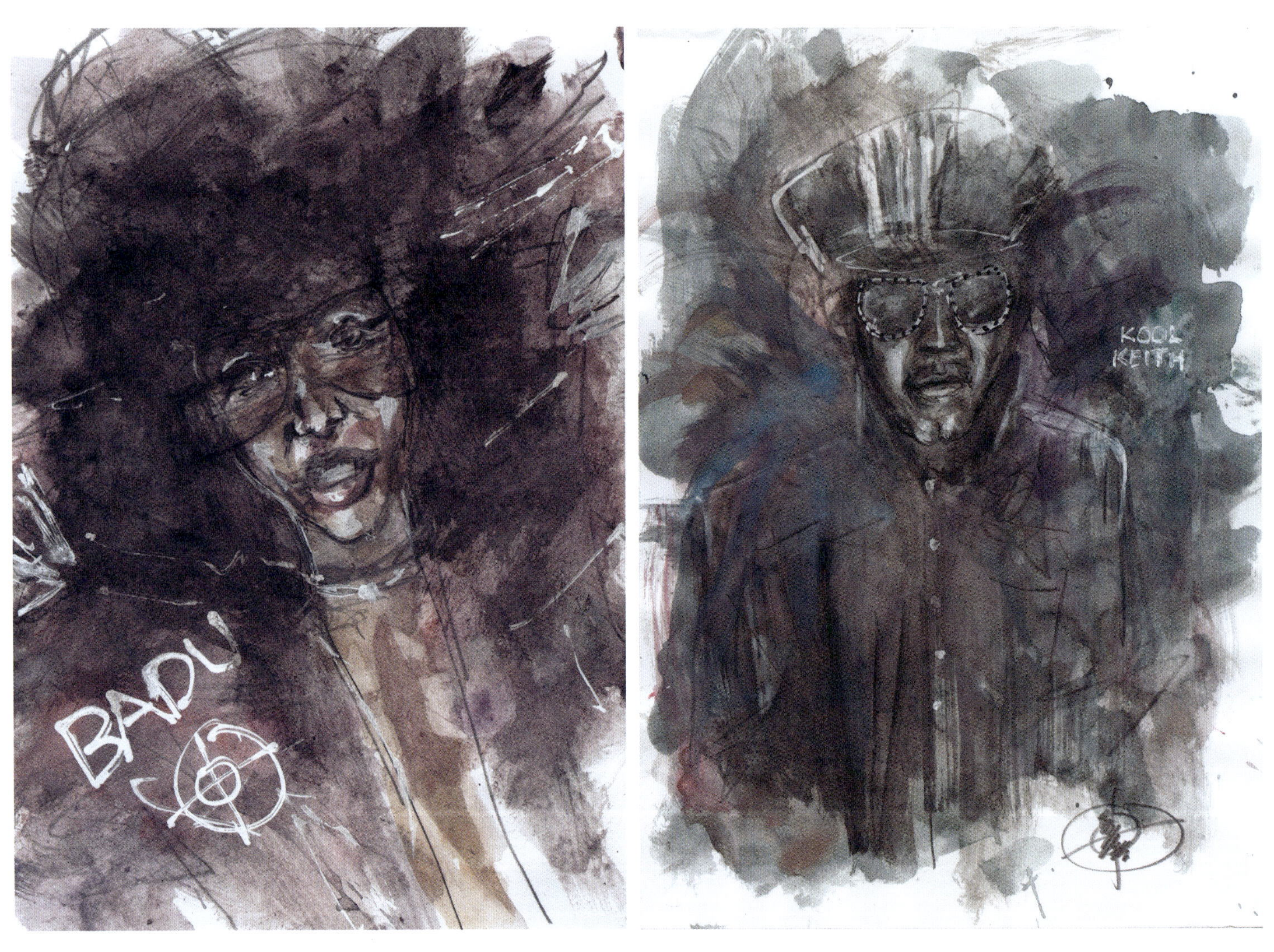

Erykah Badu marches to her own drum of freedom. She's no joke.

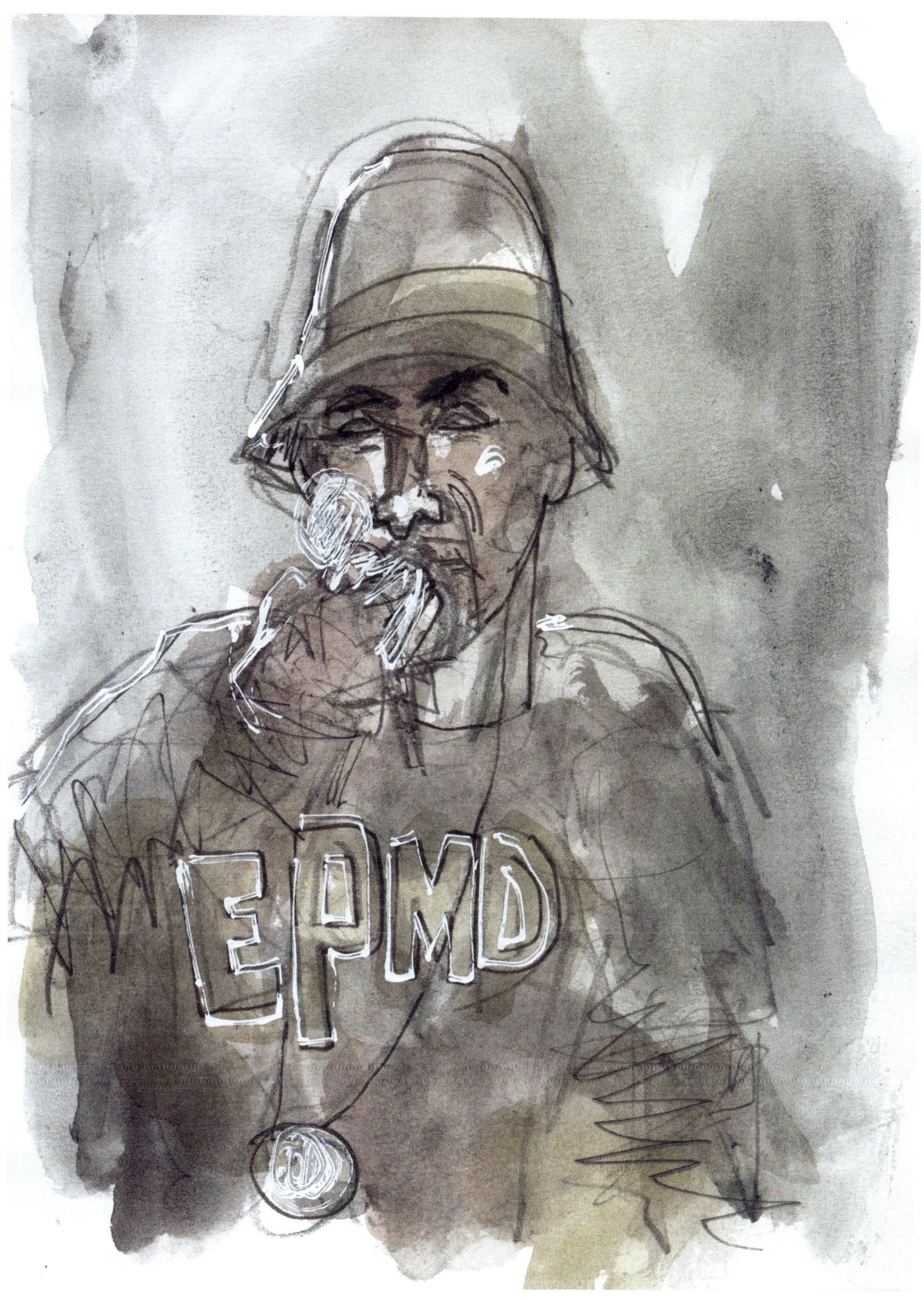

EPMD could carry on doing the same thing for 50 years, they have the formula.

I think collectives are important. Every little area of the business counts. Having great concern for people and understanding how everybody helps each other is what brings longevity. But you need to be careful of the feet you step on, because they might be attached to a behind that you have to kiss.

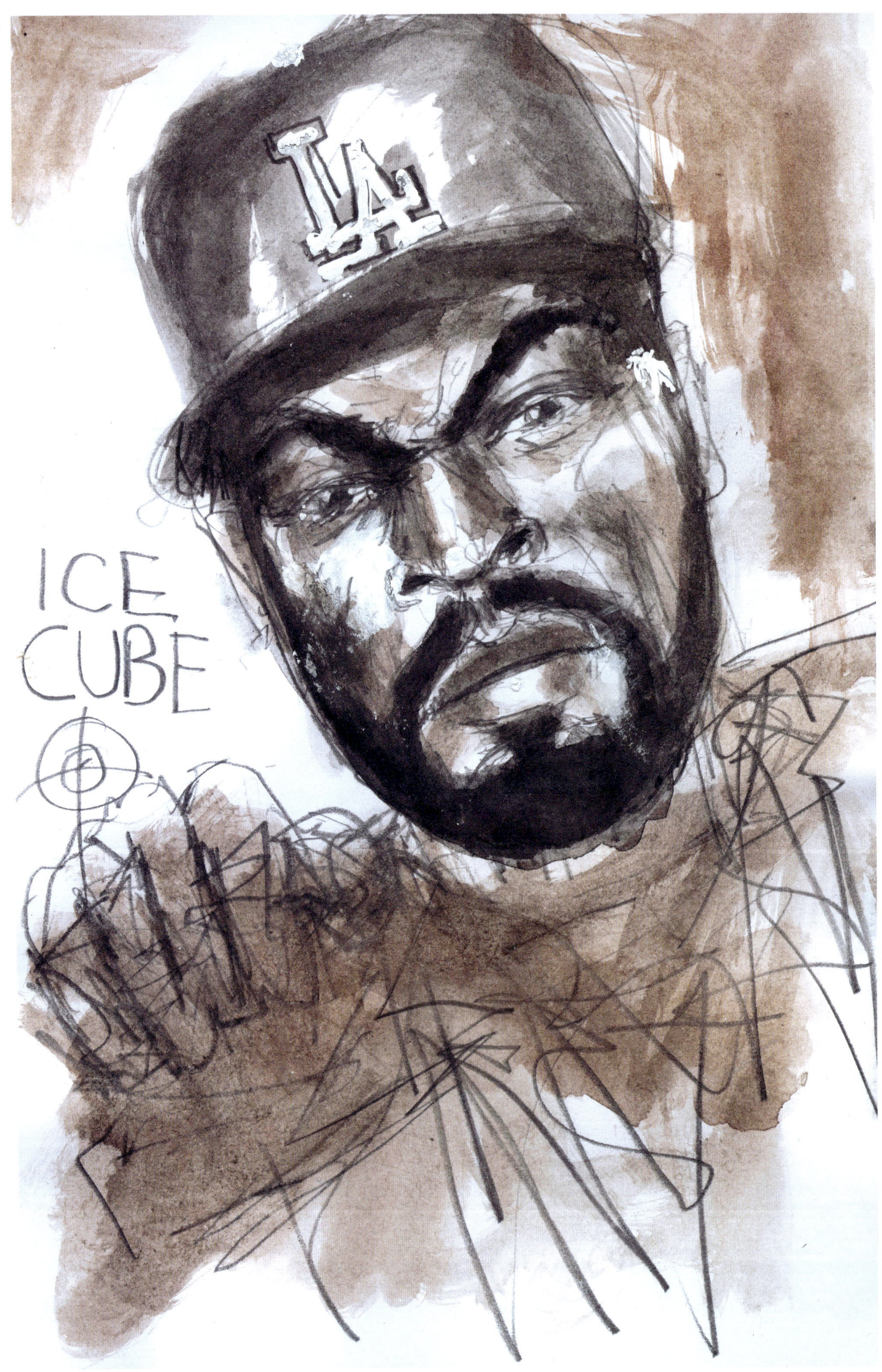
LA
ICE
CUBE

FEAR OF A BLACK PLANET

When Ice Cube left NWA I said he should stay with them but he said it was impossible. I told my team that we had to figure something out. We didn't want to jar their situation but Cube wasn't going to go back, so we agreed to help him make his first album, *AmeriKKKa's Most Wanted*. That's when shit changed. After NWA's *Straight Outta Compton* came Cube's record and our next record, *Fear of a Black Planet*.

'Burn Hollywood Burn' came from Big Daddy Kane visiting me at Greene St. Recording in New York while Cube was there working out the beginnings of *AmeriKKKa's Most Wanted*. Kane and I had been talking about collaborating on a song. I said the title, 'Burn Hollywood Burn', and Cube said, 'Yo, I wanna be down on that shit.' Kane and I thought 'Fuck it, why not?'

It was hell to get our three record companies to agree to us collaborating on one song. Damn lawyers.

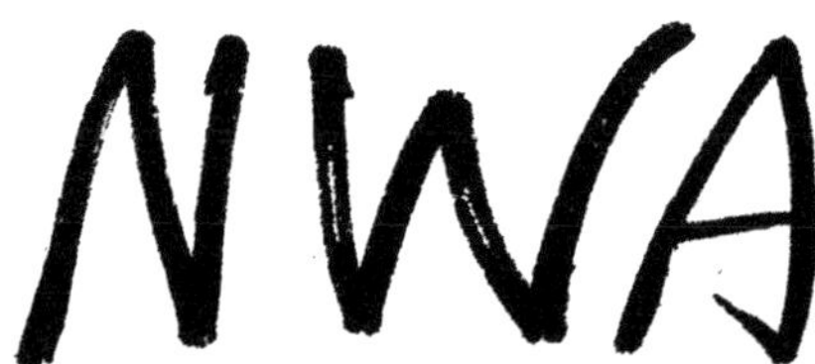

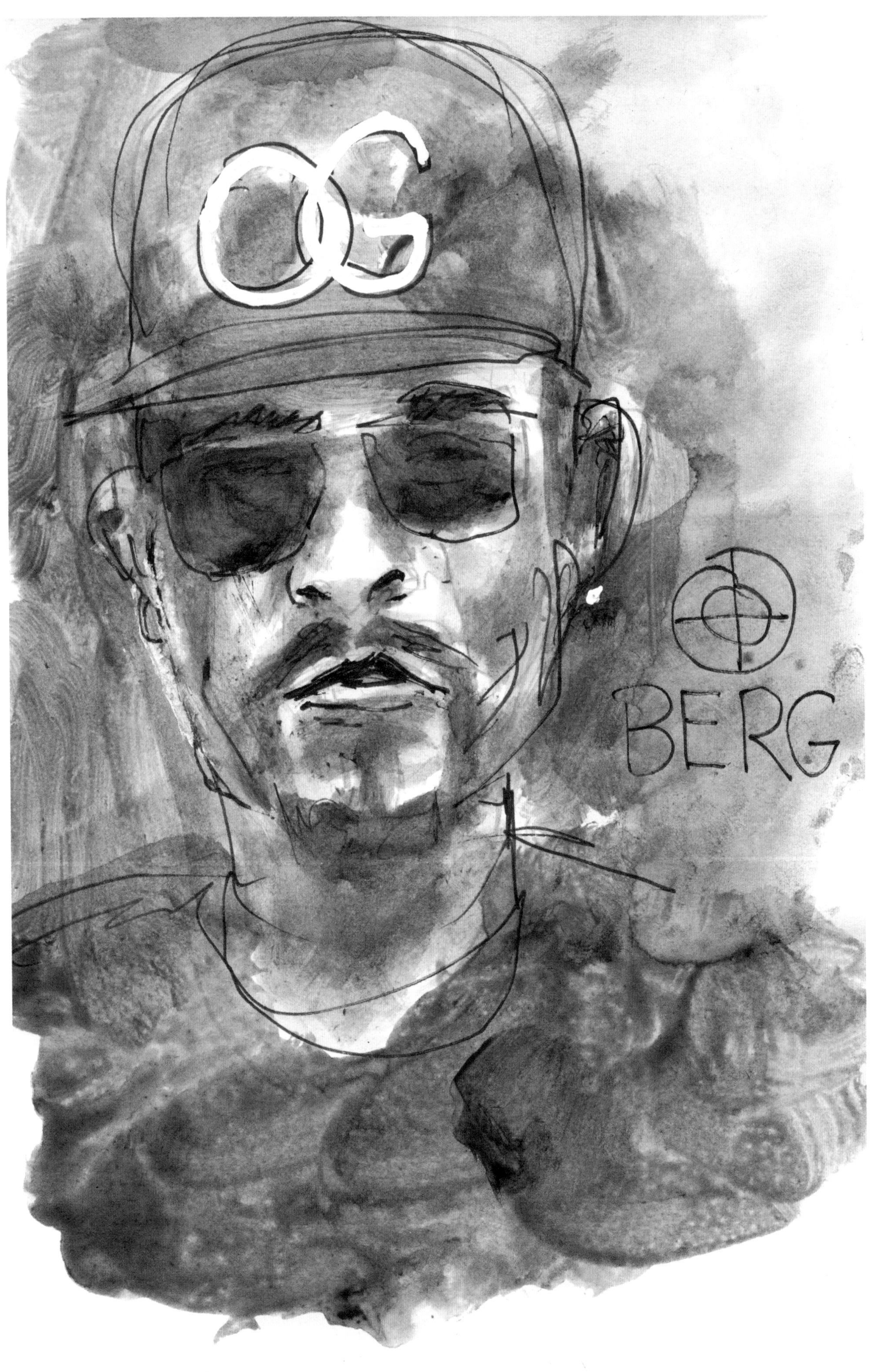
OG
BERG

Ice-T, or Iceberg, as I call him. My brother from another mother.

Ice T's album *O.G. Original Gangster* was the epitome of LA street culture broken down by the doctor philosopher himself. I have always looked up to Iceberg. He's one of the few rappers that has age seniority over me. The first rapper to put out a book, first rapper to head a documentary and festival: the Art of Rap. Iceberg is one of the most engaging live rap performers ever. He's like the Alice Cooper of rap, very forward in presenting a stage atmosphere fitting his words. He had the Rhyme Syndicate bring the LA streets to every city he played.

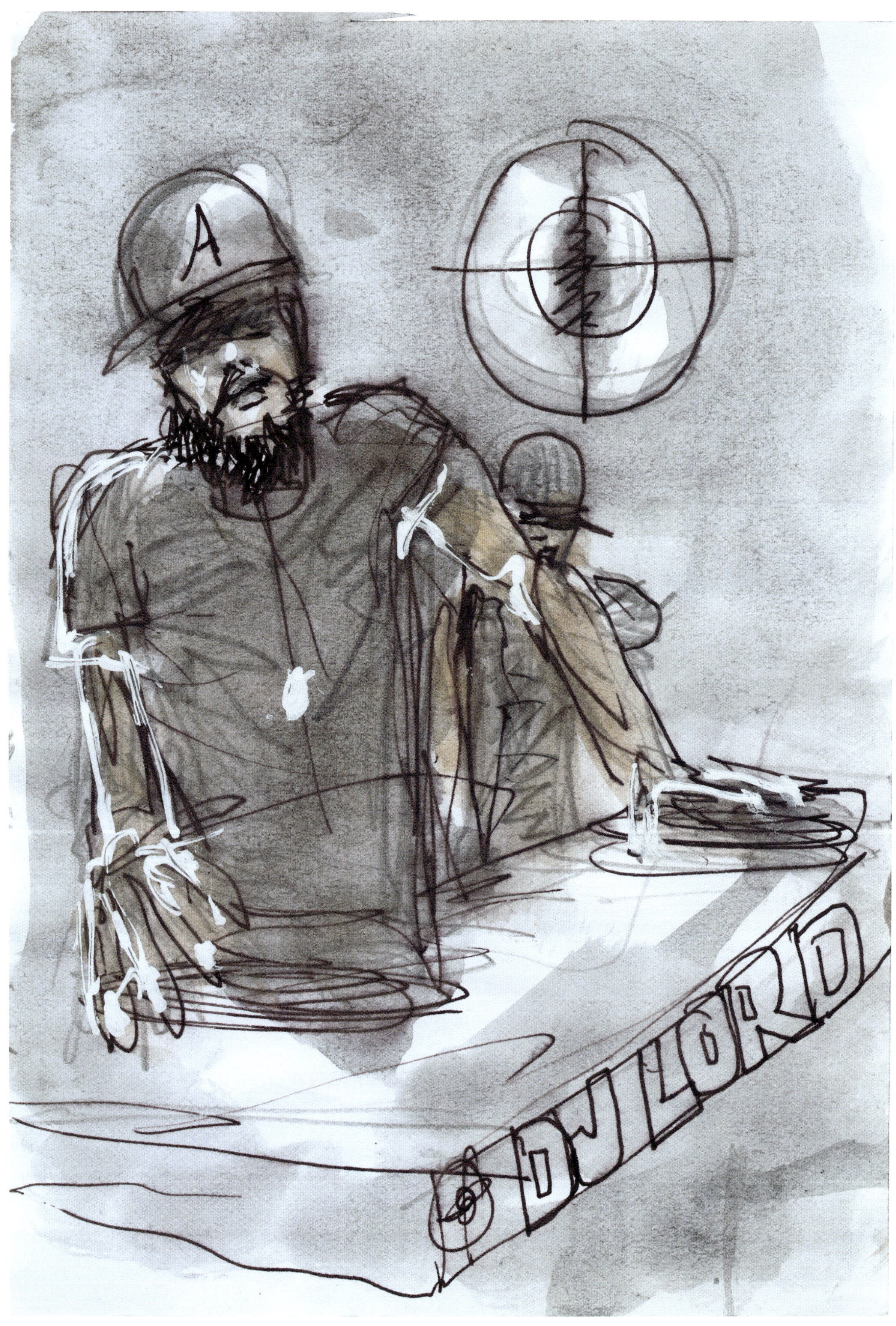
A
DJ LORD

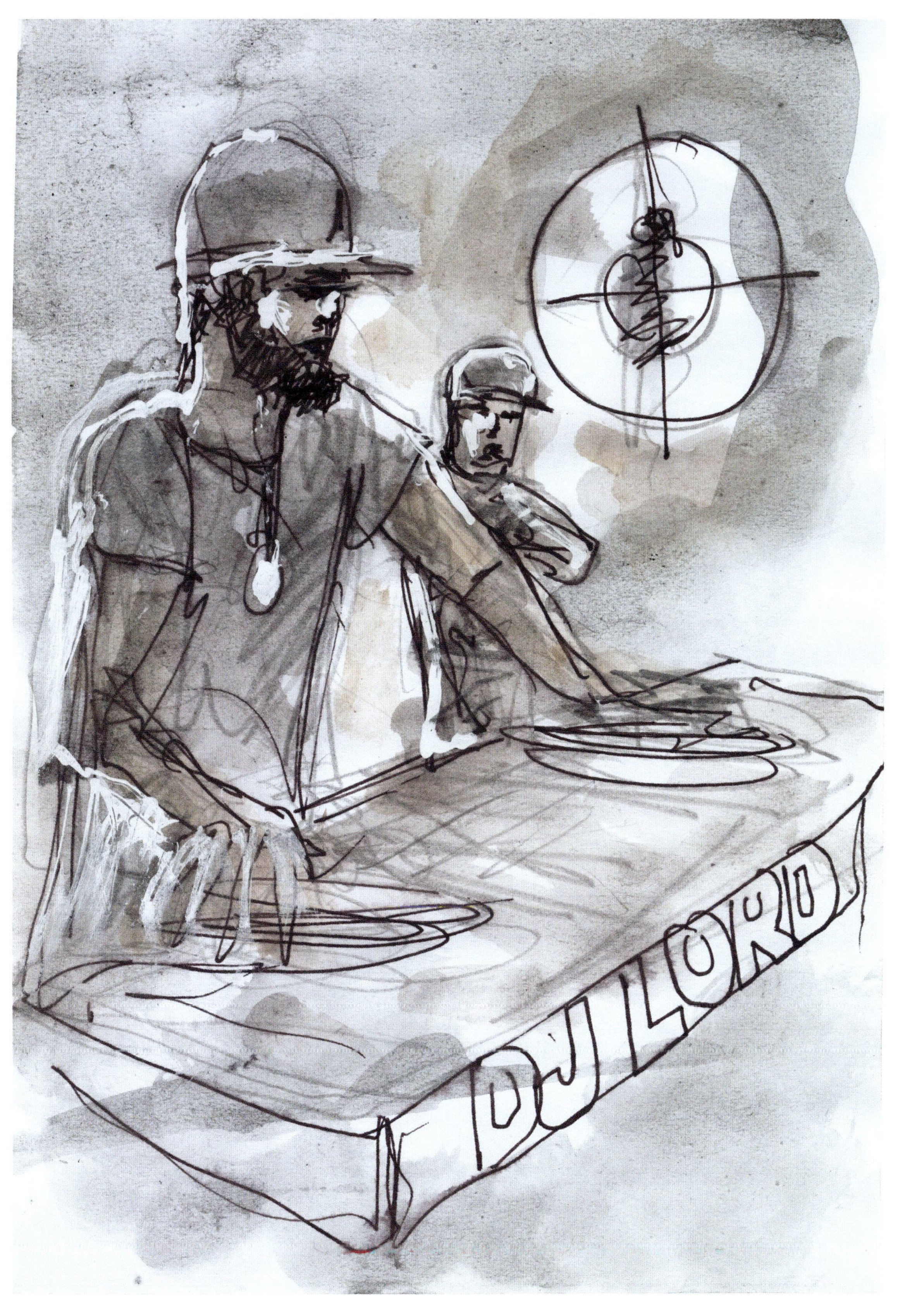

DJ Lord is one of the greatest turntablists in the world.

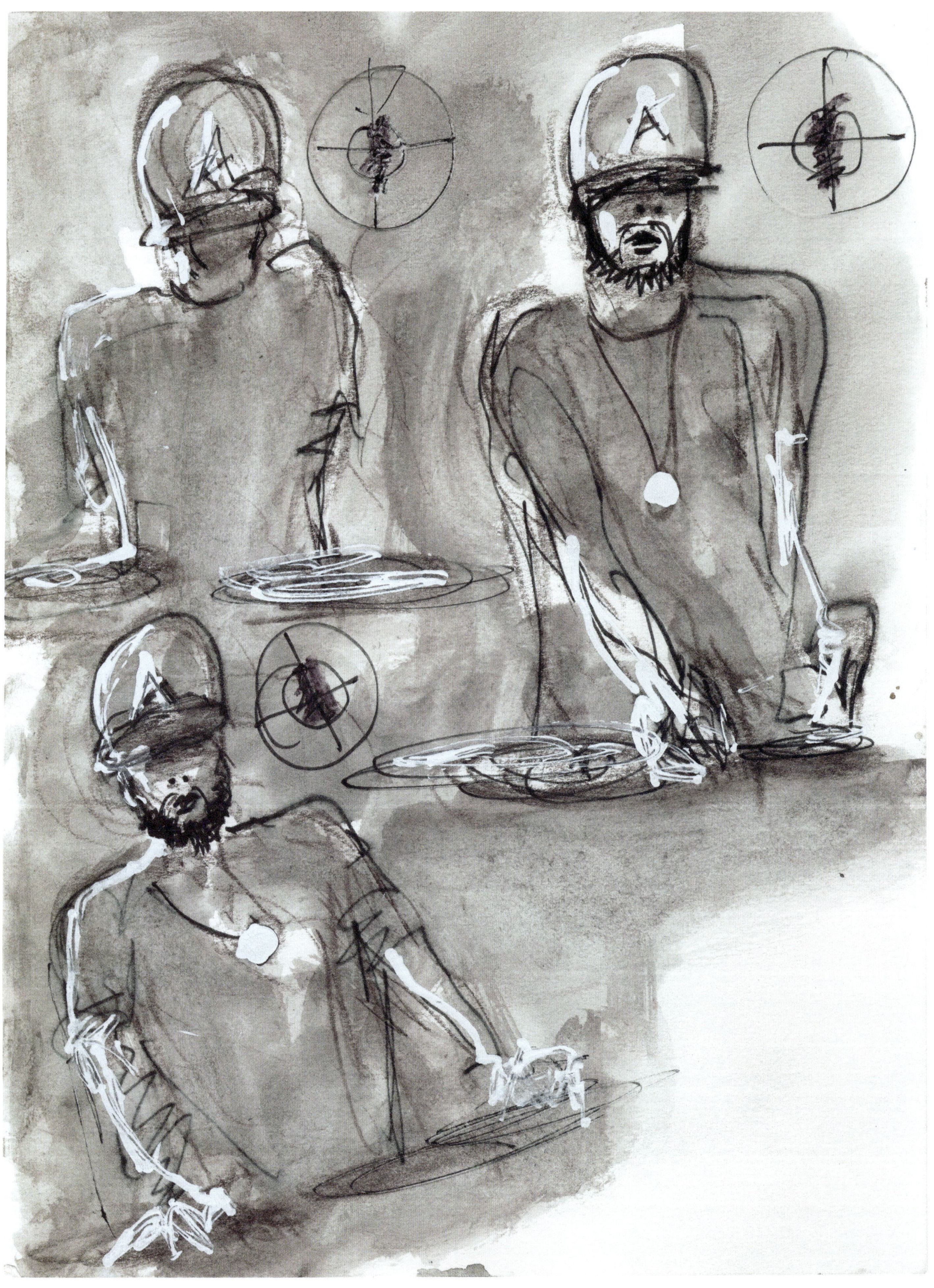

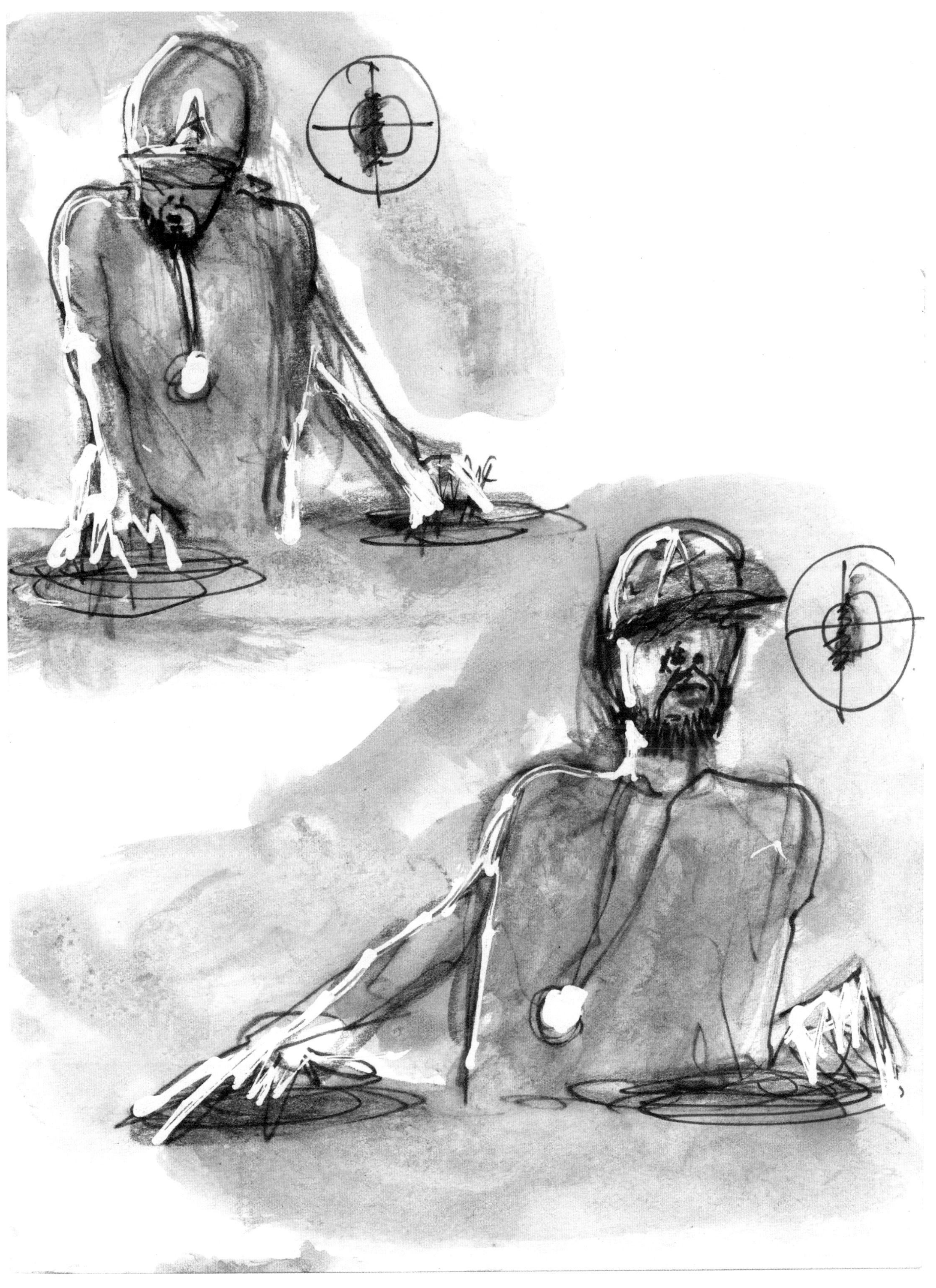

PUMP UP THE VOLUME

HOW CLOSE CAN YOU DANCE GET W THE HEAT

We don't get Grammys and shit like that. It's an incestuous circle. We've always operated outside the circle and attacked the circle, which makes our existence harder sometimes. When we got into the Rock and Roll Hall of Fame, we felt we were properly curated.

I got the phone call and told the rest of the group. We looked forward to the induction ceremonies; to be in the company of all those legendary artists was fantastic. We're musicologists, so everyone in that room meant something to us.

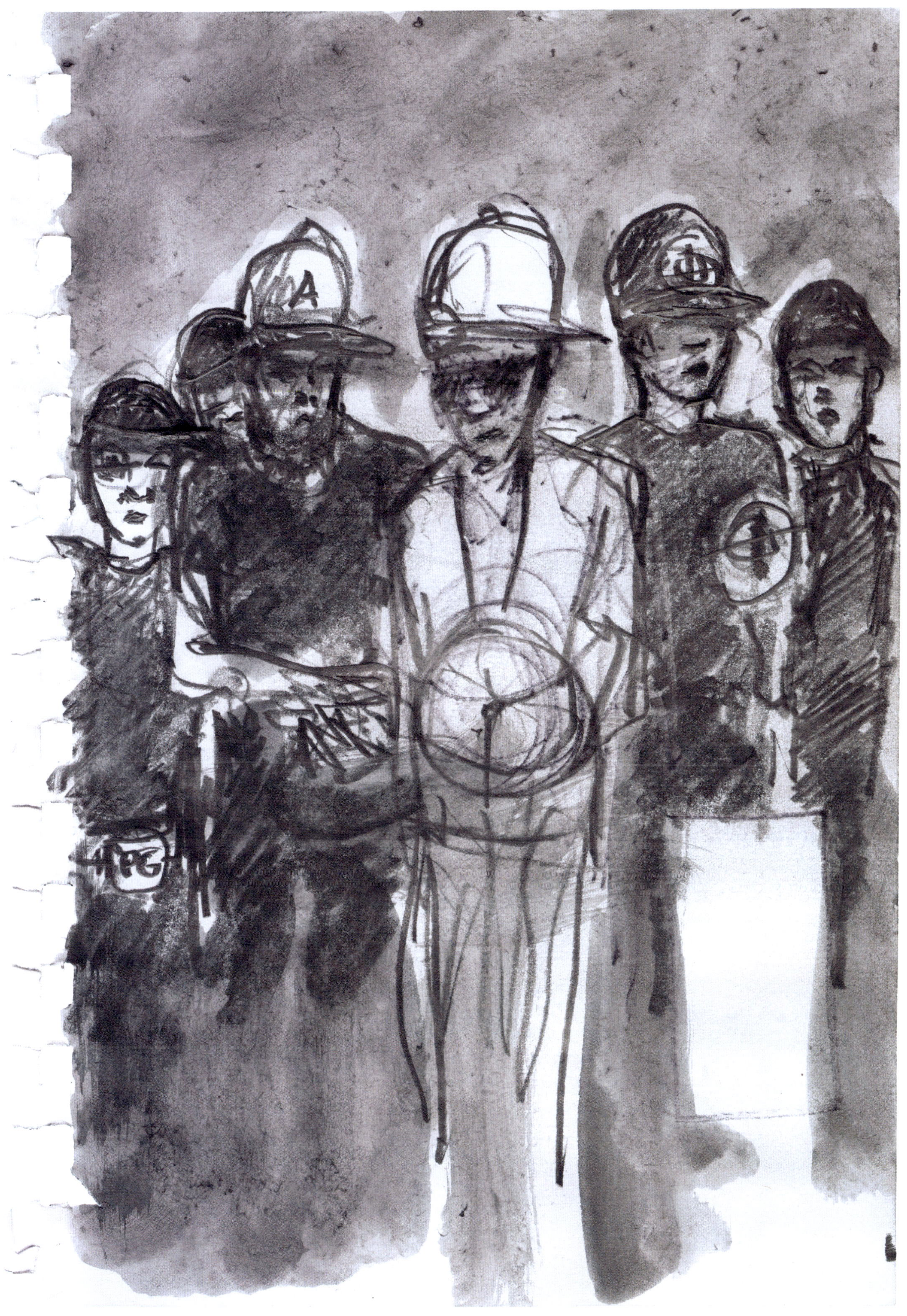
A
PG

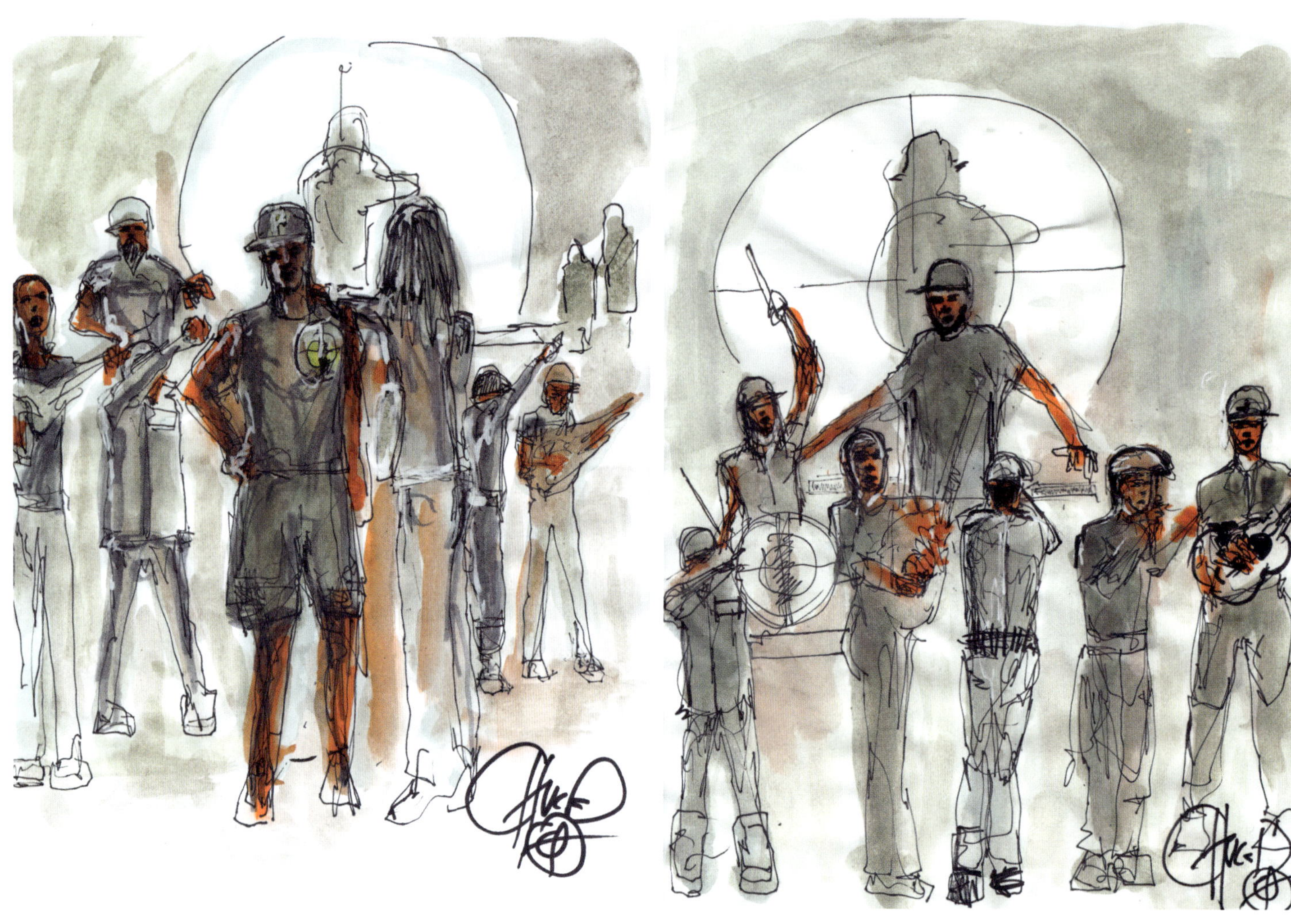

ROCK AND ROLL HALL OF FAME

I took the Rock and Roll Hall of Fame very seriously. I grew up as a sports fan, and I know that a hall of fame is very different than an award for being the best of the year, but it was a nod to the longevity of our accomplishment. When it comes to Public Enemy, we did it on our own terms. Hip-hop is a part of rock and roll because it comes from DJ culture. DJ culture is the embodiment of all genres and all recorded music, if you actually pay attention to it.

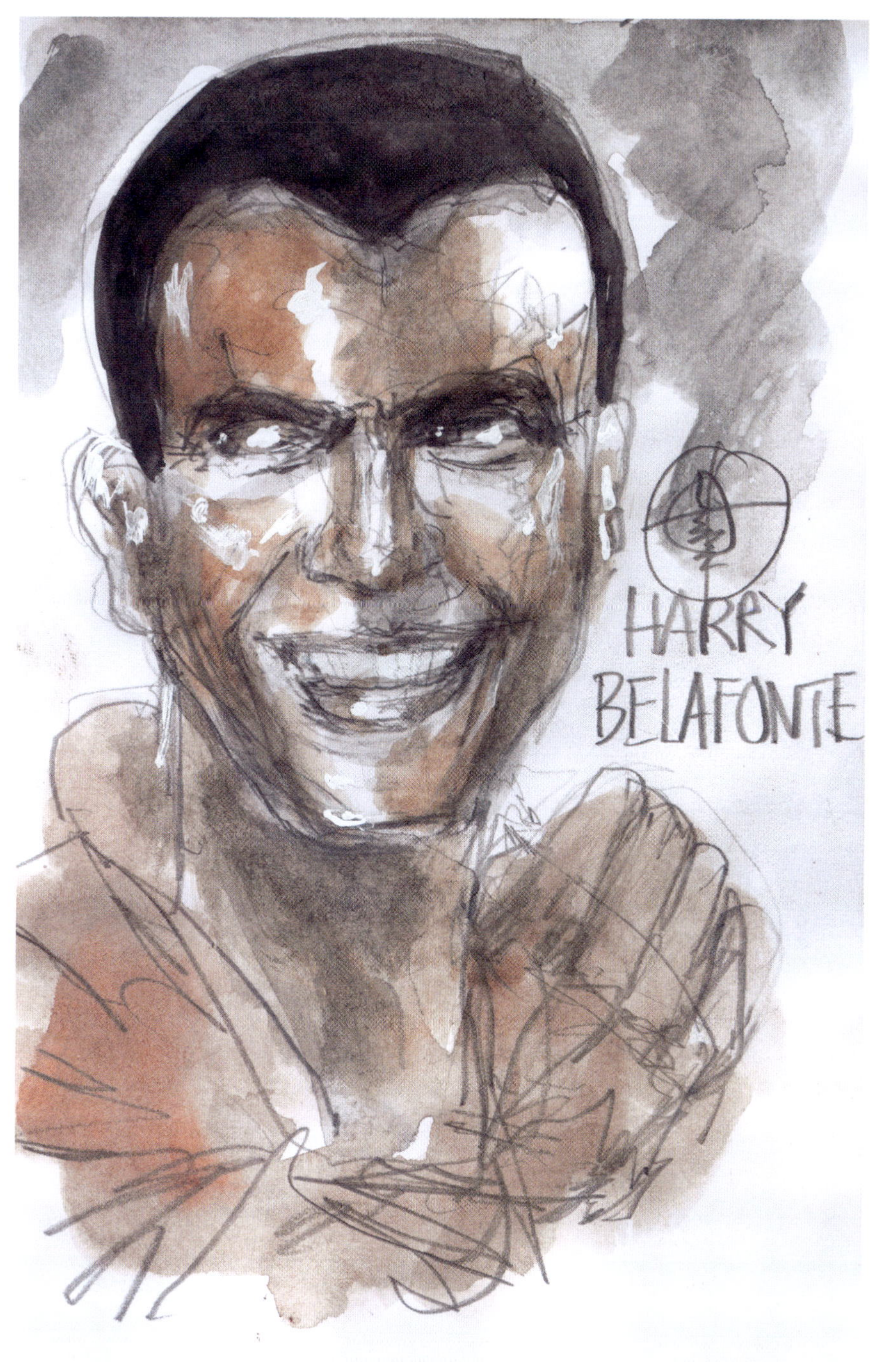

Harry Belafonte was a big deal in my house, even before I was born.

I've known no better feeling than being introduced by him at the Rock and Roll Hall of Fame night. That was something we had really pushed to make happen, because how many times do you see octogenarians, especially those of colour, speak their minds about what's going on in the world – the atrocities, the malfeasance by government? Harry Belafonte spoke to that.

It's important for a person like myself to understand the magnitude that he had 50 years ago and still has today. He is the voice of the voiceless. If you're the one that's seen, you have to be a sight for the unseen and a thinker for the unthought of.

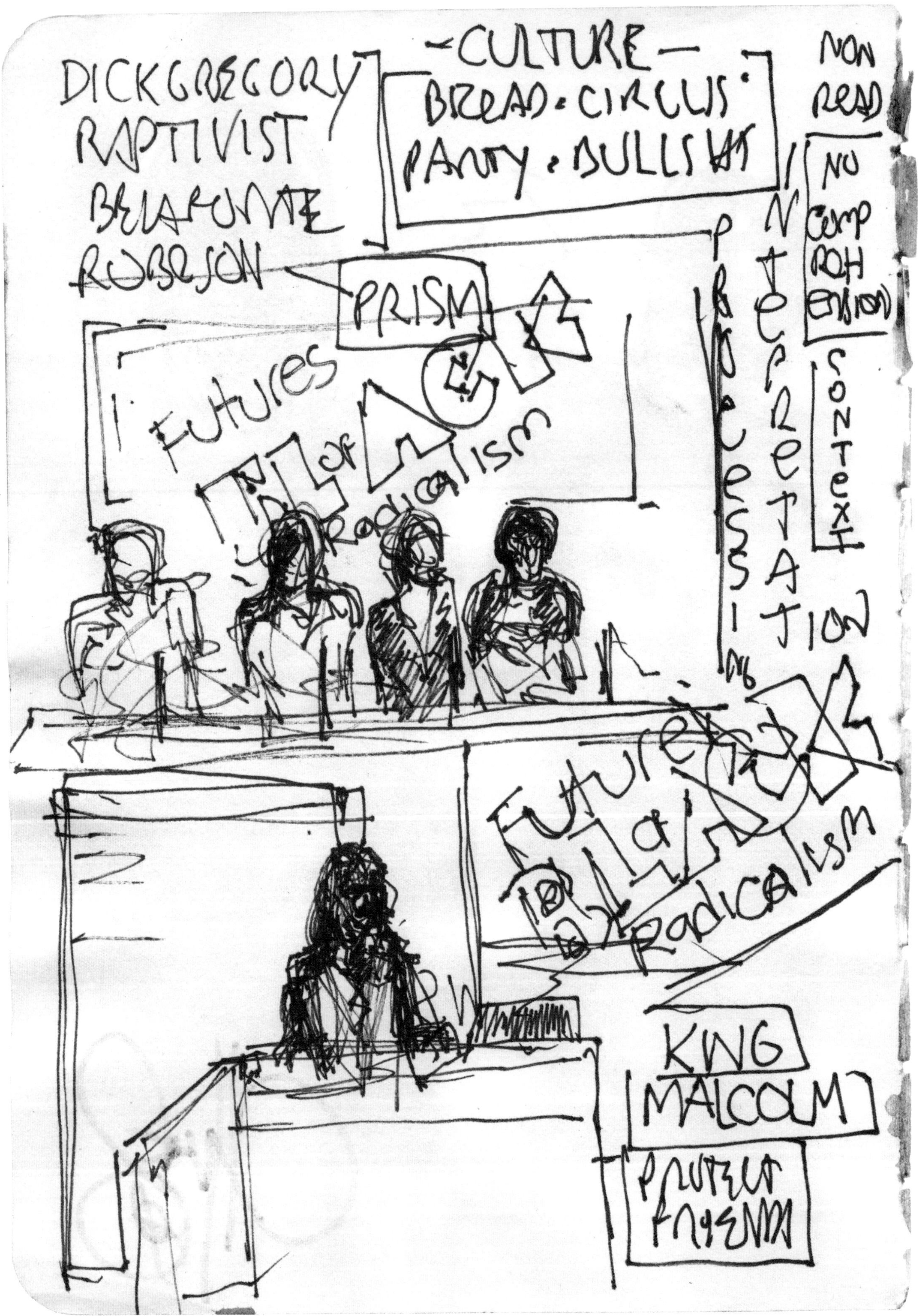

DICK GREGORY
BELAFONTE
ROBESON
CULTURE
BREAD • CIRCUS
NON READ
NO COMPREHENSION
CONTEXT
INTERPRETATION
PRISM
Futures of Black Radicalism
Futures of Black Radicalism
KING
MALCOLM

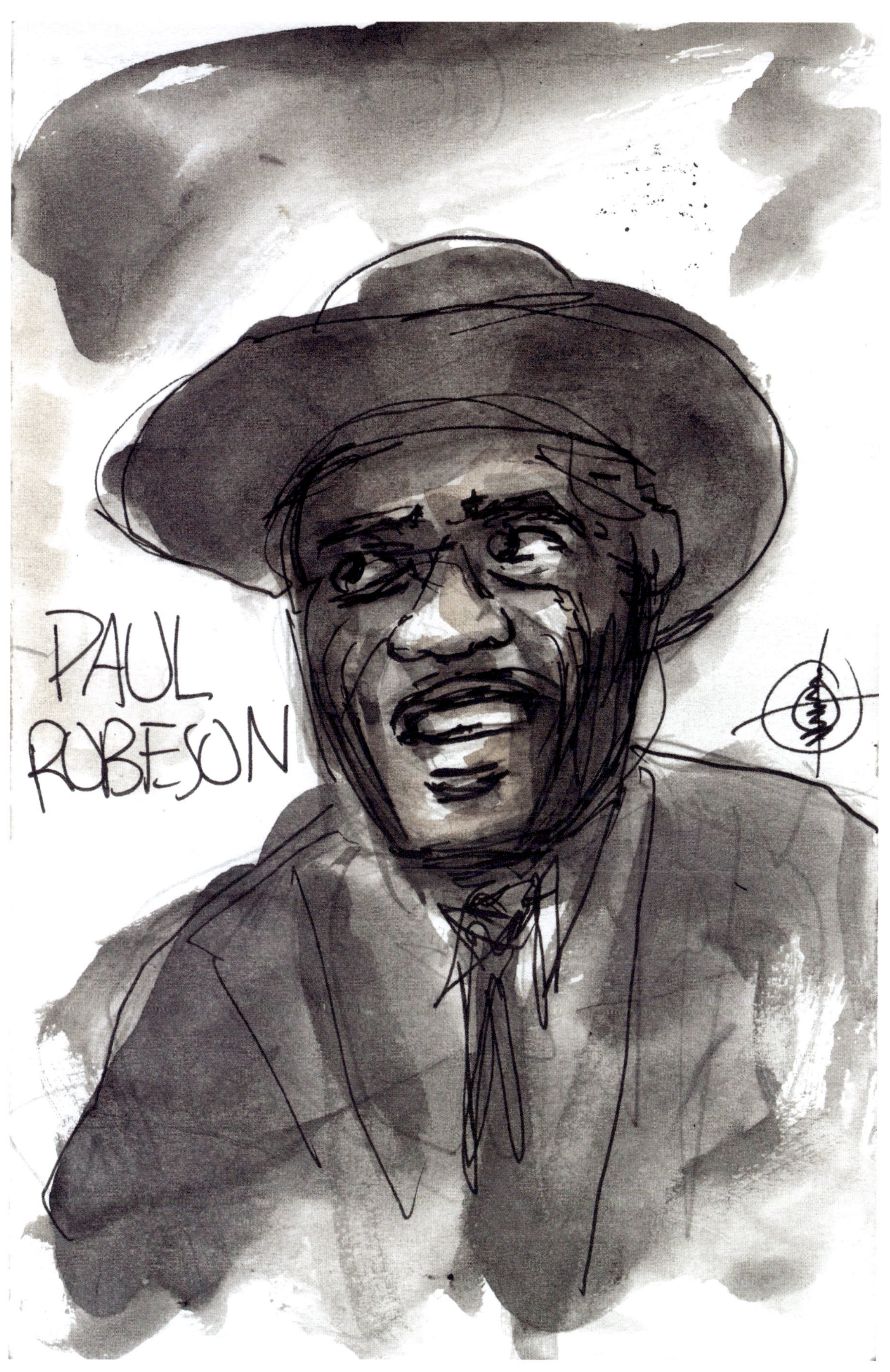

If you study Paul Robeson, you'll understand why I am a culturalist.

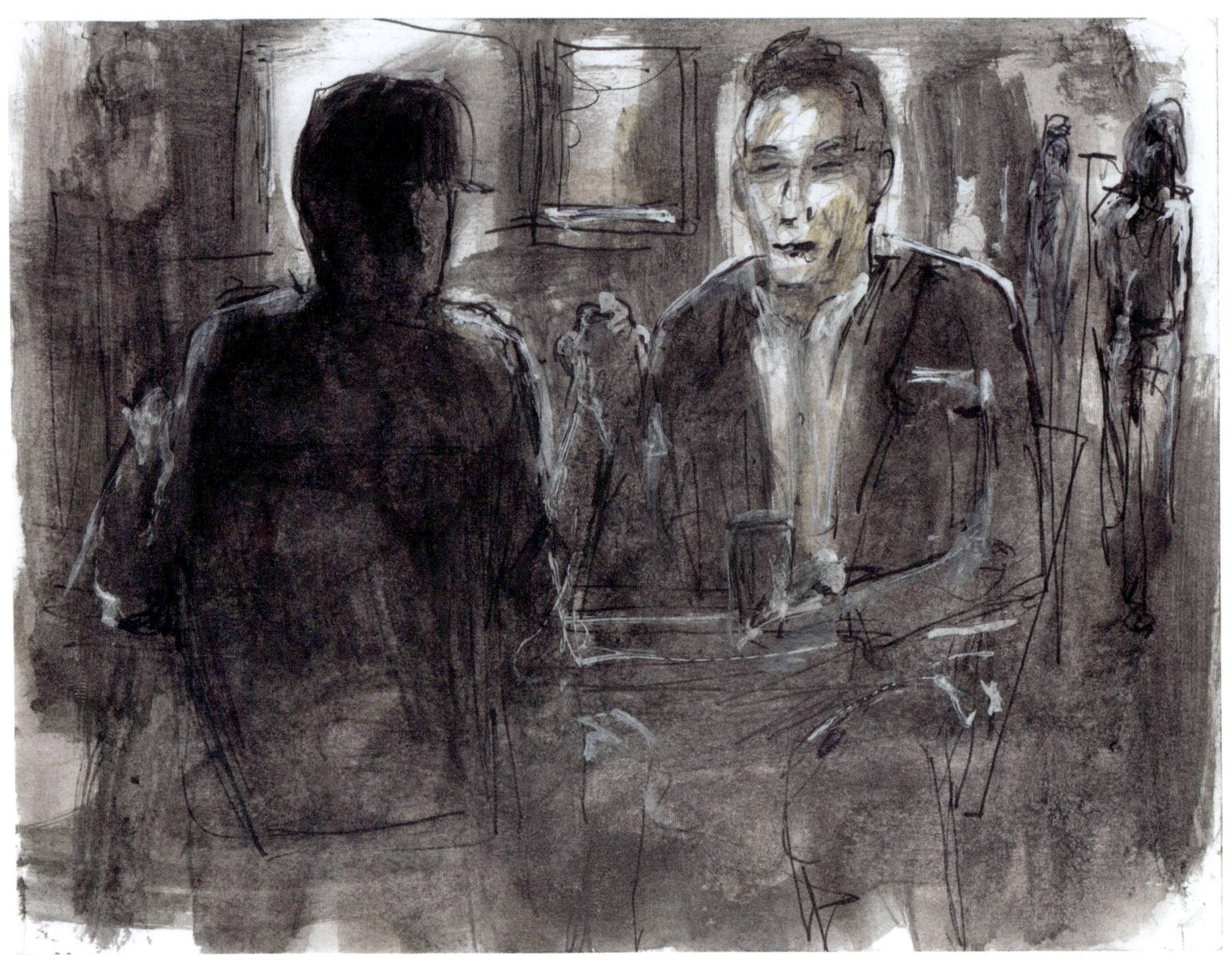

This was the scene after Public Enemy and Rush were inducted into the Rock and Roll Hall of Fame in 2013. This is me and the great drummer Neil Peart in a silent moment of relief.

Public Enemy has included around 50 people. This wasn't a three-man group that came up like Ad-Rock, MCA and Mike D of the Beastie Boys. I still have conversations with these people and we can always pick up right where we left off. I might not be able to fix their problem, but they all know that they can come to me. We're wedded to each other, we're family. The barbecue can get a little... you know... but it's a family barbecue. I don't tell stories on any of my guys, so anything you hear you're going to hear from someone else. Those that know don't tell, and those that tell don't know.

I don't take the credit for making Public Enemy what it is. I've done a lot of things outside of Public Enemy, but I know that I carry the PE cloak, cape and banner with me. So, therefore, I can't be out of character, because it points back to the group.

Everybody else can afford to do their own thing without being tied to Public Enemy. But I'm alright to be stuck with it; it's not a bad place to get stuck.

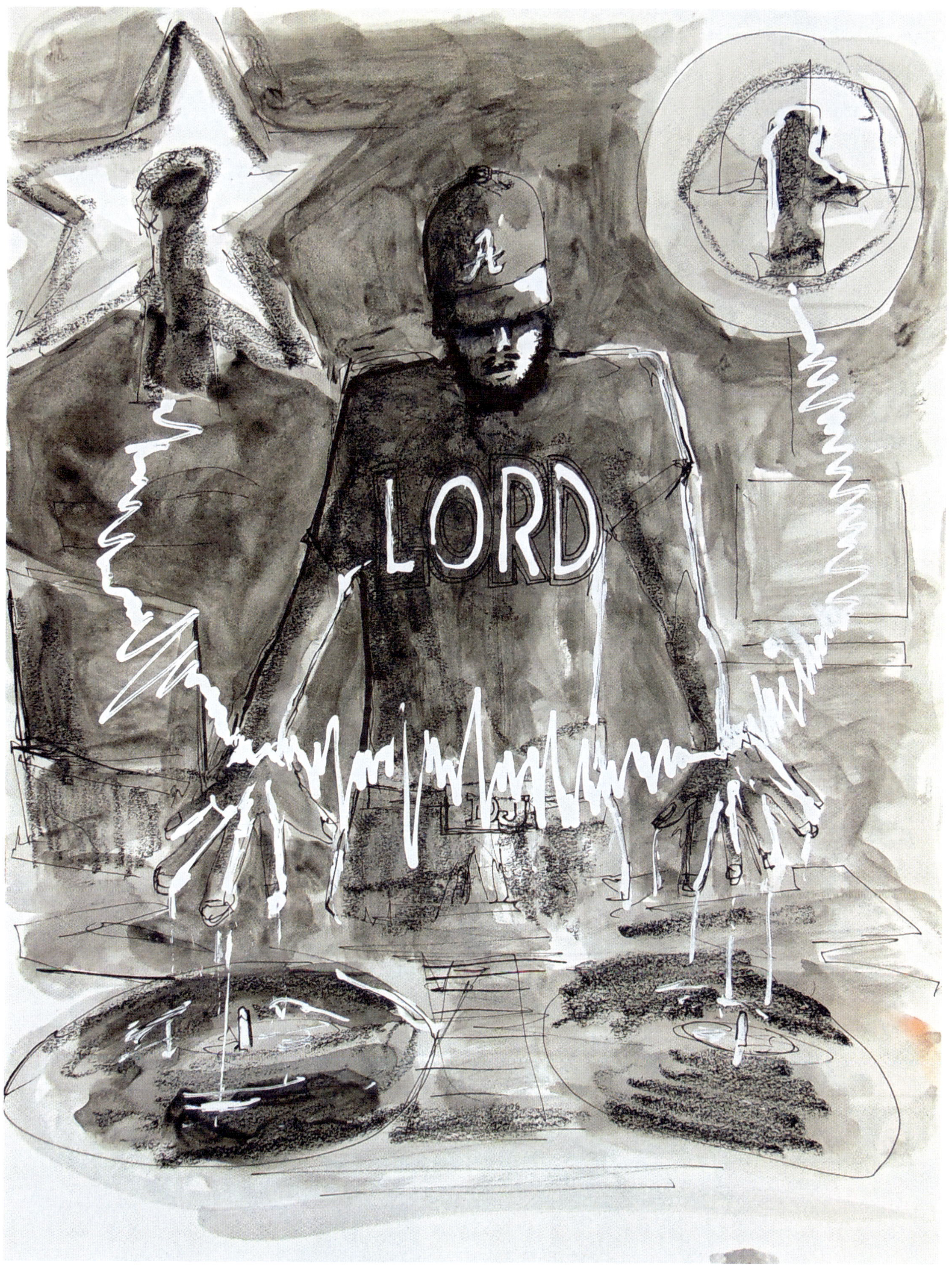
LORD

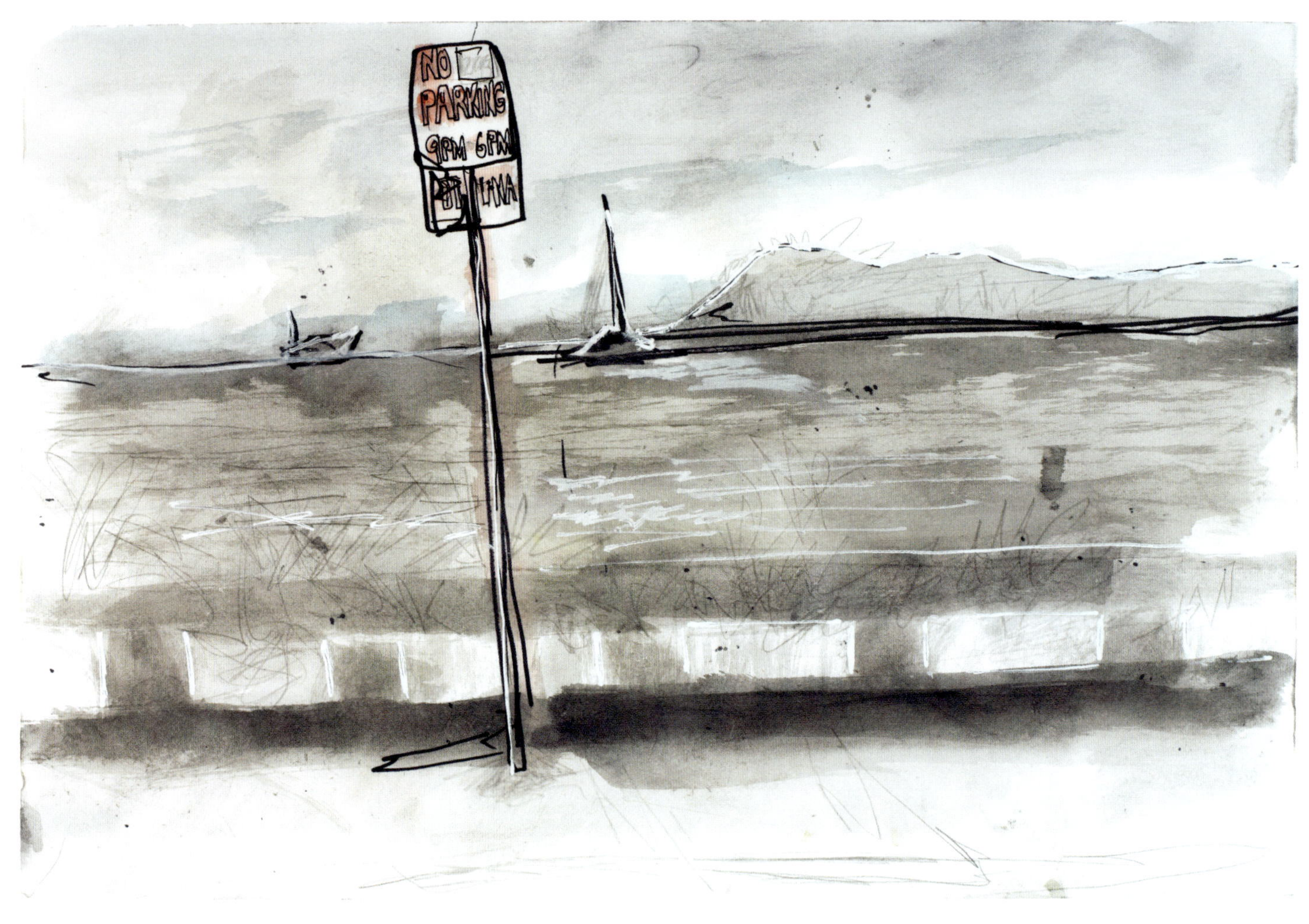

I've written my best records while driving, ever since the first in 1986. It's an energy I continue to use. The number one thing is to be safe and keep your eyes on the road, but I still keep a pad and a pen in the car for when I'm driving and an idea comes.

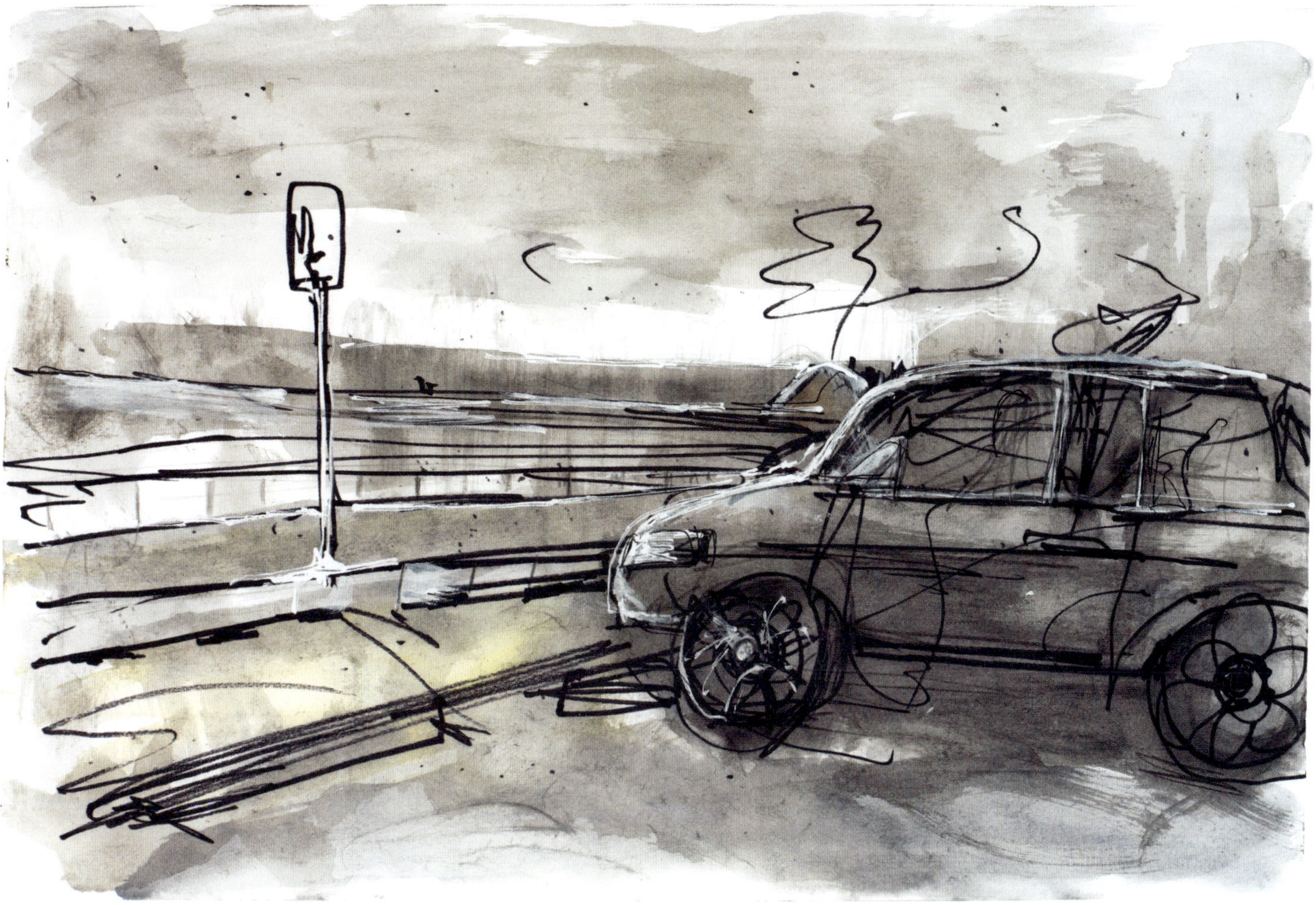

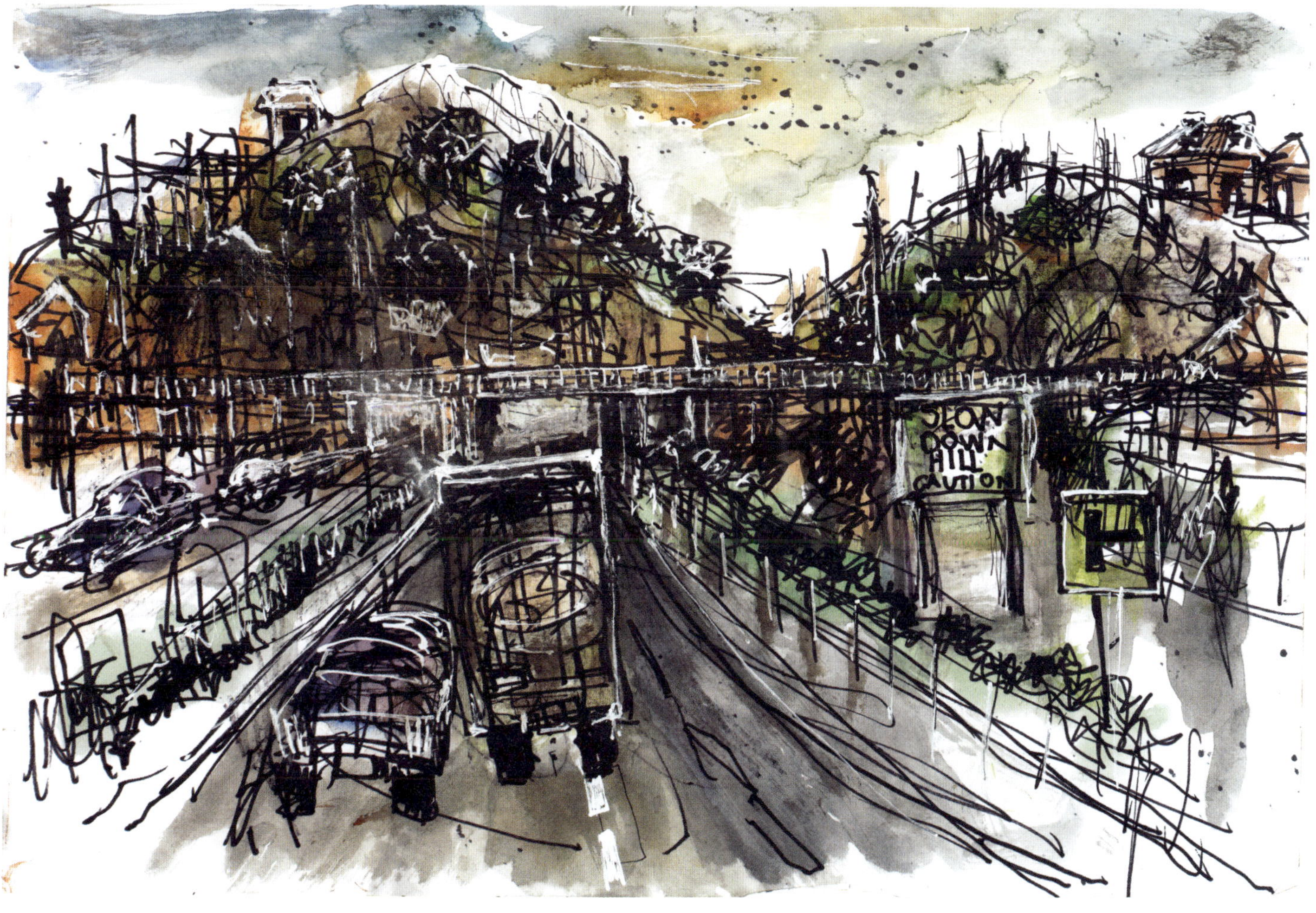

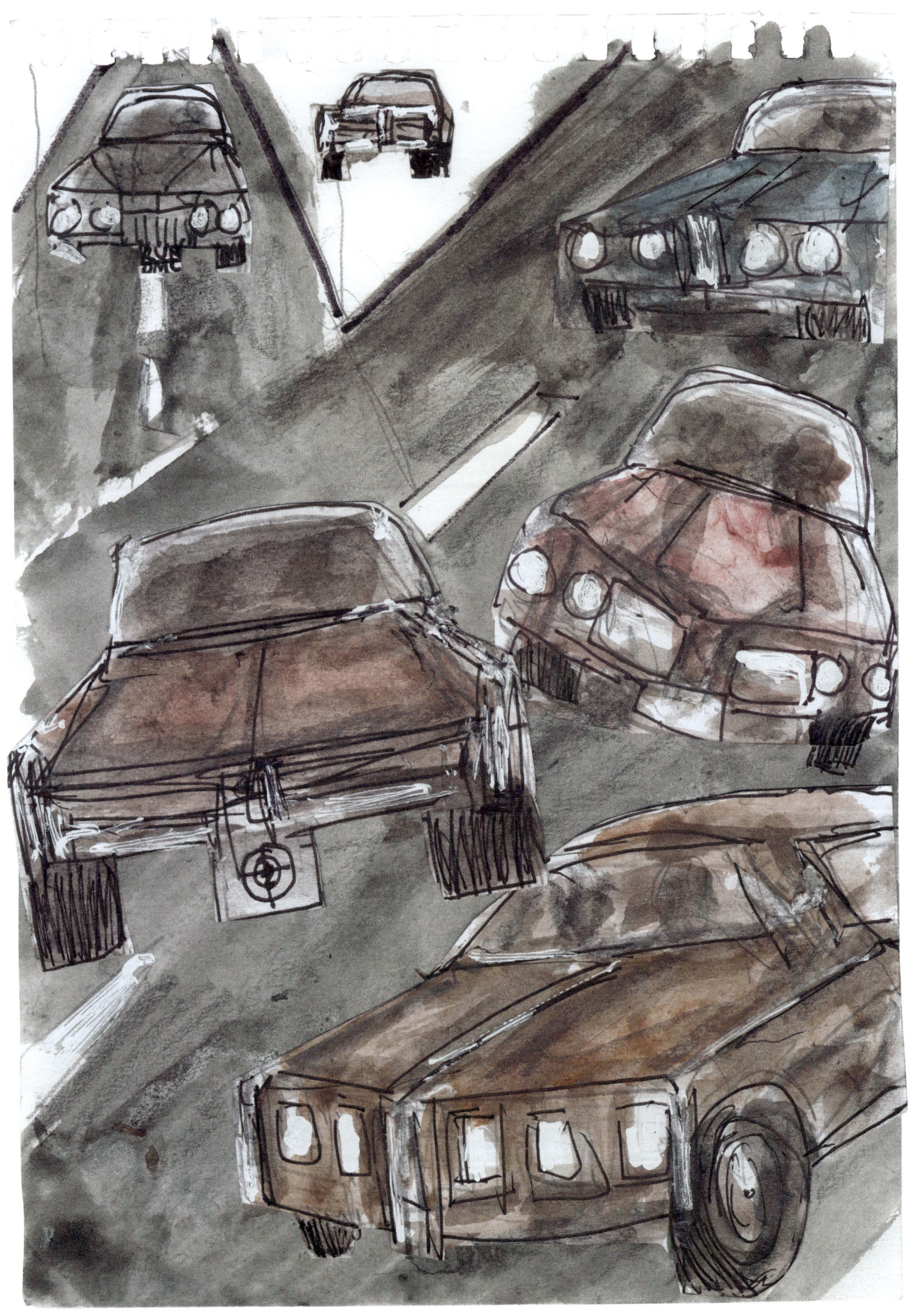
BMC

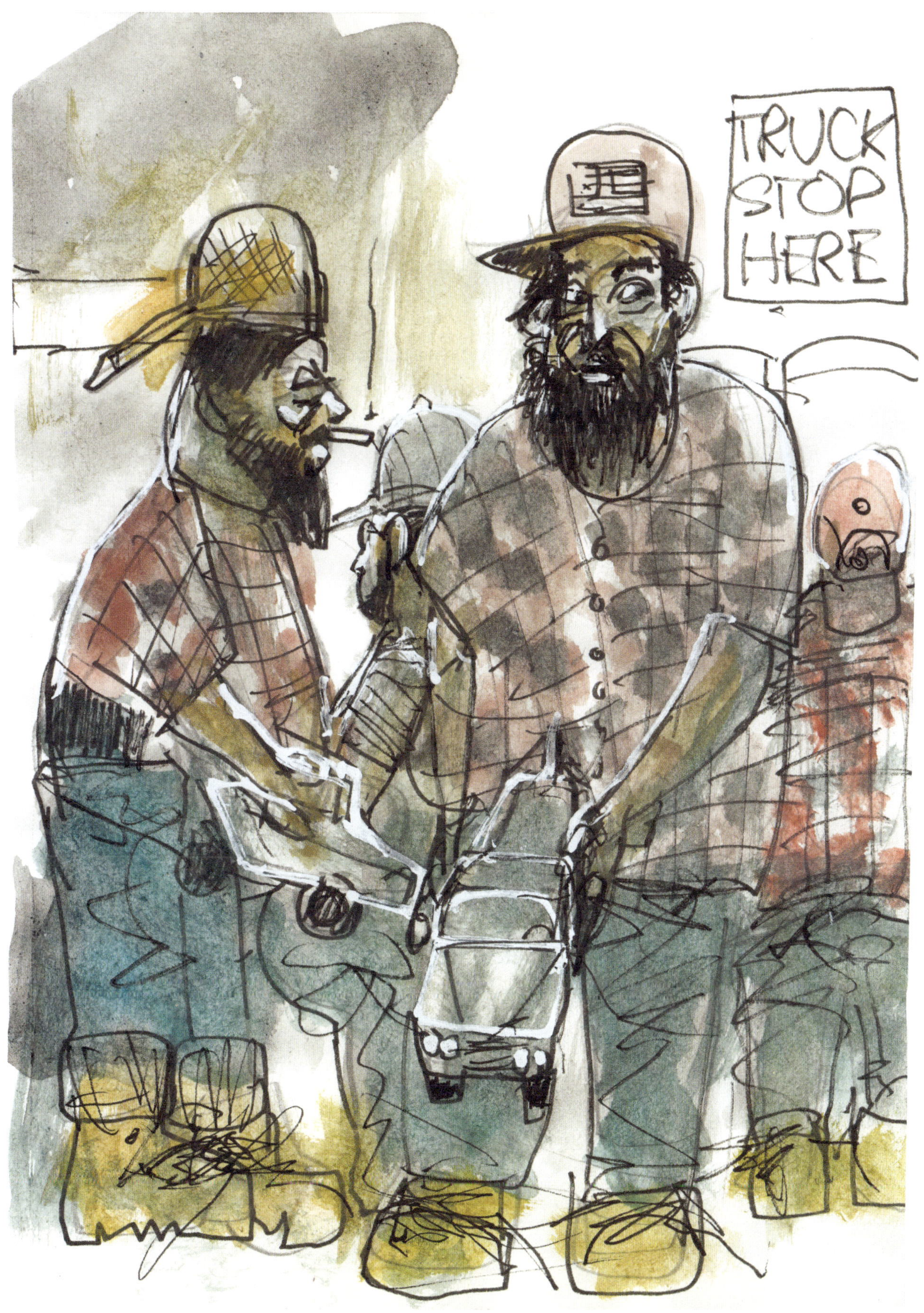

The US interstate highways are a culture of their own. The trucks are metal dinosaurs.

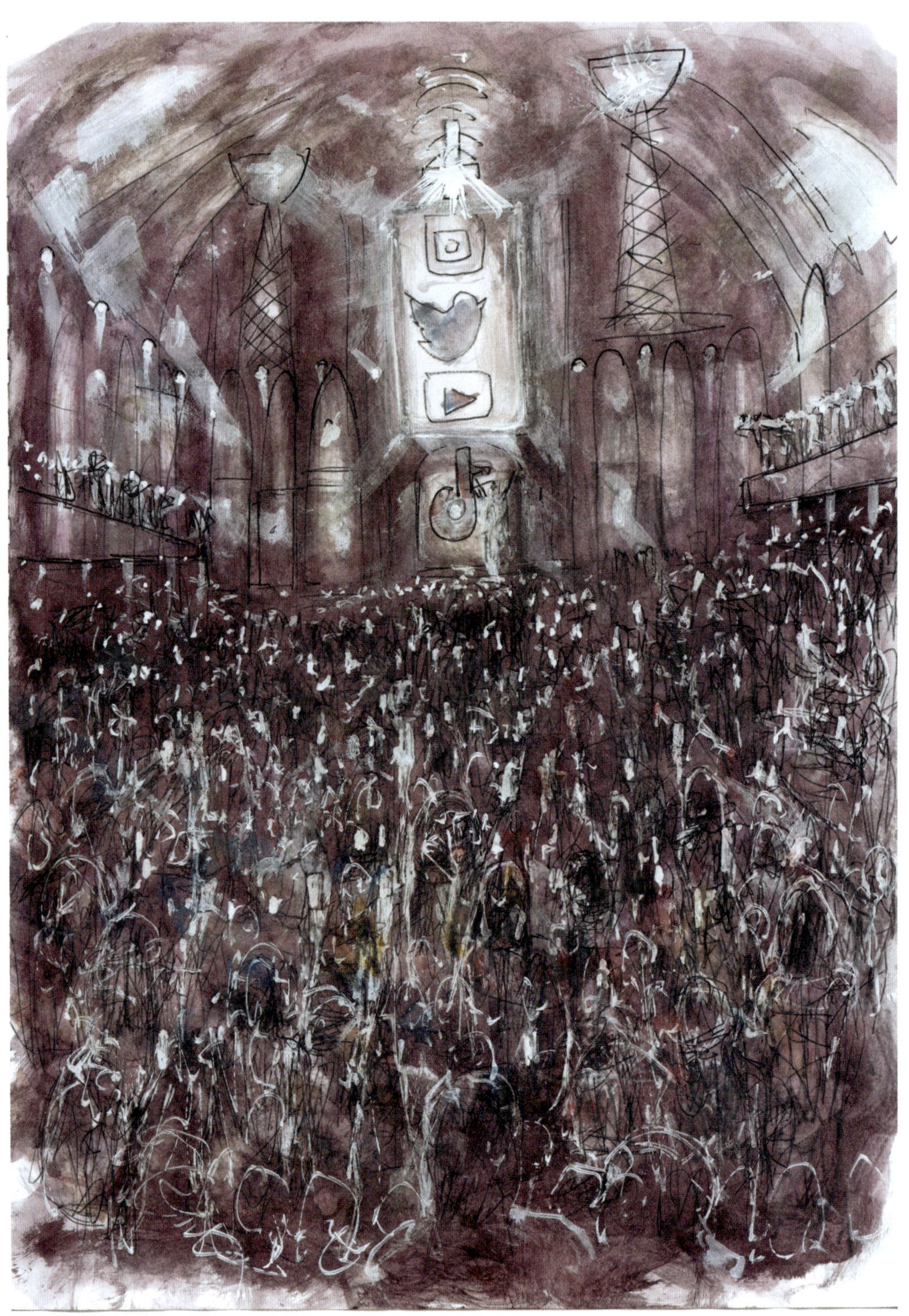

MEDIA

I'm sure when Henry Ford made the Model T he couldn't foresee drag racing, people doing figure of eights in parking lots, drunk driving... all of that. He just wanted people to be able to get from A to B economically in a horseless carriage. That happens with technology. Younger generations grow up with it and use it in a different way from the original idea.

I try to tell people to use these things as tools more than gadgets. Prince was right when he said that we should look to manage our gadgets, or else they'll start managing us. That's where we're at right now because what comes through on the other side of the transmission will master you if you don't watch it.

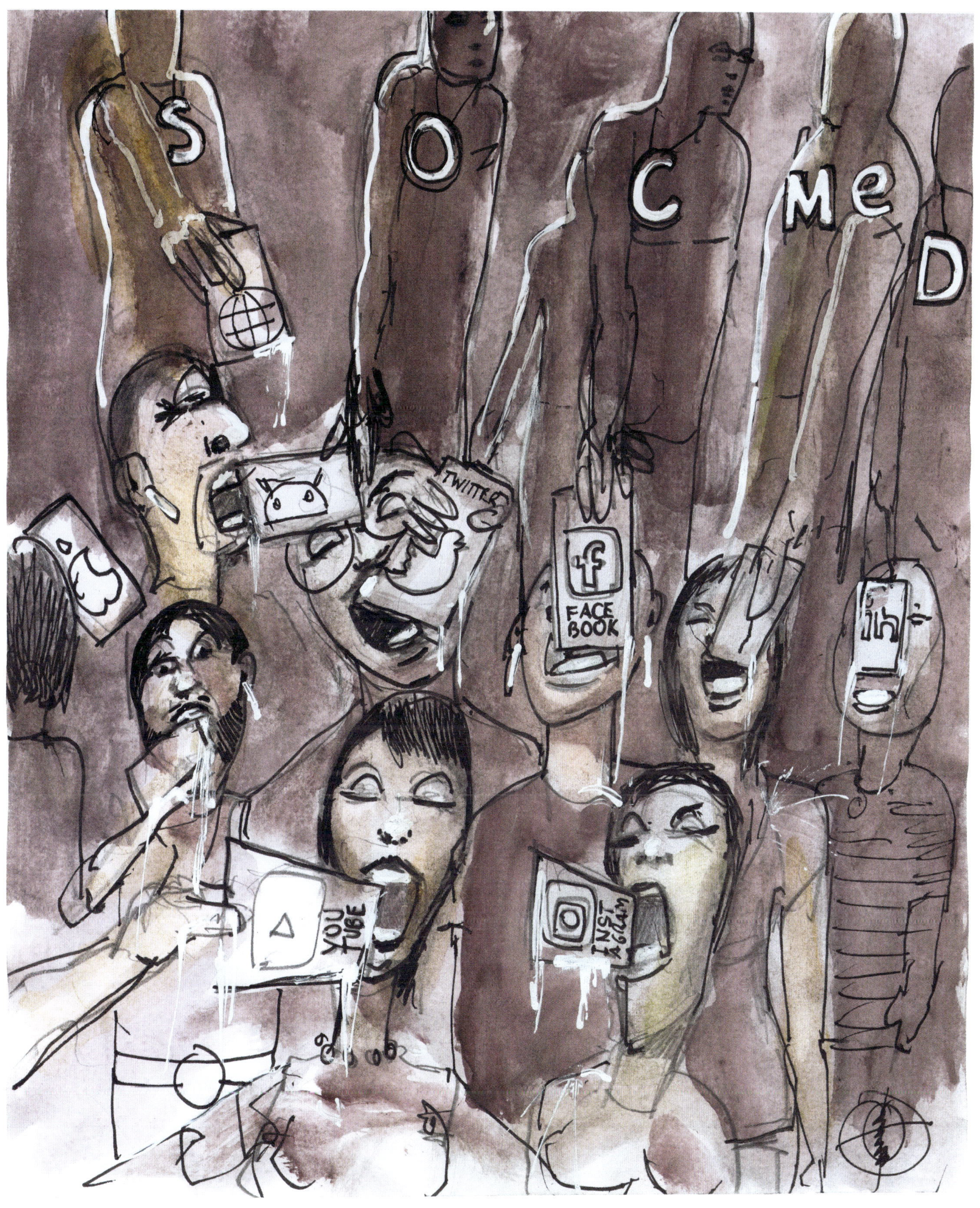

Things that start out as a tool end up as a toy.

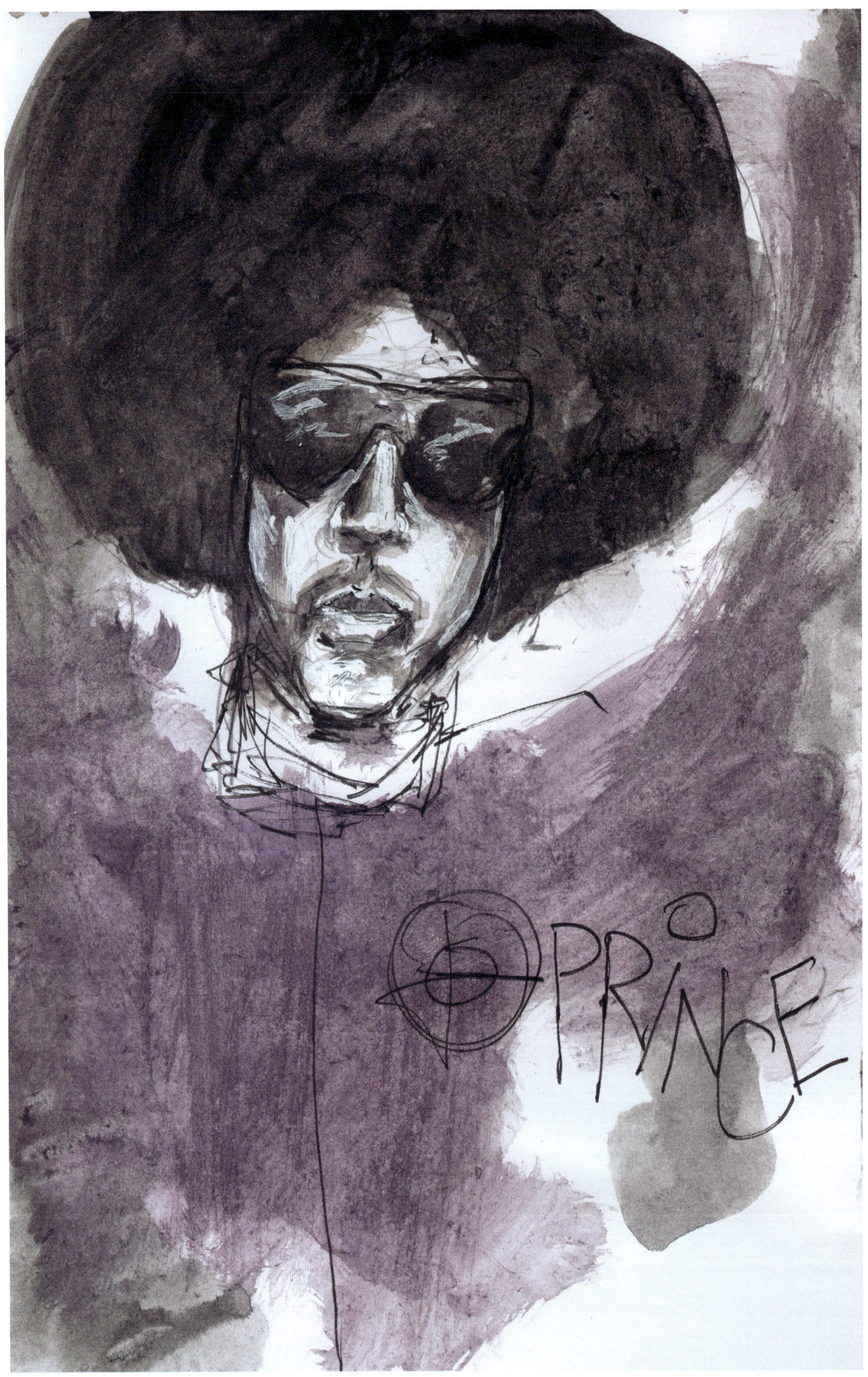
PRINCE

Prince was always from the future.

Prince is a maestro, up there in the same conversation as Duke Ellington and Louis Armstrong. For black folks, he signifies the past, present and future. I recorded with him in 1999 – which was mind-blowing – but the really tripped-out thing was he had a garage sale on the lawn of Paisley Park. Someone would ask him about a guitar with a tag on it and he'd say, 'I'll give you $60 off that one.' What the fuck, man? A garage sale at Paisley Park and Prince is out there giving price breaks!

We went inside and spoke while listening to the track. After I was done rapping he told me to go and wait for him in the lobby. I could see him through a window and it looked like he was making a salad... he was tossing tape around like a chef! He knew every aspect of that studio. Half an hour later, he invited me back in and it was done.

Prince passed only a few months after my dad. It was the day before what would have been my dad's birthday, so I was already swelled up ready for 22 April and then that happened.

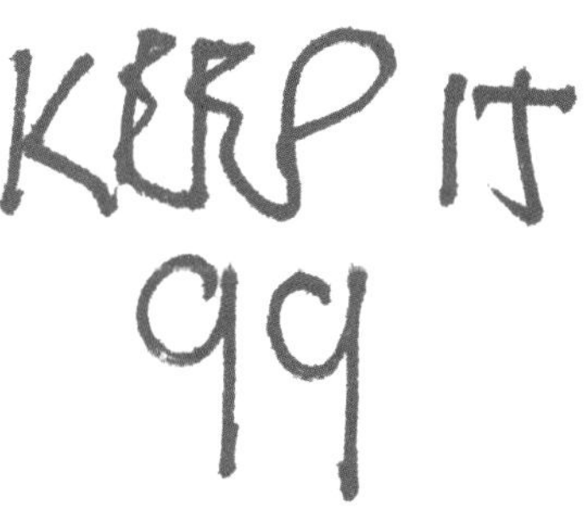

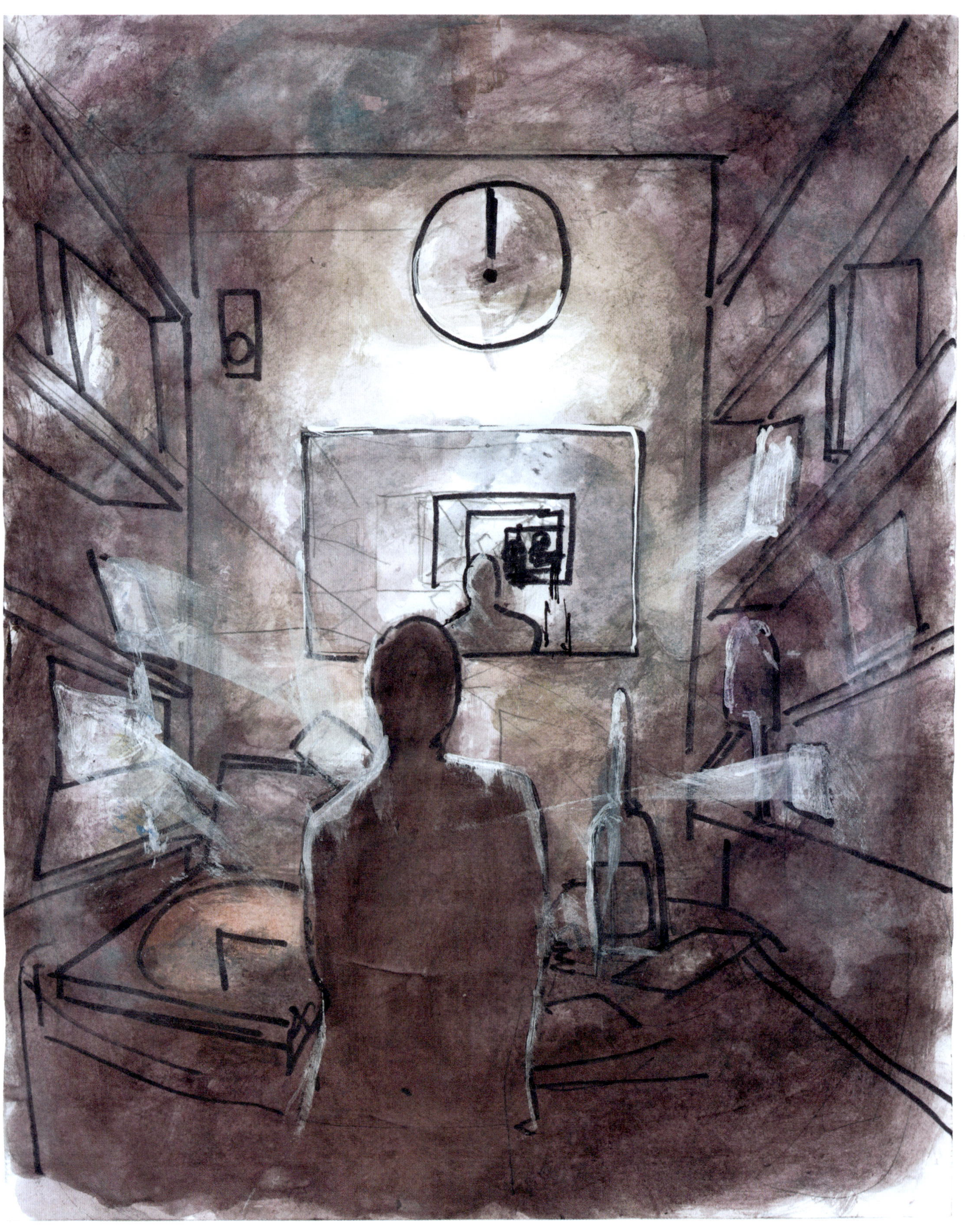

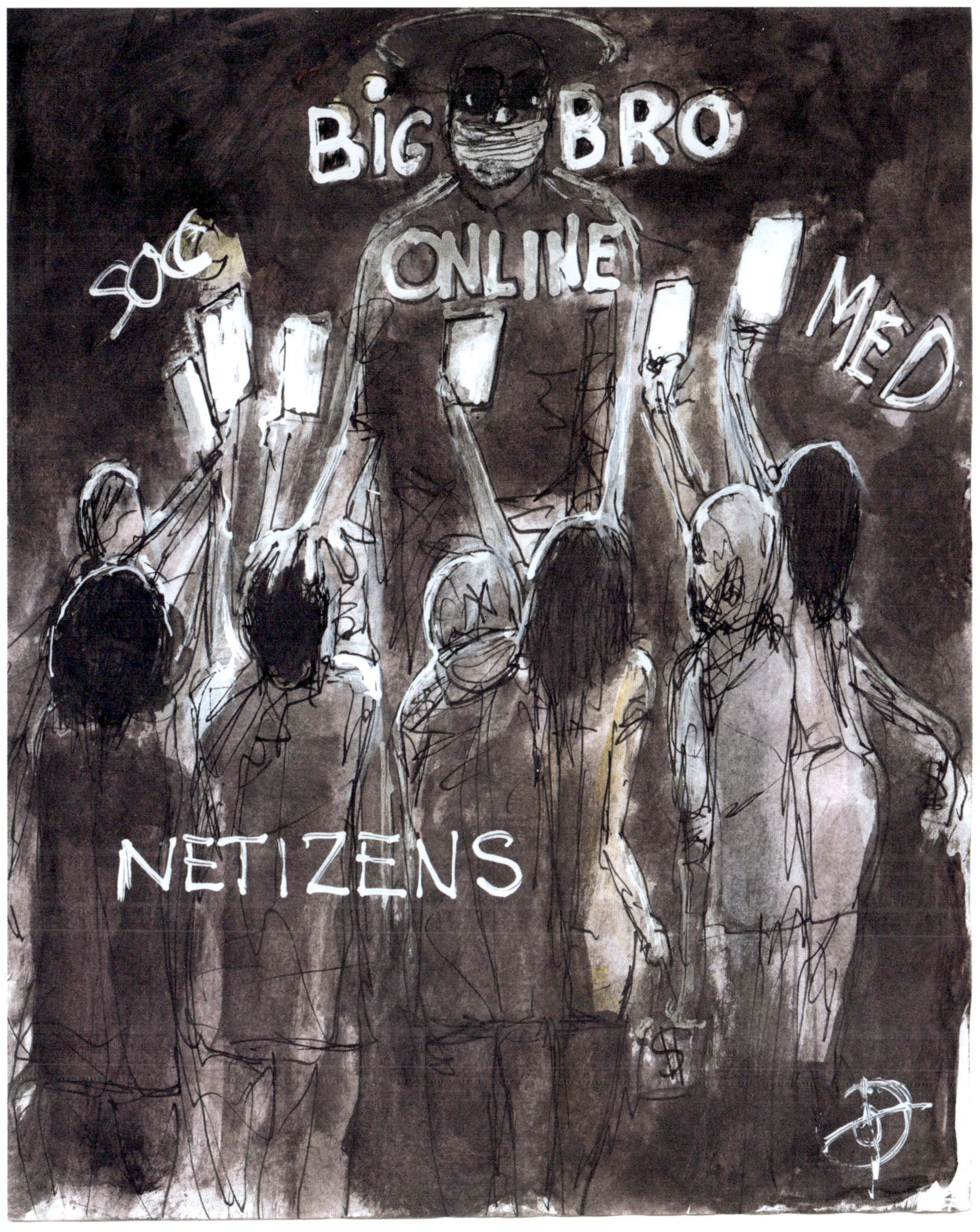

There are a lot of people who are accustomed to being citizens. You grow up aiming to reach a certain category and then you live in that box for the rest of your life. The pandemic wiped that off. For the first time, citizens have become netizens. All of a sudden, most of our communicating is done through technology.

People might have a cyber understanding, but there's no such thing as net etiquette. People are not net-literate, they were thrust into this world and now they're trying to figure out what it means to be a netizen. That all happened in the past few years, and it took everybody off guard. Like, who am I in this world?

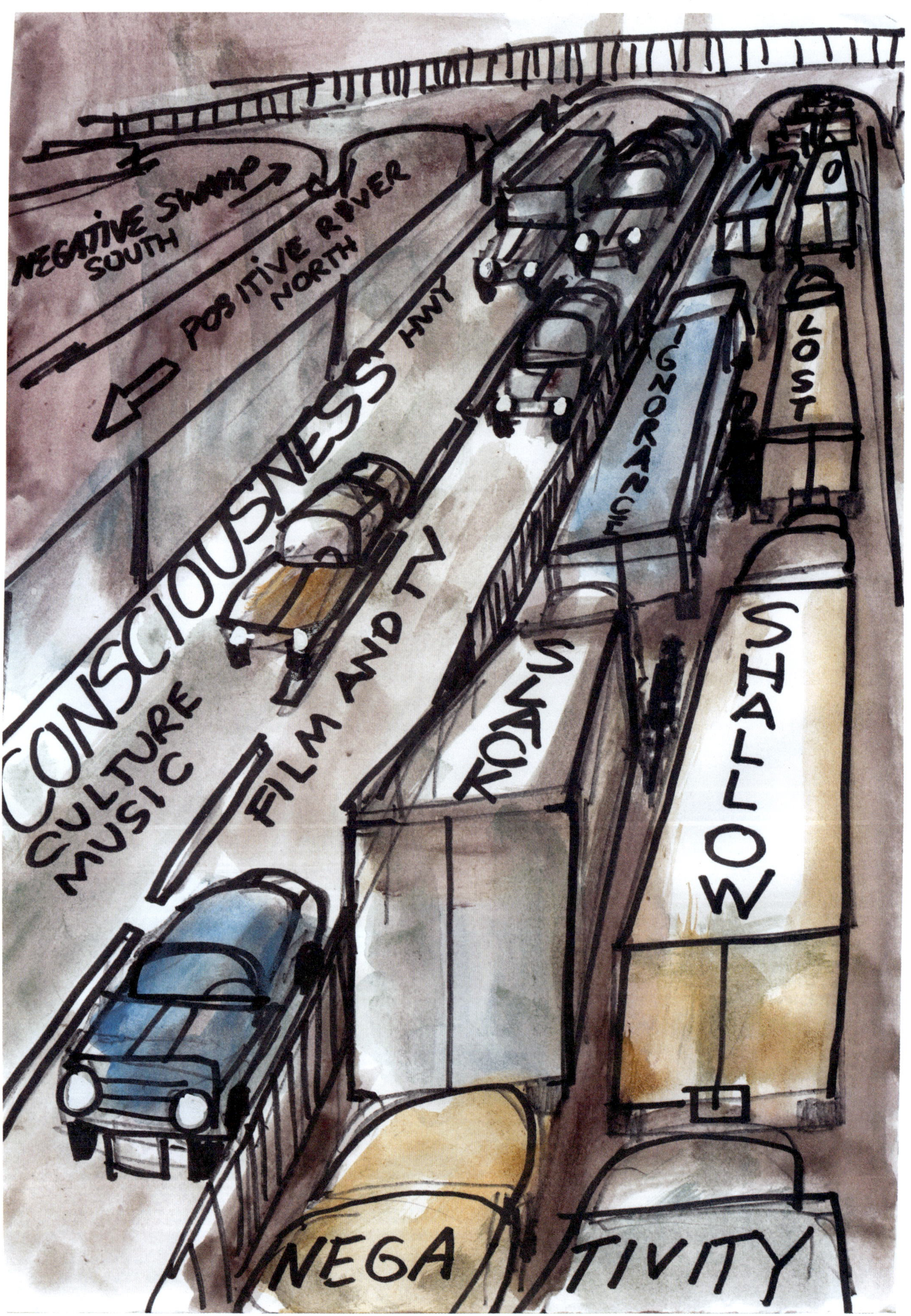
NEGATIVE SWAMP SOUTH
POSITIVE RIVER NORTH
CONSCIOUSNESS HWY
CULTURE MUSIC
FILM AND TV
IGNORANCE
LOST
SLACK
SHALLOW
NEGA TIVITY

The designed narrative against consciousness.

Art is subjective and people have their tastes, but usually these tastes are acquired based on learning. If you have a great time with something, it's best to know what it is versus what it ain't. Education helps you enjoy music even more. You find that not only do you dig it, but you want to engage with it. That was an early goal of Public Enemy, to find leaders who, by digging what they dug, showed people that they could do something life-enhancing. The arts give you a plan for everyday living. Not having that focus can lead to boredom and over-consumption.

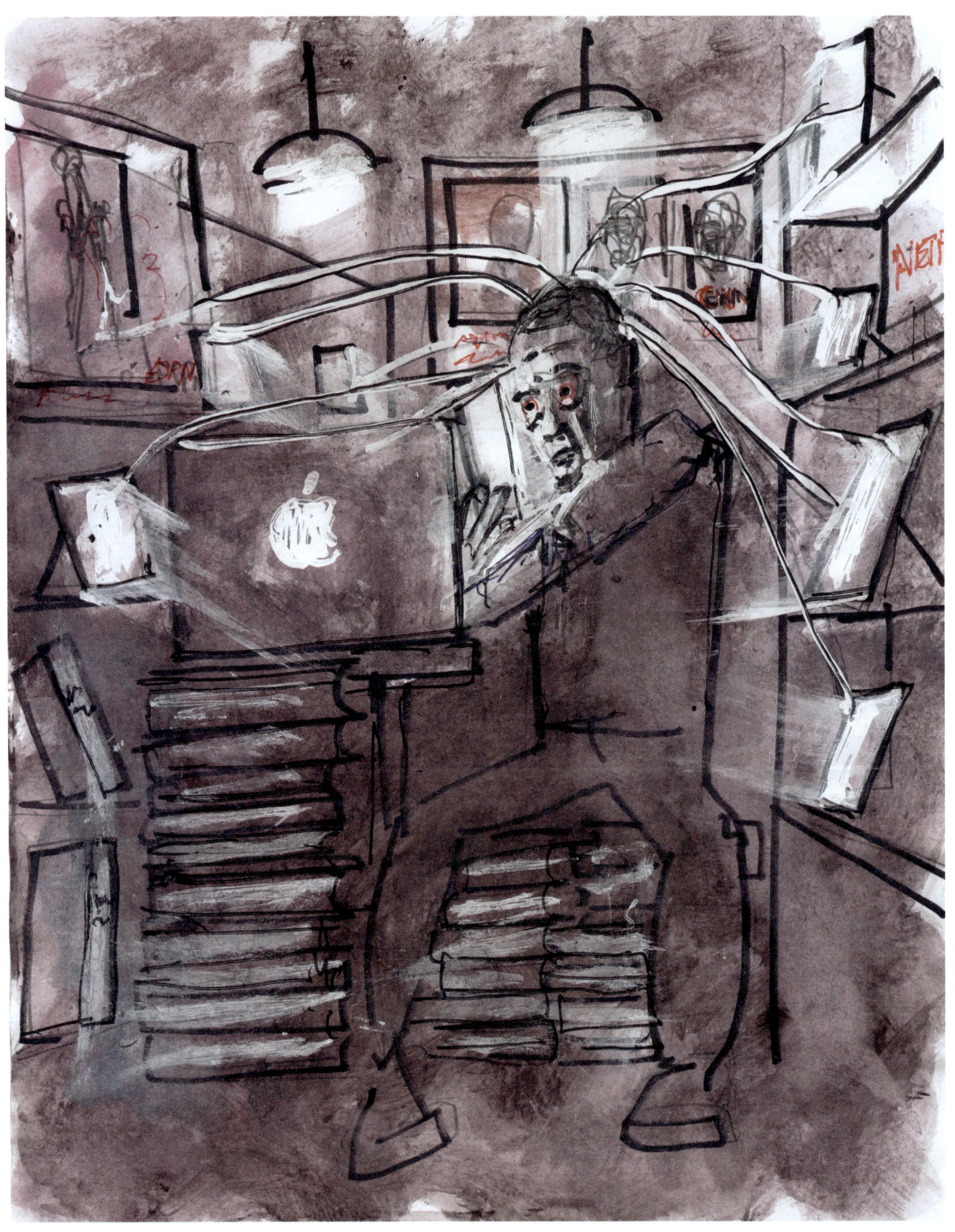

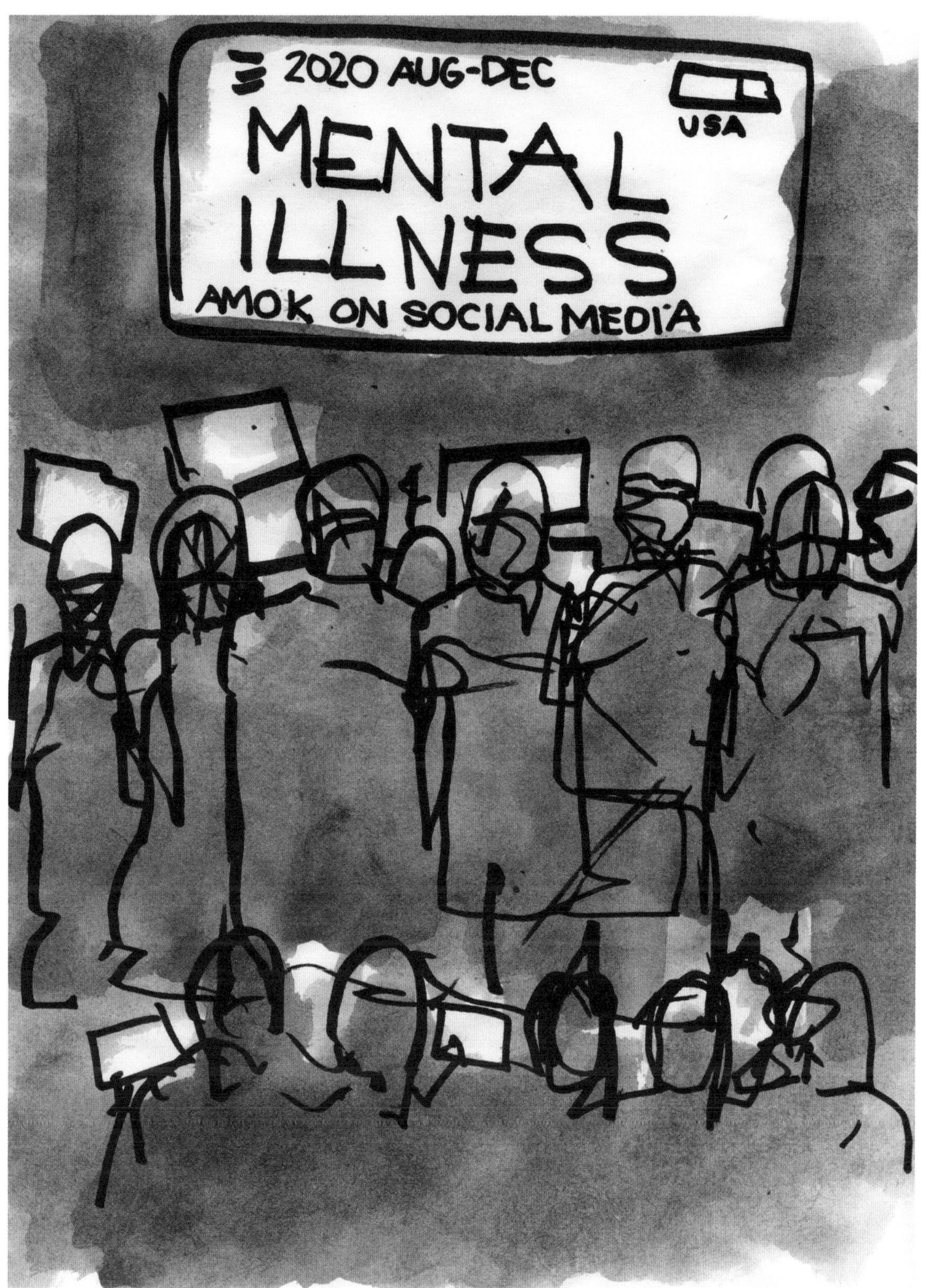

Social media I always say is soc-med. It's when 'the masses' get transformed into 'them asses', sucking their gadget and inhaling digital gases.

If somebody has an opinion they're going to go on to social media in a flash to elaborate on it, whereas a song is on a delay. It could be written within the course of what's going on, but it doesn't come out of the blocks first. With a song you can envelop the moment, you can enhance the moment, but you're just not going to get it out at the top of the moment.

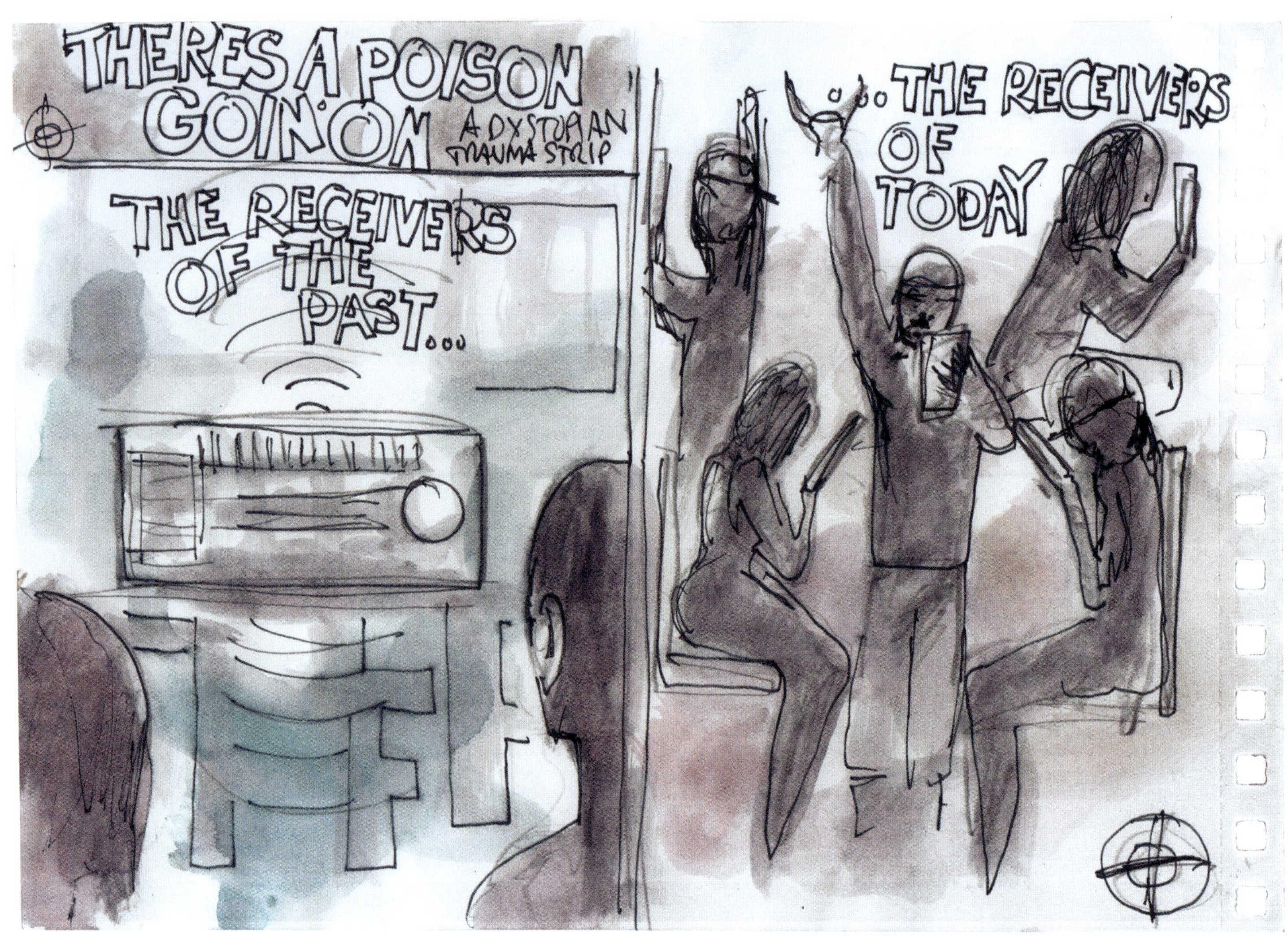

The internet has replaced a lot of the news. You have to pay attention to the major media, and I'm not saying you have to believe it, but it's important to pay attention. They're the number one propaganda feeders of the planet. So, as well as getting information by talking and relating to people at the grassroots level, you gotta get your news from the powers that be, like *the New York Times* and Rupert Murdoch.

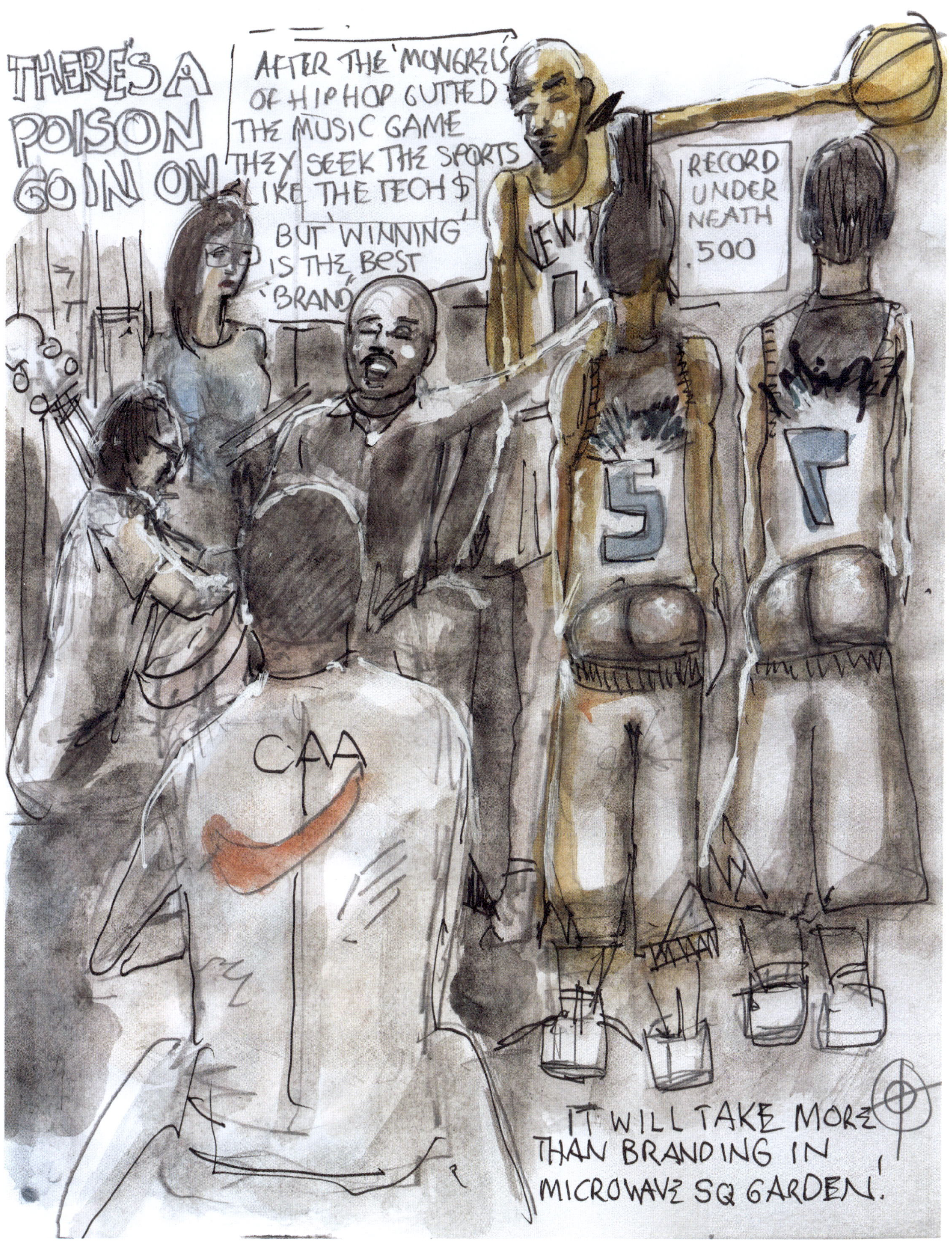
THERE'S A POISON GO IN ON
AFTER THE MONGRELS OF HIP HOP GUTTED THE MUSIC GAME THEY SEEK THE SPORTS LIKE THE TECH $
BUT WINNING IS THE BEST "BRAND"
RECORD UNDER NEATH .500
CAA
IT WILL TAKE MORE THAN BRANDING IN MICROWAVE SQ GARDEN!

THERE'S A POISON GOIN ON!

The record industry doesn't make opportunities for black people in business roles. Look at record companies, management companies, but, more importantly, look at lawyers and accountants. You won't find too many brothers and sisters in those areas. Maybe it's because a lot don't know these positions are there to be taken up. At the same time, the companies aren't showing any willingness to recruit minorities in these areas.

The administration of hip-hop is piss poor. We need more people from the community who love and grew up with the music to be part of the business structure taking care of it.

Rap makes a gigantic profit, which means that the industry wants to milk it for what it's worth. But they don't seem to have any interest in long-term career development for hip-hop acts the way they do with pop or rock acts. I think most companies prefer to have groups that are disposable, so they won't have to get involved with big contracts. They'd like to have 10 young groups this year and then replace them with 10 different young groups the next year so they can pay beginner's royalties.

I try to create avenues by running the SpitSLAM Record Label Group and RapStation, so artists can come and do their thing.

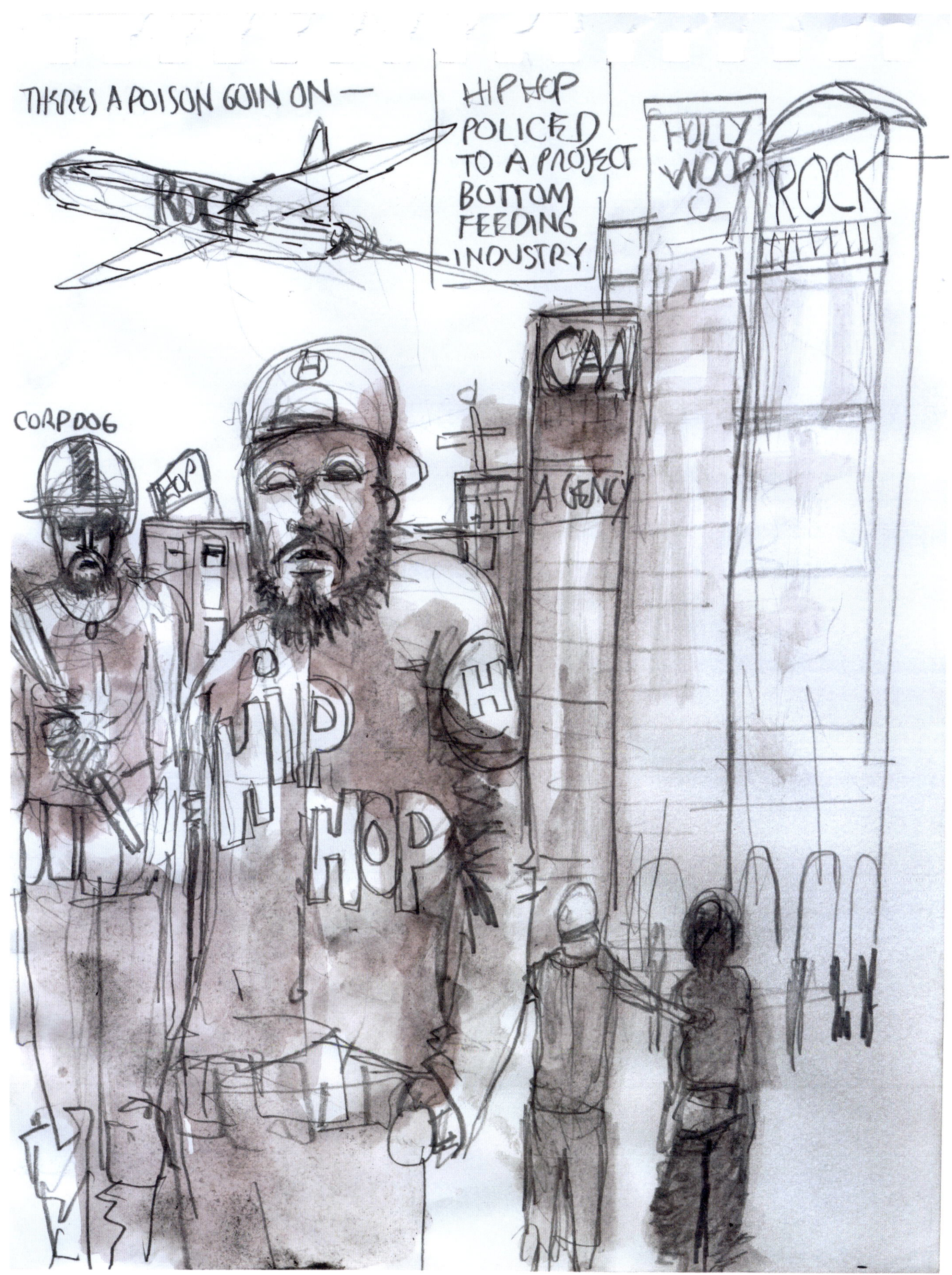
THERES A POISON GOIN ON —
ROCK
HIP HOP
POLICED
TO A PROJECT
BOTTOM
FEEDING
INDUSTRY
HOLLY
WOOD
ROCK
CAA
AGENCY
CORPDOG
HOP
HIP
HOP

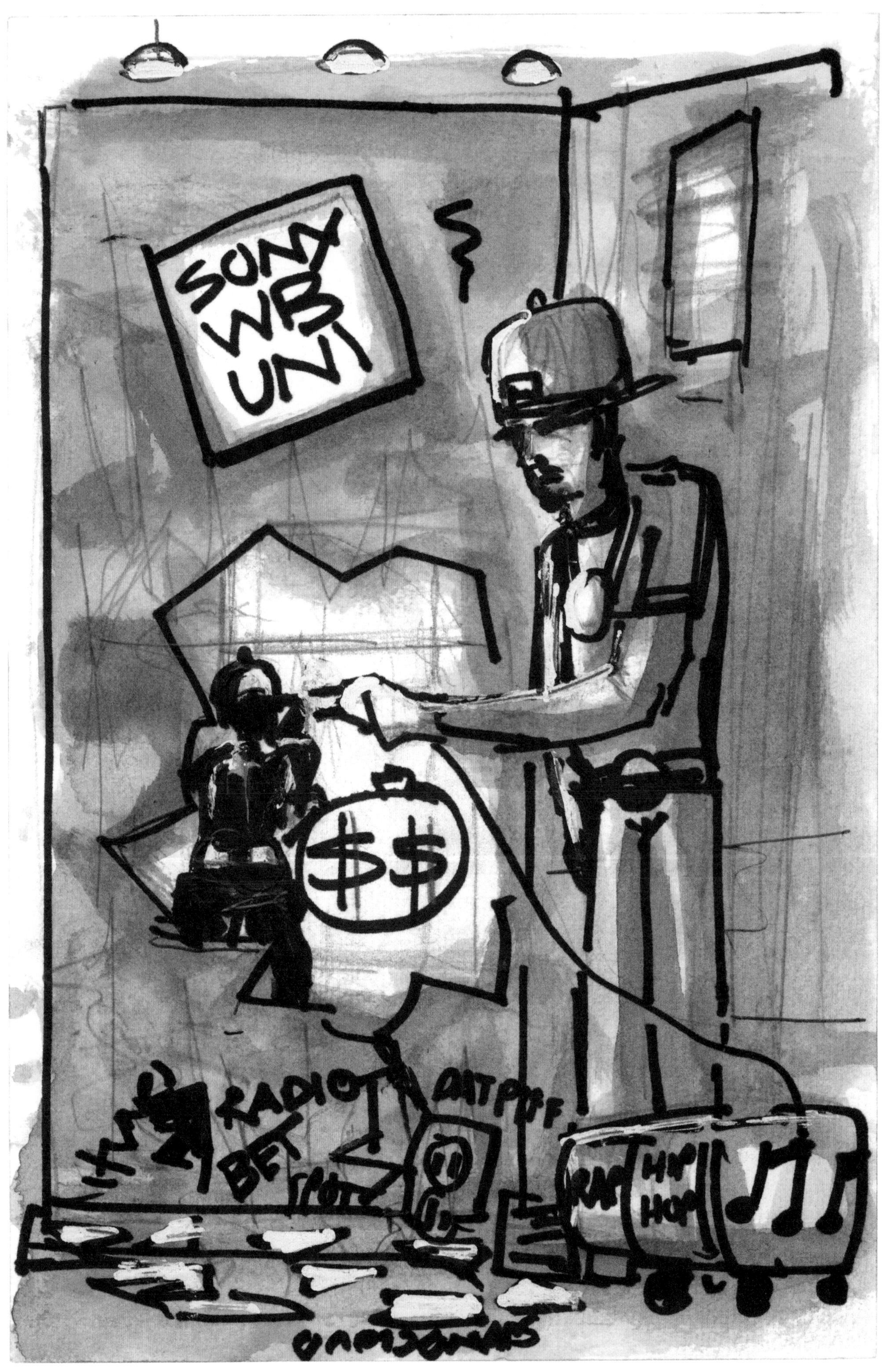
SONY
WB
UNI
$$
RADIO
BET
RAP
HIP HOP

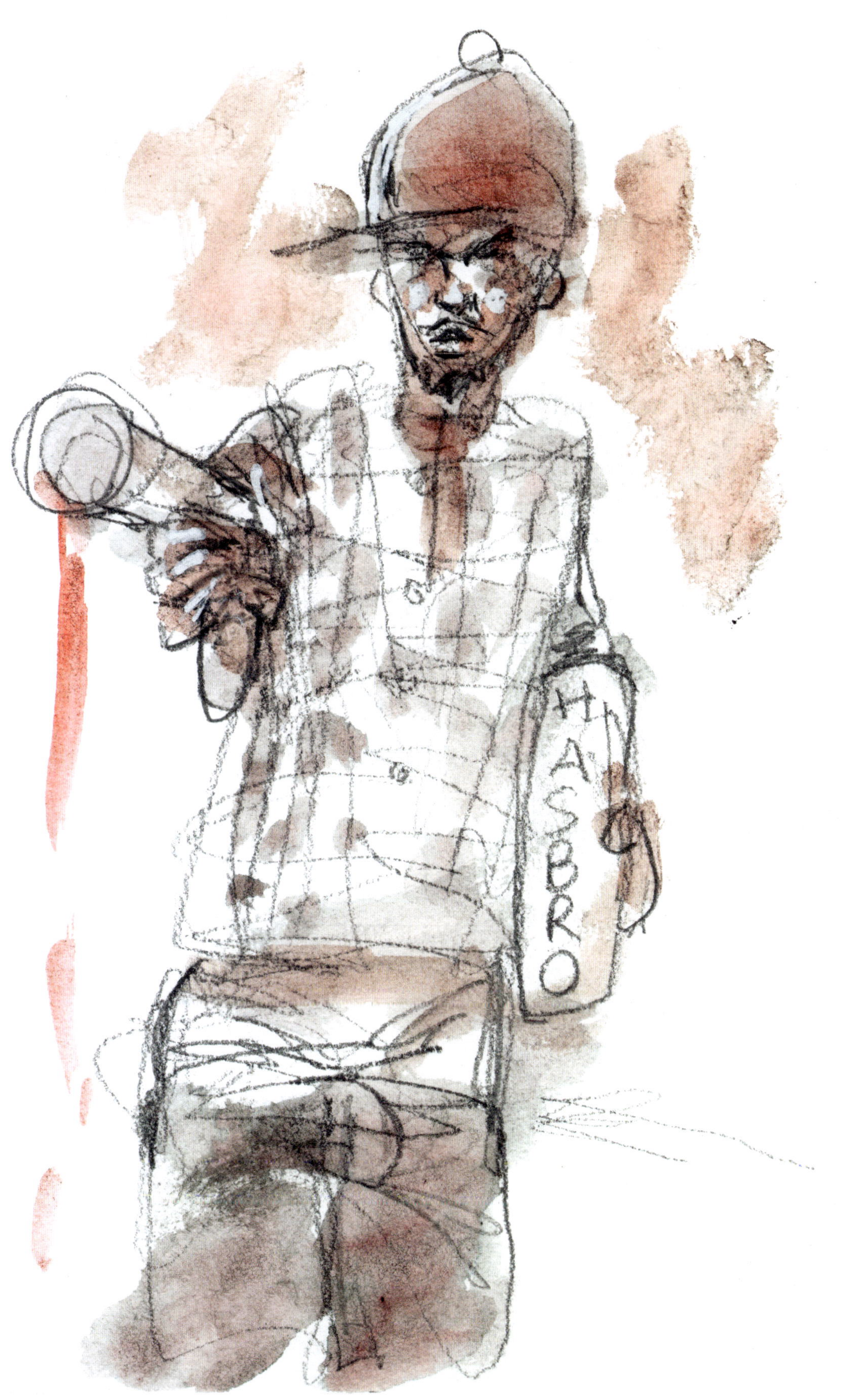

The record business has turned into something else. Since Hasbro bought Death Row Records they've been the ones writing rapper's cheques for beats and songs.

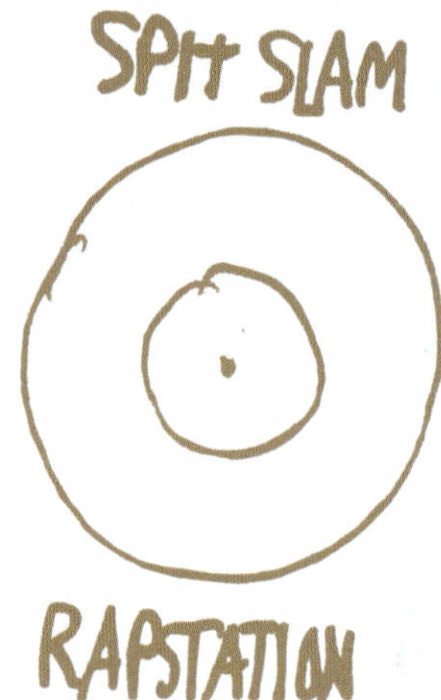

I illustrate for SpitSLAM and its artists. This is super strong Long Island spitter Kris Payne.

There's a young spirit that's really rebelling against the status quo in the record industry. With social media and downloads, artists are realising that they can be their own record labels – that's going to make for some big changes. But I don't think the internet properly curates all the great music that's out there. The artists are there, but the curators are not.

That's what radio can do so well. Radio stations are the best communicators. RapStation, the station I'm involved in, is an innovative network of specialist rap radio channels. For example, there's Planet Earth Planet Rap, which covers the mind-blowing movements occurring in hip-hop and rap music all over the world, not just in the US and the UK.

Then there's Hip-Hop Gods, which only plays artists who have had careers of 15 years or more, and She Movement, which is all women. There are more women doing hip-hop than ever before. In the Nineties, the heads of the hip-hop record companies hated women. It was the same with rappers that were gay. My argument was, and always will be, that hip-hop is about being who you are and not trying to be somebody else. Trying to silence those autonomous voices is not hip-hop.

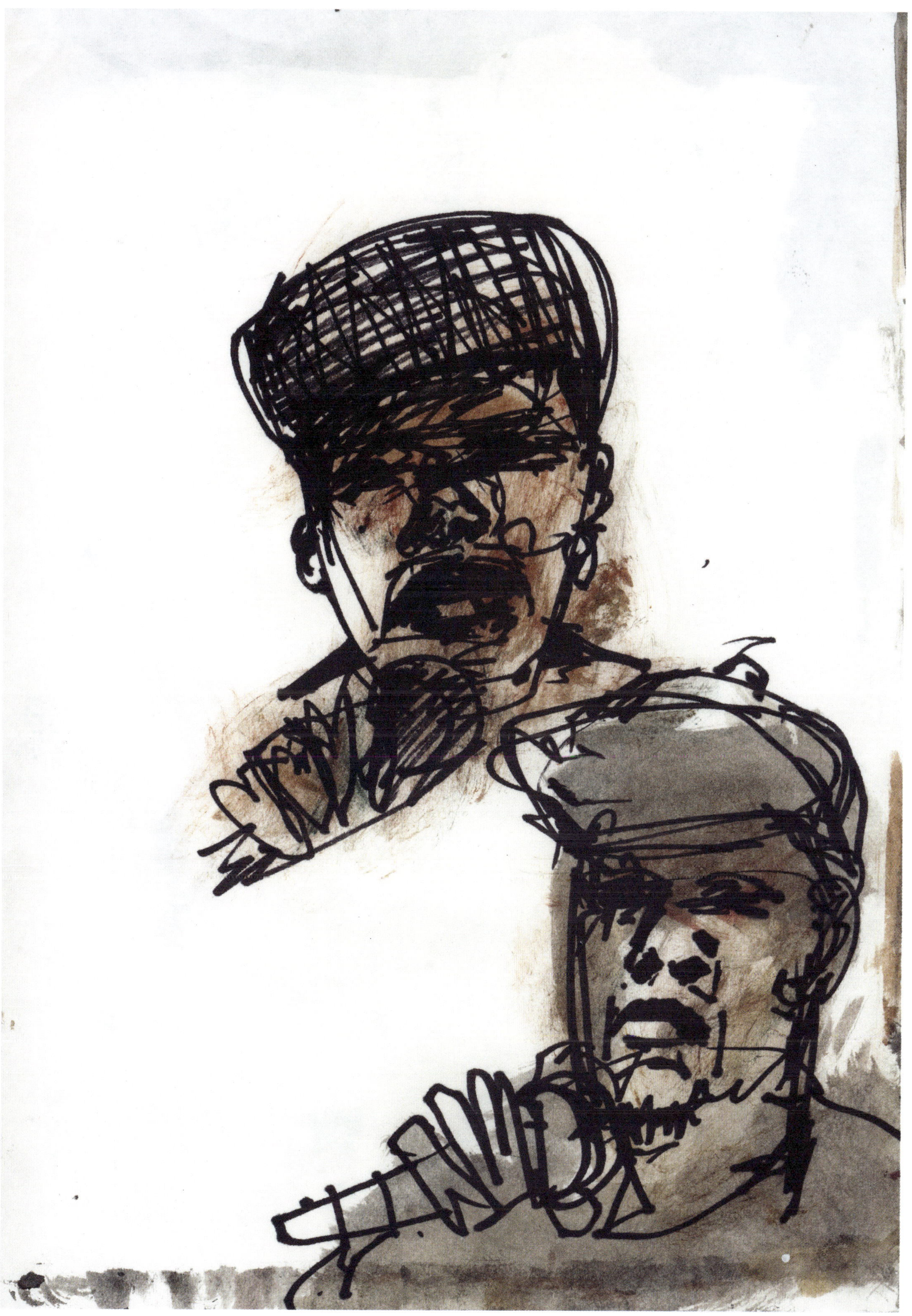

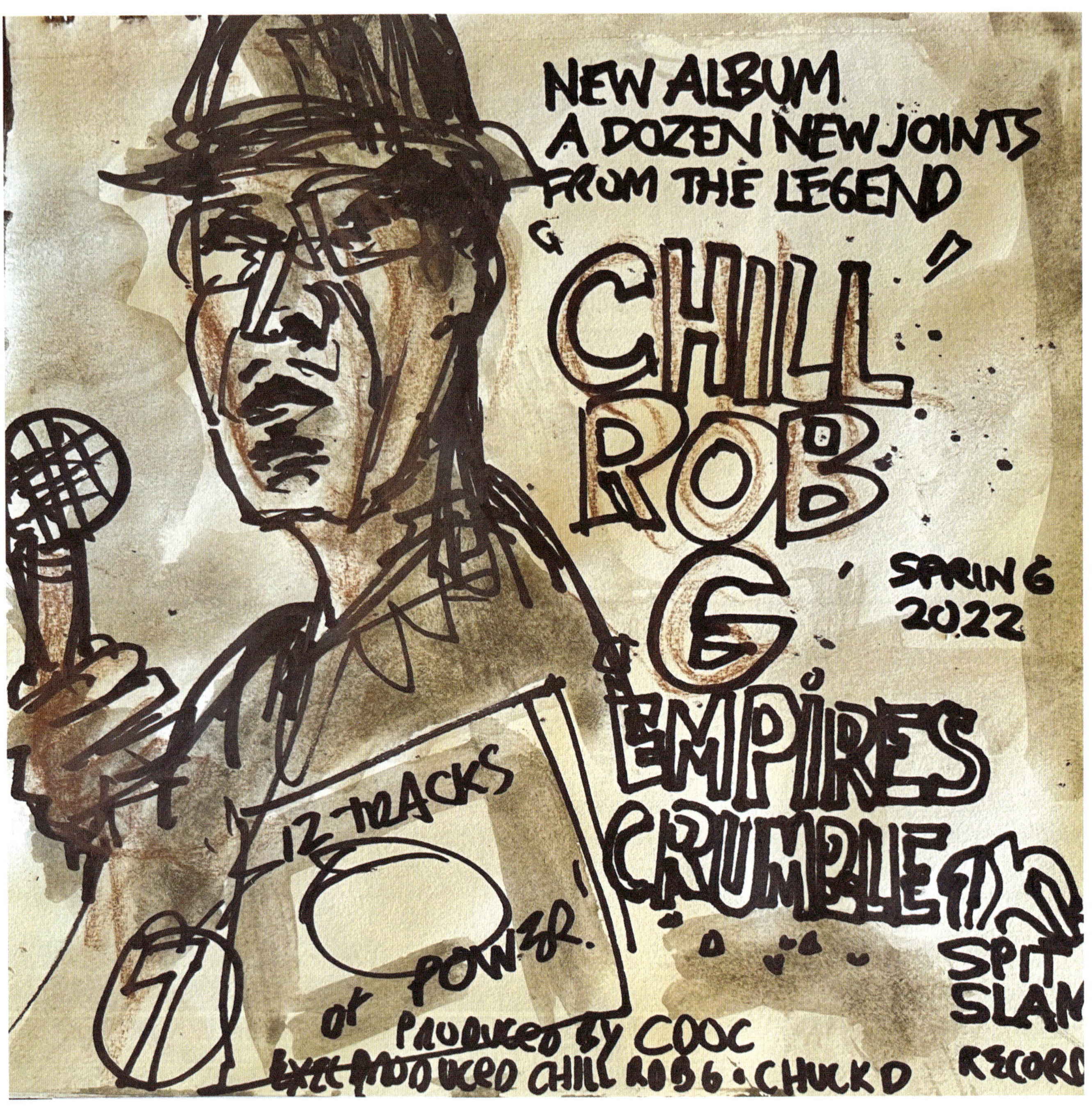

SpitSLAM has a group of artists that are interested in putting their own points of view out into the world.

We try to get their voices and music heard, so that's my calling. I have no purpose if I can't provide a service to somebody who wants to excel in the arts. This is loose-line work for Canadian artists Anime Oscen and Hive (opposite, left), who brought out an EP called *North Country* on SpitSLAM.

Pops Smash (opposite, right) is another SpitSLAM artist. He claims to be the first 60-year-old rapper. He brags about his age as an advantage. He's happily stuck in 1979. He keeps the party on and on to the break of dawn. This is his art of attraction.

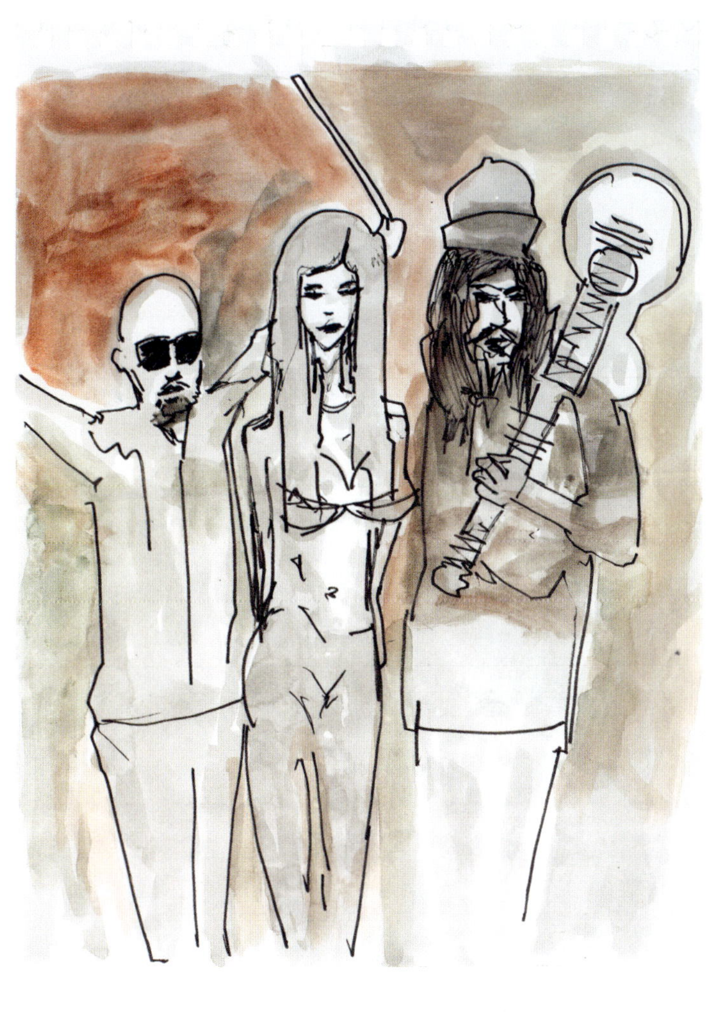

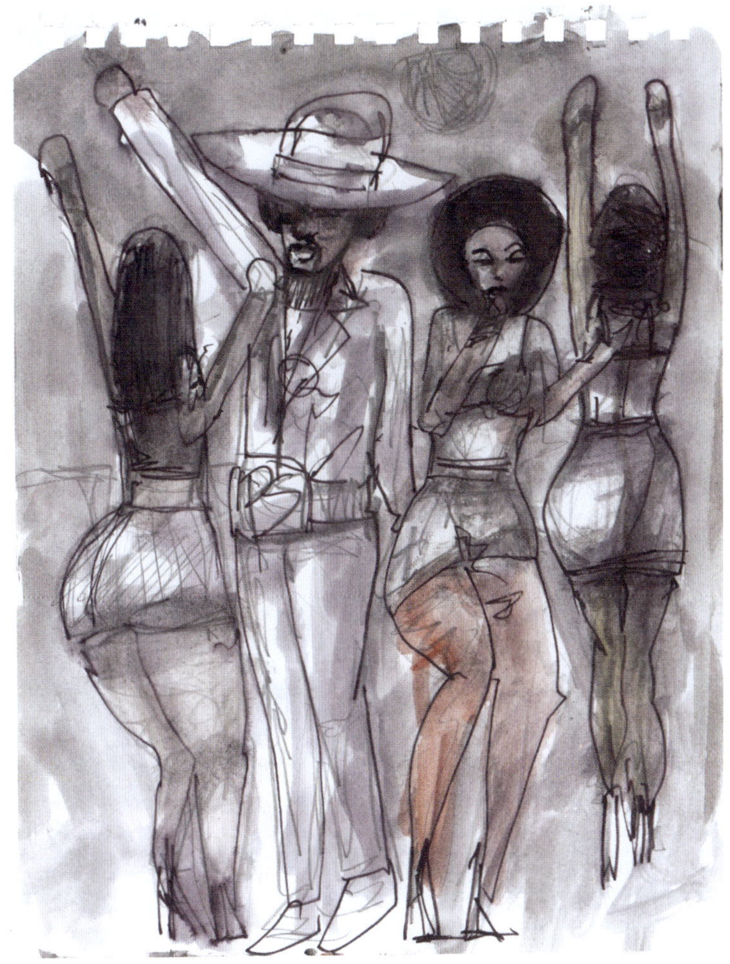

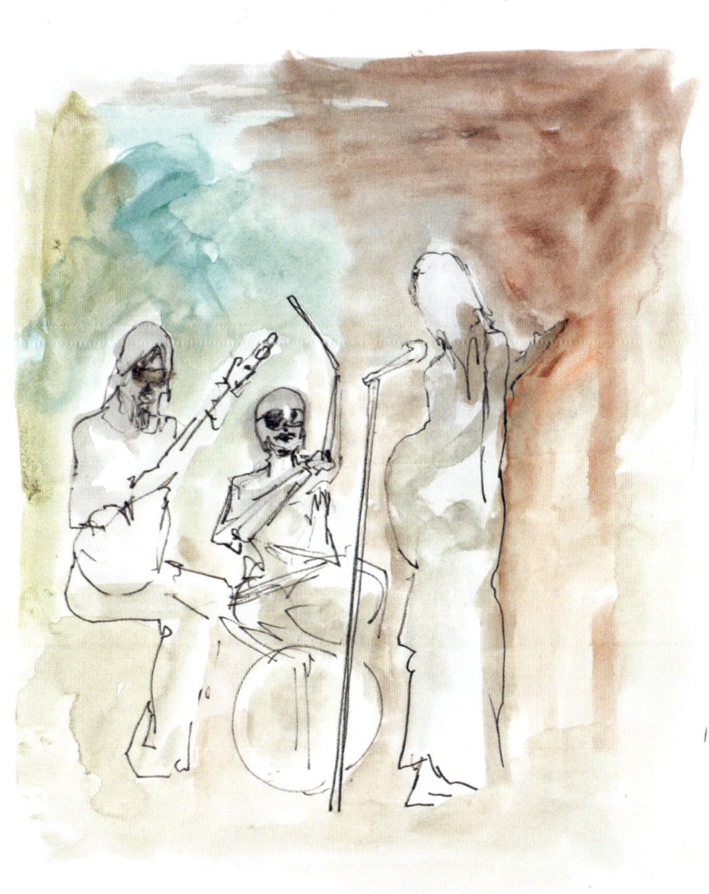

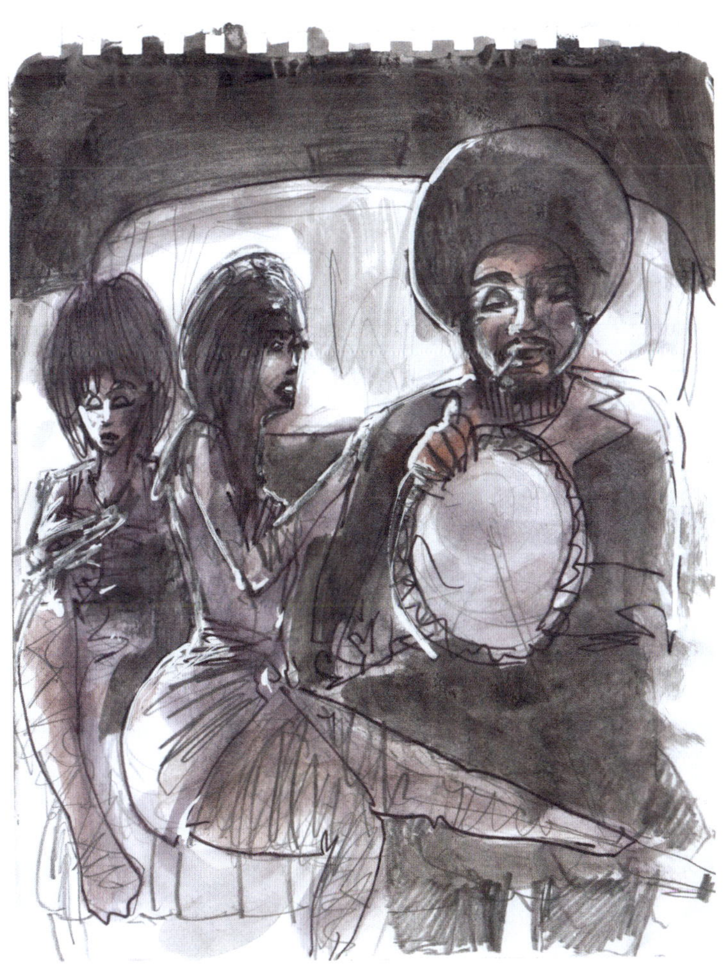

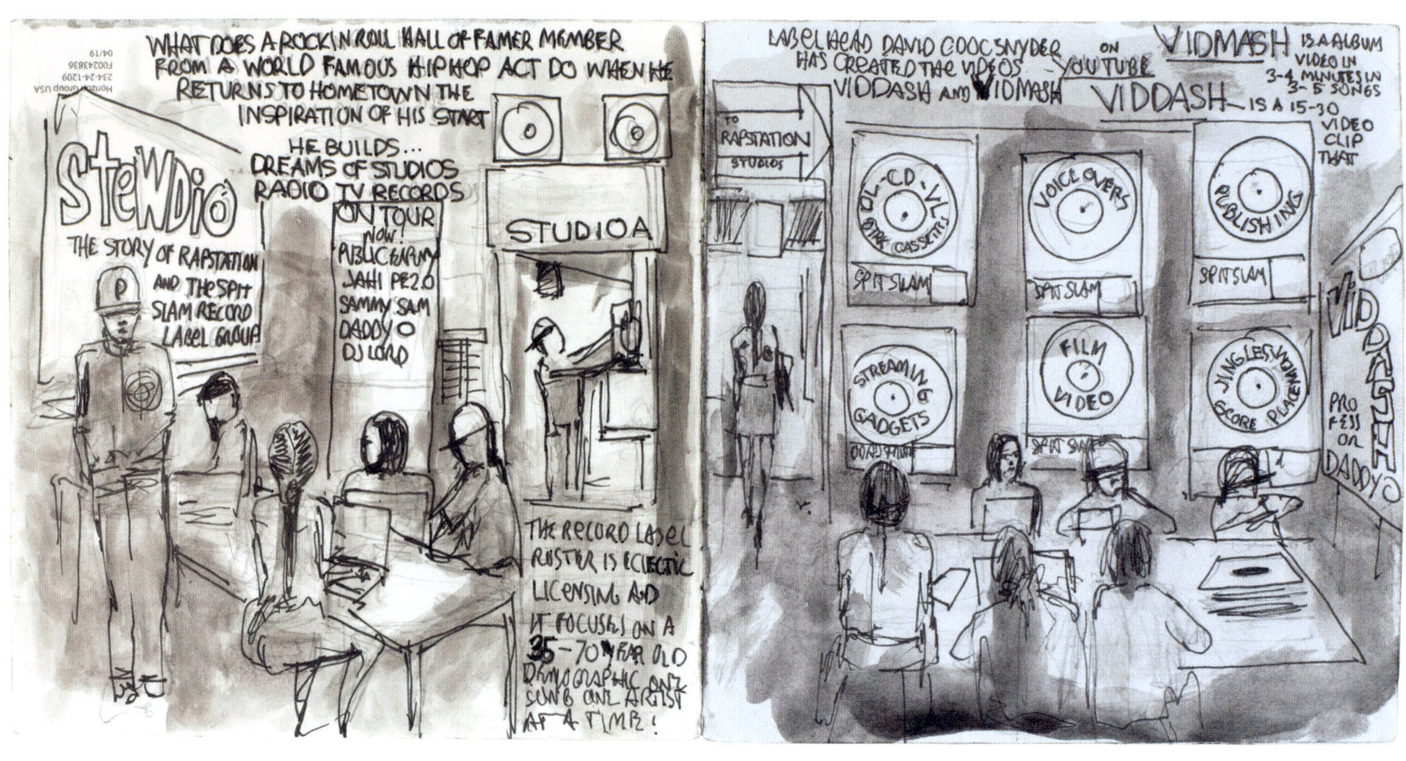
WHAT DOES A ROCK IN ROLL HALL OF FAMER MEMBER FROM A WORLD FAMOUS HIPHOP ACT DO WHEN HE RETURNS TO HOMETOWN THE INSPIRATION OF HIS START
HE BUILDS... DREAMS OF STUDIOS RADIO TV RECORDS
STEWDIO
THE STORY OF RAPSTATION AND THE SPIT SLAM RECORD LABEL GROUP
ON TOUR NOW! PUBLIC ENEMY JAHI PE2.0 SAMMY SAM DADDY O DJ LORD
STUDIO A
THE RECORD LABEL ROSTER IS ECLECTIC LICENSING AND IT FOCUSES ON A 35-70 YEAR OLD DEMOGRAPHIC
HAS CREATED THE VIDEOS ON YOUTUBE VIDDASH AND VIDMASH
VIDMASH IS A ALBUM VIDEO IN 3-4 MINUTES IN 3-5 SONGS
VIDDASH IS A 15-30 VIDEO CLIP THAT
TO RAPSTATION STUDIOS
VOICE OVERS
PUBLISHING
SPIT SLAM
STREAMING GADGETS
FILM VIDEO
VIDDASH
PRO FESS OR DADDY O

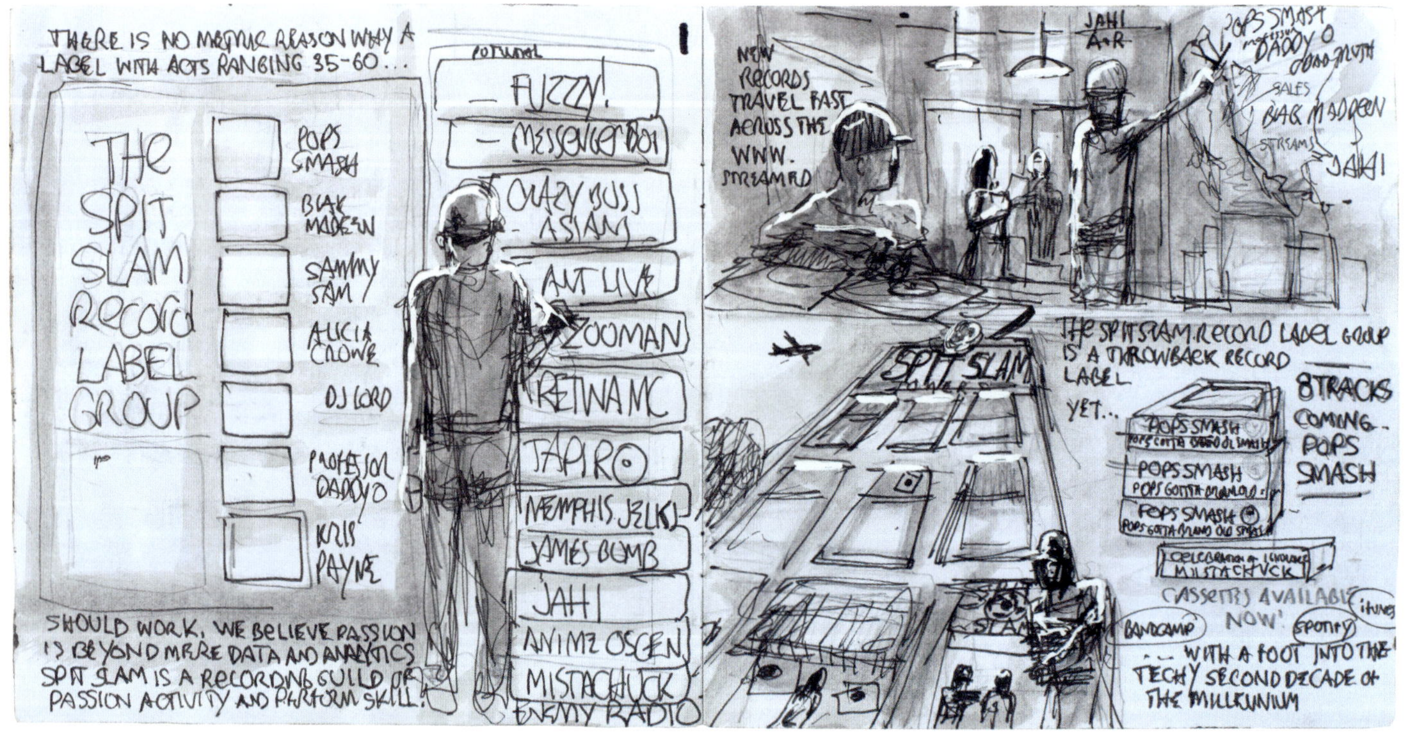
THERE IS NO MATURE REASON WHY A LABEL WITH ACTS RANGING 35-60...
THE SPIT SLAM RECORD LABEL GROUP
POPS SMASH
BLAK MADEEN
SAMMY SAM
ALICIA CLOWE
DJ LORD
PROFESSOR DADDY O
KRIS PAYNE
FUZZY!
ANT LIVE
ZOOMAN
RETINA MC
TAPIRO
MEMPHIS JELKS
JAMES BOMB
JAHI
MISTACHUCK
ENEMY RADIO
SHOULD WORK. WE BELIEVE PASSION IS BEYOND MERE DATA AND ANALYTICS SPIT SLAM IS A RECORDING GUILD OF PASSION ACTIVITY AND PERFORM SKILL!
NEW RECORDS TRAVEL FAST ACROSS THE WWW. STREAMED
JAHI A+R
POPS SMASH
SALES
BLAK MADEEN
STREAMS
JAHI
SPIT SLAM
THE SPIT SLAM RECORD LABEL GROUP IS A THROWBACK RECORD LABEL YET...
8TRACKS COMING POPS SMASH
POPS SMASH
MISTACHUCK
CASSETTES AVAILABLE NOW!
BANDCAMP
SPOTIFY
ITUNES
... WITH A FOOT INTO THE TECHY SECOND DECADE OF THE MILLENNIUM

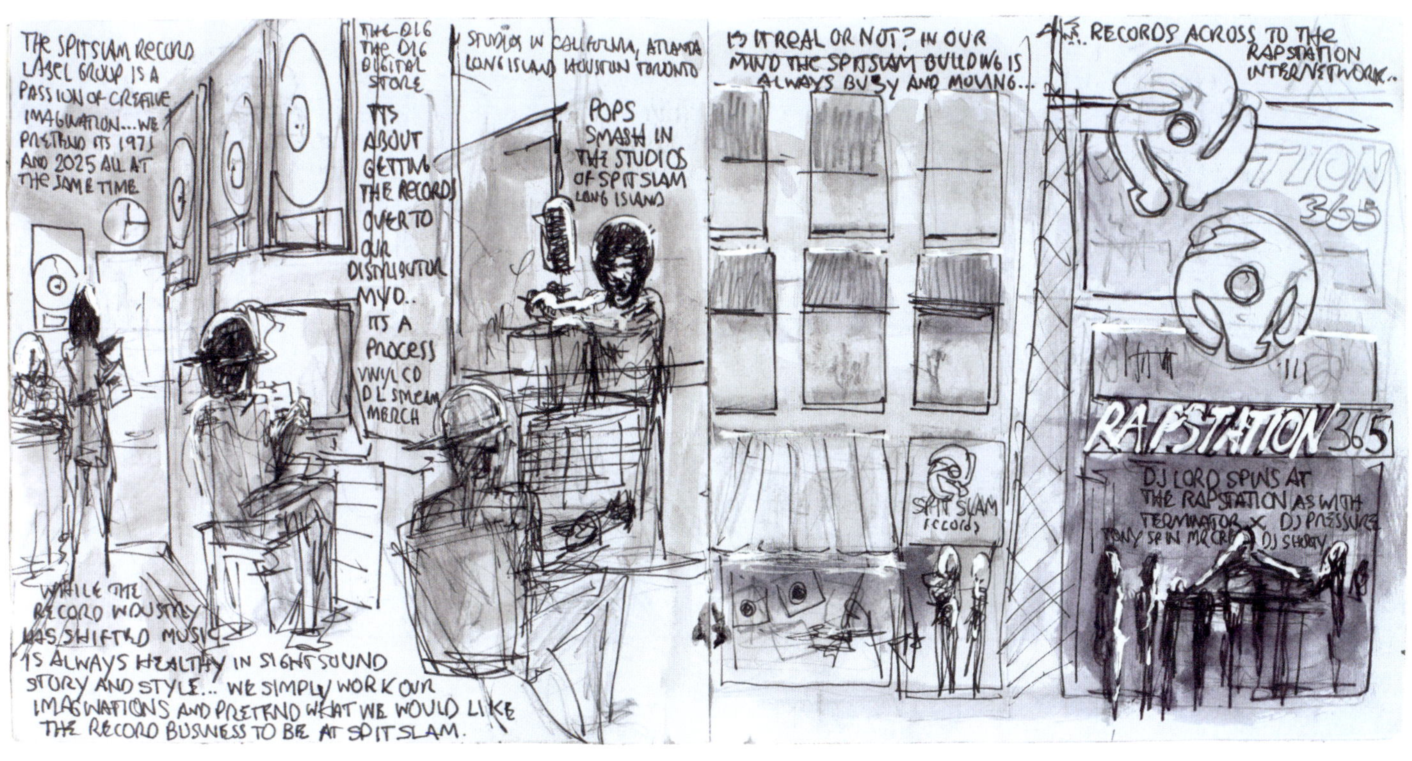
THE SPITSLAM RECORD LABEL GROUP IS A PASSION OF CREATIVE IMAGINATION... WE PRETEND ITS 1973 AND 2025 ALL AT THE SAME TIME
THE DIG DIGITAL STORE
ITS ABOUT GETTING THE RECORDS OVER TO OUR DISTRIBUTOR MVD.. ITS A PROCESS VINYL CD DL STREAM MERCH
STUDIOS IN CALIFORNIA, ATLANTA LONG ISLAND HOUSTON TORONTO
POPS SMASH IN THE STUDIOS OF SPITSLAM LONG ISLAND
WHILE THE RECORD INDUSTRY HAS SHIFTED MUSIC IS ALWAYS HEALTHY IN SIGHT SOUND STORY AND STYLE... WE SIMPLY WORK OUR IMAGINATIONS AND PRETEND WHAT WE WOULD LIKE THE RECORD BUSINESS TO BE AT SPITSLAM.
IS IT REAL OR NOT? IN OUR MIND THE SPITSLAM BUILDING IS ALWAYS BUSY AND MOVING...
SPITSLAM records
... RECORDS ACROSS TO THE RAPSTATION INTERNETWORK..
TION 365
RAPSTATION 365
DJ LORD SPINS AT THE RAPSTATION AS WITH TERMINATOR X, DJ PRESSURE TONY SPIN MR CR DJ SHORTY

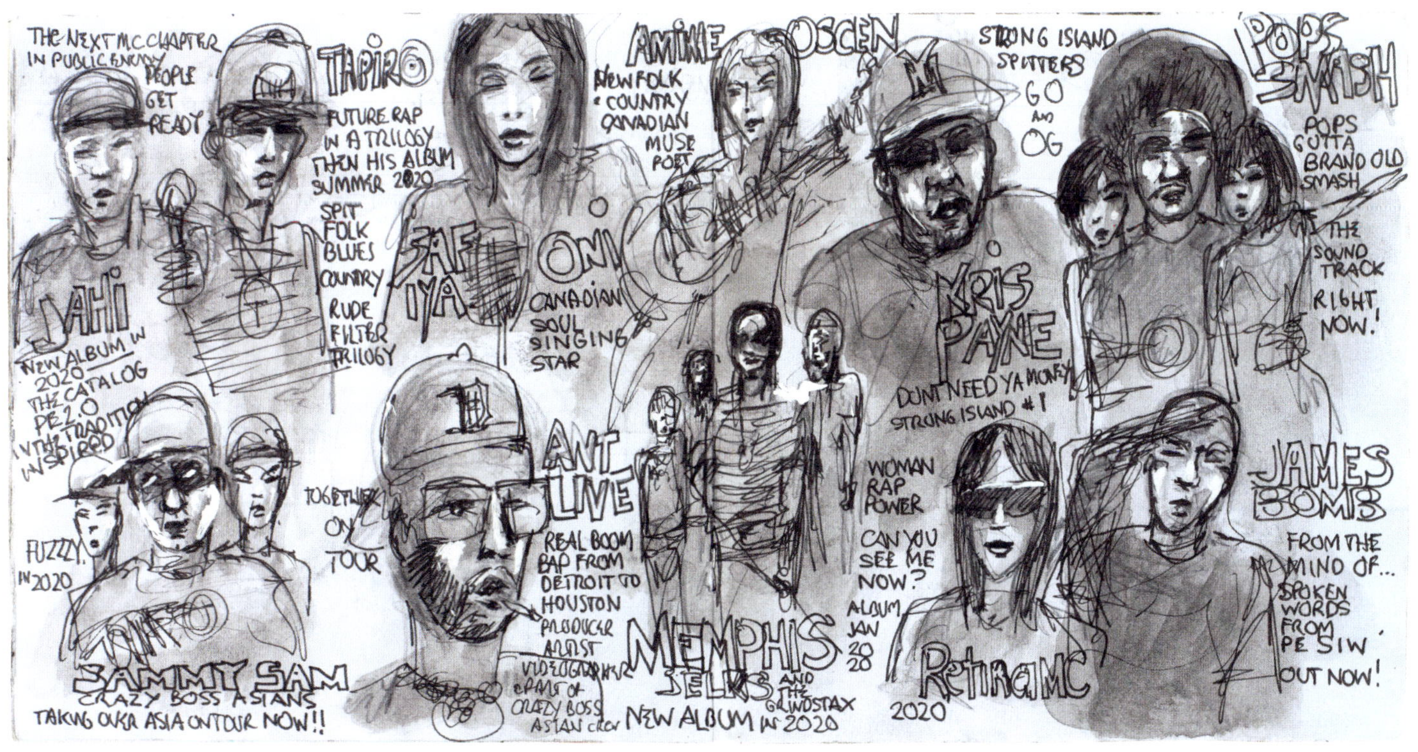
THE NEXT MC CHAPTER IN PUBLIC ENEMY PEOPLE GET READY
JAHI
NEW ALBUM IN 2020 THE CATALOG PE 2.0 IN THE TRADITION INSPIRED
TAPIRO
FUTURE RAP IN A TRILOGY THEN HIS ALBUM SUMMER 2020
SPIT FOLK BLUES COUNTRY RUDE FILTER TRILOGY
SAFIYA
ONI
CANADIAN SOUL SINGING STAR
AMIKE
NEW FOLK & COUNTRY CANADIAN MUSE POET
OSCEN
STRONG ISLAND SPITTERS GO AN OG
KRIS PAYNE
DONT NEED YA MONEY STRONG ISLAND #1
POPS SMASH
POPS GOTTA BRAND OLD SMASH
THE SOUND TRACK RIGHT NOW!
FUZZZY. IN 2020
SAMMY SAM
CRAZY BOSS ASIANS
TAKING OVER ASIA ON TOUR NOW!!
TOGETHER ON TOUR
ANT LIVE
REAL BOOM BAP FROM DETROIT TO HOUSTON PRODUCER ARTIST VIDEOGRAPHER
MEMPHIS SELKS AND THE GRINDSTAX
NEW ALBUM IN 2020
WOMAN RAP POWER
CAN YOU SEE ME NOW?
ALBUM JAN 2020
RetnaMC
2020
JAMES BOMB
FROM THE MIND OF... SPOKEN WORDS FROM PE SIW
OUT NOW!

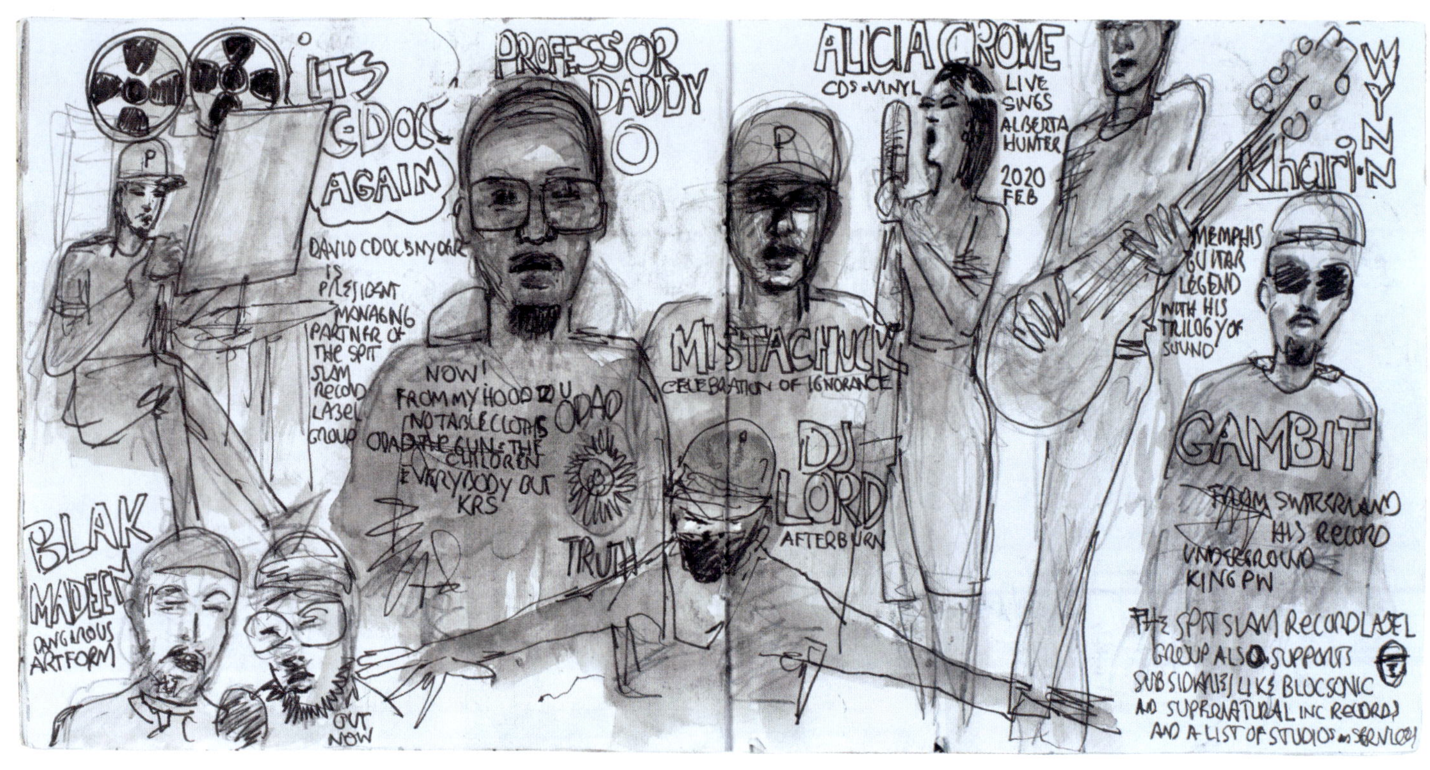
ITS C-DOC AGAIN
PROFESSOR DADDY O
ALICIA CROWE
CDs + VINYL
LIVE SINGS ALBERTA HUNTER
2020 FEB
WYNN
Khari
MEMPHIS GUITAR LEGEND WITH HIS TRILOGY OF SOUND
MISTACHUCK
CELEBRATION OF IGNORANCE
DJ LORD
AFTERBURN
GAMBIT
UNDERGROUND KINGPIN
BLAK MADEEN
DANGEROUS ARTFORM
OUT NOW
KRS
TRUTH
THE SPIT SLAM RECORD LABEL GROUP ALSO SUPPORTS SUBSIDIARIES LIKE BLOCSONIC AND SUPERNATURAL INC RECORDS AND A LIST OF STUDIOS AND SERVICES

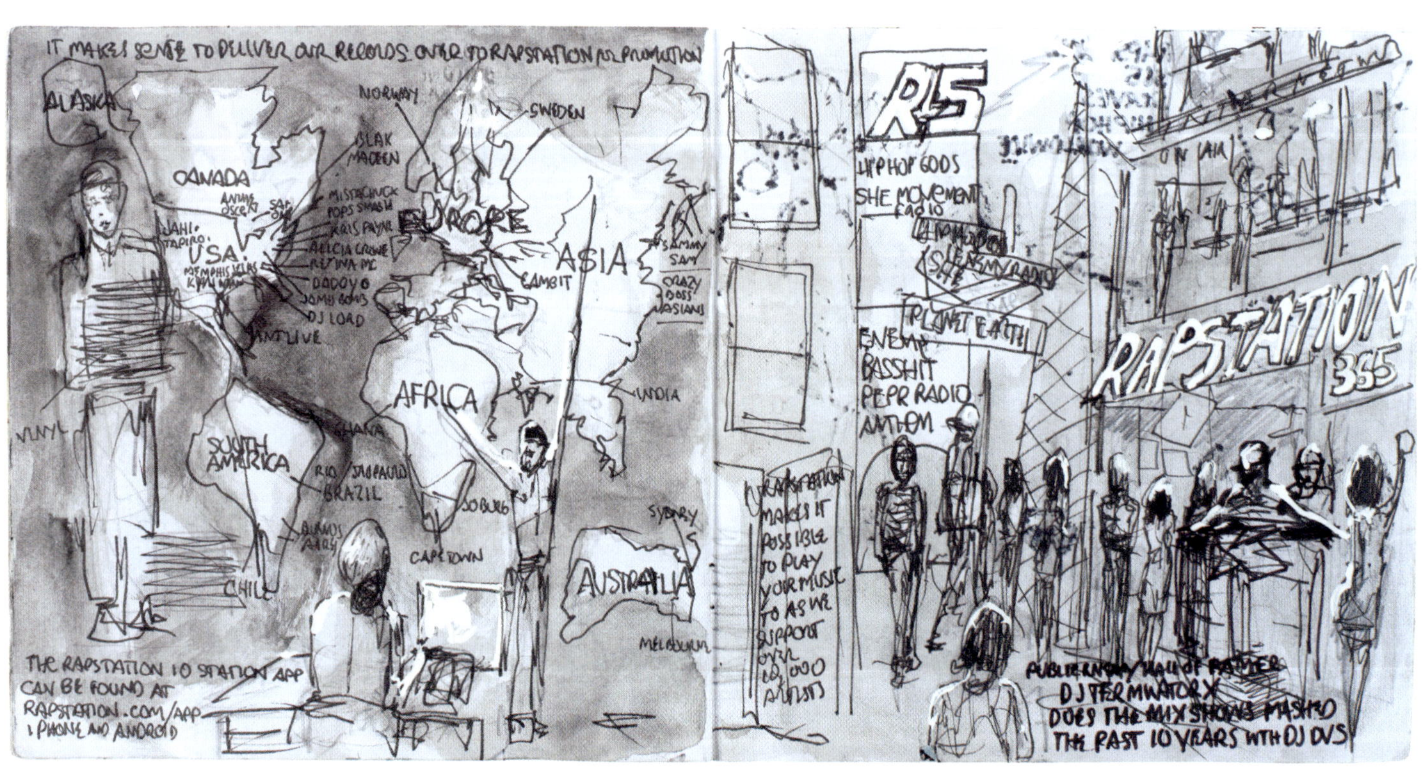
IT MAKES SENSE TO DELIVER OUR RECORDS OVER TO RAPSTATION FOR PROMOTION
ALASKA
CANADA
NORWAY
SWEDEN
BLAK MADEEN
EUROPE
ASIA
USA
MISTACHUCK
ALICIA CROWE
DADDY O
DJ LORD
GAMBIT
AFRICA
INDIA
SOUTH AMERICA
BRAZIL
CAPETOWN
SYDNEY
AUSTRALIA
MELBOURNE
VINYL
THE RAPSTATION 10 STATION APP CAN BE FOUND AT RAPSTATION.COM/APP IPHONE AND ANDROID
R5
HIP HOP GODS
SHE MOVEMENT RADIO
PLANET EARTH
BASSHIT
PEPR RADIO
ANTHEM
RAPSTATION 365
DJ TERMINATOR X
THE PAST 10 YEARS WITH DJ DVS

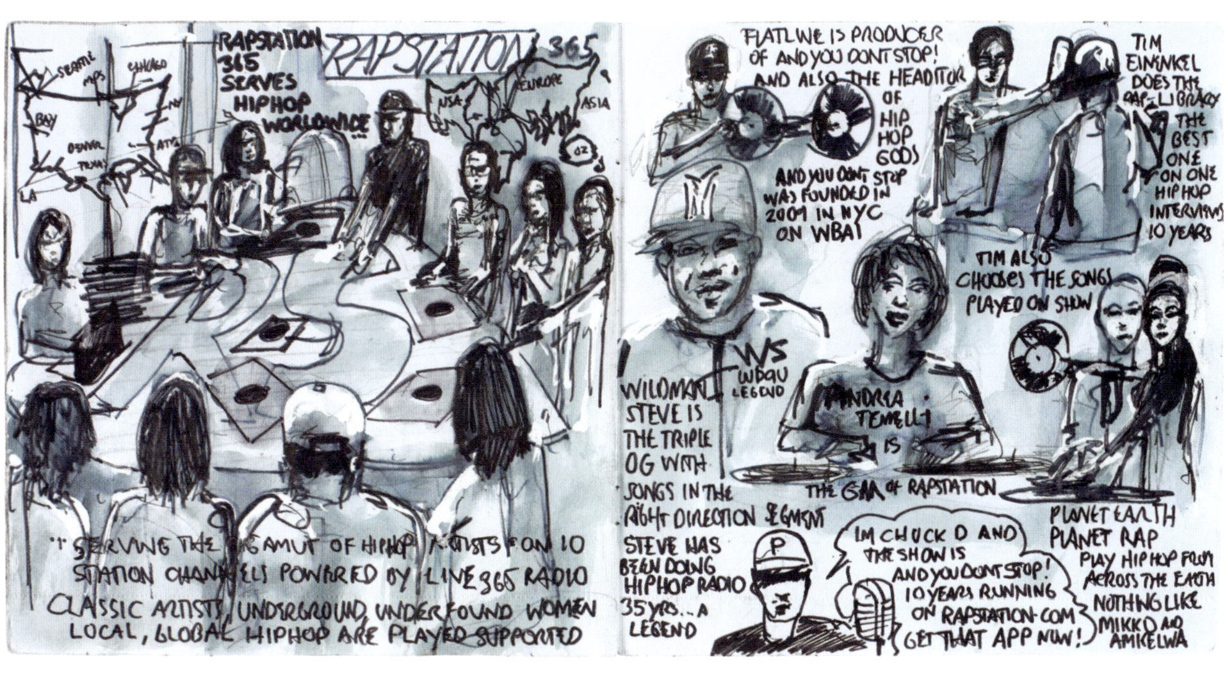

RAPSTATION 365 SERVES HIPHOP WORLDWIDE
RAPSTATION 365
SEATTLE
CHICAGO
BAY
NY
DENVER
ATL
TEXAS
LA
USA
EUROPE
ASIA
OZ
"I SERVING THE GAMUT OF HIPHOP ARTISTS ON 10 STATION CHANNELS POWERED BY LIVE 365 RADIO
CLASSIC ARTISTS, UNDERGROUND, UNDERFOUND WOMEN LOCAL, GLOBAL HIPHOP ARE PLAYED SUPPORTED
FLATLINE IS PRODUCER OF AND YOU DONT STOP! AND ALSO THE HEADITOR OF HIP HOP GODS
AND YOU DONT STOP WAS FOUNDED IN 2009 IN NYC ON WBAI
TIM EINENKEL DOES THE RAP-LIBRARY THE BEST ONE ON ONE HIPHOP INTERVIEWS 10 YEARS
TIM ALSO CHOOSES THE SONGS PLAYED ON SHOW
WS WBAU LEGEND
WILDMAN STEVE IS THE TRIPLE OG WITH SONGS IN THE RIGHT DIRECTION SEGMENT
ANDREA TEMELLI IS THE GM OF RAPSTATION
STEVE HAS BEEN DOING HIPHOP RADIO 35 YRS... A LEGEND
IM CHUCK D AND THE SHOW IS AND YOU DONT STOP! 10 YEARS RUNNING ON RAPSTATION.COM GET THAT APP NOW!
PLANET EARTH PLANET RAP
PLAY HIPHOP FROM ACROSS THE EARTH NOTHING LIKE MIKKO AND AMIKELWA

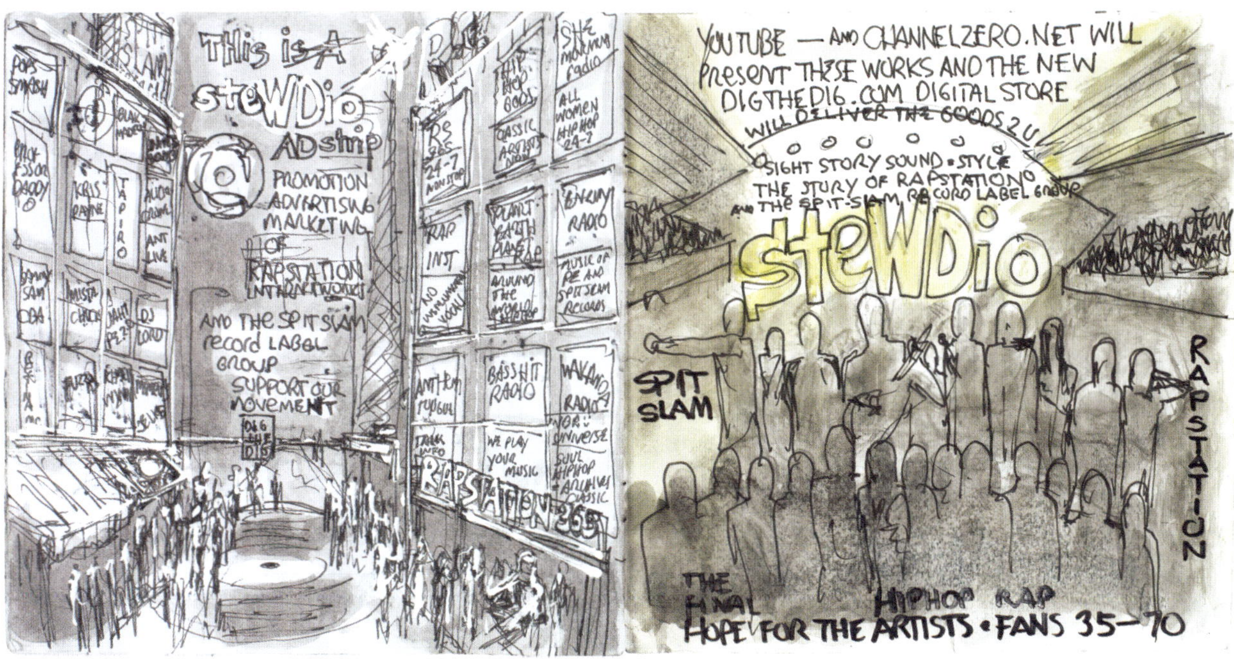

THIS IS A stewDio ADstrip
PROMOTION ADVERTISING MARKETING OF RAPSTATION INTERNETWORKS
AND THE SPIT SLAM record label group support our movement
SHE MORNING radio
HIP HOP GODS
CLASSIC ARTISTS
ALL WOMEN HIPHOP 24-7
PLANET EARTH PLANET RAP
RAP INST
BASSHIT RADIO
WAKANDA RADIO
WE PLAY YOUR MUSIC
RAPSTATION 365
YOUTUBE — AND CHANNELZERO.NET WILL PRESENT THESE WORKS AND THE NEW DIGTHEDIG.COM DIGITAL STORE WILL DELIVER THE GOODS 2 U
SIGHT STORY SOUND • STYLE THE STORY OF RAPSTATION AND THE SPIT-SLAM RECORD LABEL GROUP
stewDio
SPIT SLAM
RAPSTATION
THE FINAL HIPHOP RAP HOPE FOR THE ARTISTS • FANS 35–70

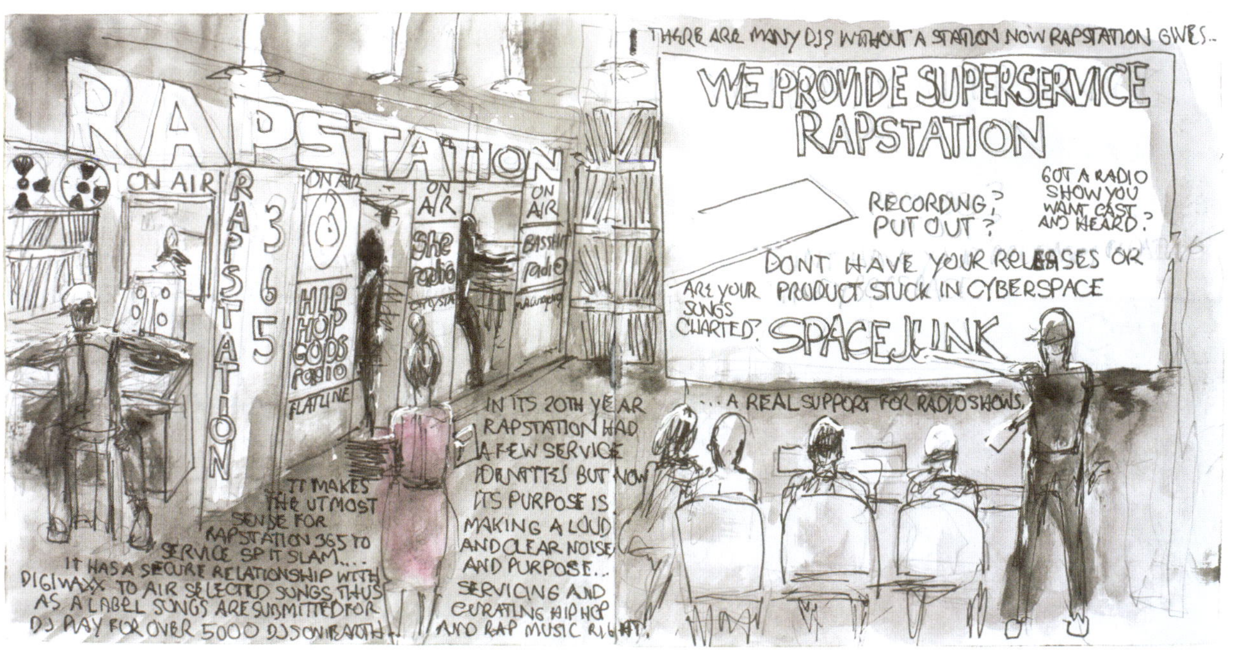

RAPSTATION
ON AIR
RAPSTATION
365
ON AIR
HIP HOP GODS RADIO
FLATLINE
ON AIR
she radio
ON AIR
BASSHIT radio
IT MAKES THE UTMOST SENSE FOR RAPSTATION 365 TO SERVICE SPIT SLAM...
IT HAS A SECURE RELATIONSHIP WITH DIGIWAXX TO AIR SELECTED SONGS THUS AS A LABEL SONGS ARE SUBMITTED FOR DJ PLAY FOR OVER 5000 DJS ON EARTH...
IN ITS 20TH YEAR RAPSTATION HAD A FEW SERVICE FORMATTES BUT NOW ITS PURPOSE IS MAKING A LOUD AND CLEAR NOISE AND PURPOSE... SERVICING AND CURATING HIPHOP AND RAP MUSIC RIGHT.
THERE ARE MANY DJS WITHOUT A STATION NOW RAPSTATION GIVES...
WE PROVIDE SUPERSERVICE RAPSTATION
RECORDING? PUT OUT?
GOT A RADIO SHOW YOU WANT CAST AND HEARD?
DONT HAVE YOUR RELEASES OR PRODUCT STUCK IN CYBERSPACE
ARE YOUR SONGS CHARTED?
SPACEJUNK
...A REAL SUPPORT FOR RADIO SHOWS.

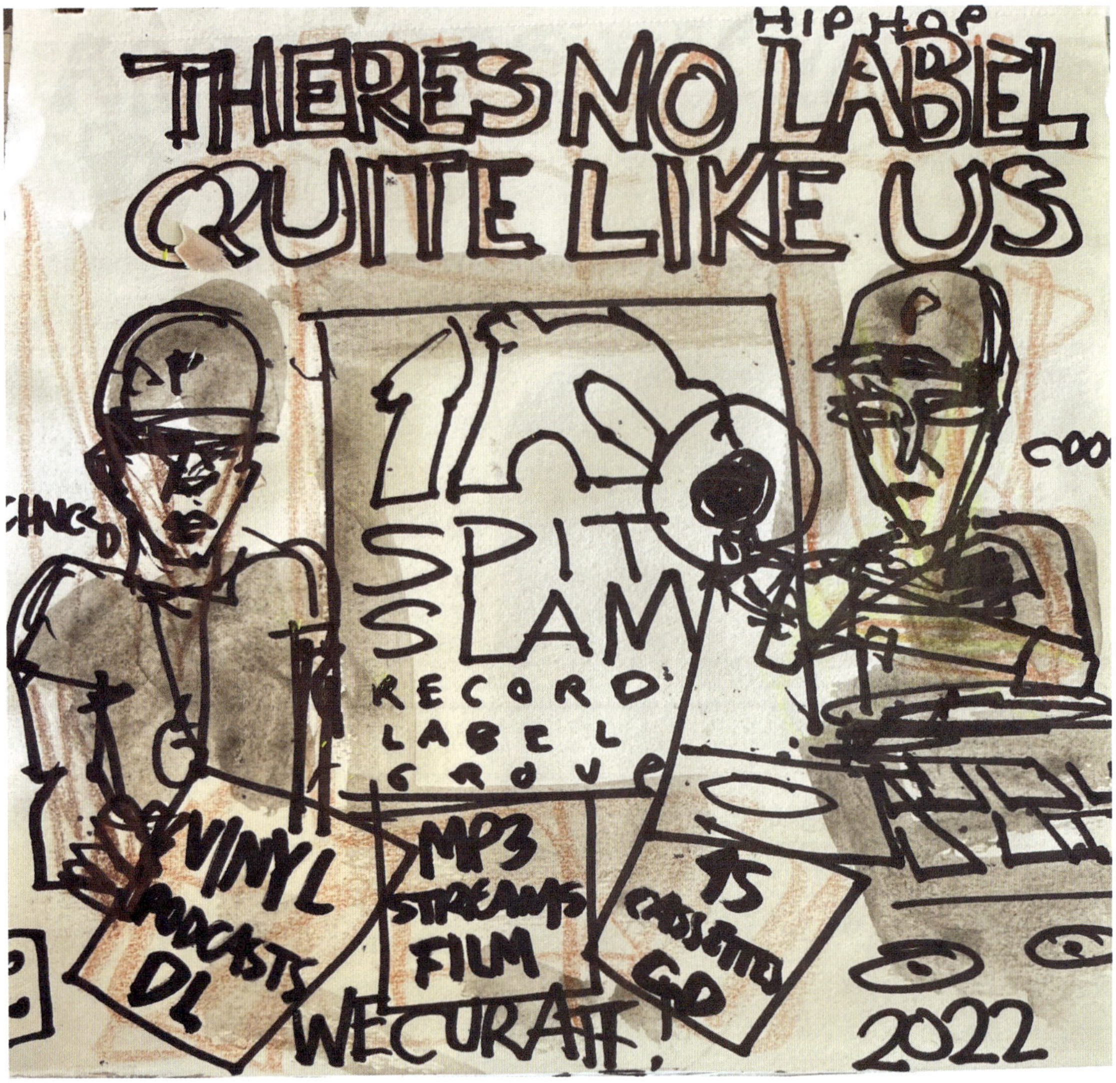

HIP HOP
THERES NO LABEL
QUITE LIKE US
SPIT
SLAM
RECORD
LABEL
GROUP
VINYL
PODCASTS
DL
MP3
STREAMS
FILM
CASSETTES
CD
WE CURATE!
2022

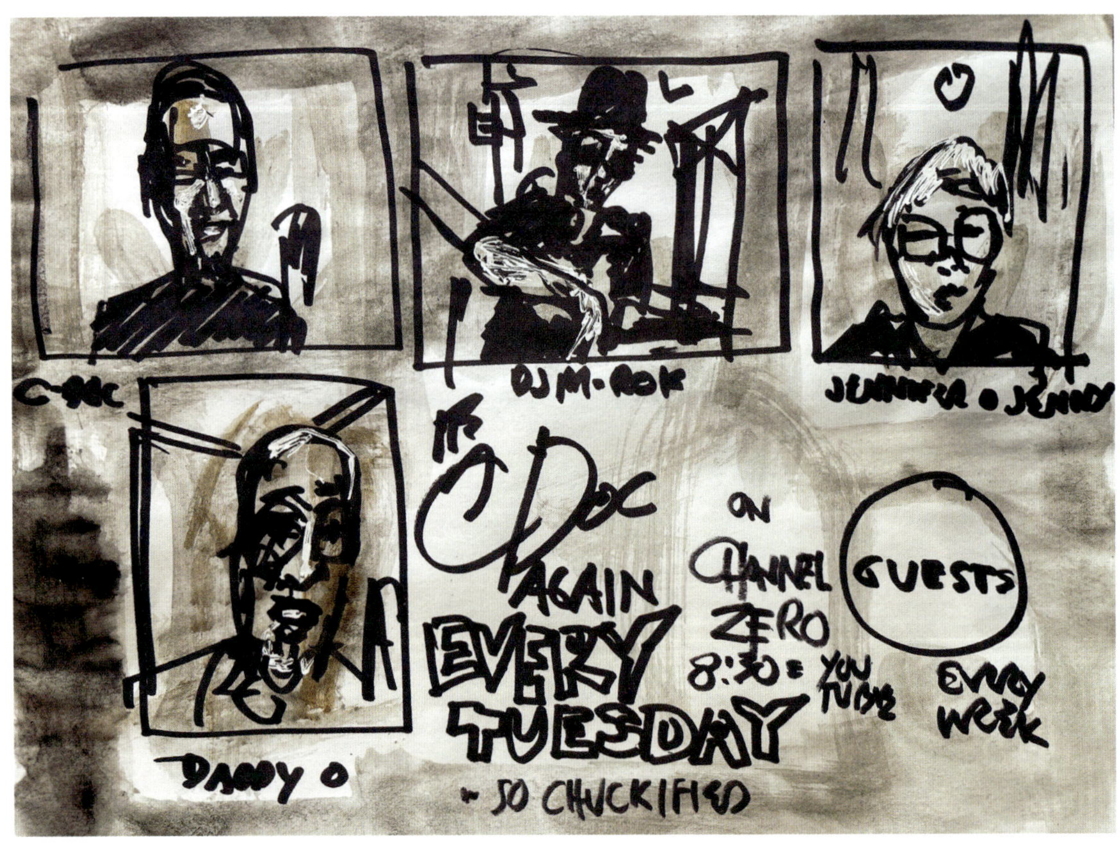
C-DOC
DJ M-ROK
C DOC
AGAIN
ON
CHANNEL
ZERO
GUESTS
EVERY
TUESDAY
8:30 = YOU TUBE
EVERY WEEK
SO CHUCKIFIED

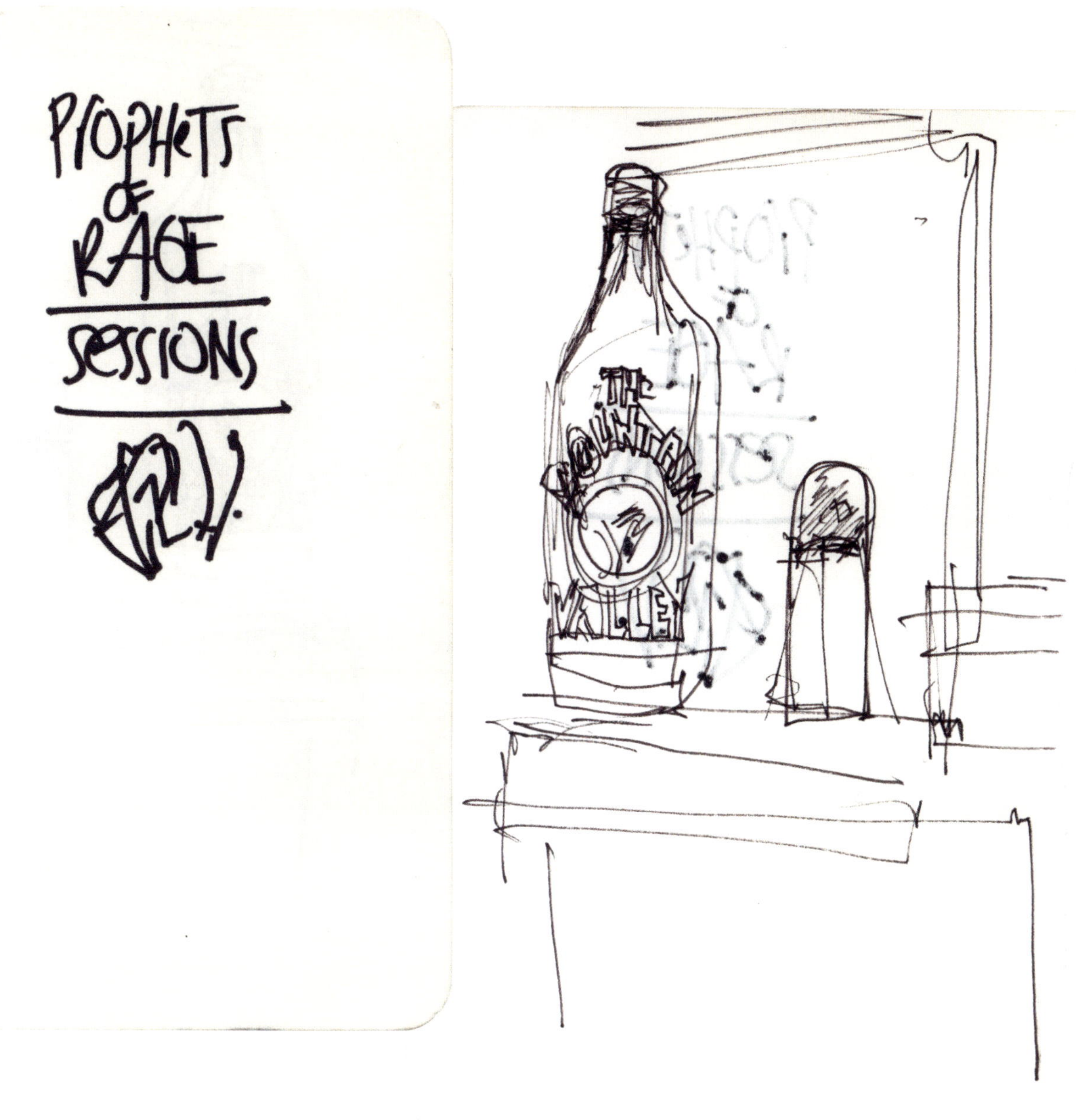

Tom Morello looked at the monstrousness of what was happening in 2016 with the election and realised he had to do more than just tweet about it. So, he created a task force of revolutionary-minded, forward-thinking artists who weren't afraid to say and do the things that needed to be said and done, and he called it Prophets of Rage.

As well as Tom Morello, who has reinvented the way the guitar does its work, Prophets of Rage also features B-Real from Cypress Hill – the straw that stirs the drink. He is the charismatic leader, microphone A. Next is the great turntablist DJ Lord. As Tom Morello makes the guitar sound like a turntable, DJ Lord makes the turntable sound like a guitar. The bassist, Tim Commerford, goes to war every night, rocking to millions of fanatics. And then, of course, there's the hard as hell Brad Wilk on drums.

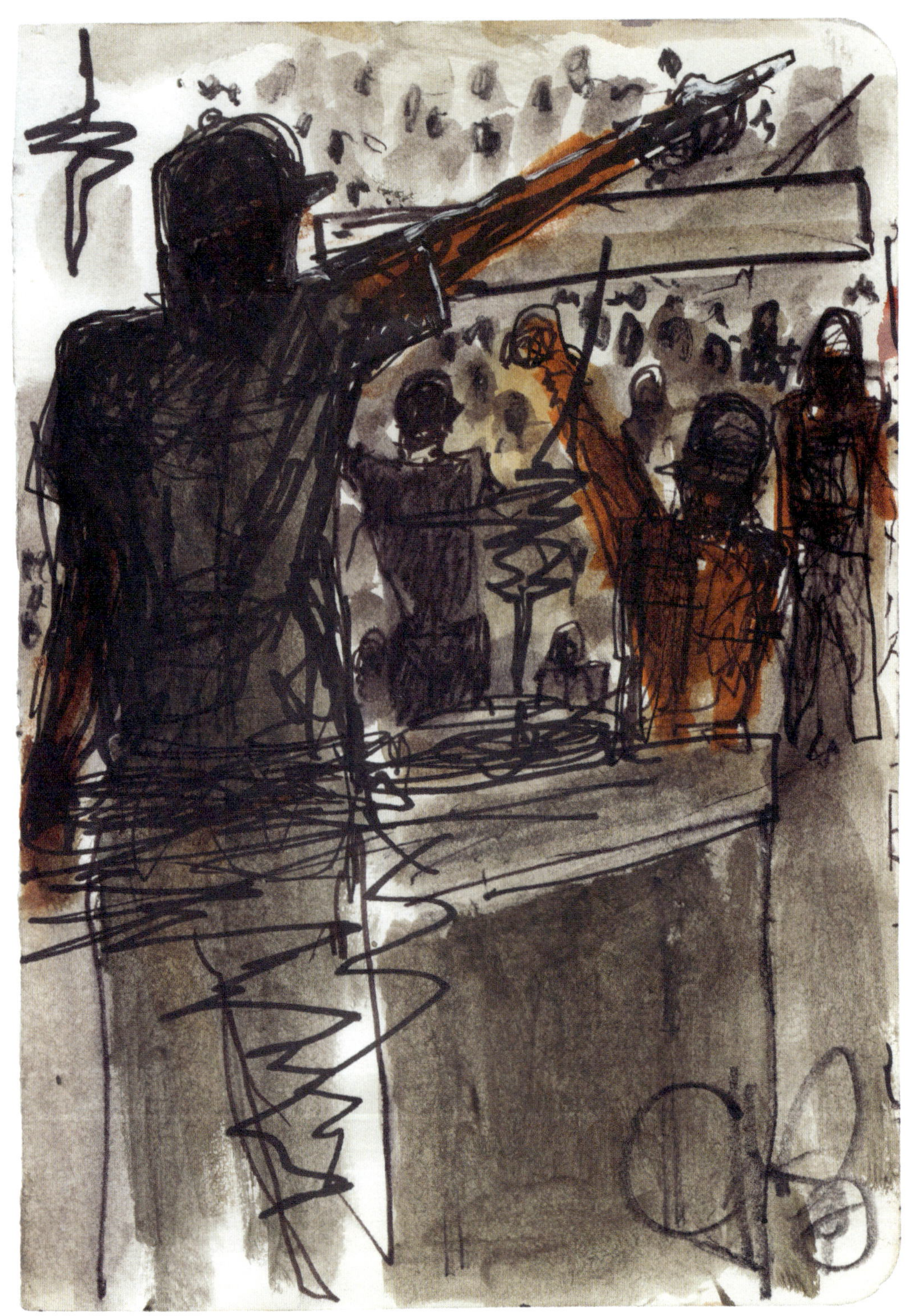

When I ventured out and took on Prophets my dad had just passed. He was a man I talked to almost every day of my life for 55 years, so the void was tremendous. He kept me grounded when I was loose. The silence without him was unbelievably powerful and the only way I could fill the silence was by speaking powerfully.

Prophets of Rage gave me four years of unbelievable, unstoppable brotherhood. It was a totally life-fixing, beautiful opportunity to get out of that space I was in.

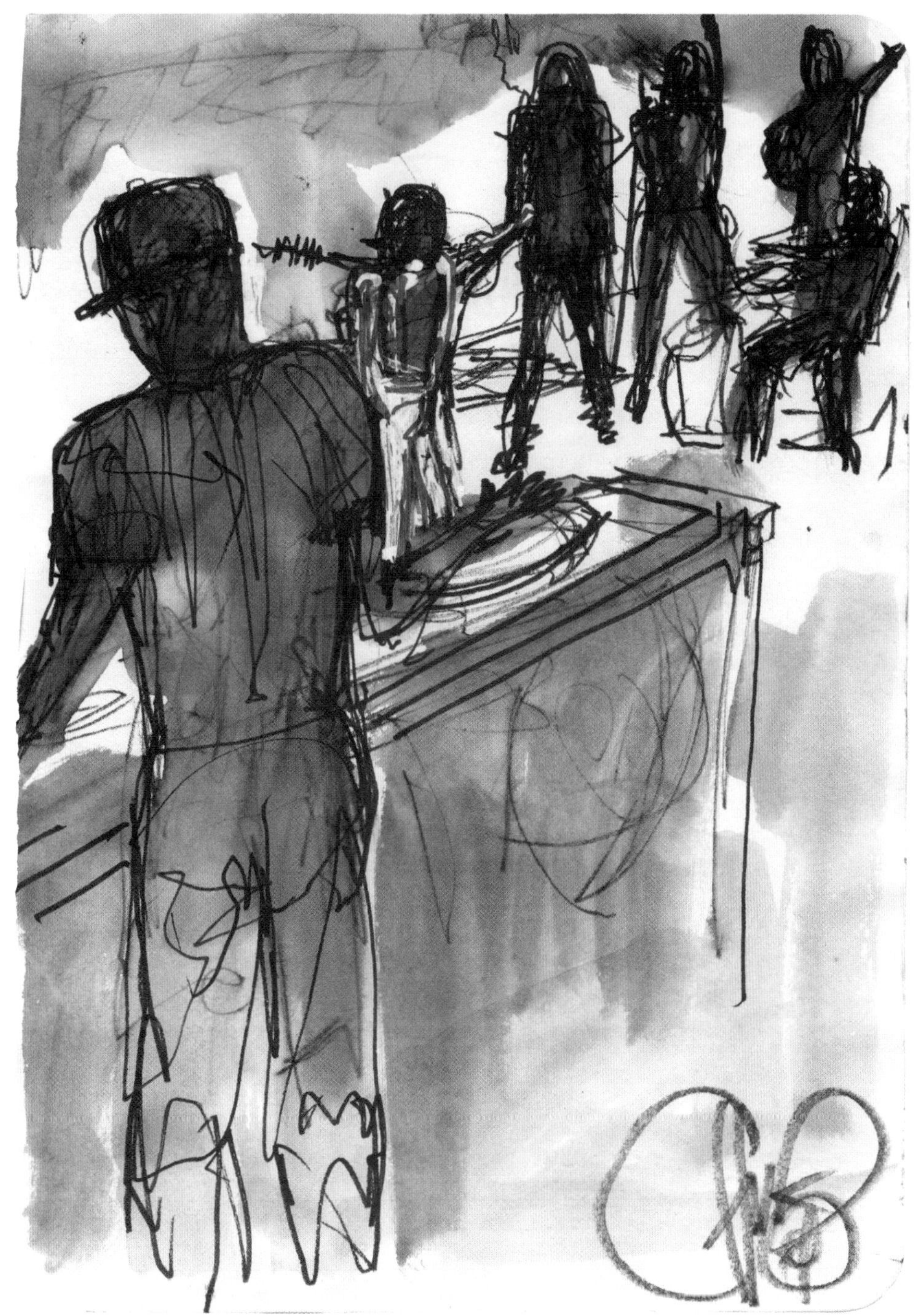

Prophets of Rage weren't afraid to be categorised as a political band, but how can a band *not* be political? Everything is political once you pay attention. If you're 25 years old and trying to pay for your apartment, you better get fucking political in some sort of way. It's a mistake to think that young people don't want to hear about what's happening and what affects them. And I think Rage Against the Machine, Cypress Hill and Public Enemy spoke to that. We encouraged people to make their own independent decisions.

Most Americans have got no idea what people in other territories think about their country. If you gave them an international point of view they'd be surprised. We've played three continents in front of 2.7 million people. We went to all kinds of places and it didn't matter whether they were left, right, centre or whatever, they all said to us, 'What the fuck is going on with that Trump guy?'

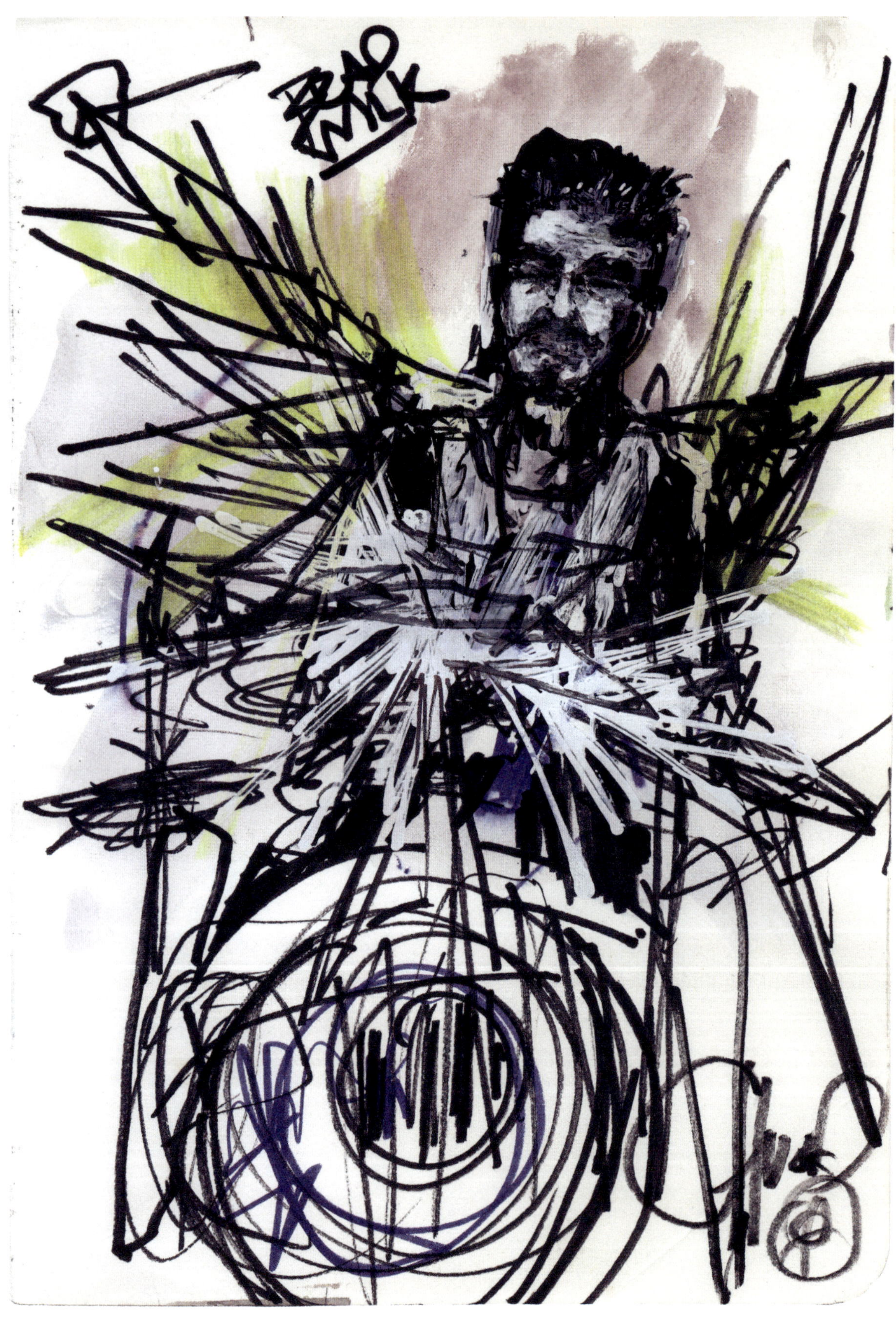

The great god of hard drums, Brad Wilk.

When people are sceptical there's only one job to do and that's to be super. With Prophets of Rage there weren't a lot of kumbaya songs. It was brutality.

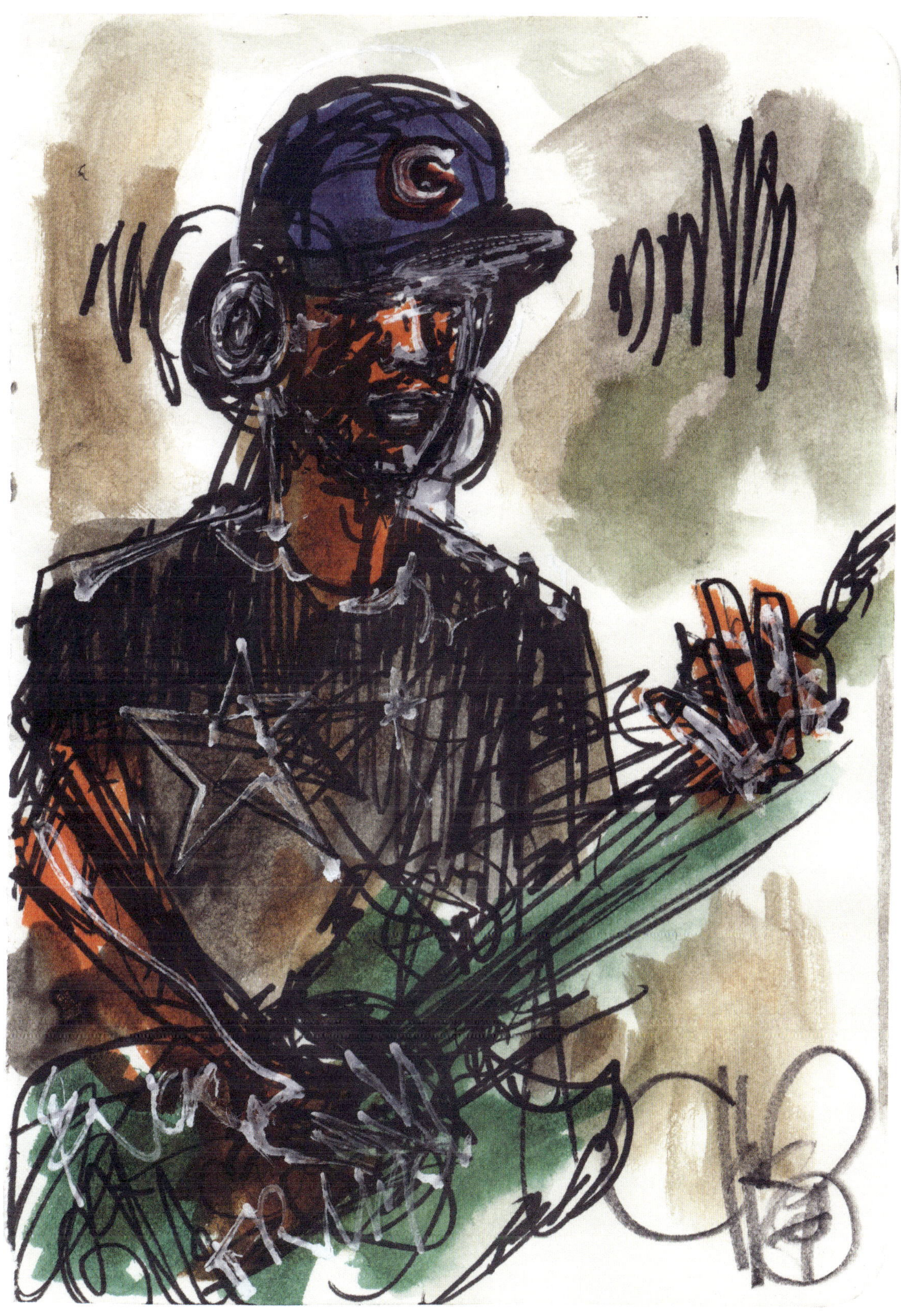

Tom coined a statement, 'The world won't fix itself.'

Things don't fix themselves, you've got to make it happen. That's how the song 'Unfuck the World' came about. If you're going to consider the world fucked, somebody's got to figure out how to unfuck it.

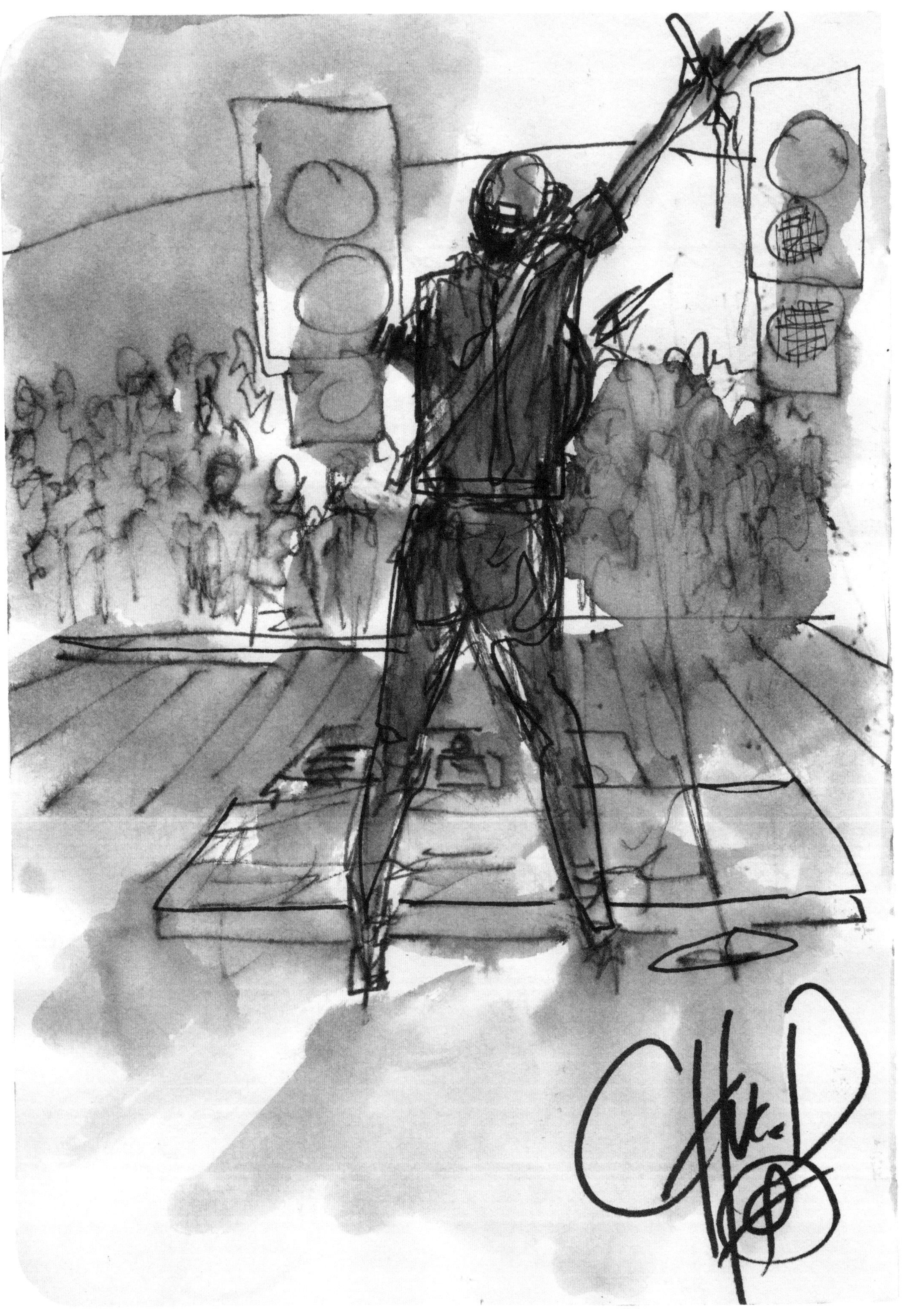

I was one of the last to be asked to join Prophets of Rage. Tom got the core of Tim, Brad and himself in place and then he reached out to me. At the time I thought my plate was already full and I was daunted by the magnitude of it.

Throughout my career I've been recruited to join things, and I've always refused at first. I've said no to Hank Shocklee, Rick Rubin, Tom Morello – usually for around a year. But Tom was insistent and I could see that to keep saying no would be a wrong turn. When my father passed I couldn't get far enough off this planet. I realised I had to try something new, as therapy.

It didn't become a reality for me until B-Real came into the picture. That's when it became clear that I could be a number two mic to his number one. I thought that would be perfect. B-Real is a phenomenal MC – one of the best of all time – and I liked the idea of working in his shadow and making the shadow stronger. Then I brought in DJ Lord so that it would be different from just fronting Rage Against the Machine 2.0.

When going in and attacking Rage Against the Machine songs, B-Real and I had to take a different approach. A 25-year-old Zack de la Rocha sounded like a knife was turning in him as he was screaming and screeching like it was the last day on Earth on these tracks. We couldn't compete with that, but we made up for it with power and execution.

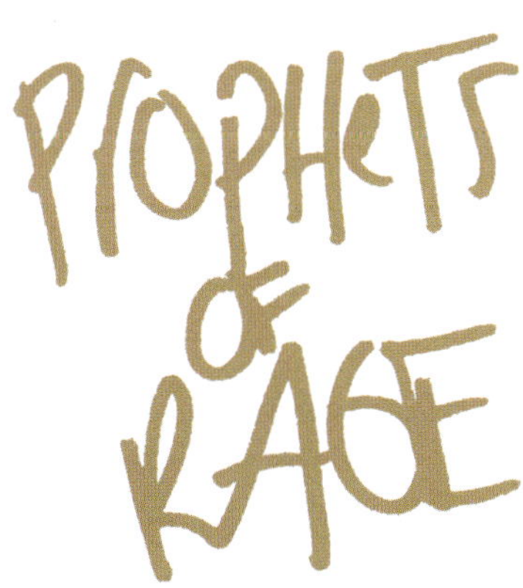

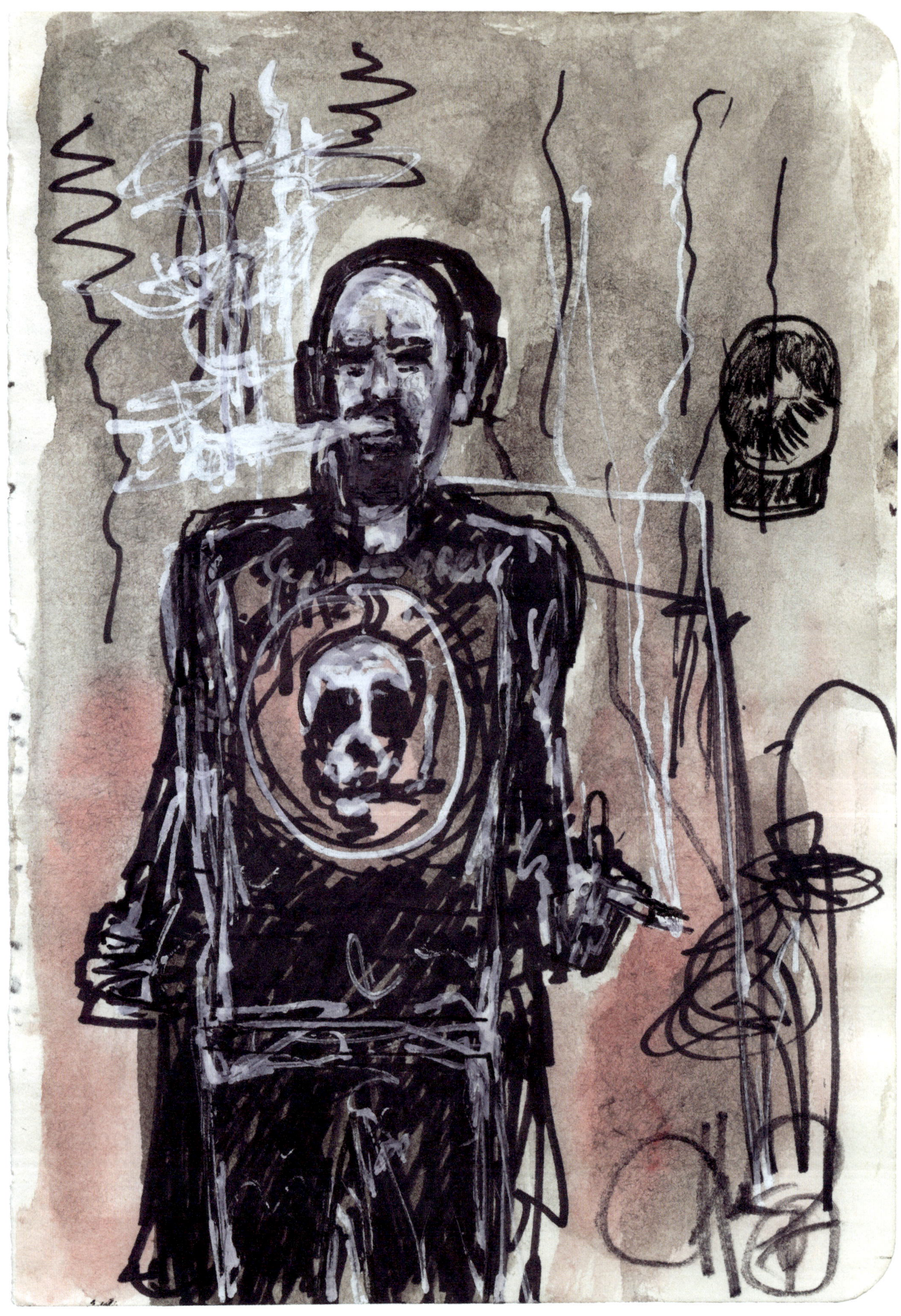

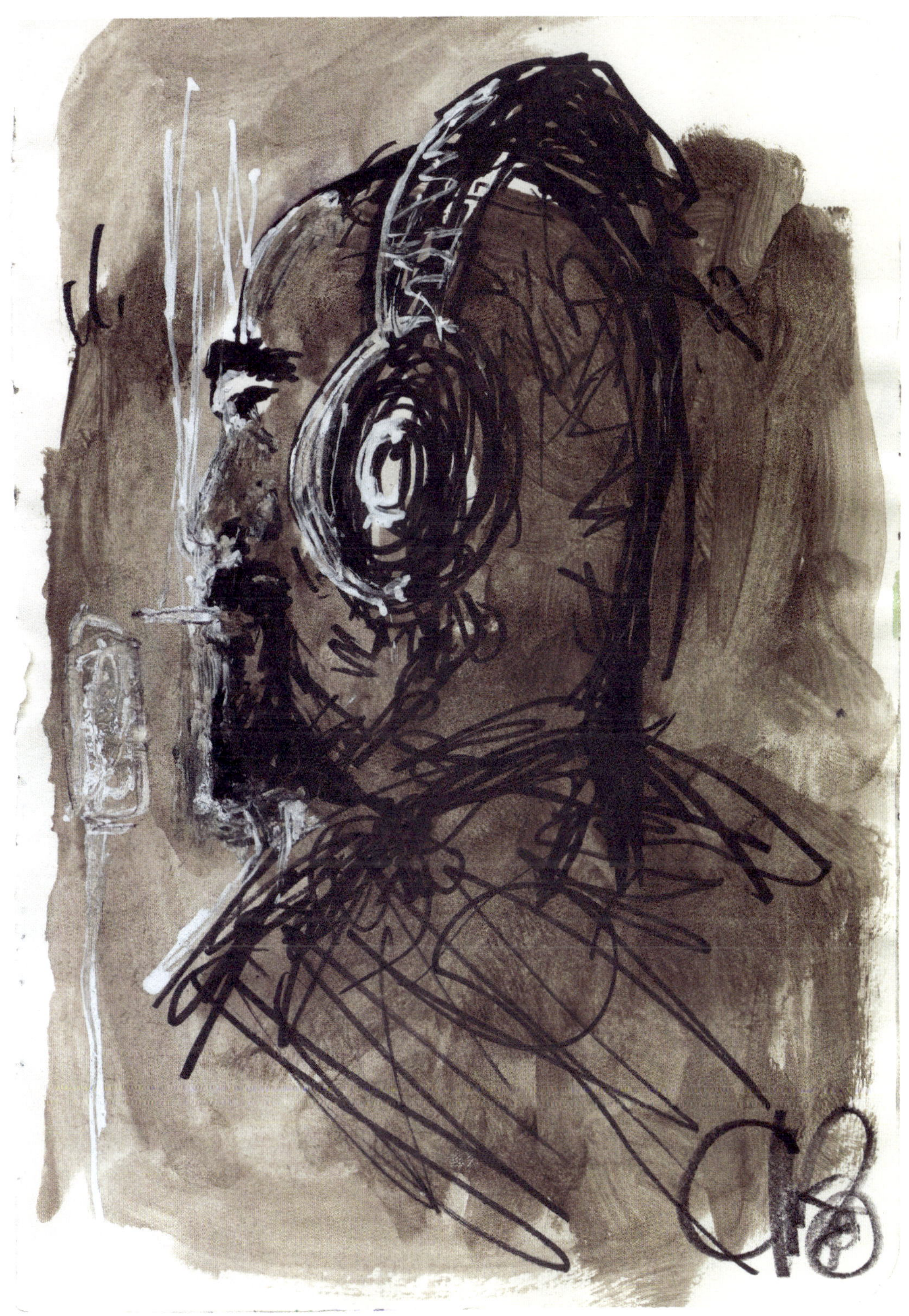

This is a capture of the mighty B-Real in action during our first time in the studio as Prophets of Rage. It introduced us to the blessings of smoke.

If you can come up with an illustrious title first, that makes it easier to write the song. Sometimes an idea will come, by divine intervention, and you cap it with a title.

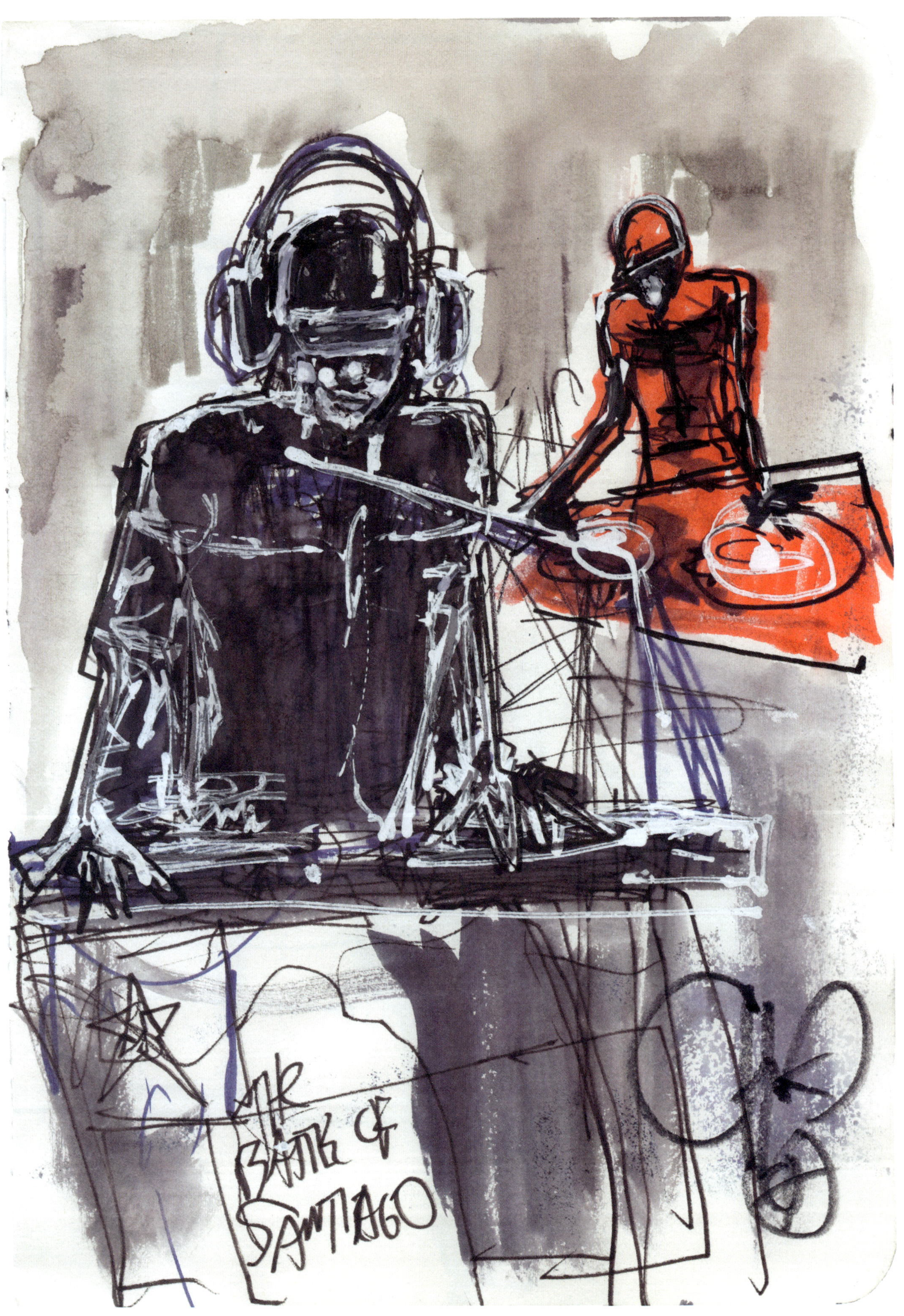
THE
BATTLE OF
SANTIAGO

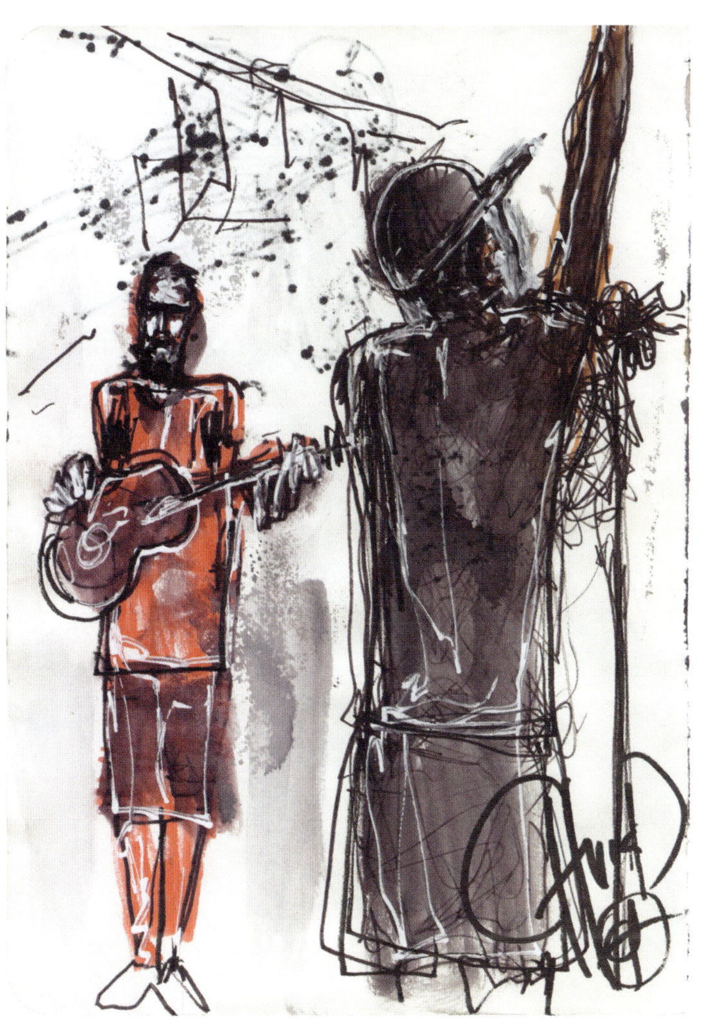

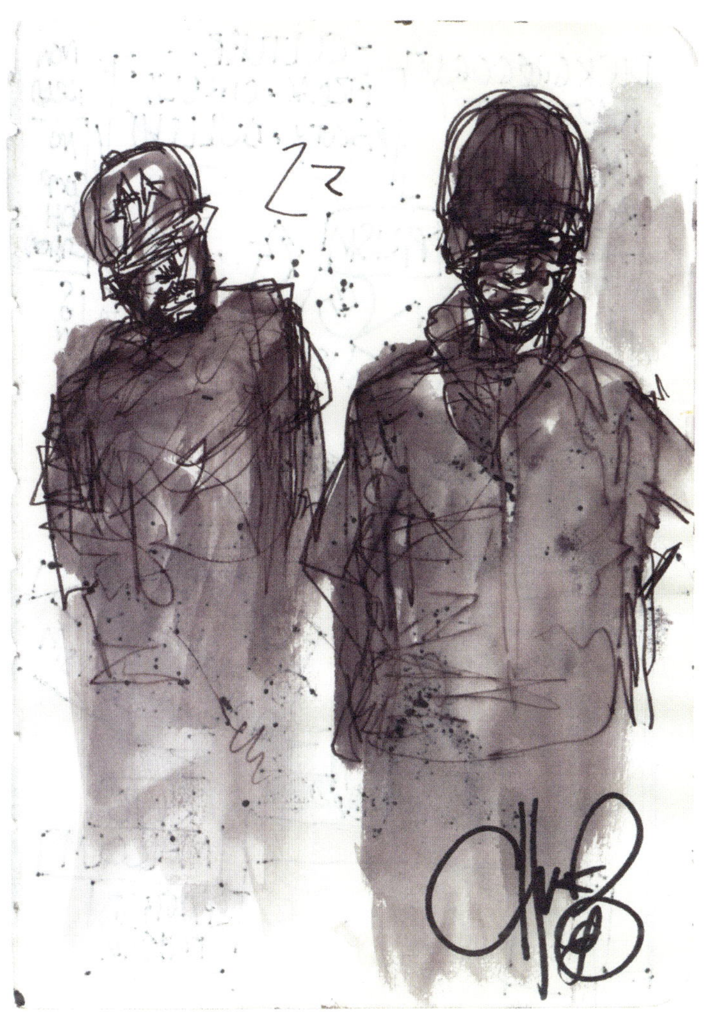

You have to be badass on the stage, you have to be relentless. With Prophets of Rage our attitude was we don't care if you like us or not, we will convince you with this performance that you have to unfuck the world. Music is a universal language that crosses timelines, gender lines, barriers, genres, and that's what we did.

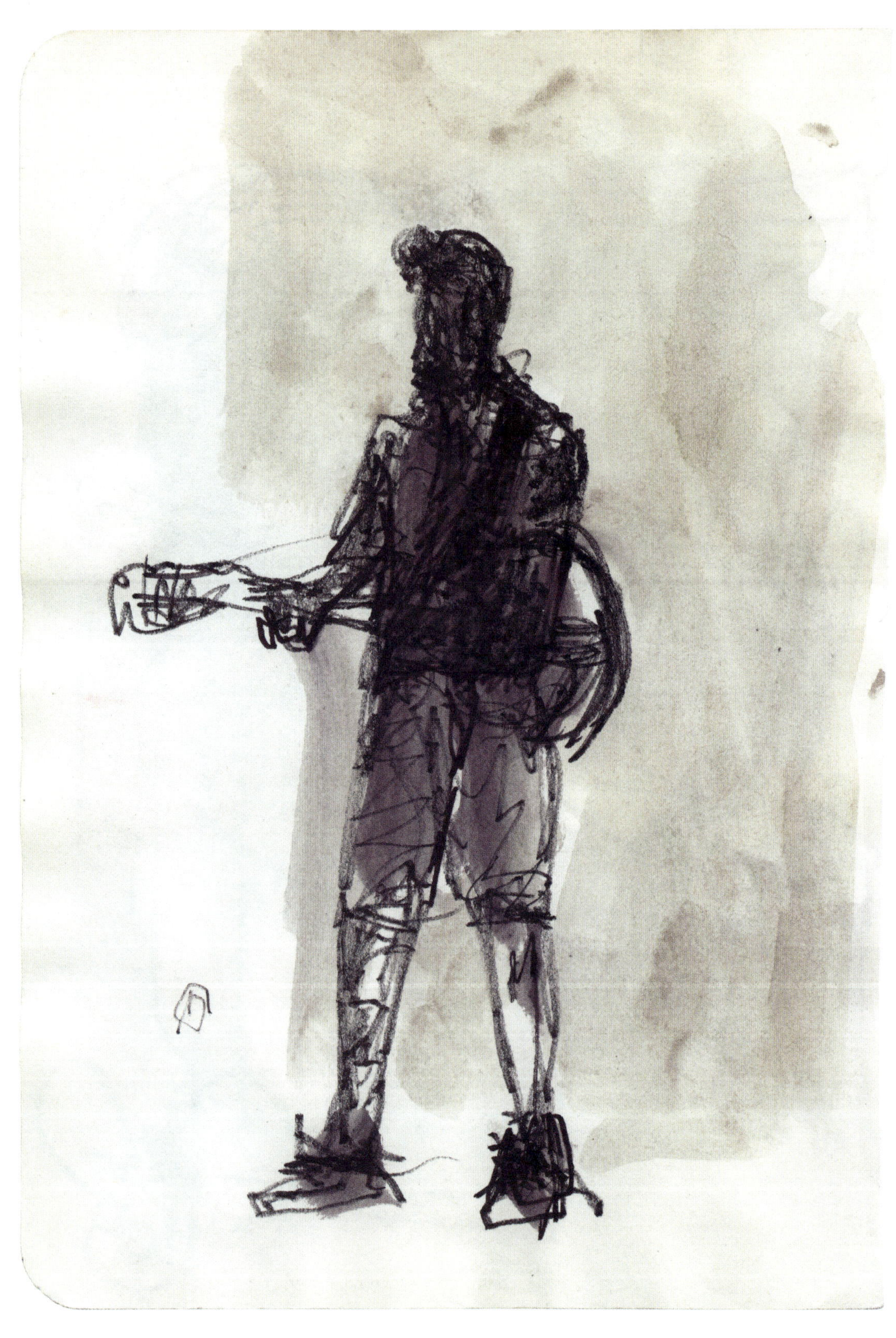

The great Tim Commerford of Rage Against the Machine and Prophets of Rage, sketched from the front and the back. He is the funkiest bass player in rock, by far.

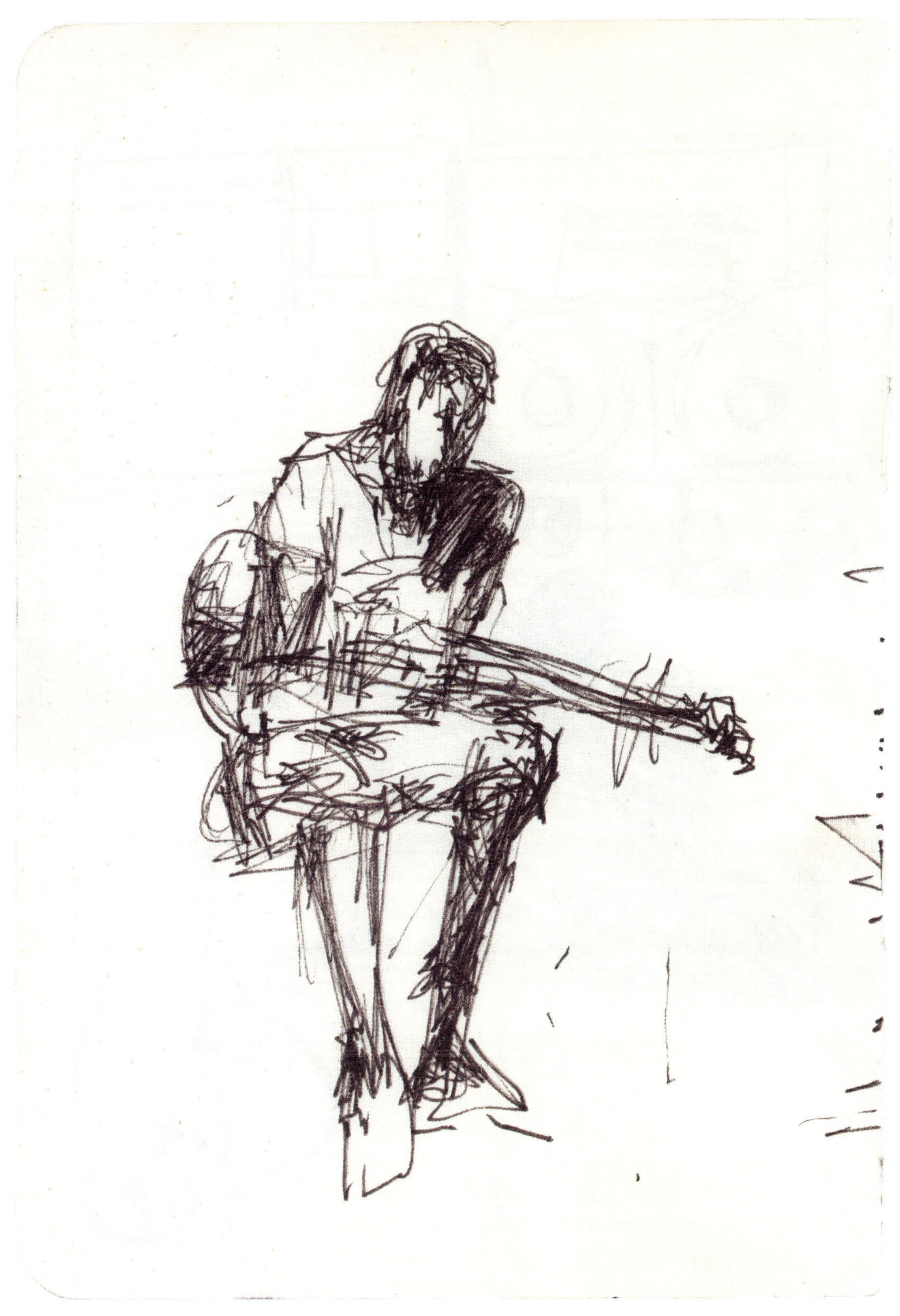

You'd think it would have been Tim, Brad and Tom writing riffs while B-Real and I worked on lyrics and Lord did scratches, but it didn't really turn out like that. It was more like Tim would do vocal parts and then B-Real might make a riff. And then Brendan O'Brien, the producer, would come in and rearrange it a bit.

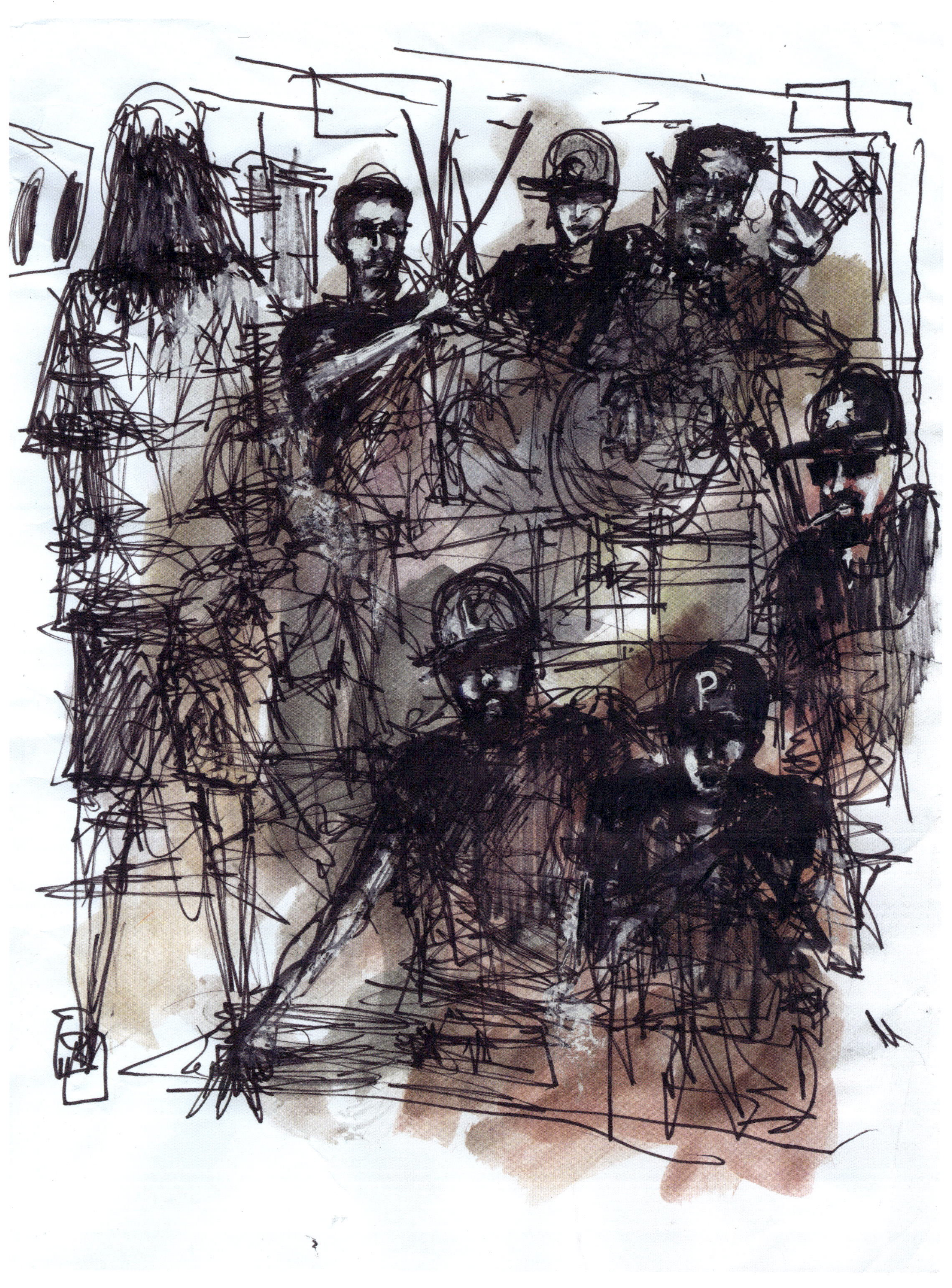

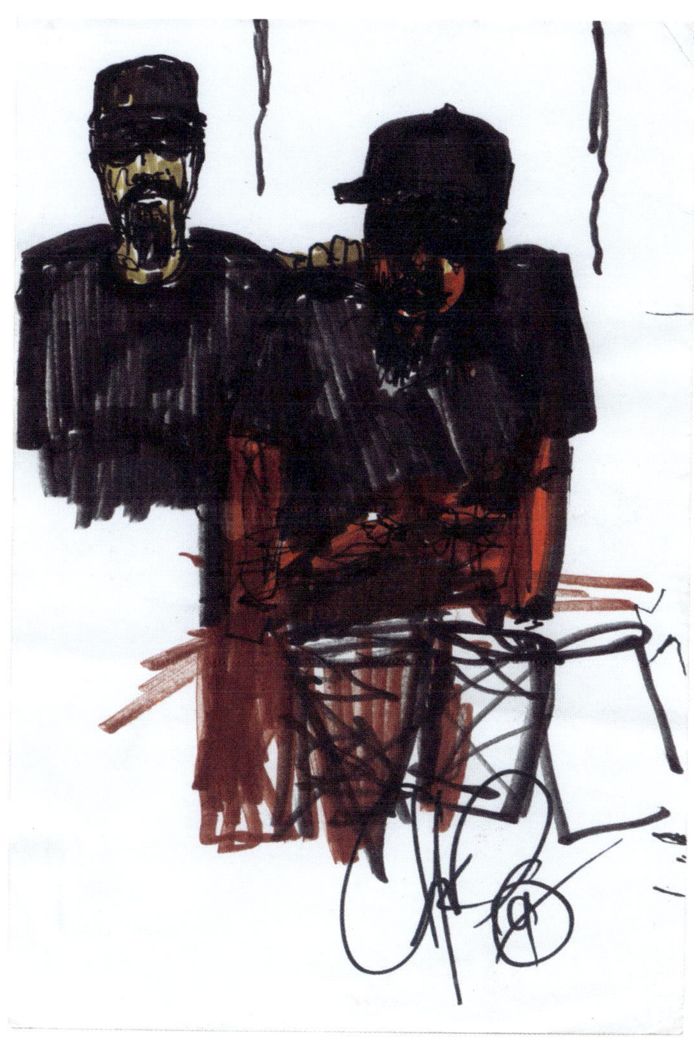

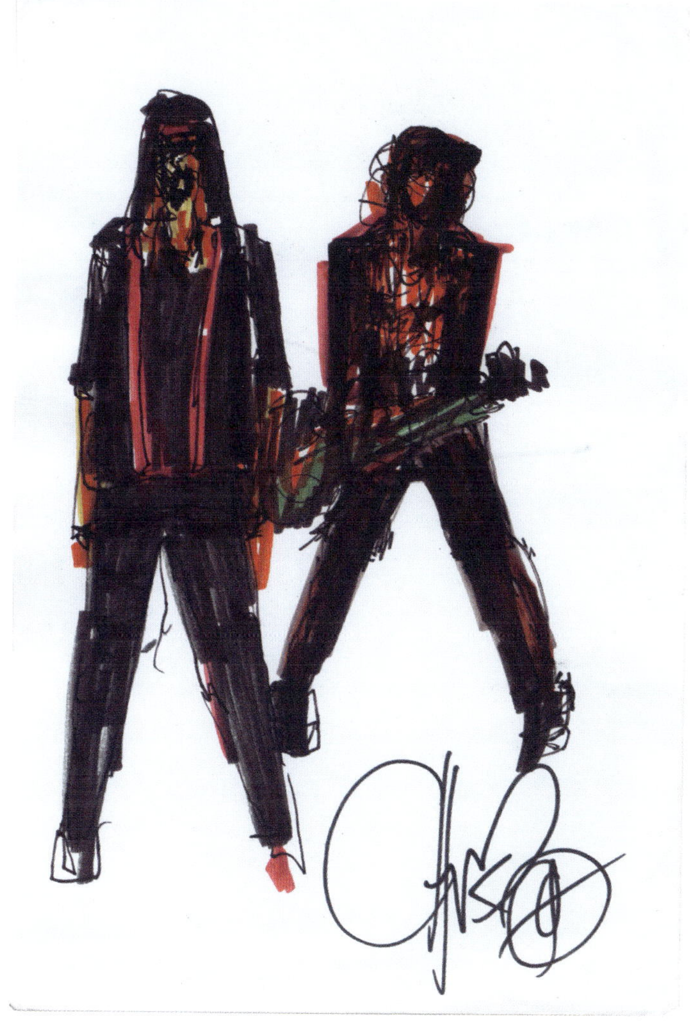

Culture brings human beings together on the same accord. That was the beauty of rap music and hip-hop at its beginnings. Hip-hop was a cultural olive branch. Collectives and revues are how hip-hop is meant to be. It's a shame how artists today are so swollen on their management, agent and record company hype, which prevents them from putting together revues featuring multiple artists. Now it's promoter, venue, artist.

Hip-hop was taken over by radio stations that wanted to turn it into pop. It wasn't a partnership, it was a takeover. You don't see radio stations take over the Rolling Stones, do you? The Stones are going to do their own thing. Prophets of Rage did their own thing.

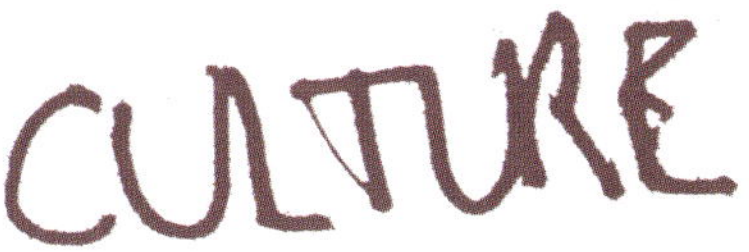

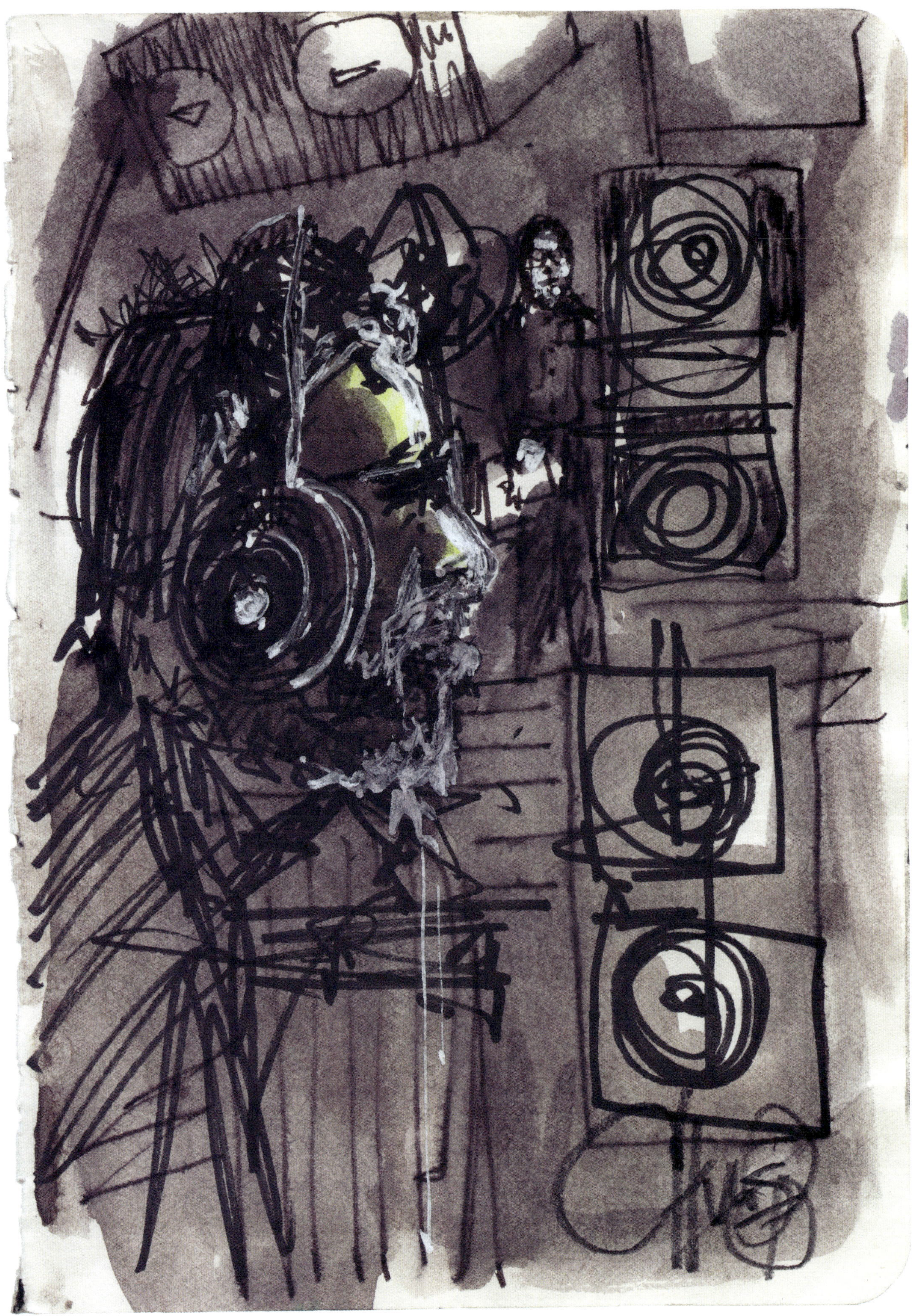

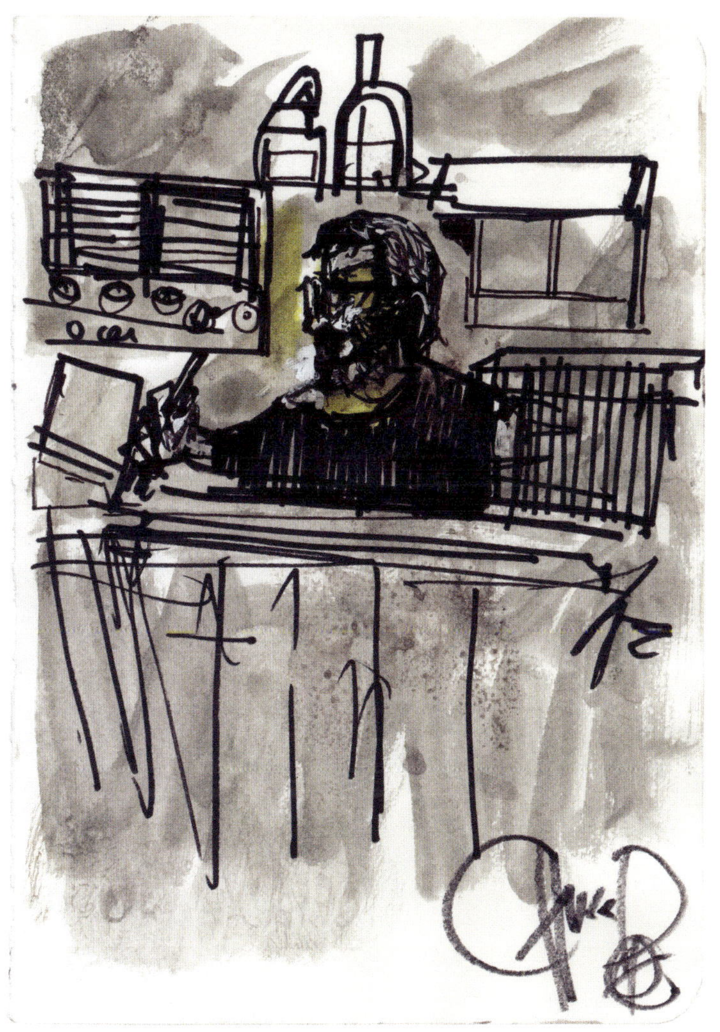

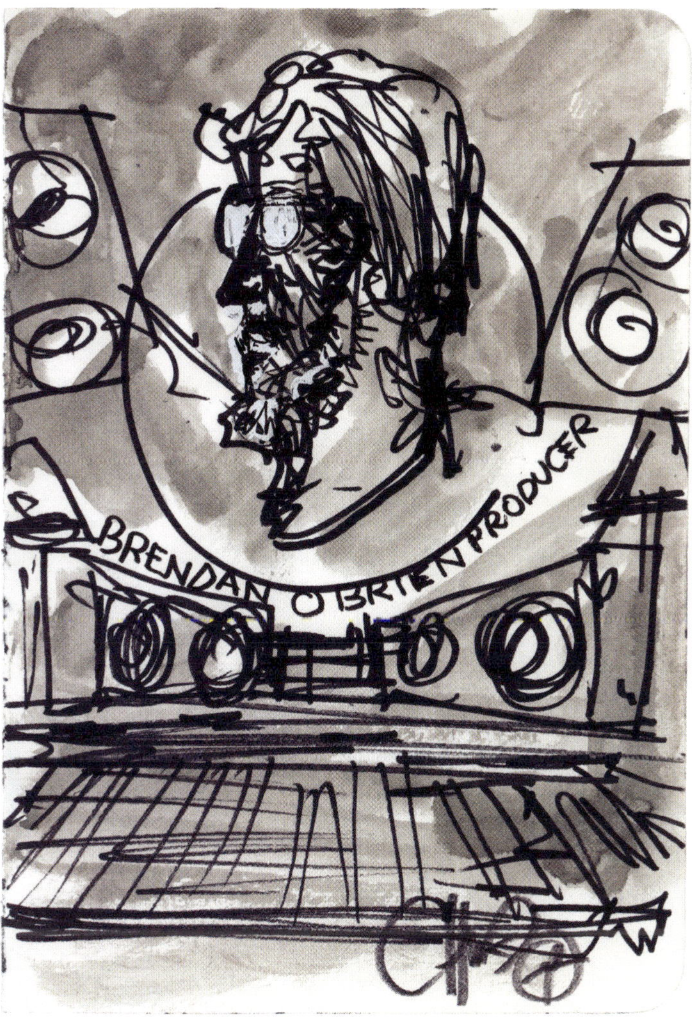

We had Brendan O'Brien and Tom Syrowski producing the first record and they weren't playing games. Many times, I wanted to do it over again but they'd say, 'You almost nailed it, let's just get it from here.' And boom, it's done.

It was a great experience working with them. Creating the album *Prophets of Rage* was almost like going back to 1987, when we made the first Public Enemy album – all of us in a room together, hashing it out.

Brendan was able to manage the spontaneous amalgamation of two MCs, a turntablist, a bass player, a drummer and a guitarist of high note into something cohesive.

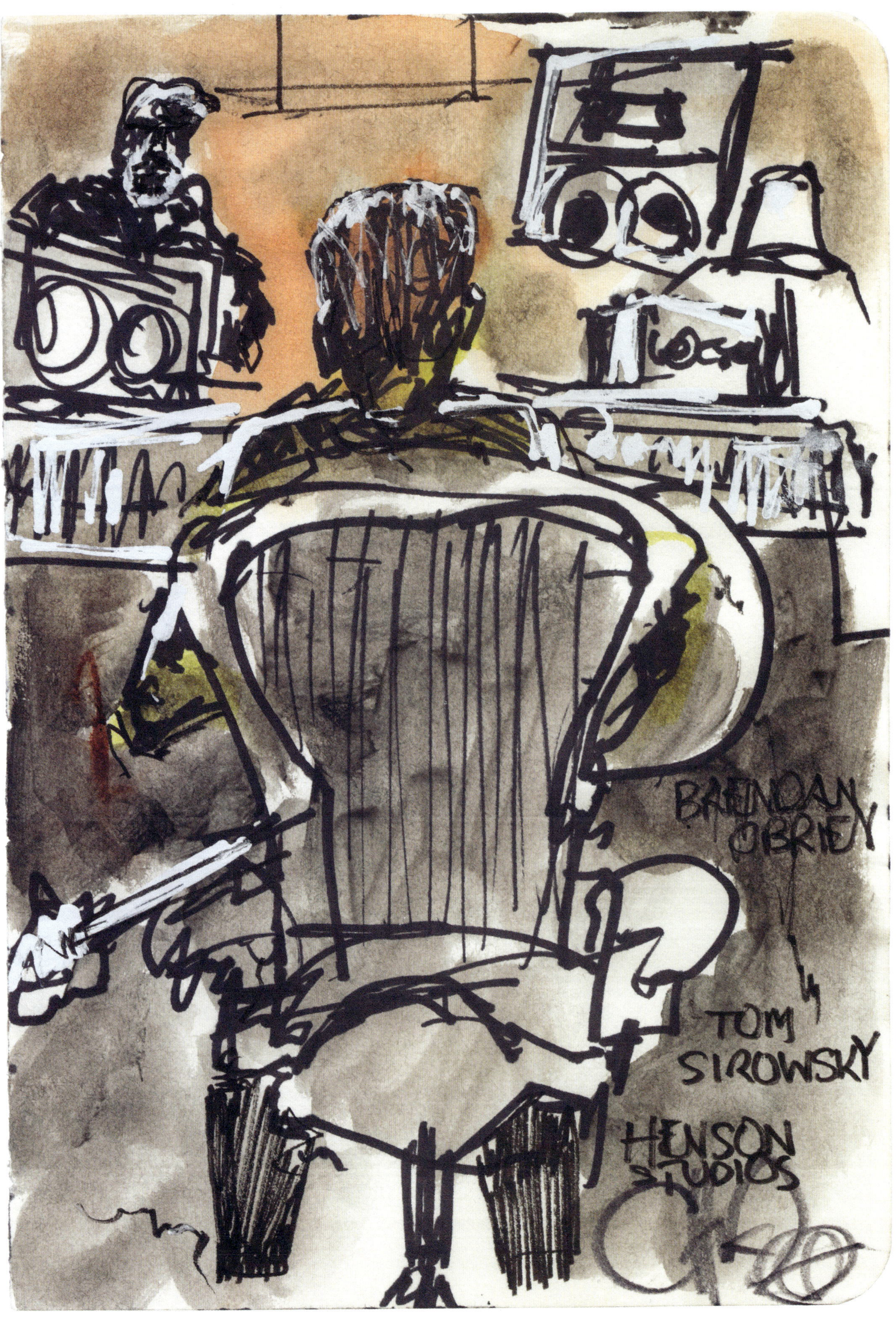
TOM SIROWSKY
HENSON STUDIOS

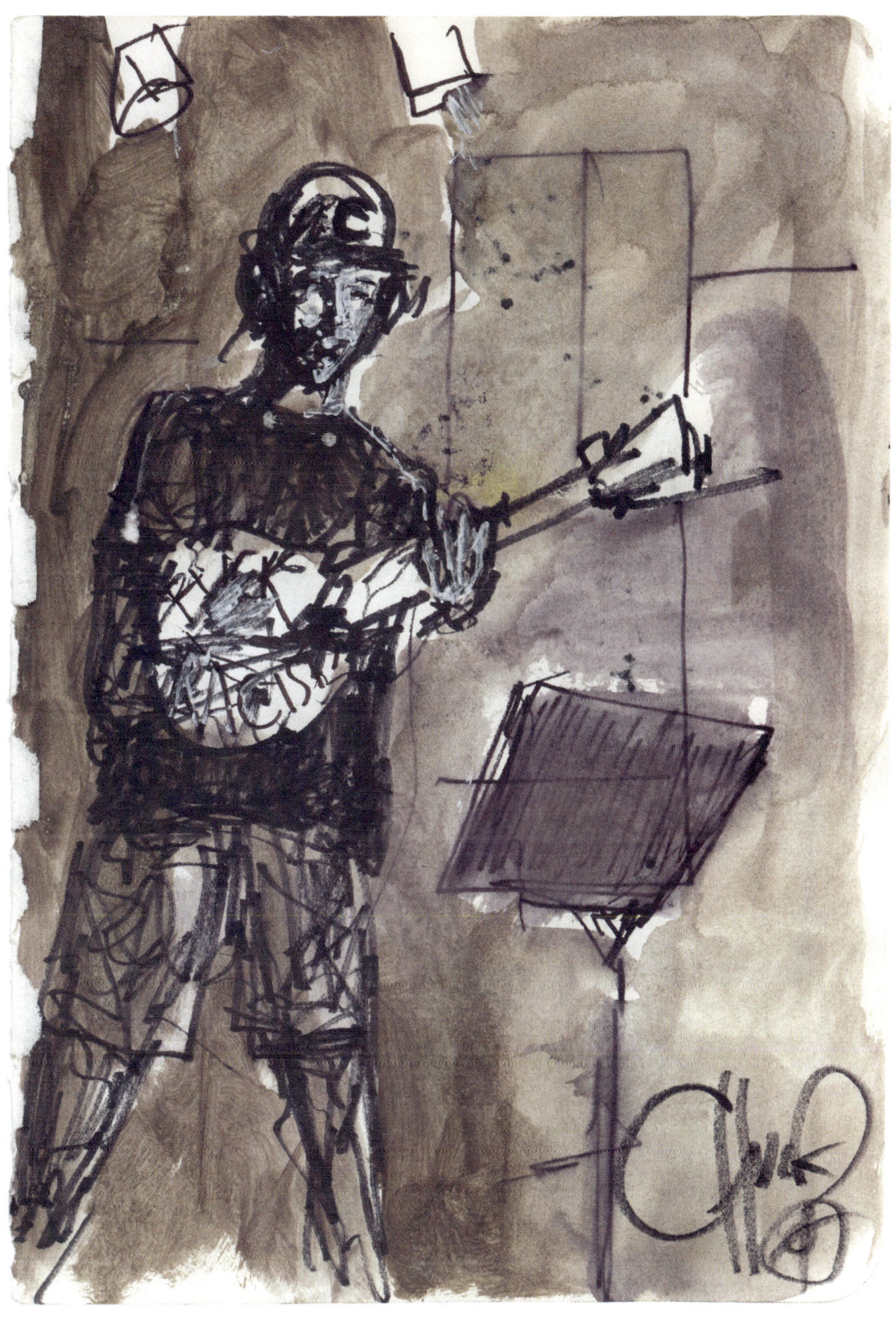

We were caught in the schism of wanting to create new songs while knowing the old songs would always be there if we needed them. When we got together to rehearse, something often came out organically that we could make into a future song. We didn't want to be always relying on something from the past.

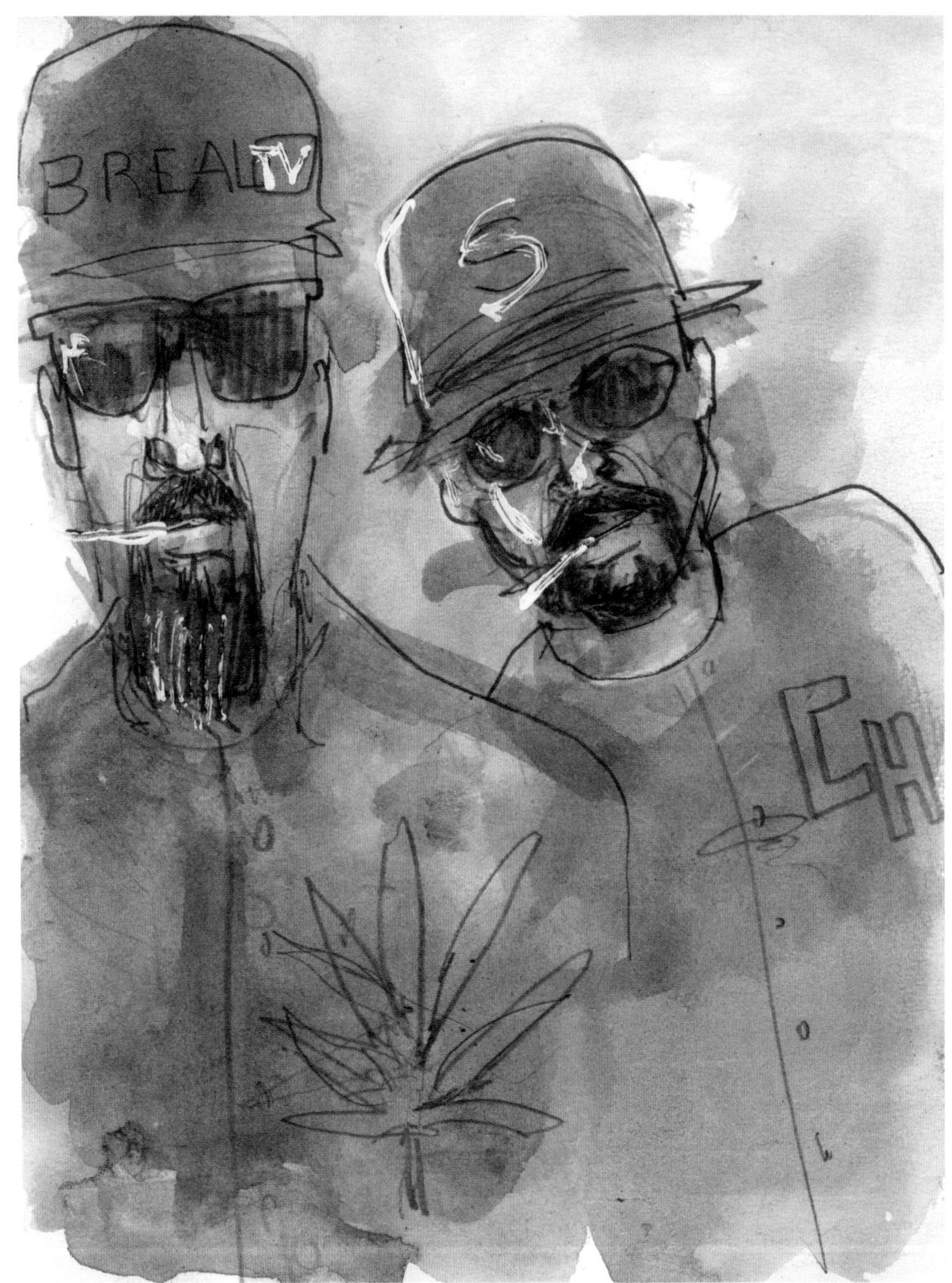

B-Real, Sen Dog and DJ Muggs formed Cypress Hill as Public Enemy in vocal reverse. The earth was opened wide by the *High Times* shamans' beliefs, songs and the connected salute to the Latino planet – previously undertapped. I was amazed nightly while on the Smokin' Grooves tour with them in 1998. Fast-forward and I'm still amazed as Cypress continues to travel the globe, just as Public Enemy does.

One time during the 1998 tour, B-Real met a woman who was pregnant and her husband asked him to give blessings for the baby. B put his hands over the woman's belly and they said a prayer together. I was stunned, but not as stunned as when we were in Prophets of Rage and we went back to the same city and met the baby that B had blessed, who was now an 18-year-old kid come to check out the show with his mom and dad. That's the most amazing thing that I've experienced ever in all my time in music. What could top that?

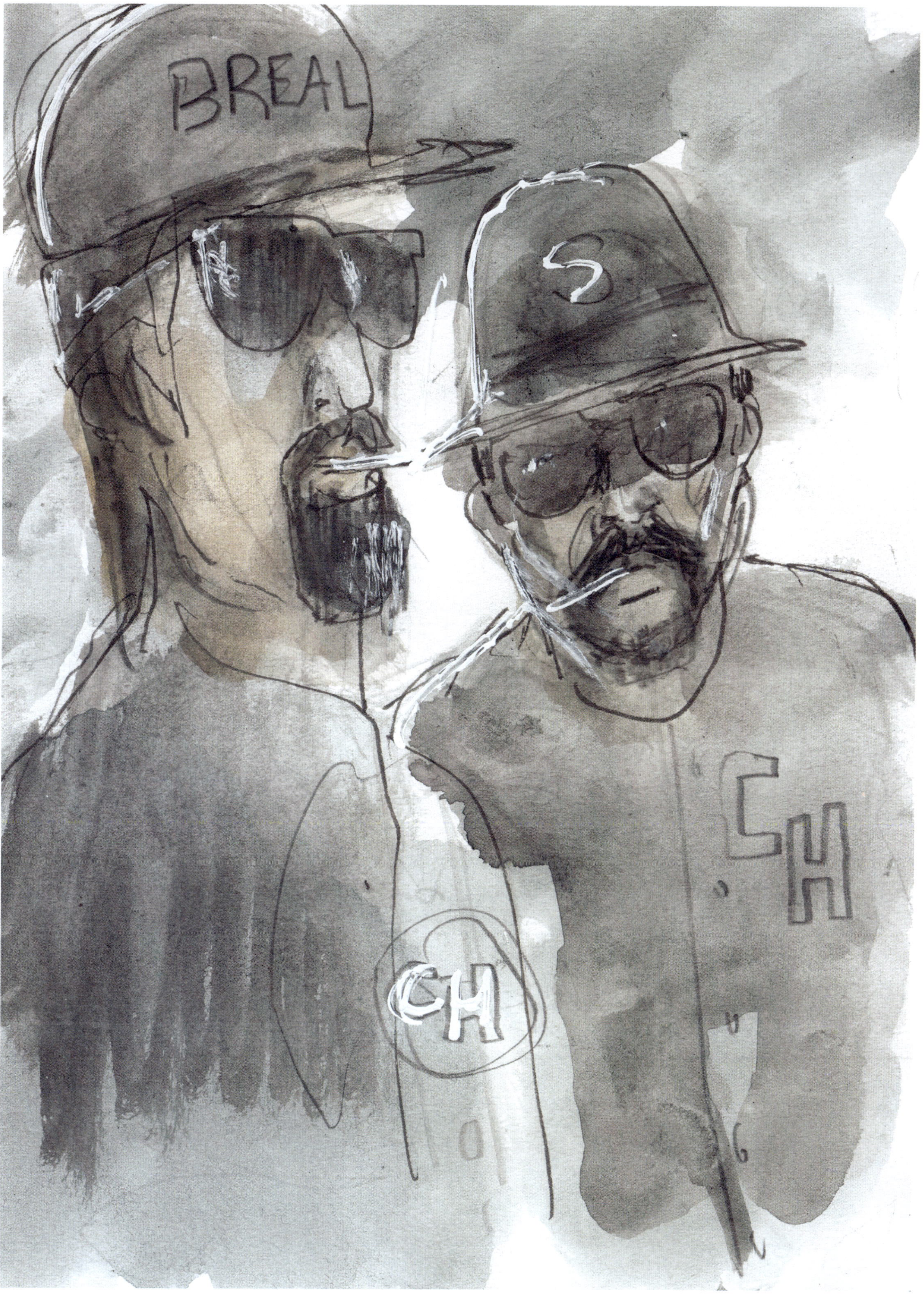
BREAL
S
CH
CH

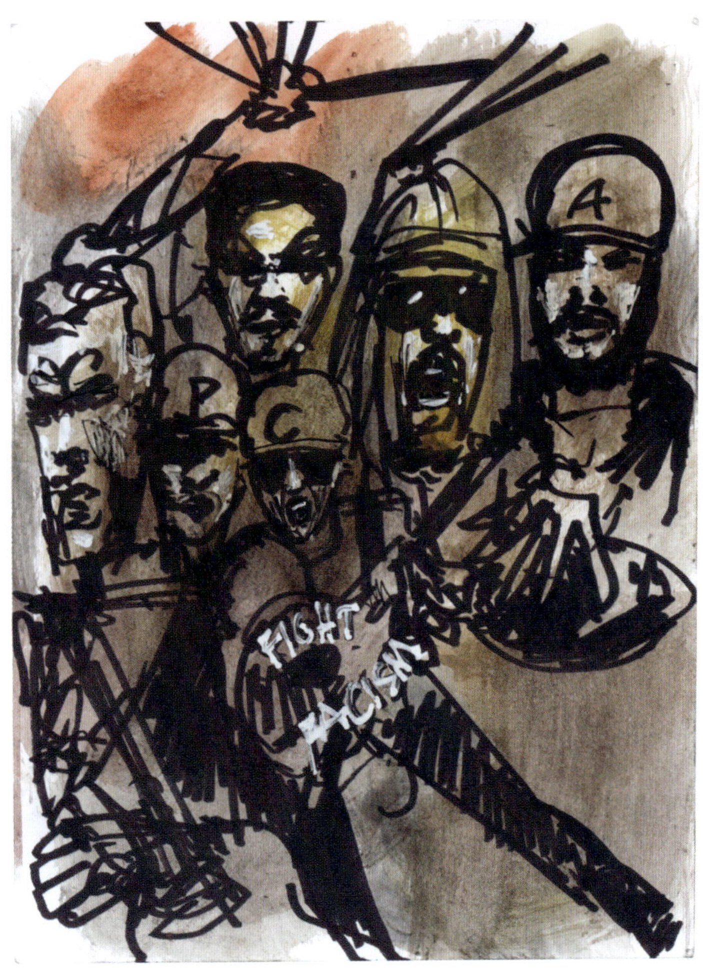

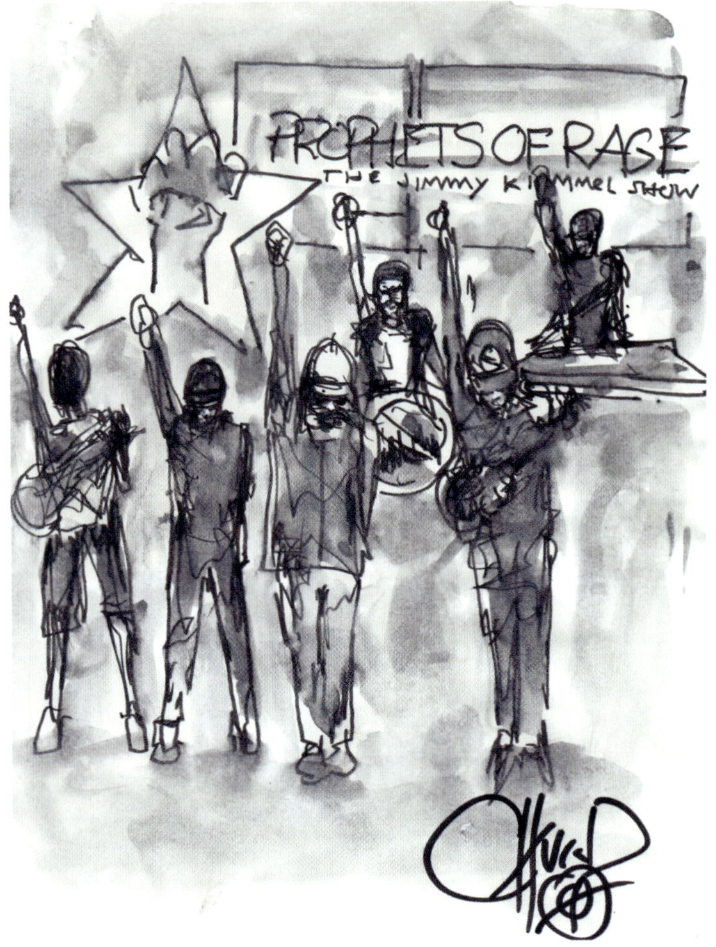

We liked to tour big. Tom often burdened himself with the tour – he's the master of that, so we left it up to him. He thought about it while we were sleeping. Overnight he'd stay up for eight hours thinking about the next day's set. I think there was pressure from our previous groups that meant our rehearsals needed to be on a higher level.

We went through different songs to have them in the repertoire, just in case we wanted to change it up. We experimented when we rehearsed, and we had a great working discovery with each other. We had a gigantic tour of the United States in 2016, and man, did we have a flow where we knew we were going to go about hitting a record. We thoroughly worked out, almost like they say in some great sports teams: 'Our practice is our heart, and it shows.'

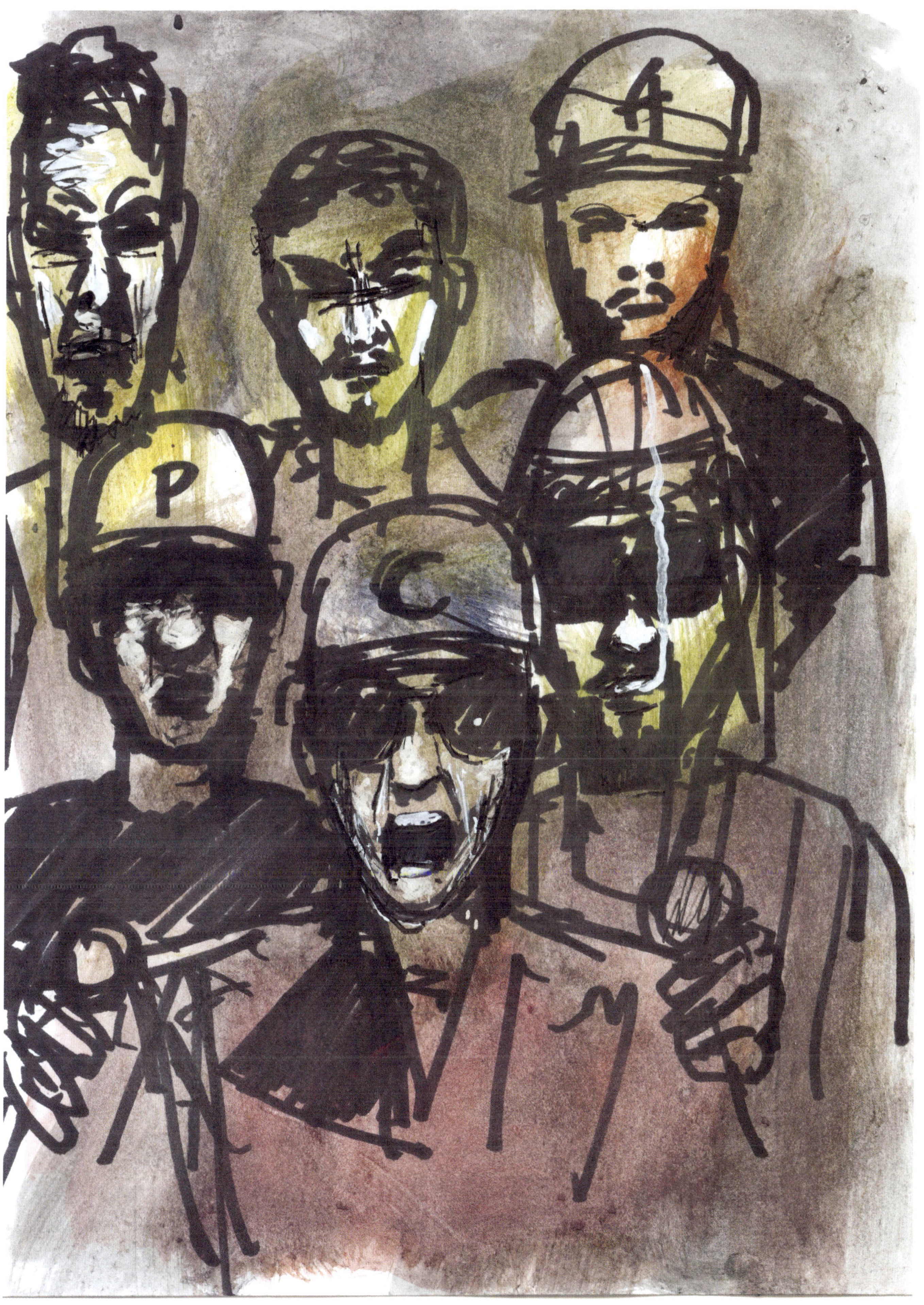

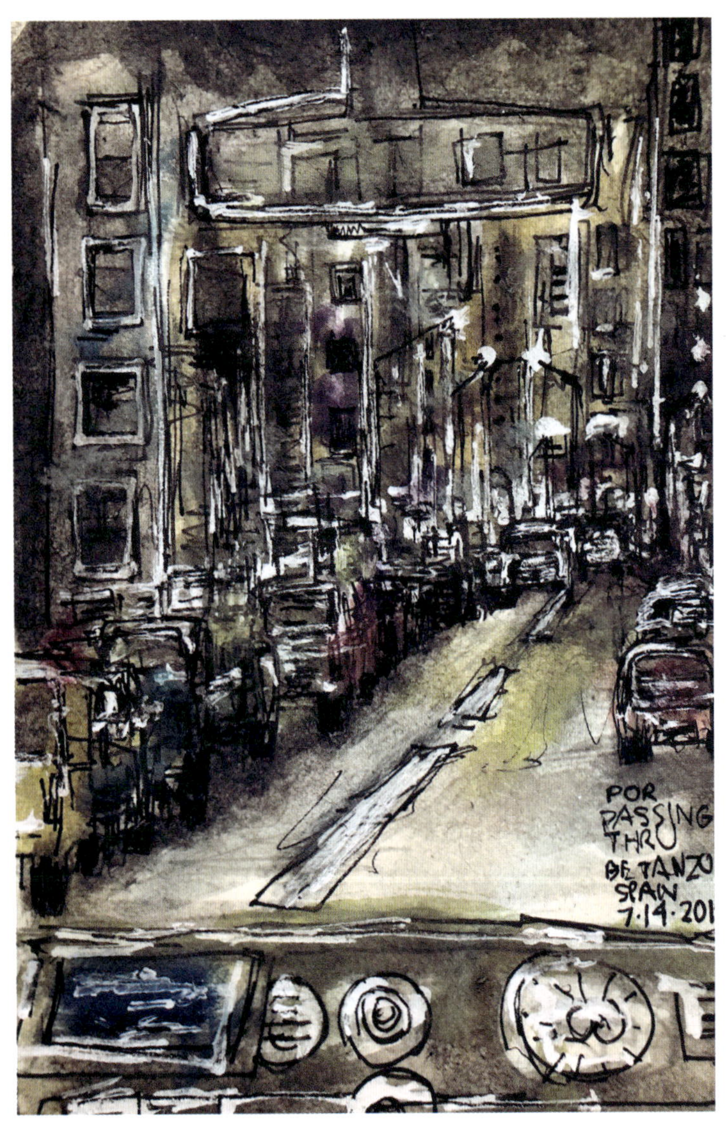

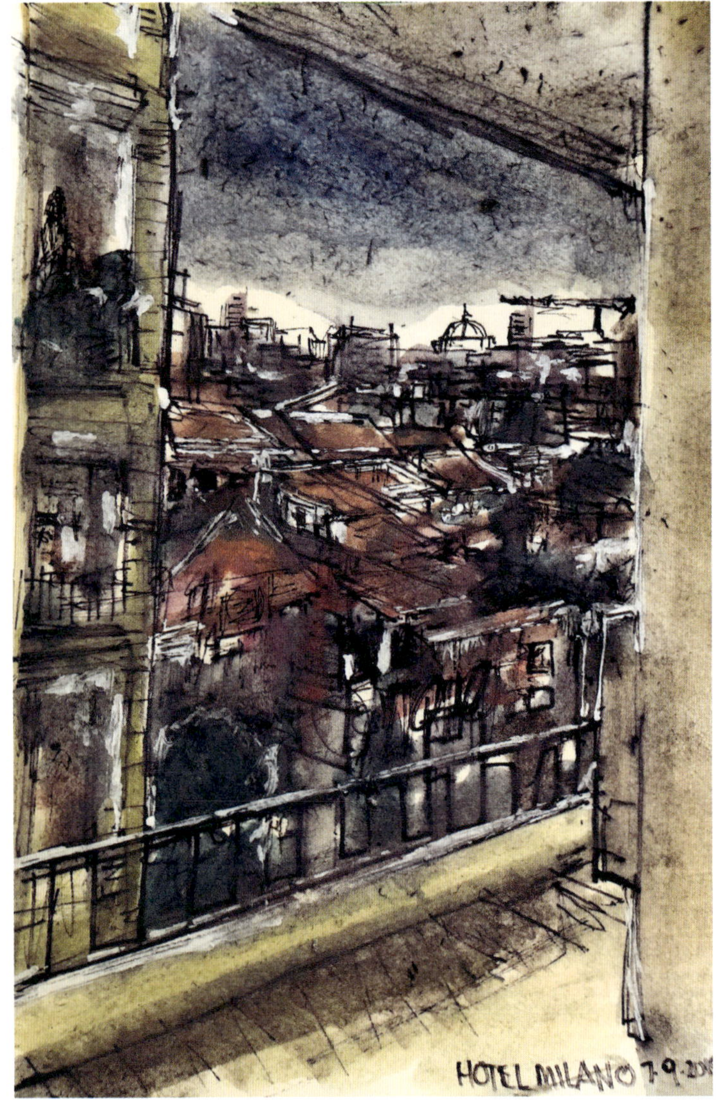

We had a lot of hotel time. While some people might have decided to go out to a city club or the hotel bar or whatever, I turned my room into an art studio. The first piece is passing through Betanzos in Spain on our way to the airport, and the second is a view through a seventh floor window at the Palazzo Parigi Hotel in Milan.

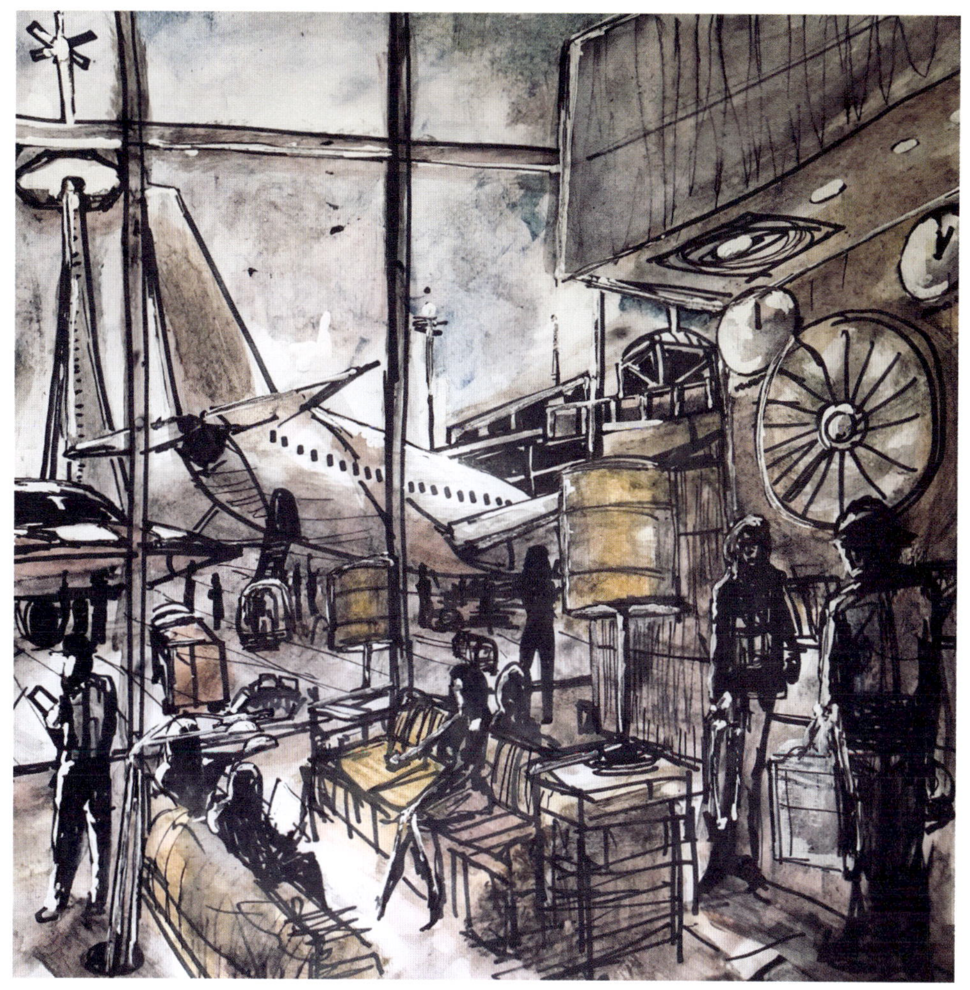

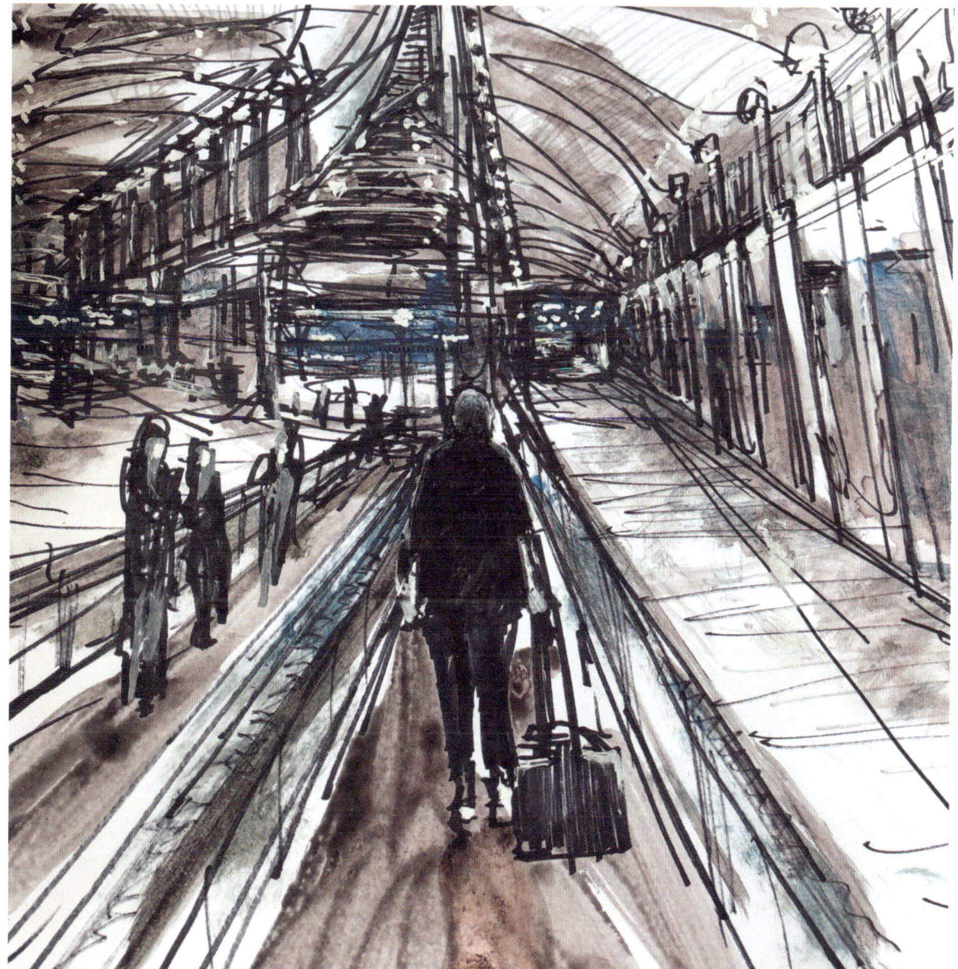

Two very different airports during the tour. At the top is Manchester Airport pre-show, and the second is Istanbul International Airport in Turkey.

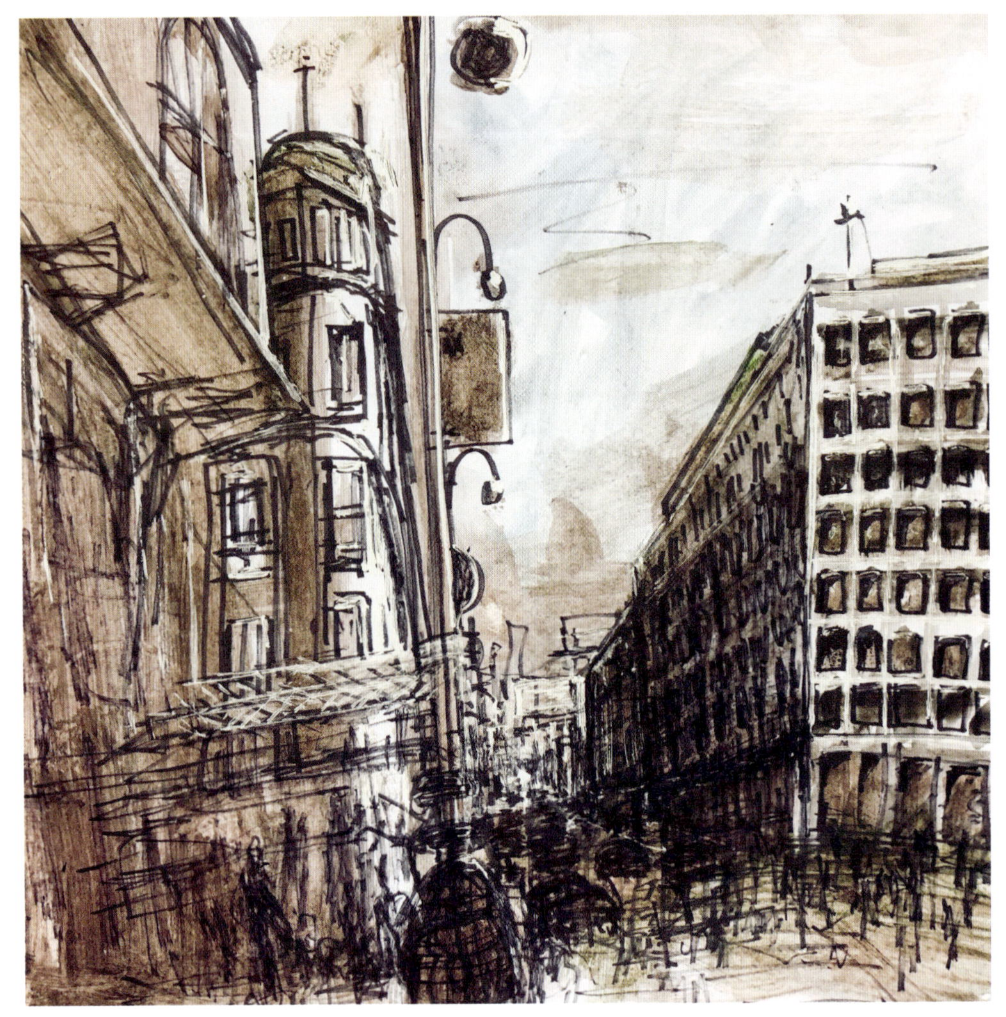

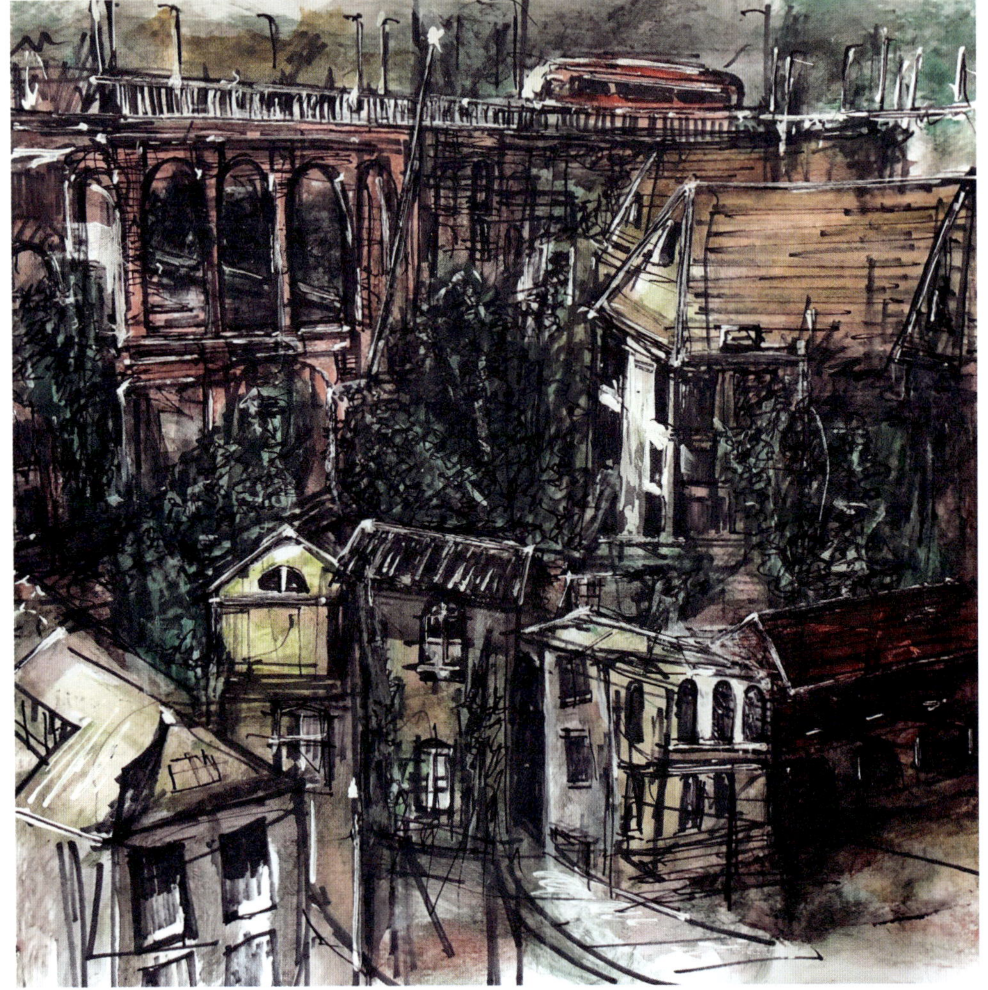

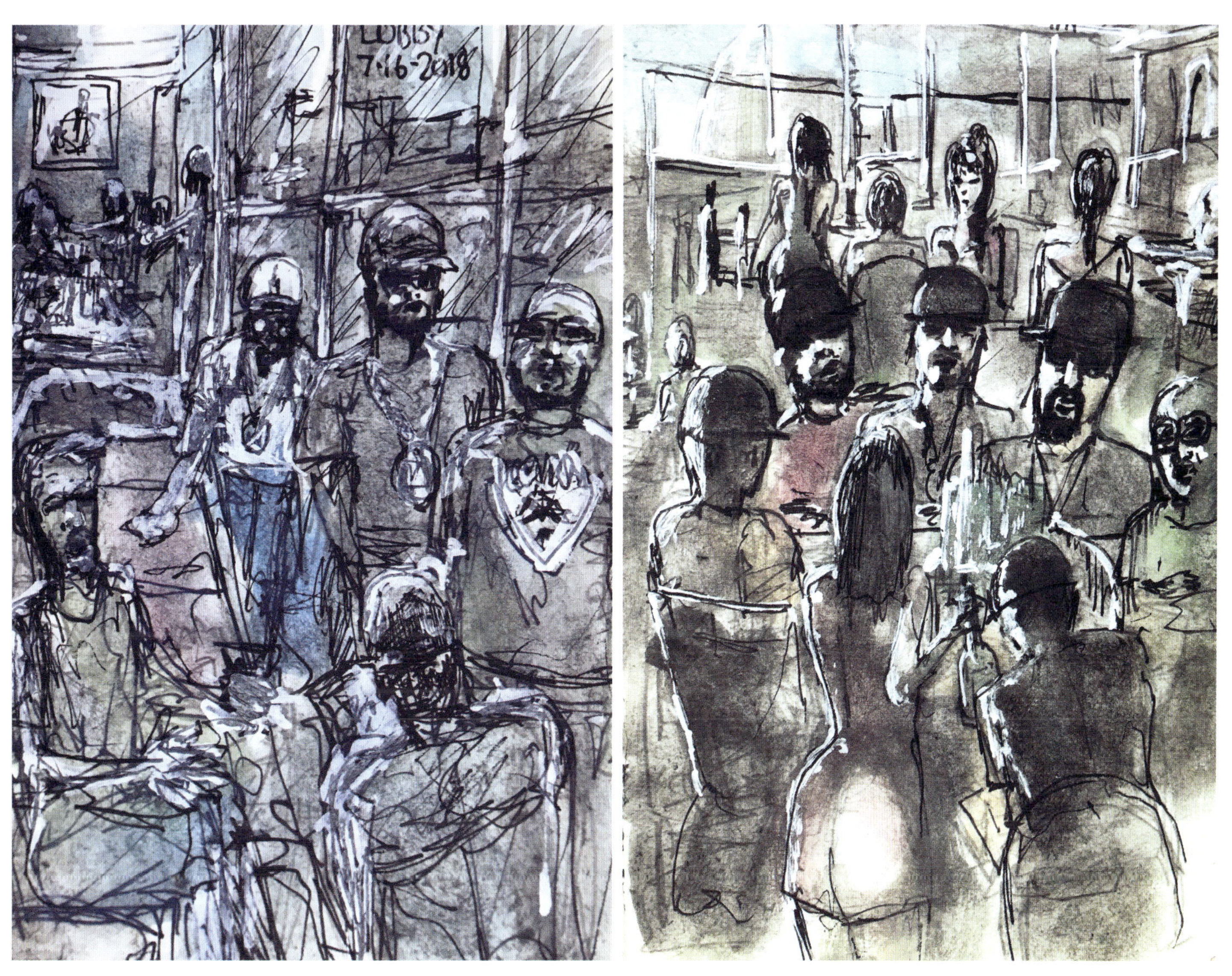

The piece on the right was the lobby of our hotel in London post-concert. On the left is a beach restaurant meeting we had in Barcelona, Spain, in July 2018.

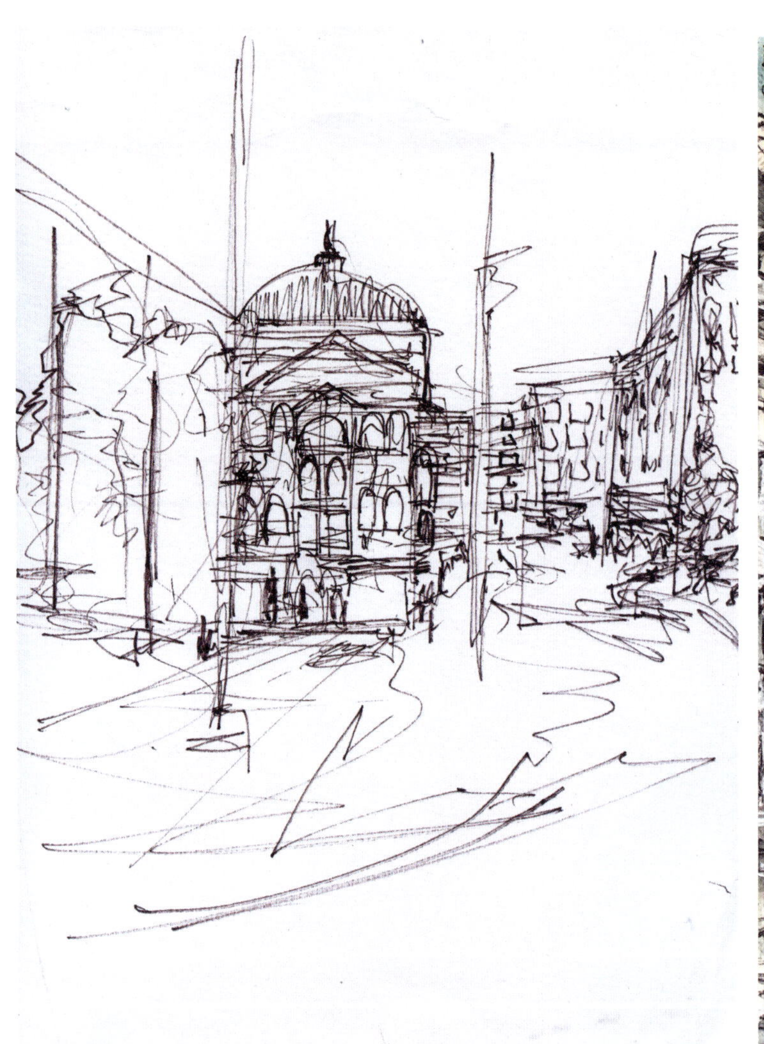

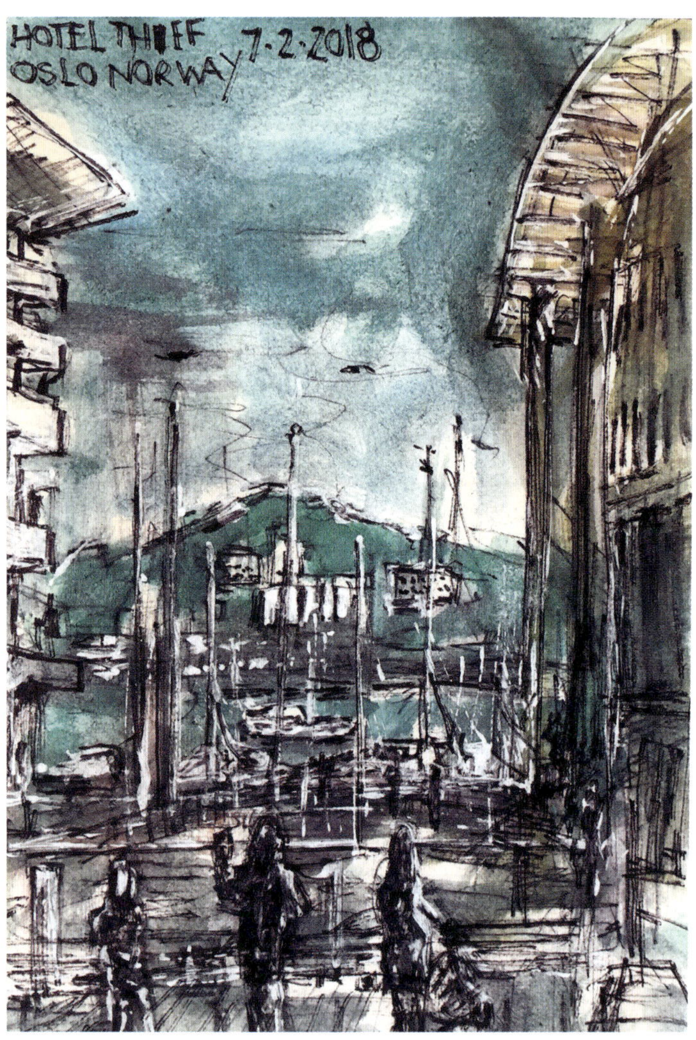

While travelling through Oslo, Norway, this central area in the city caught my eye.

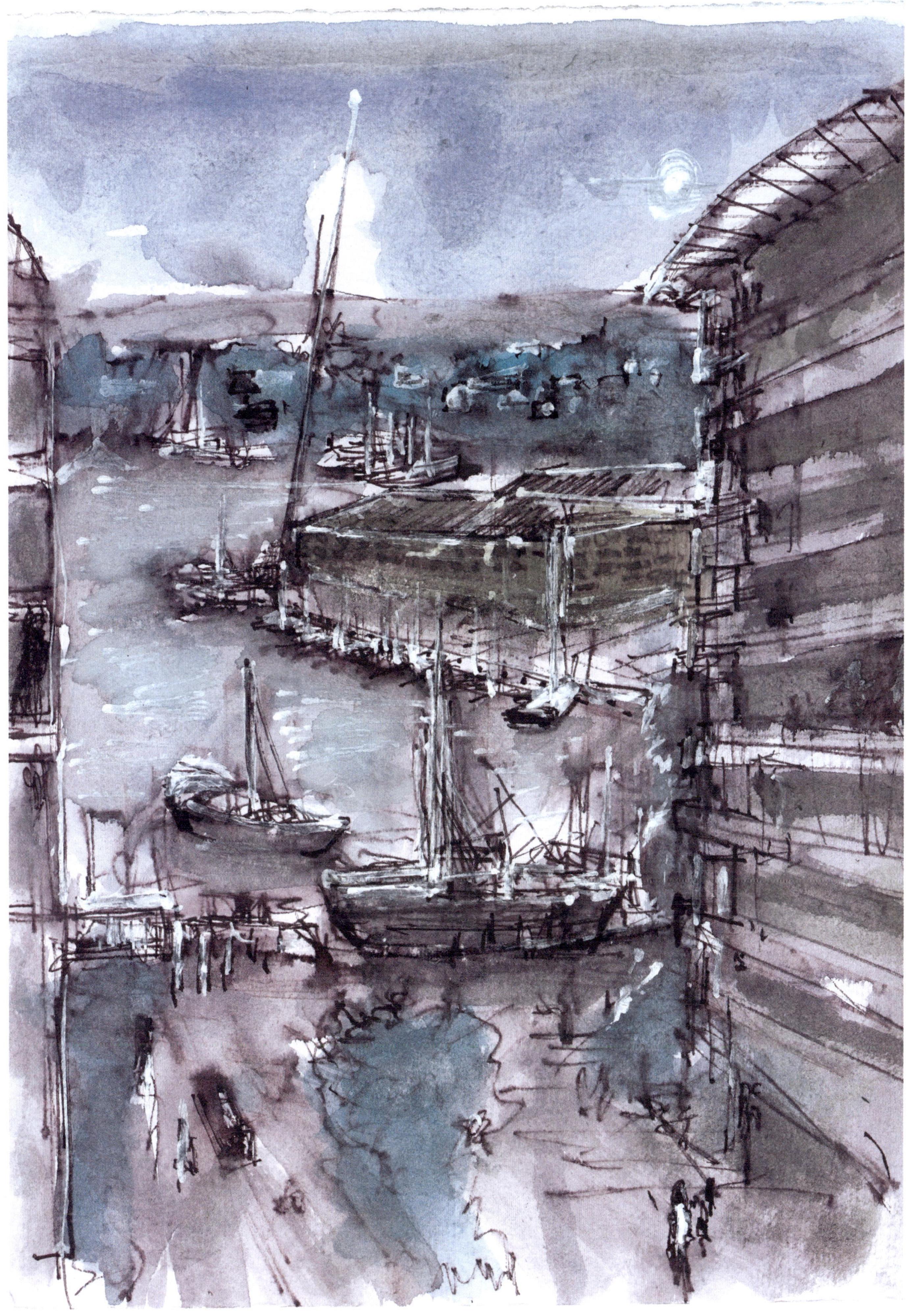

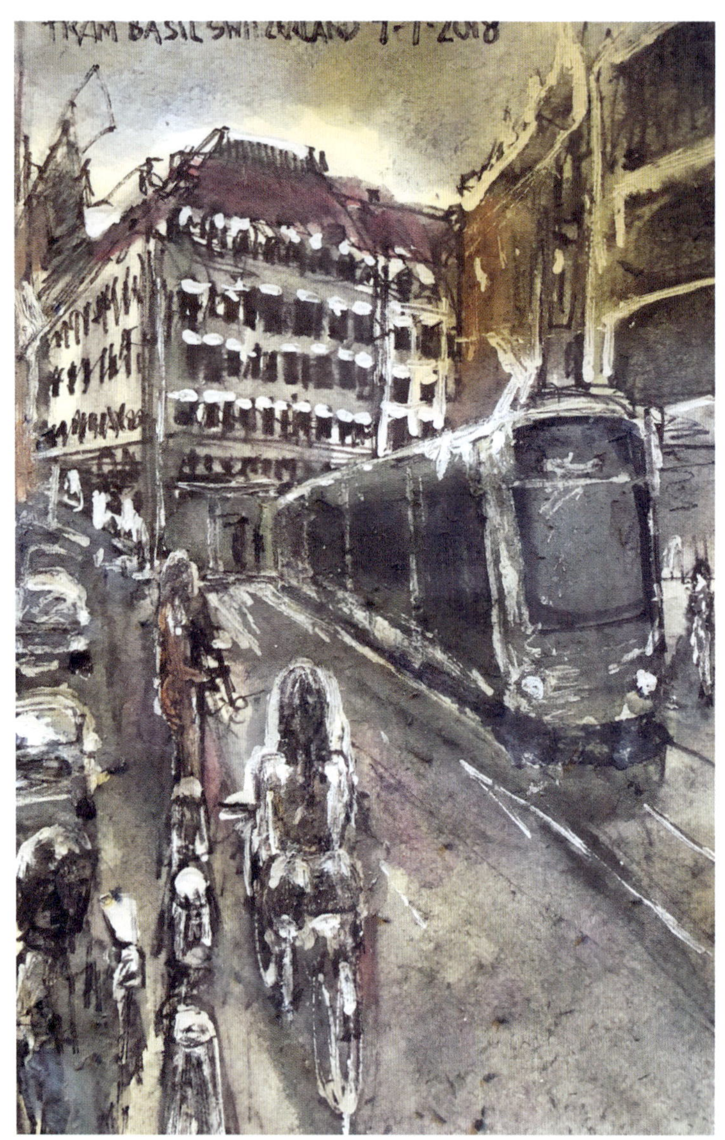
TRAM BASIL SWITZERLAND 1-7-2018

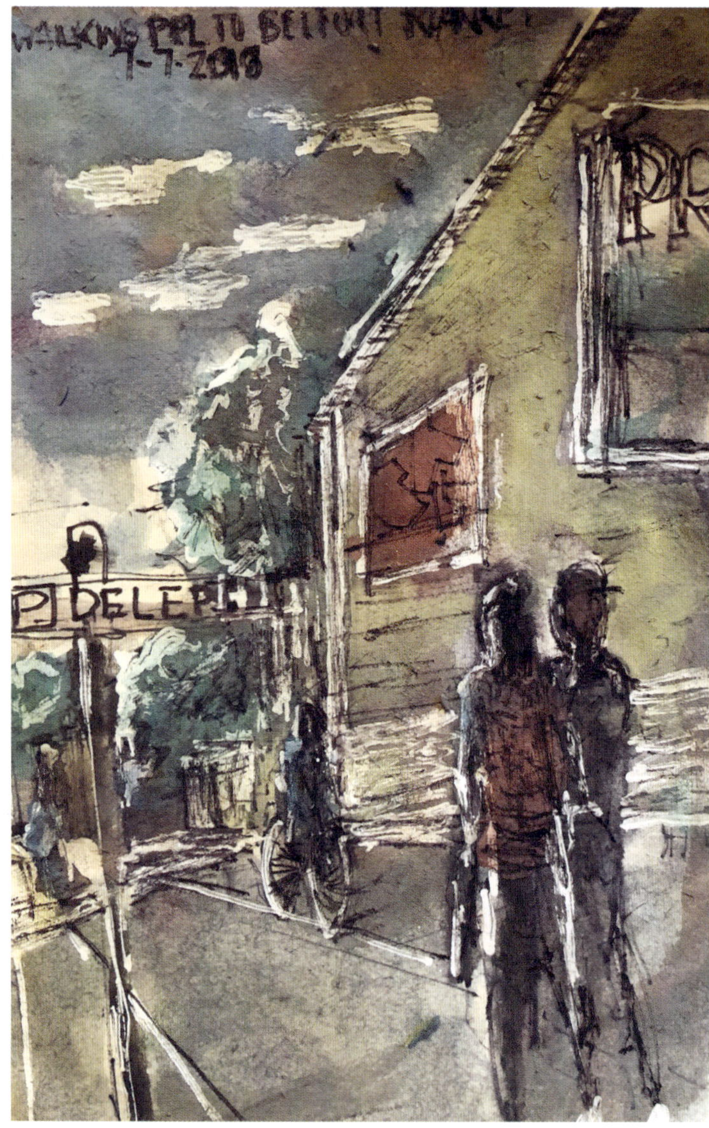
1-7-2018

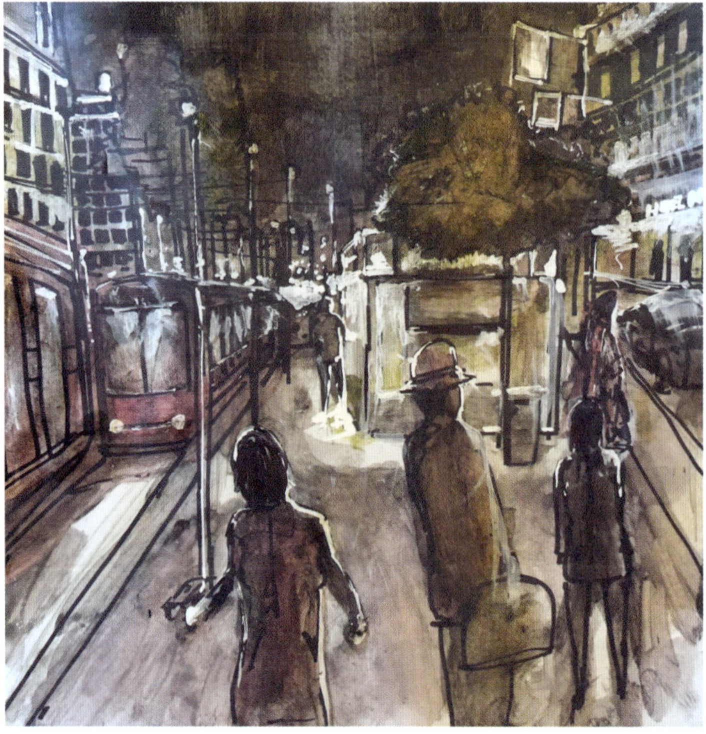

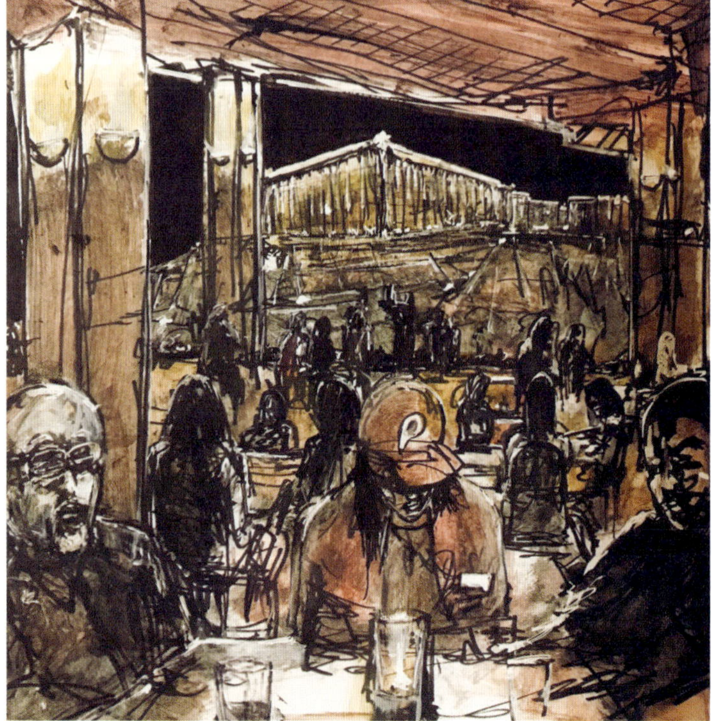

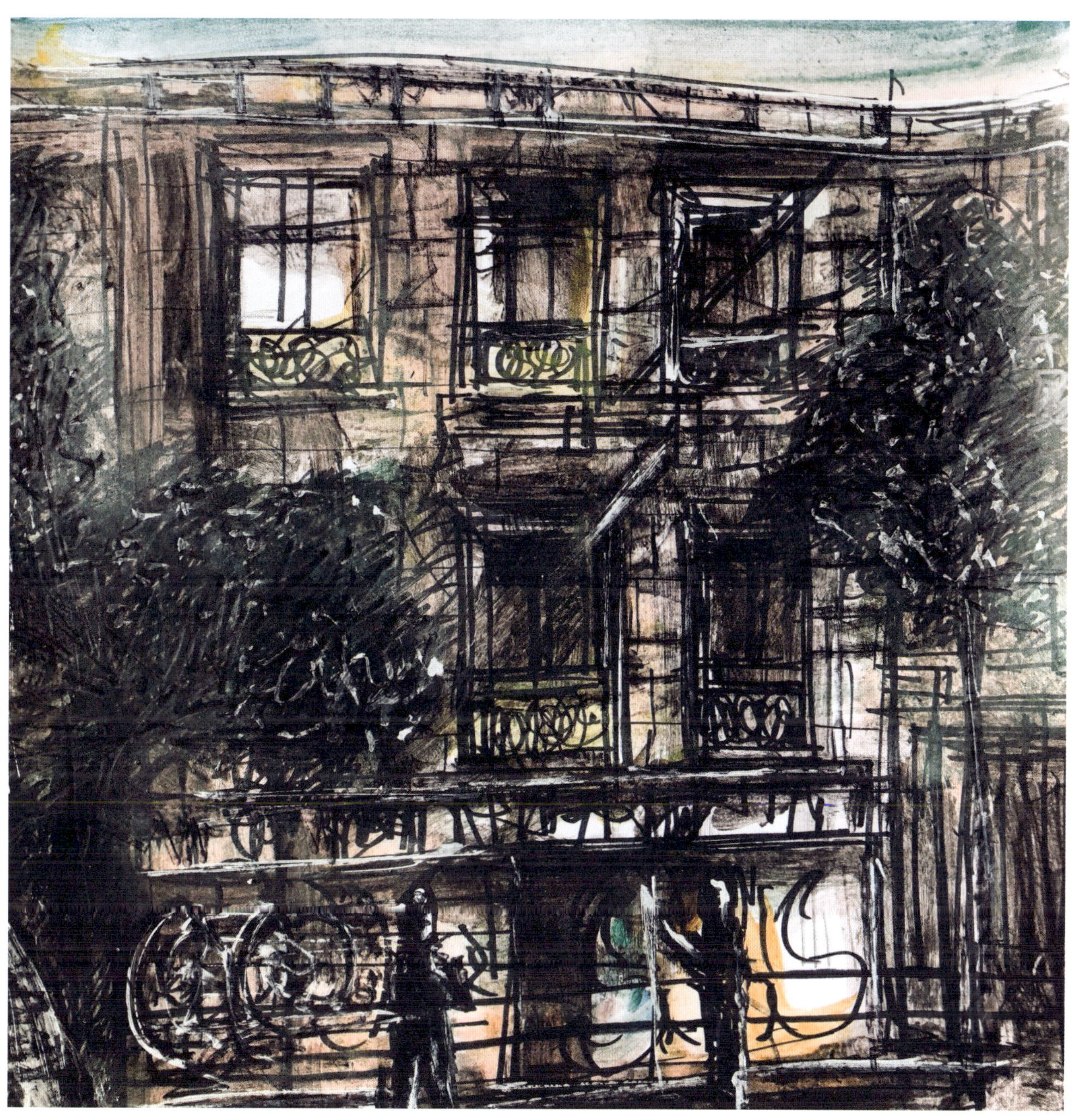

Pieces from these World Tour Sessions have ended up in four newspapers in four different countries and languages. It shows that social media can be used for progressive things too. It also shows young entertainers on tour that there is always something you can do to fill your down-time. No hotel wrecking.

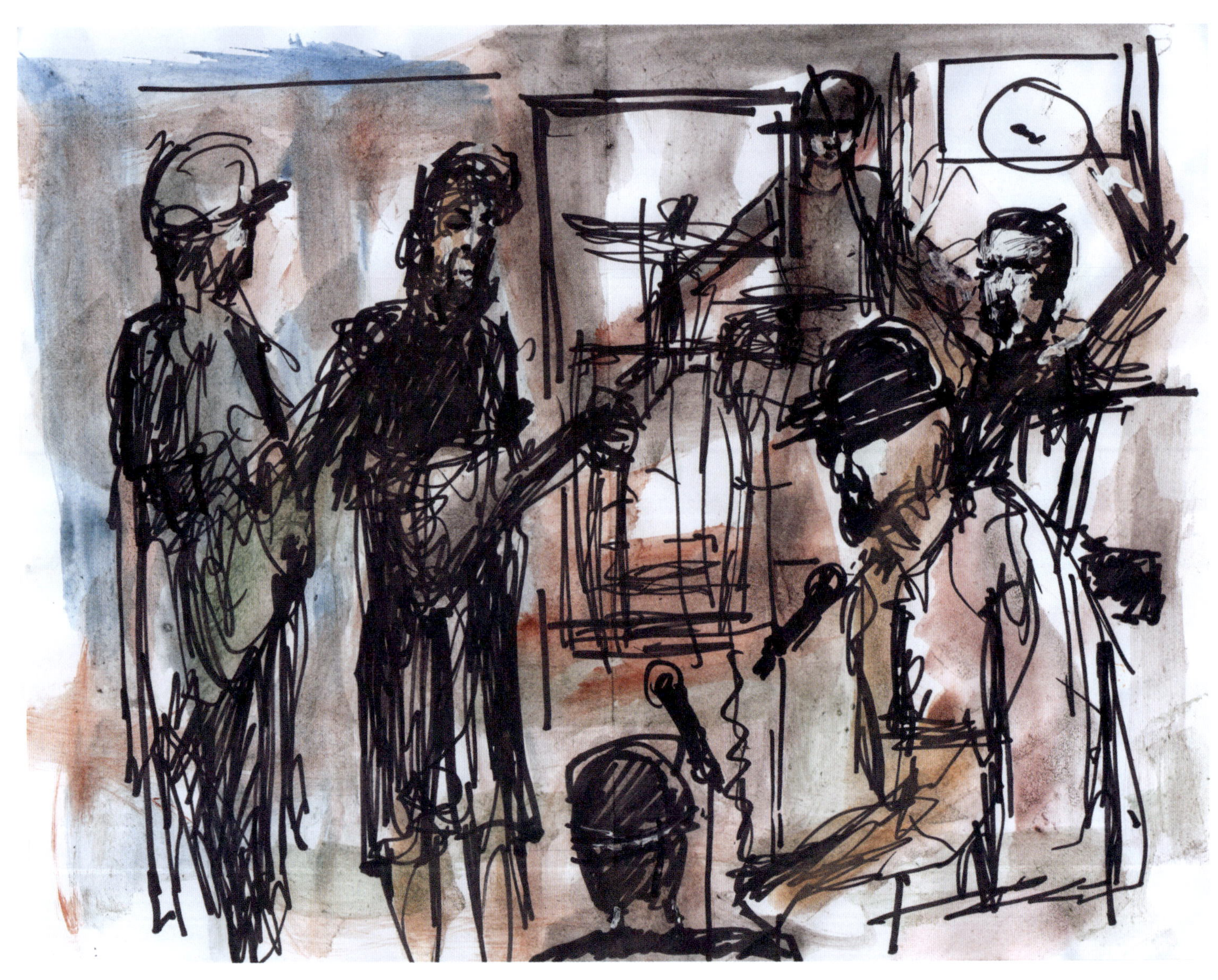

Oh man, it was a four-year university of brotherhood. Seeing the way the rock world operates gave us things to bring back into the hip-hop world. There was never one bad day – it was run like a machine. We do the thing in rap and hip-hop, but I'll tell you this much: every night we got a standing ovation for four years straight.

But it had to close out. We had to go back to our thing; Cypress had to go back, Rage Against the Machine had to reform. It happens. It's like a play, you go to the theatre and they say, 'You know what? This is the last show.'

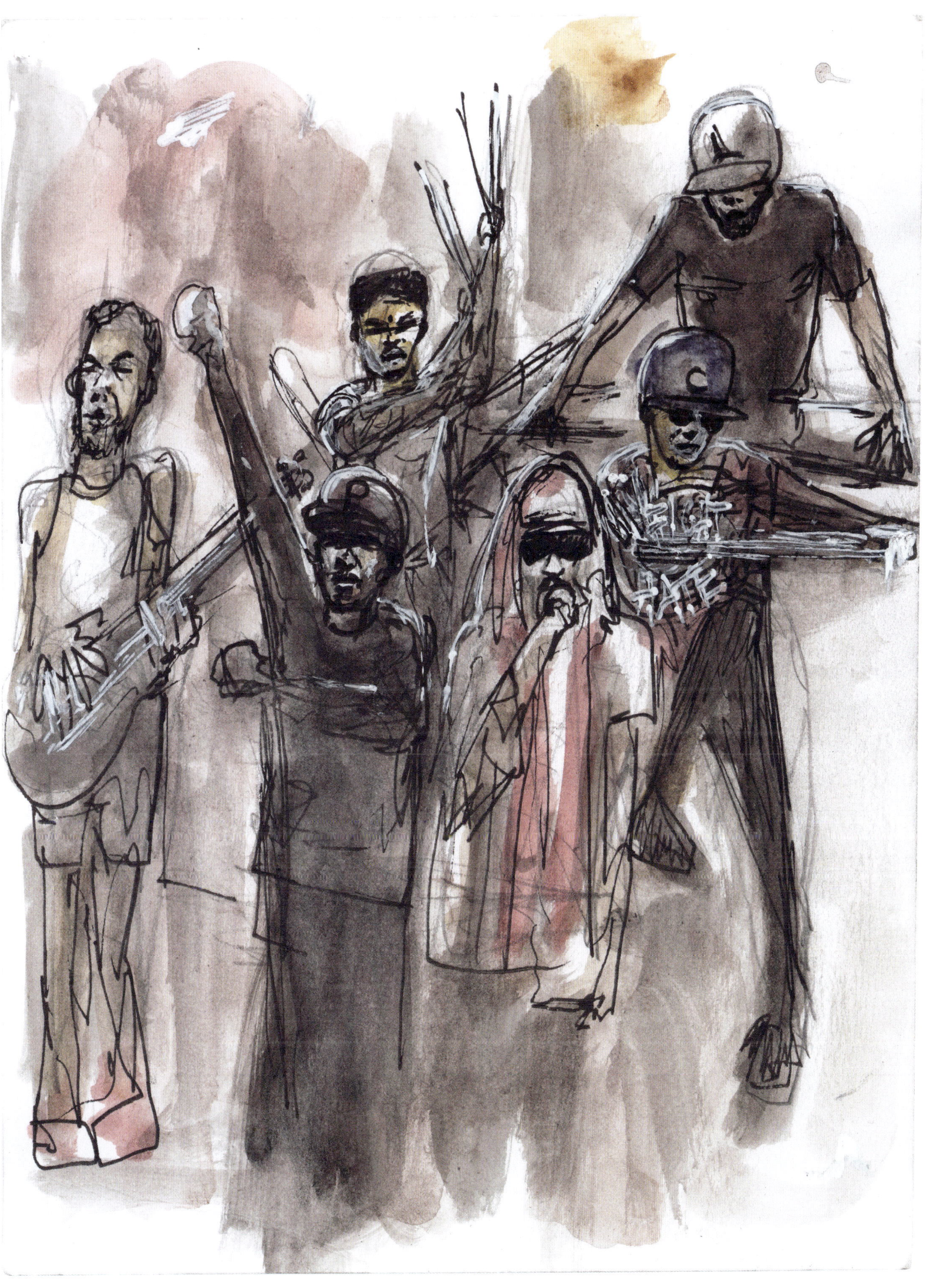

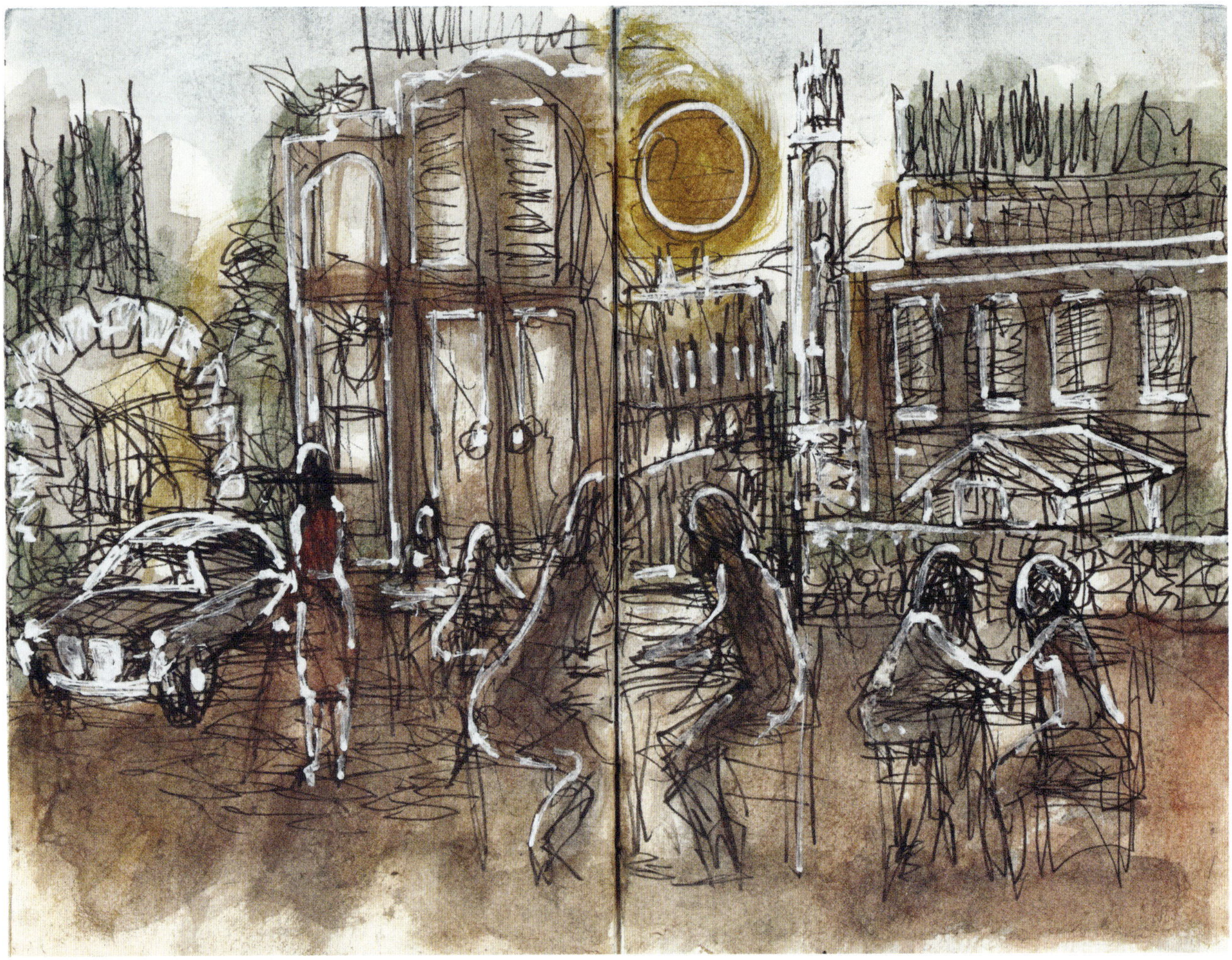

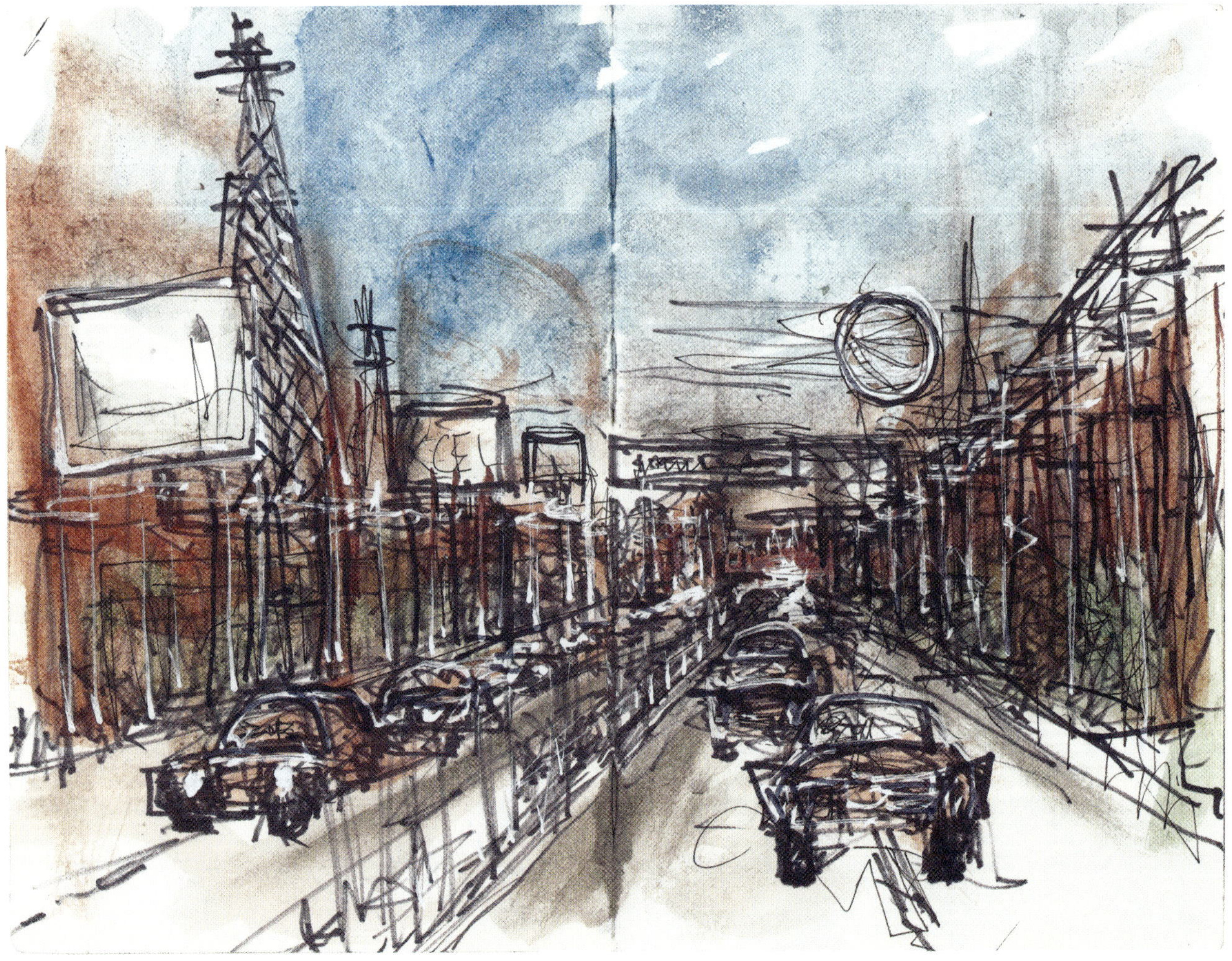

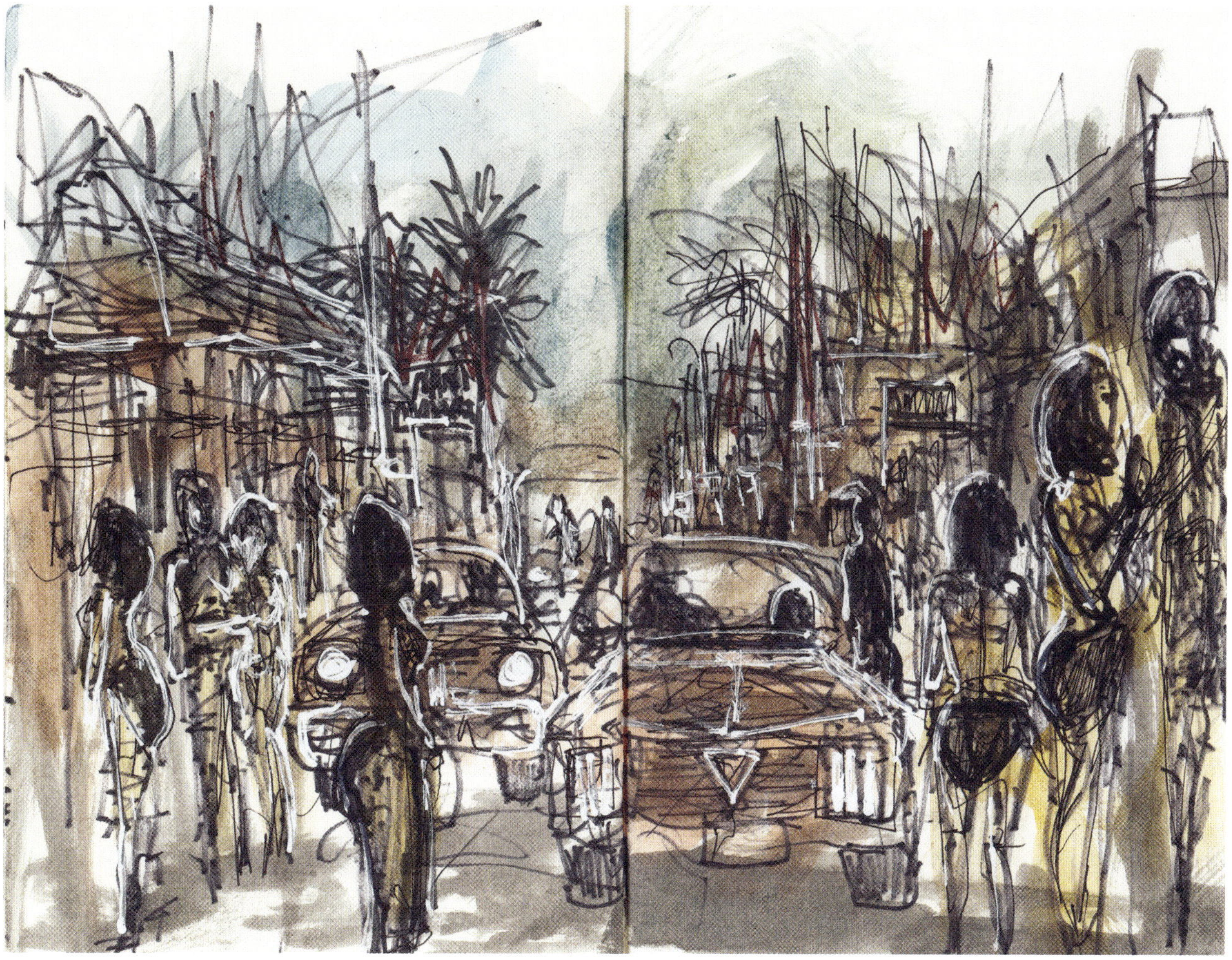

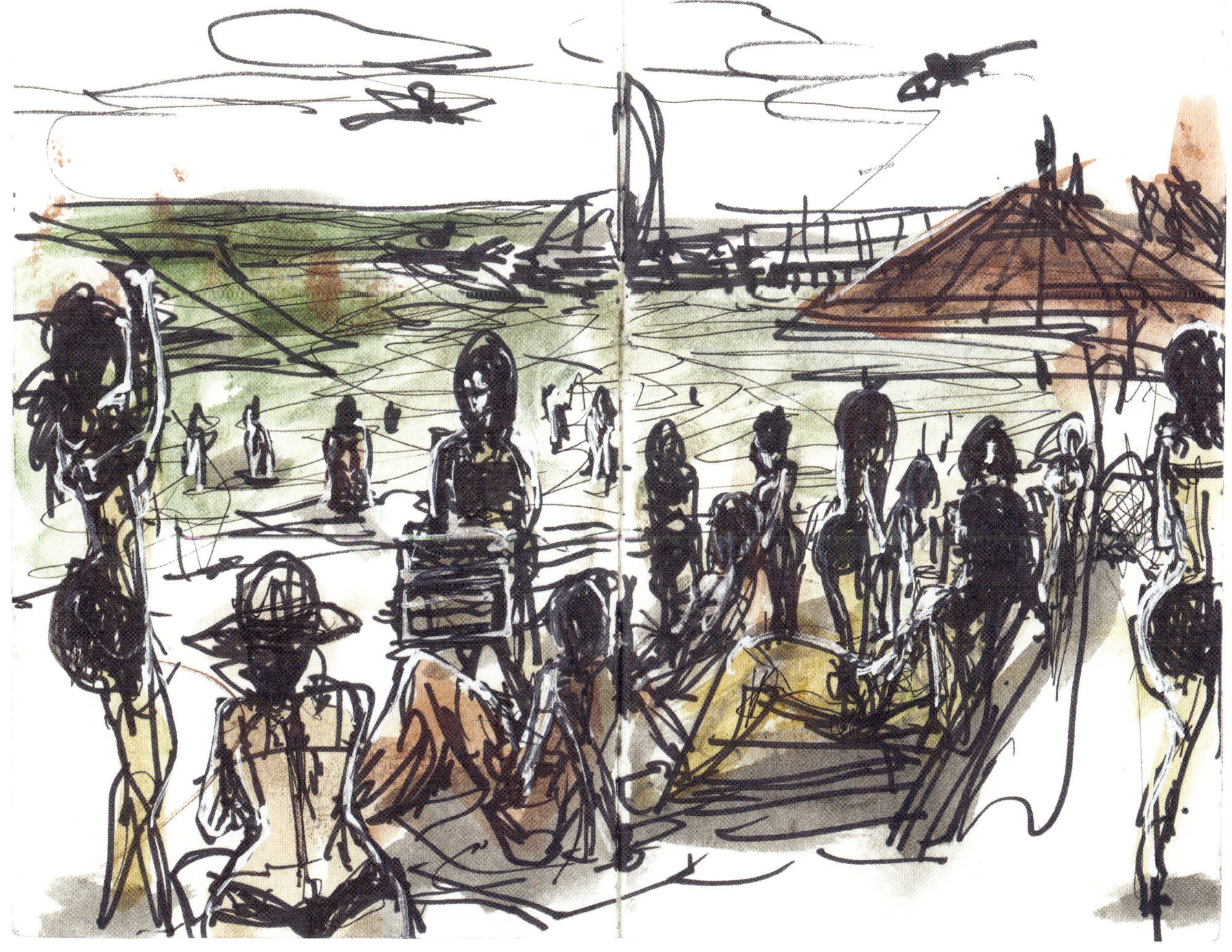

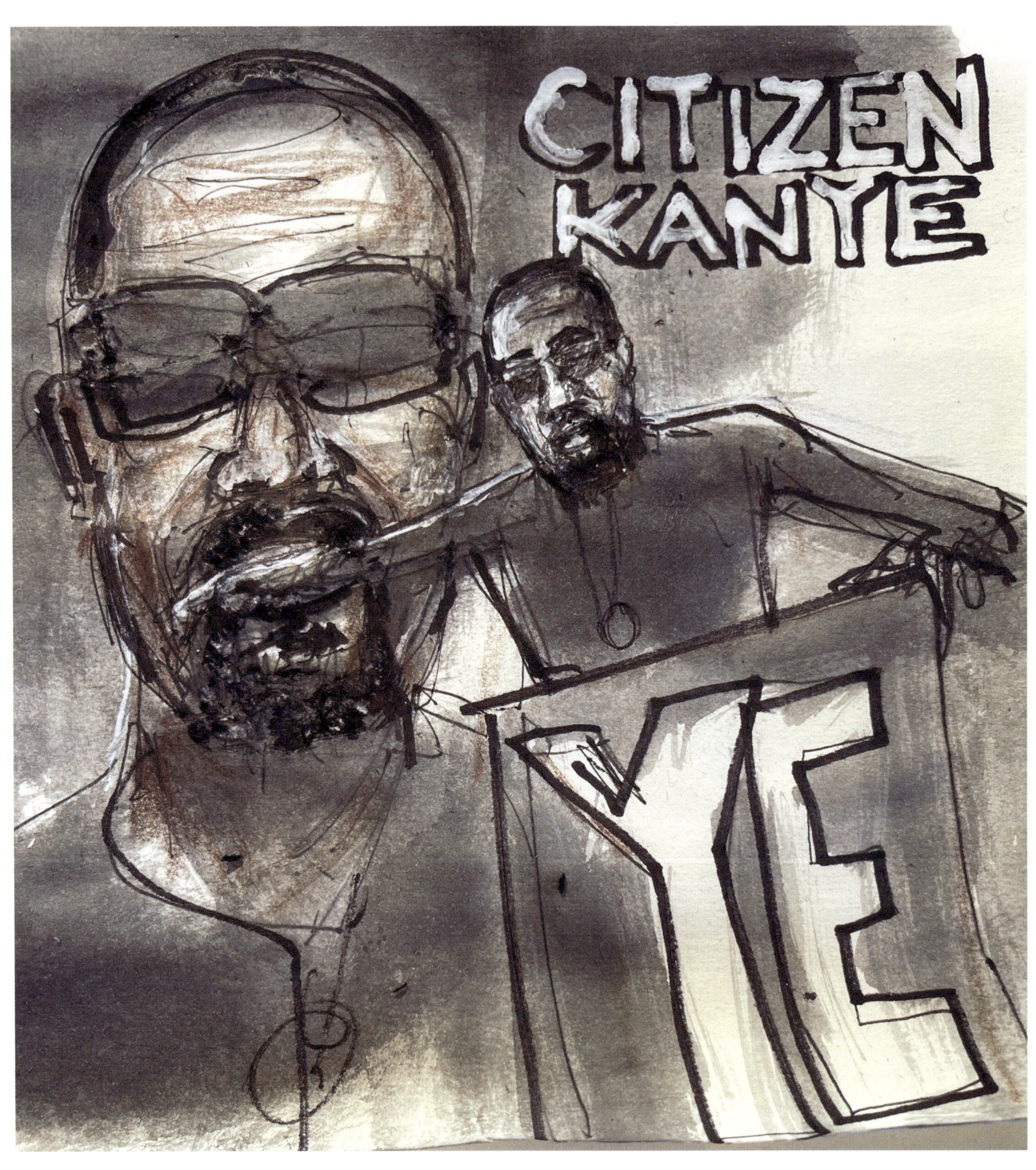

In my opinion, Kanye West doesn't just have fans, he has disciples. He done turned into a 21st-century cultural religion.

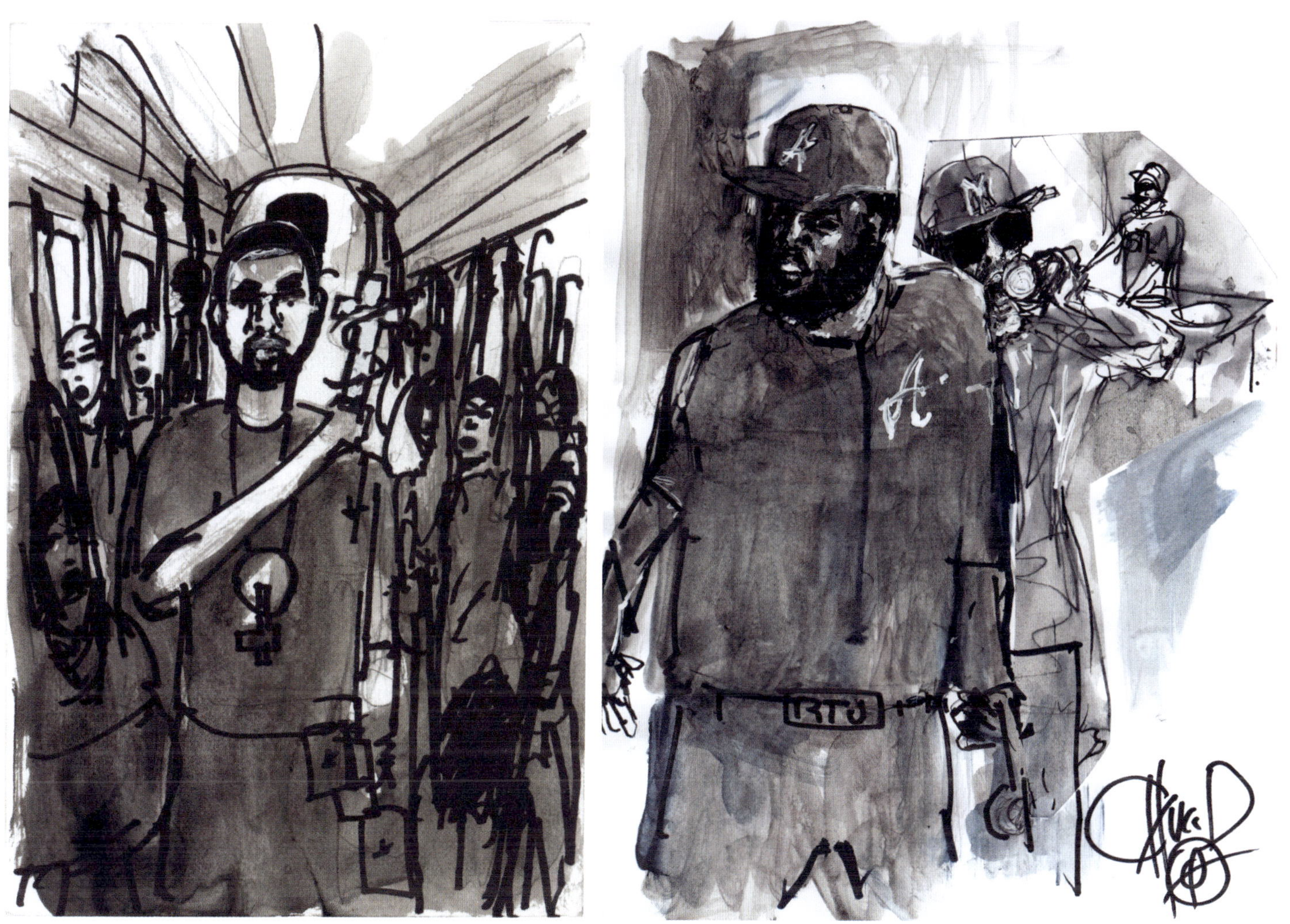

I loved the Run the Jewels (pictured right) song 'Close Your Eyes (And Count to Fuck)' – Zack de la Rocha added his instrument to the already wise Southern vet Killer Mike and El-P rounding the spit over his lab explosives. This record is like running into a Pujols swing head first, with jarring info slicing at you. If you love tender rhymes, this song is intentionally out to hurt you – with damn good reason.

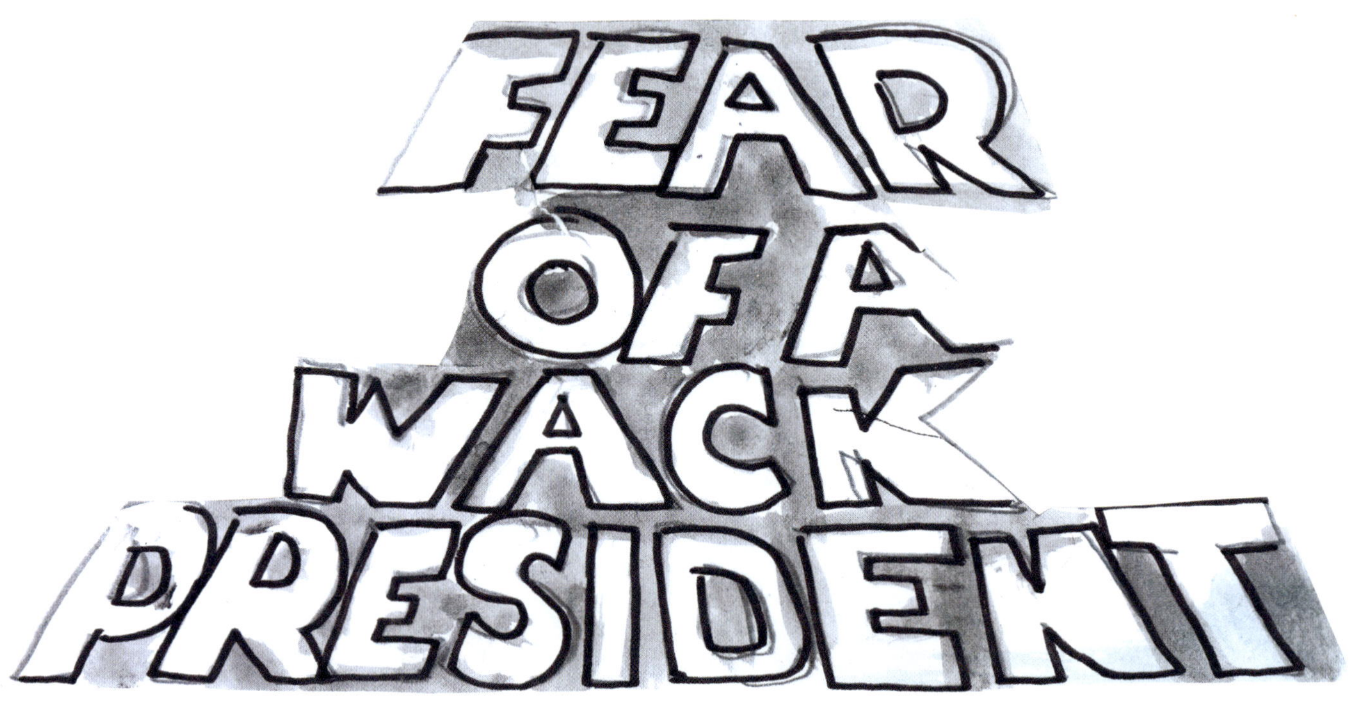

People are astonished and shocked by Donald Trump. They treat him as if he's a haunted house – they're afraid, but they go in anyway... The sign says, 'Stay away!' and they keep saying: 'Oh my God, it's so scary!' Then they see a head roll down the staircase. And they *still* think: 'What's up them steps?'

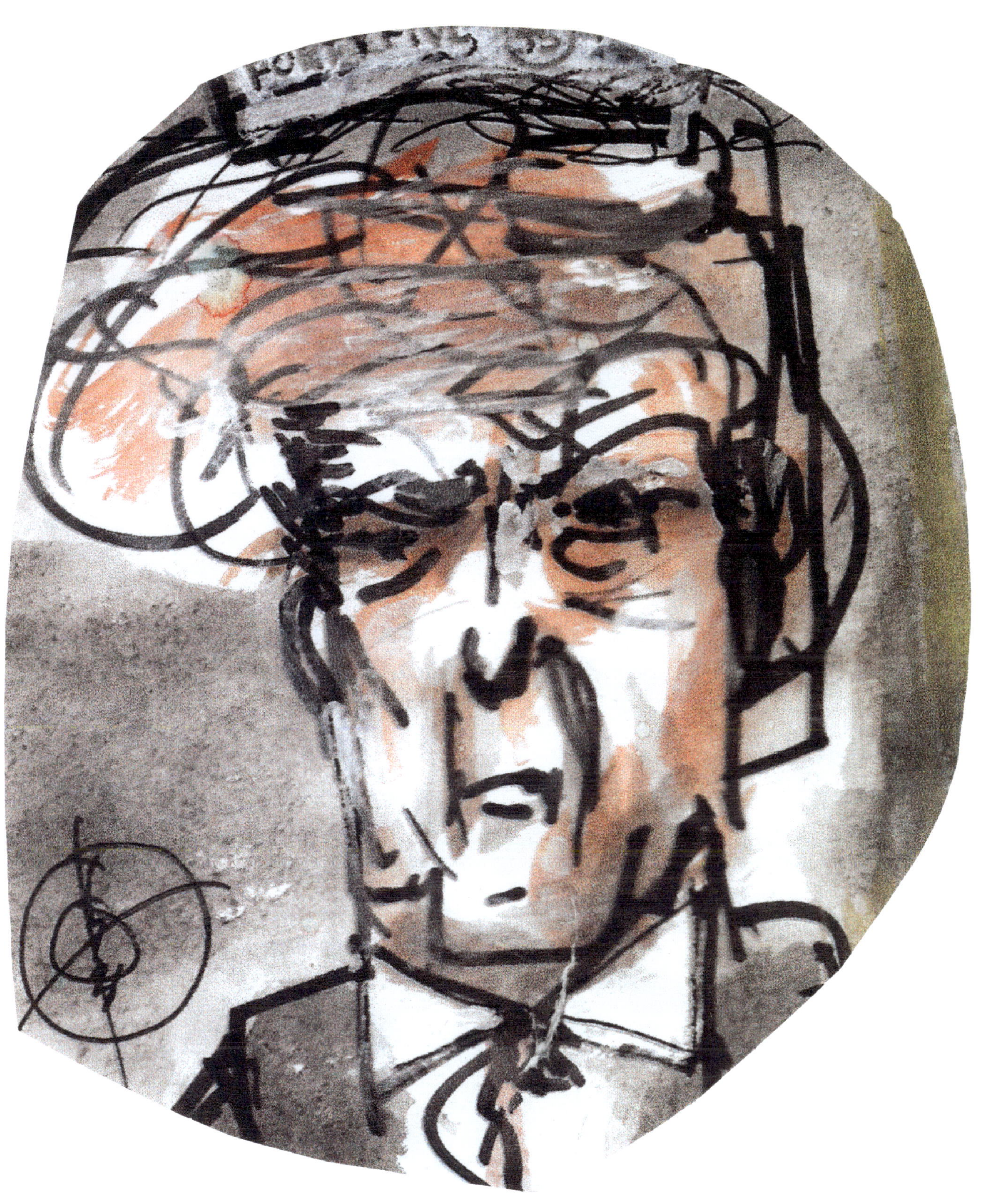

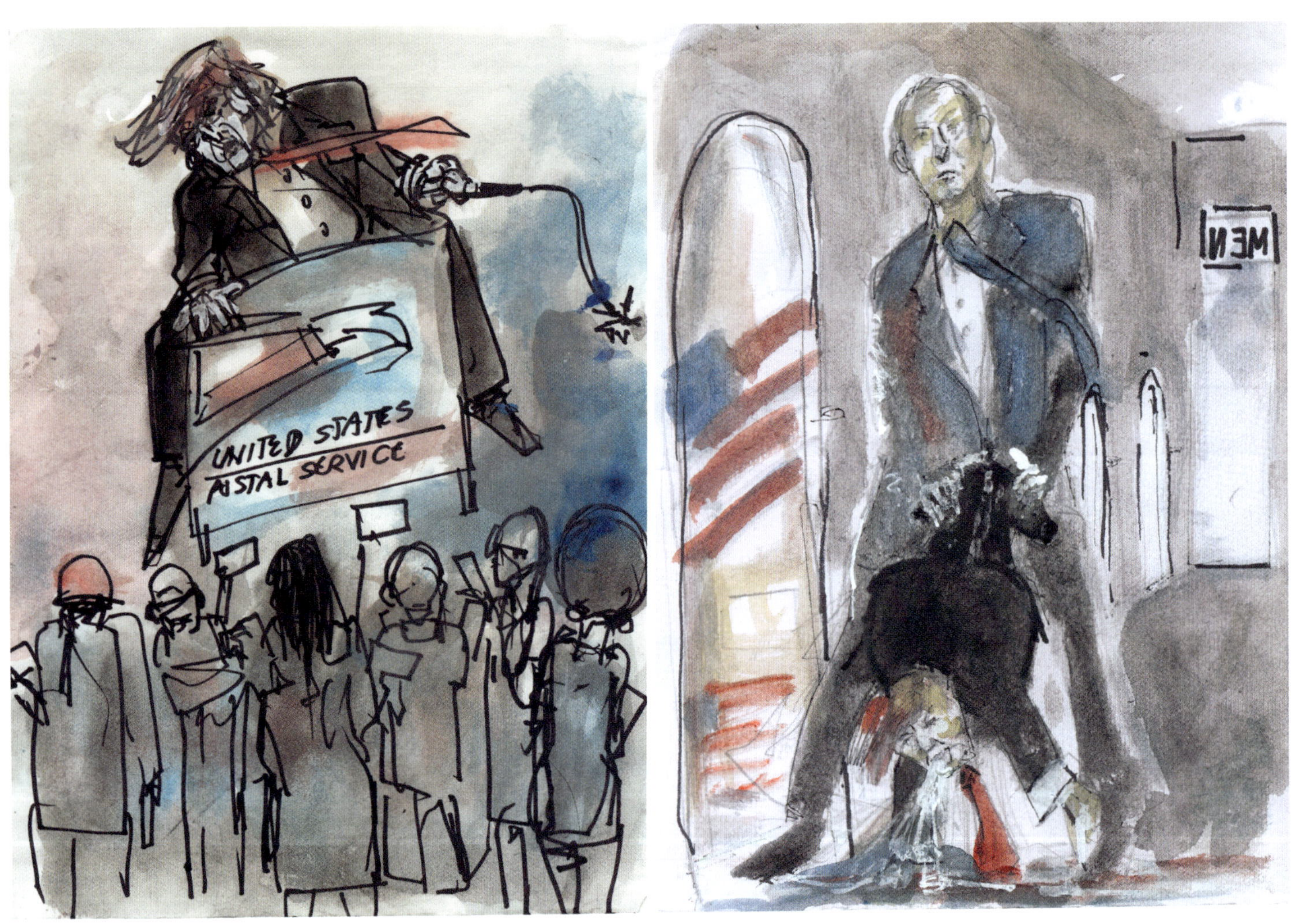

To see Trump end up in the seat of responsibility was a call to arms from the moment he got there. We went from Obama, who we had some differences with, to a person who didn't look like they were fit for any job, let alone a job in which you're responsible for millions of people. The United States was completely polarised. People were spreading hatred against black people everywhere, so we had to fight him. By fighting Trump we were fighting against twenty-first century fascism.

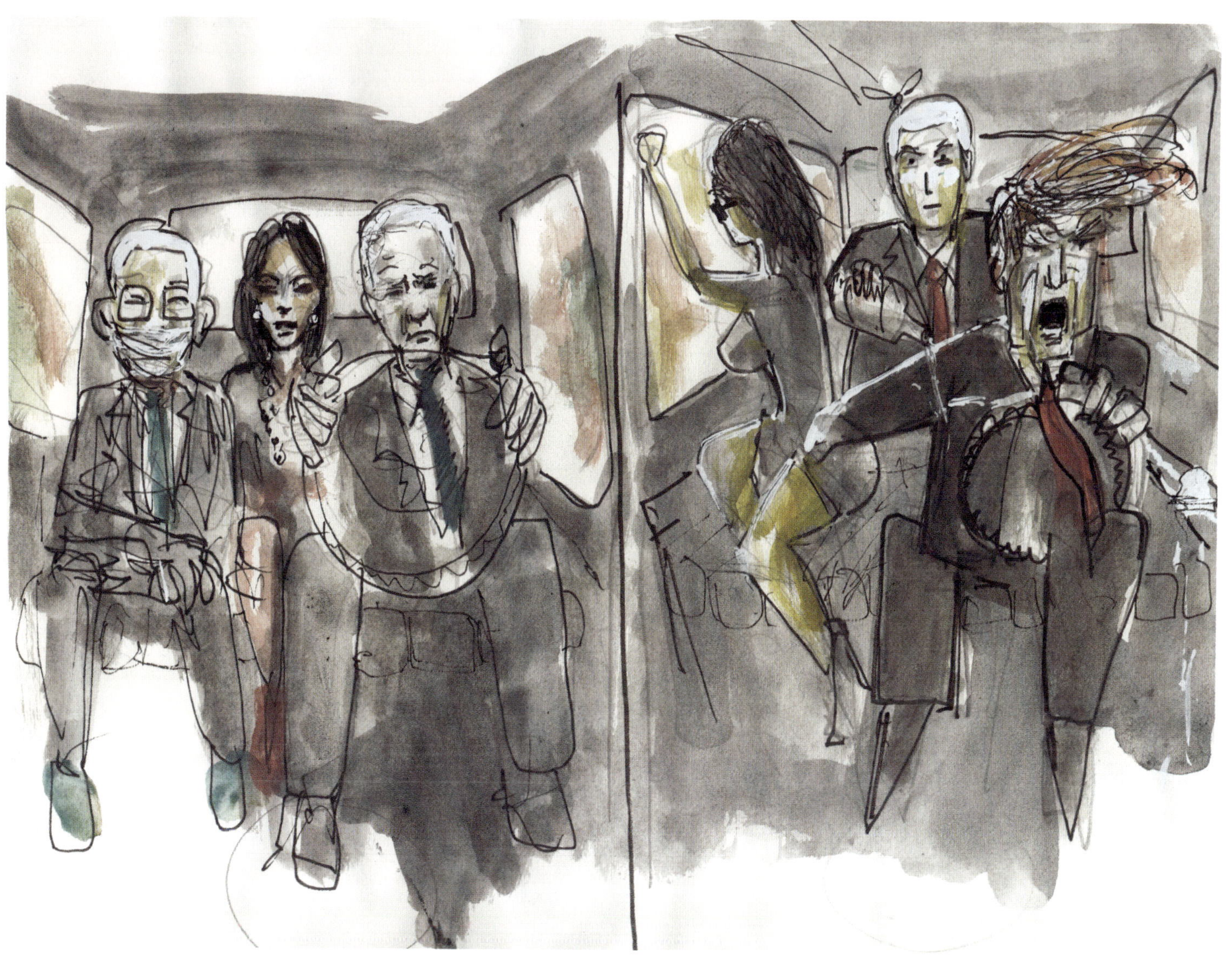

The voting system is broken, outdated and, a lot of the time, corrupt. I'm always going to tell people what's going on, challenge information and get involved in the process. My involvement with Rock the Vote in 1996 gave me a platform to be able to challenge people. It's very important for me to be involved with MTV, BET, major networks and the internet.

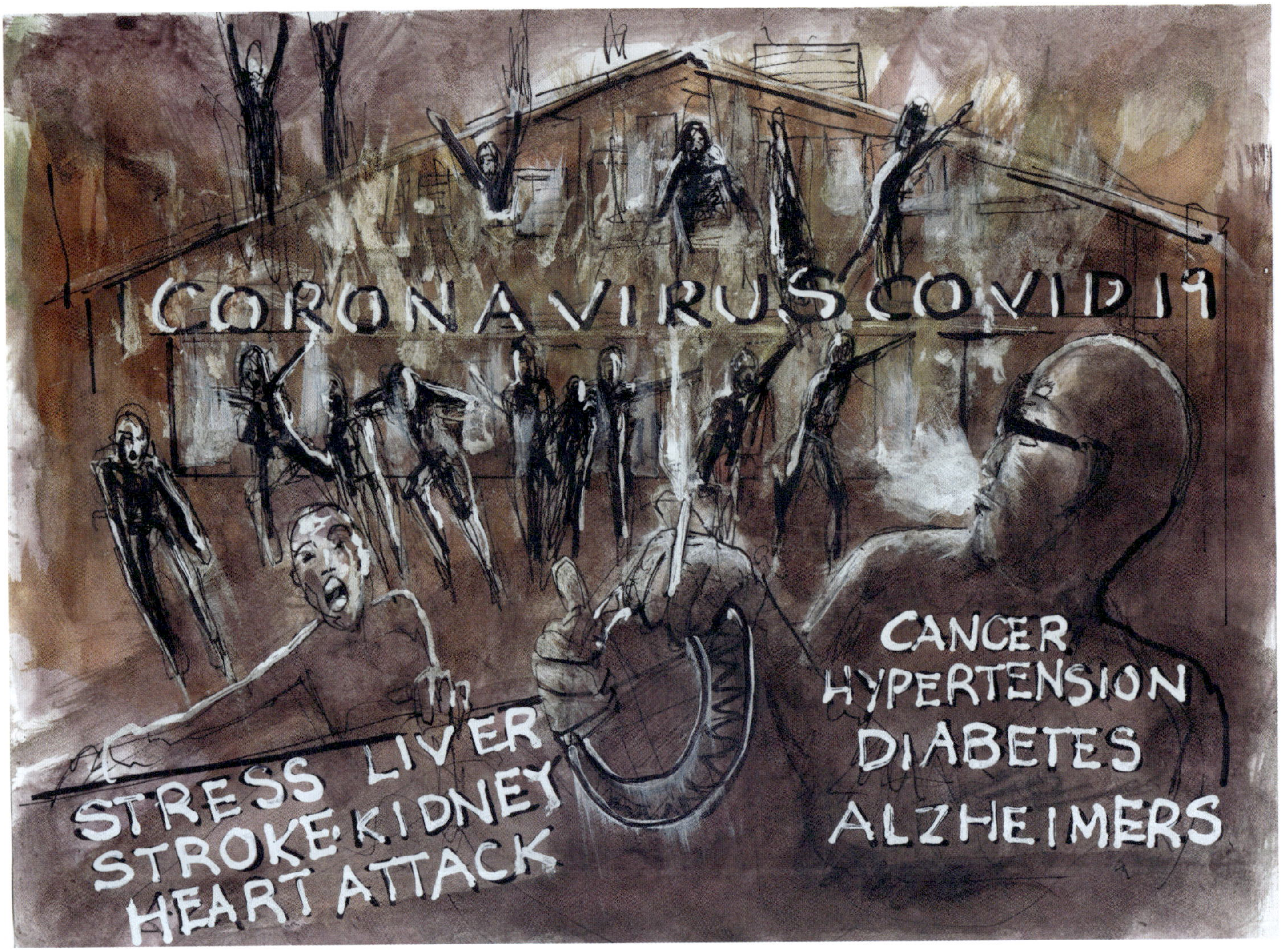

2020 was a crazy year, unlike any we've seen, yet the dude at the top had the momentum of a divisive regime.

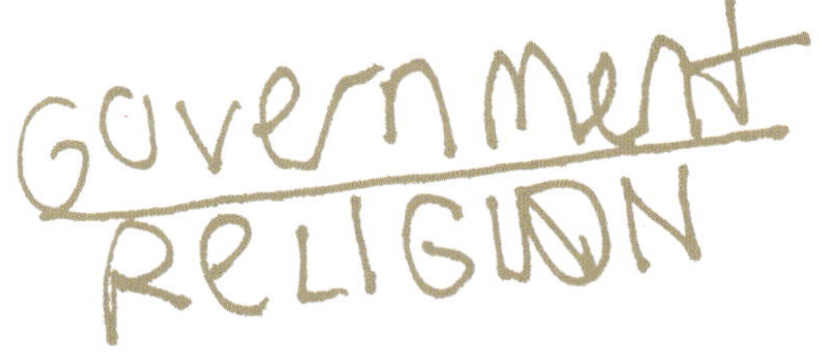

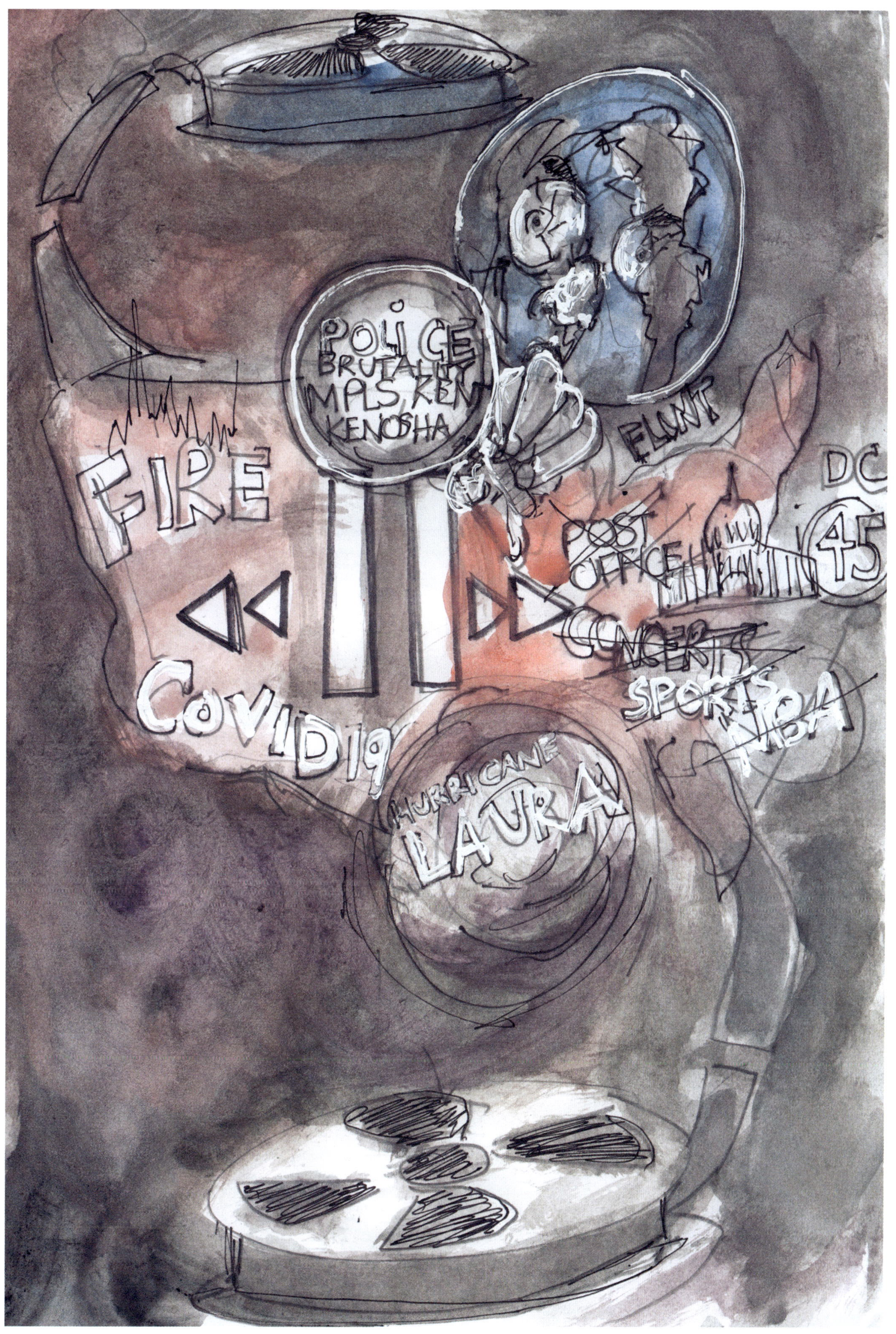
POLICE
BRUTALITY
MPLS, KEN
KENOSHA
FLINT
FIRE
DC
POST OFFICE
45
CONCERTS
SPORTS
NBA
COVID19
HURRICANE
LAURA

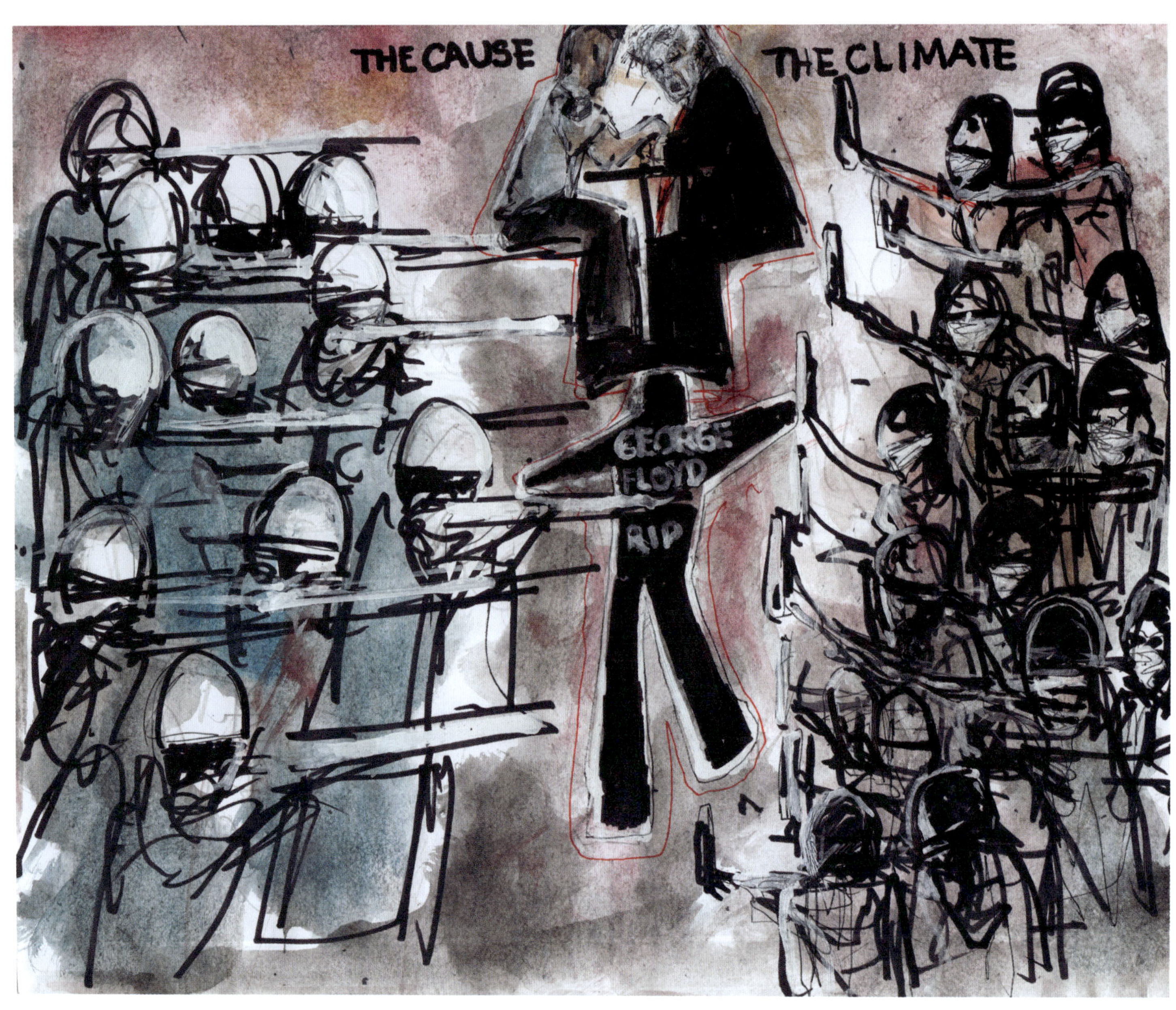

The pandemic already came with a lot of pent-up aggravation and scattered information, and then there was the murder of George Floyd.

I think that the officer in Minneapolis knew what he was doing. It looked like he was making a point to the cameras. Many people in authority get twisted and caught up on their own power, that's what I thought Derek Chauvin was on. Taking that life just like that...

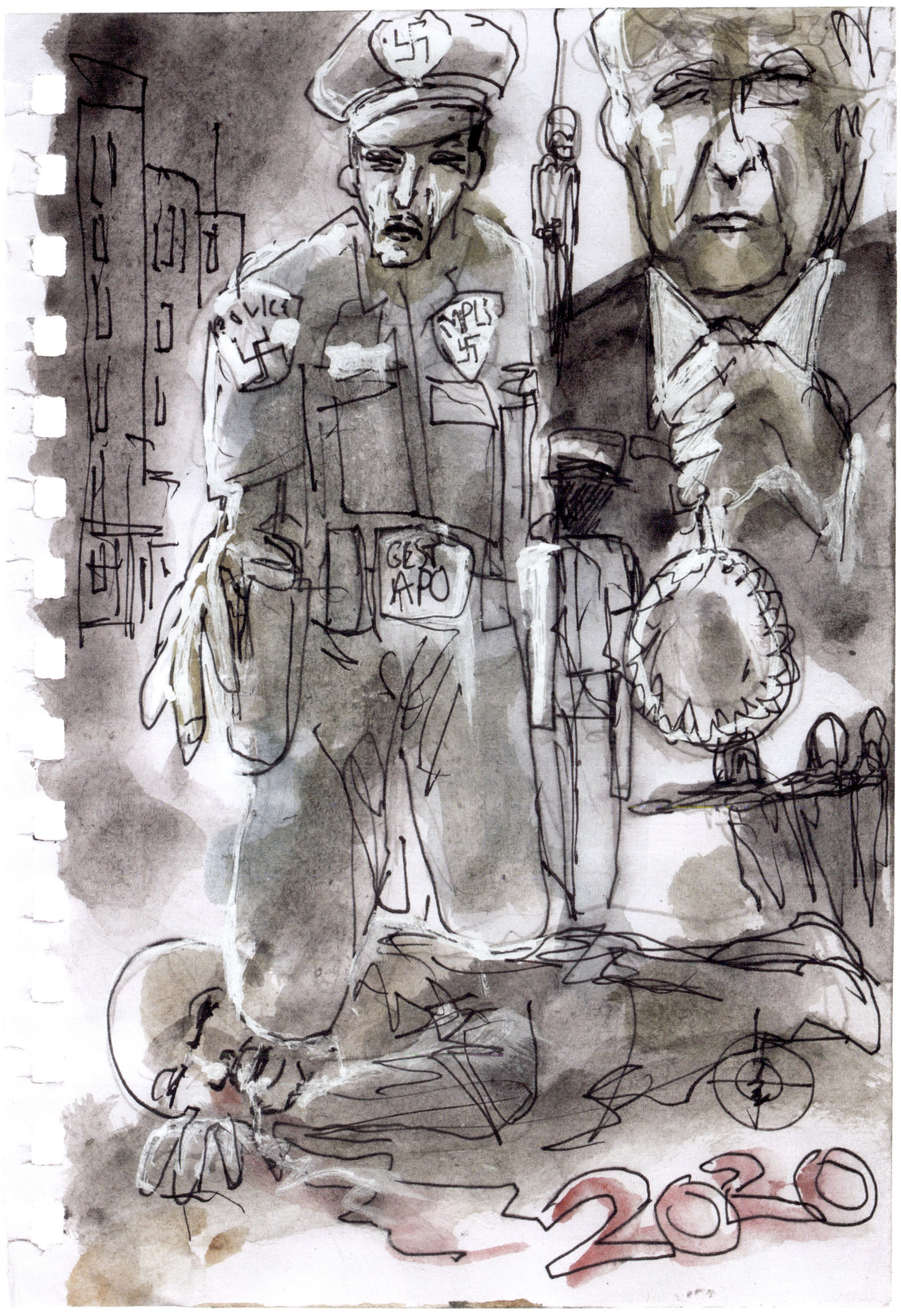
POLICE
MPLS
GEST
APO
2020

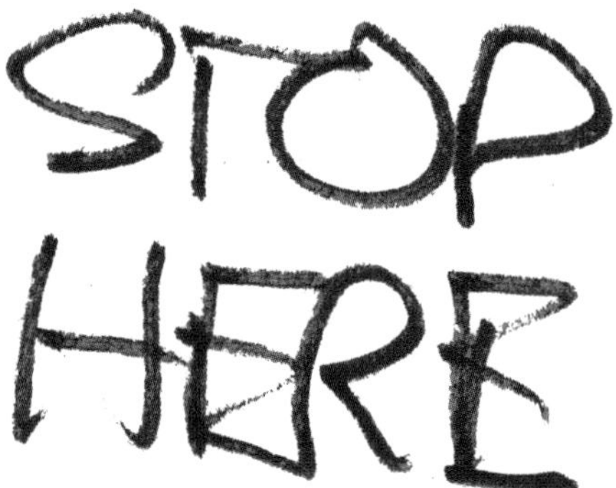

'911 Is a Joke' was about how the emergency services don't come to black neighbourhoods on time. They get there whenever they get there, but when a call comes from a white neighbourhood they get there quickly.

When the police have guns and a licence to shoot, don't stand there running your mouth when they pull you over. Just humble yourself, because you can end up a dead man very easily. We have to be wise and rise above provocation.

I talk about the three Es of enforcement, economics and education. The song 'Get the Fuck Outta Dodge' is about the black community's lack of control over one of these: enforcement. We need police from our own community, who know our people and can understand the agendas and nuances of people of colour in the hood.

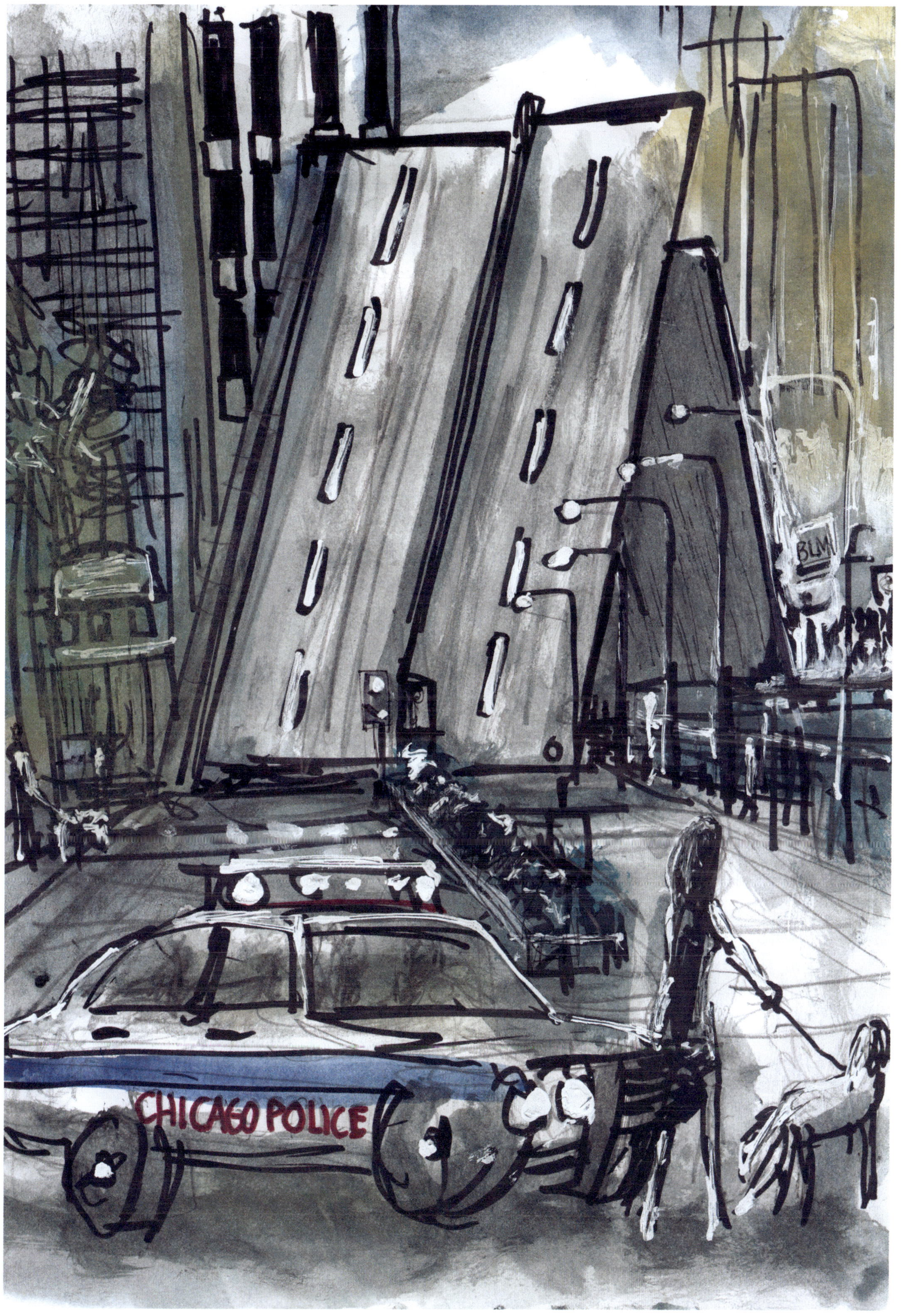
BLM
CHICAGO POLICE

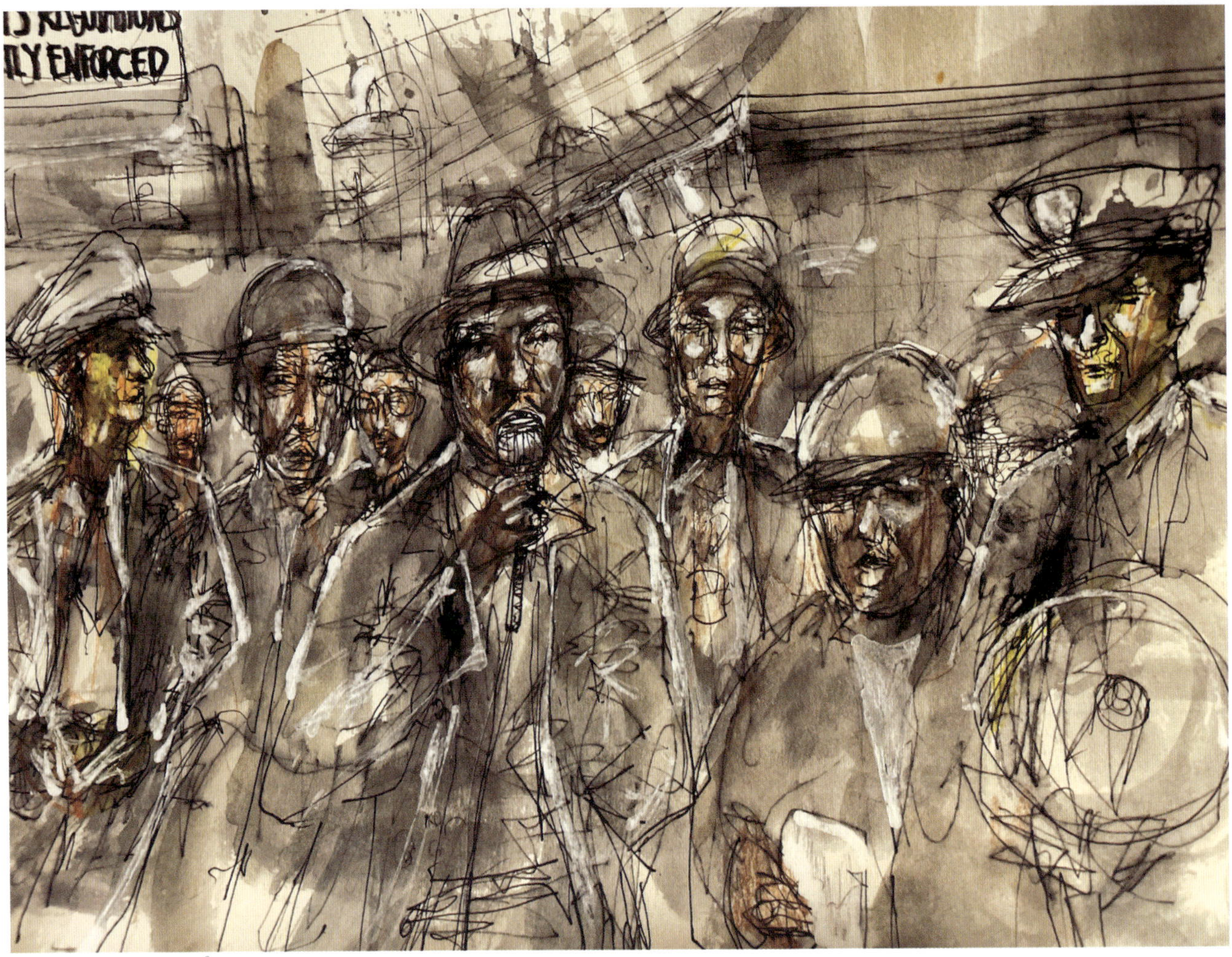

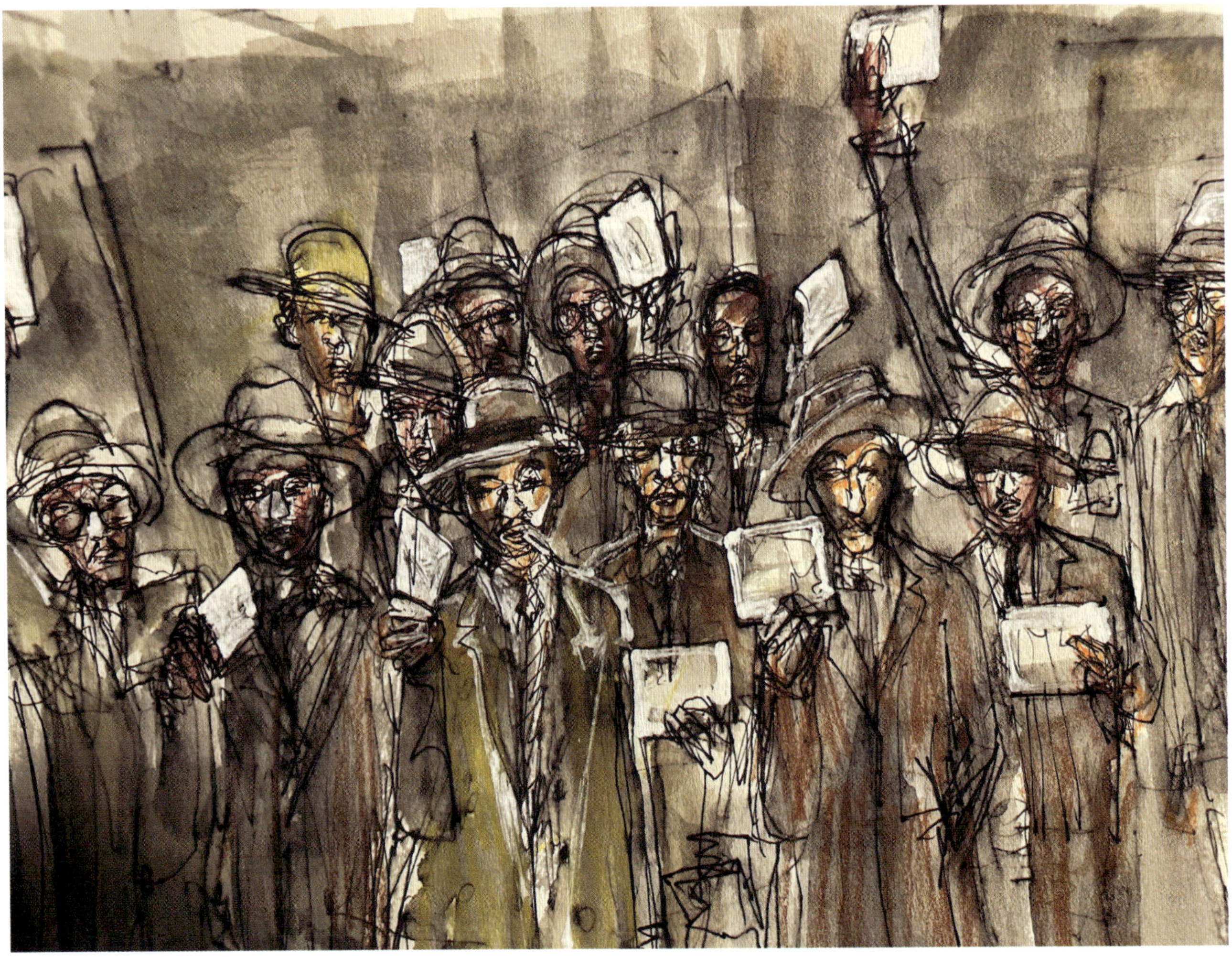

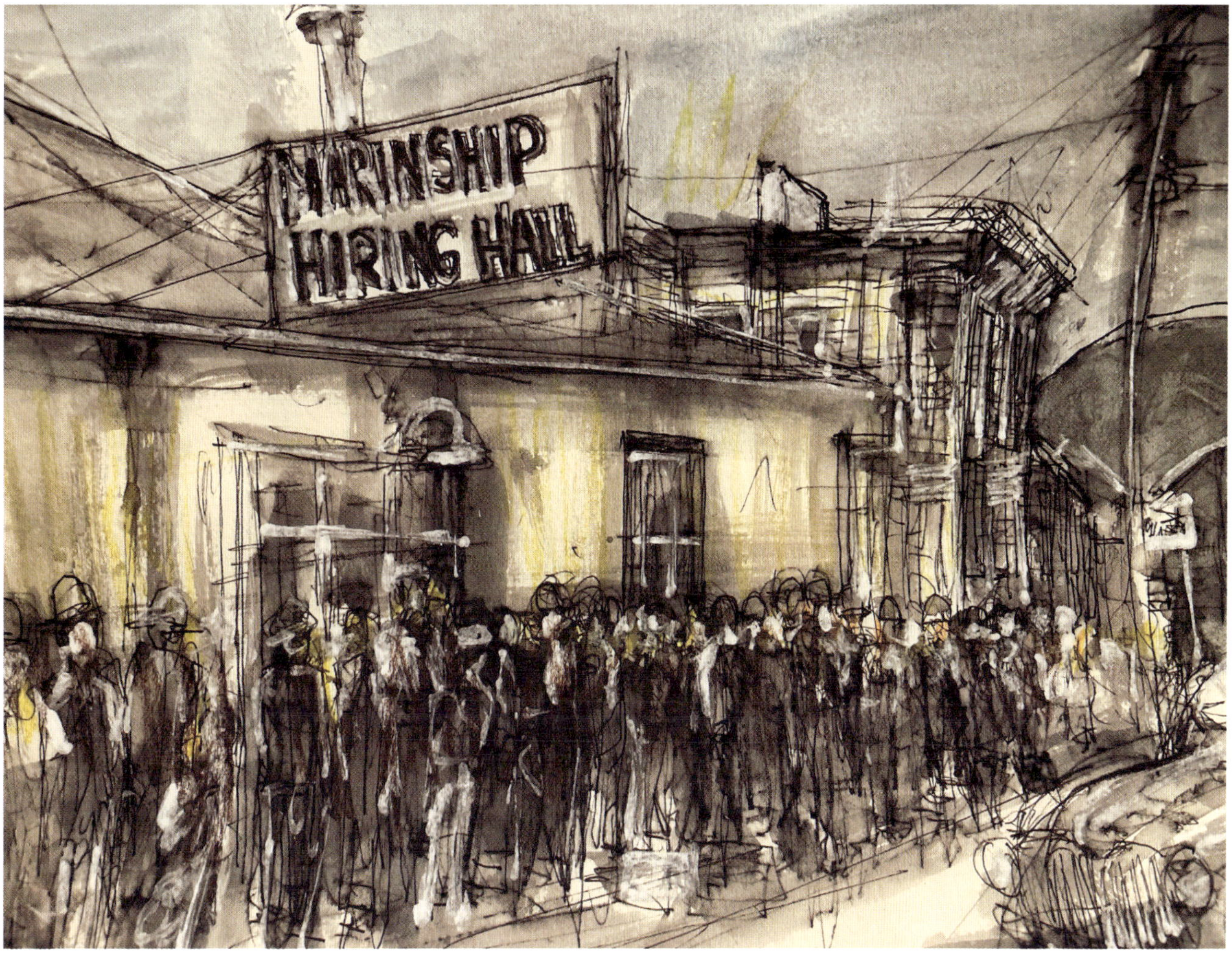

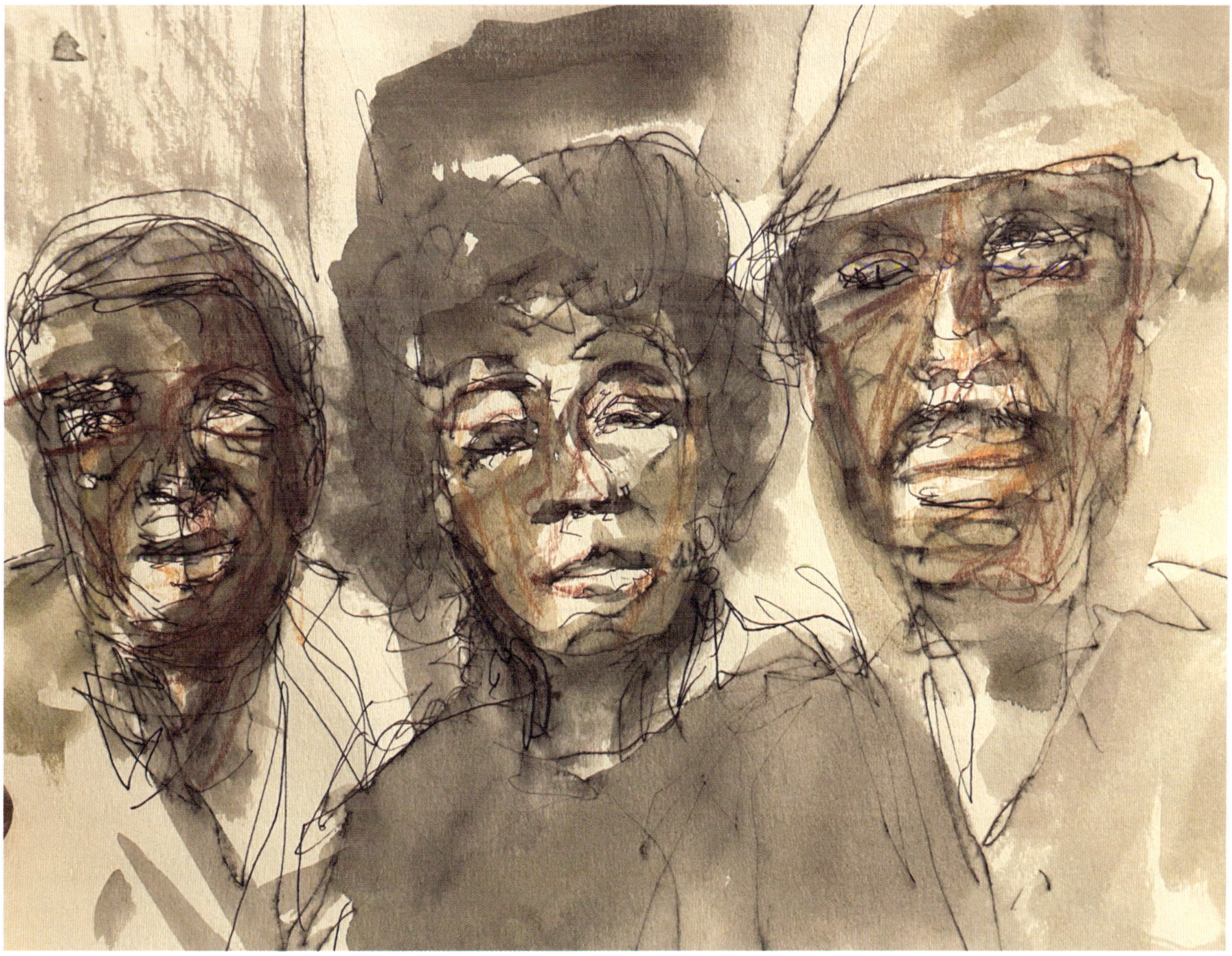

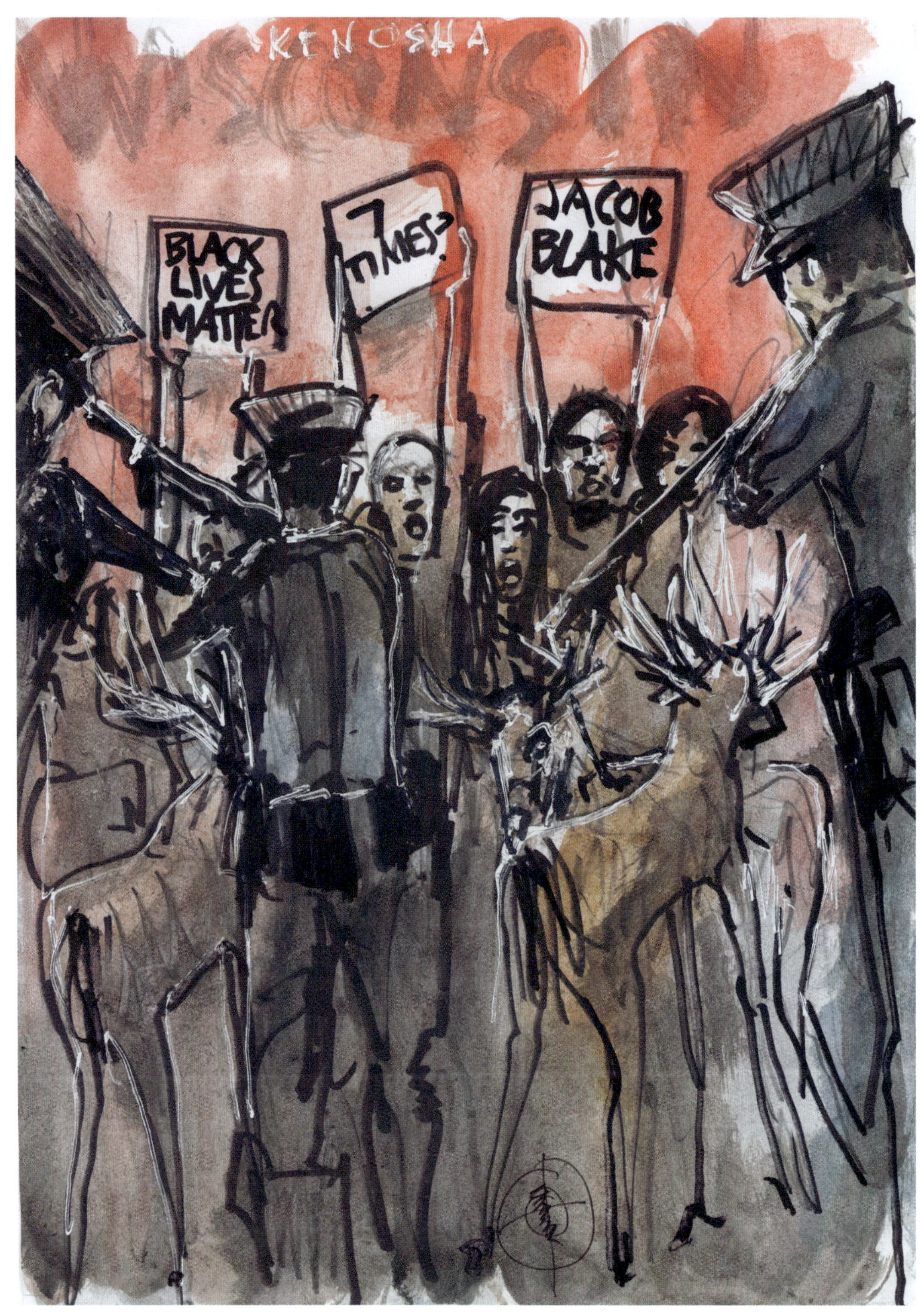

The energy of the Black Lives Matter protests spoke truth to power. The creative world that surrounds us spoke about that too, and I'd be a fool not to follow that energy. Young people are growing up with their parents telling them this is what it meant to them – they see hypocrisy in power.

A lot of people in the US think that Black Lives Matter is a violent movement, but they are wrong to see it as setting one group against another. I look at it as a push for peace that involves everybody. Yes, all lives matter, but no lives matter if black lives don't.

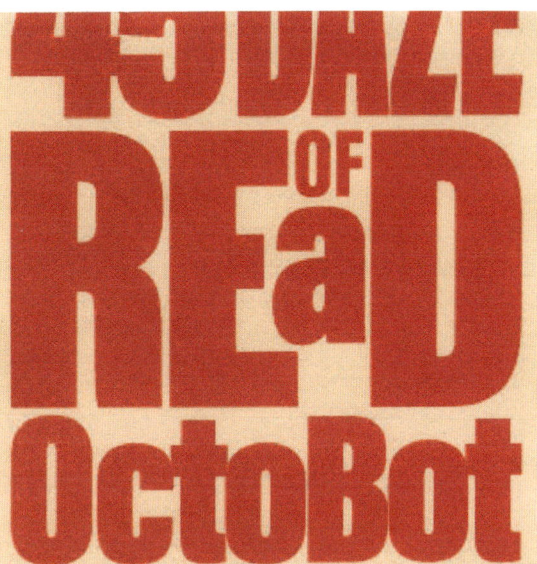

FLIES, DYES AND THE LIES OF 45 AS THE WORLD CRIES

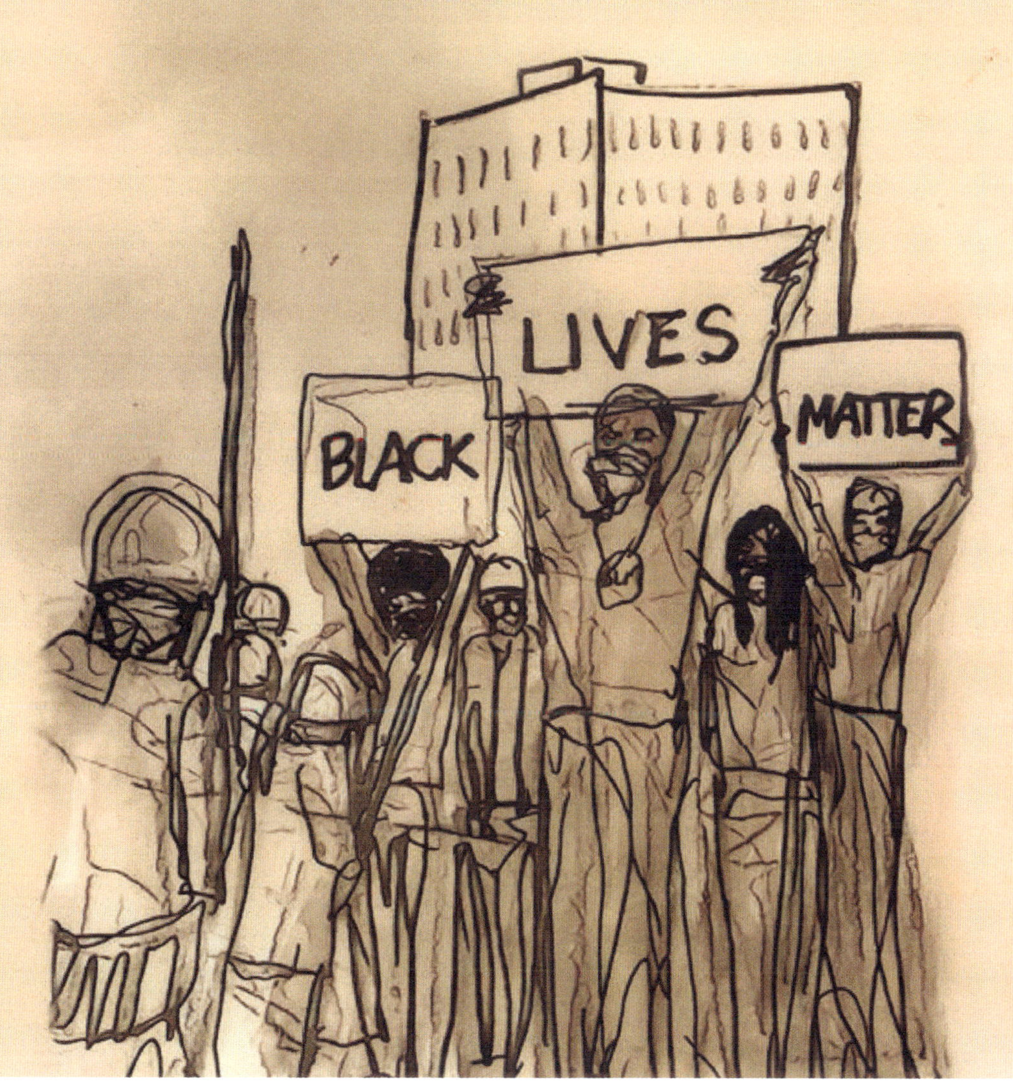

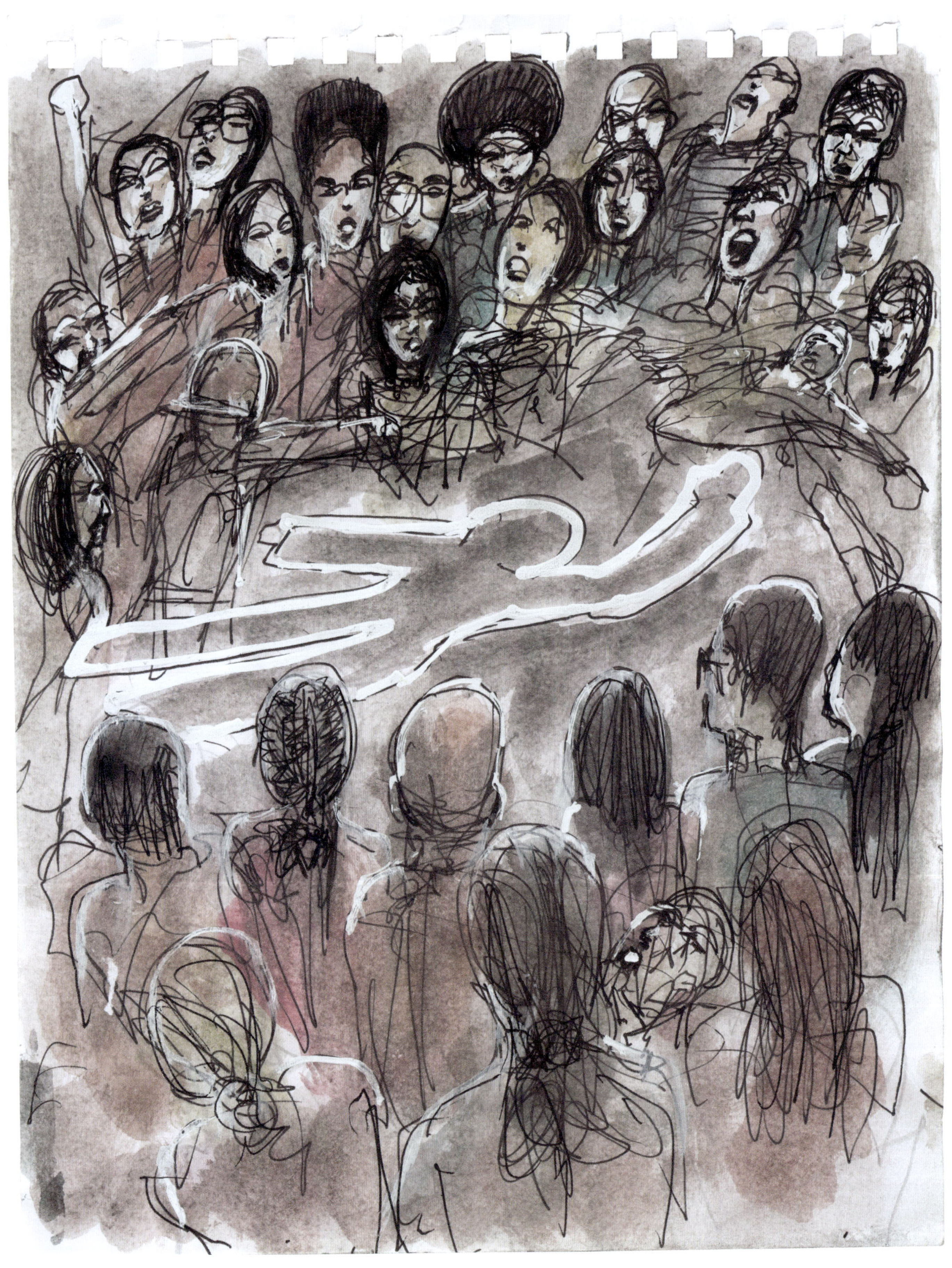

Black Lives Matter is responding to a gaping need and they're being vocal about it the best way they can. I didn't go to Ferguson, but I salute everyone who did. Life is a fight, man. In the middle of the smoke, you fight to breathe.

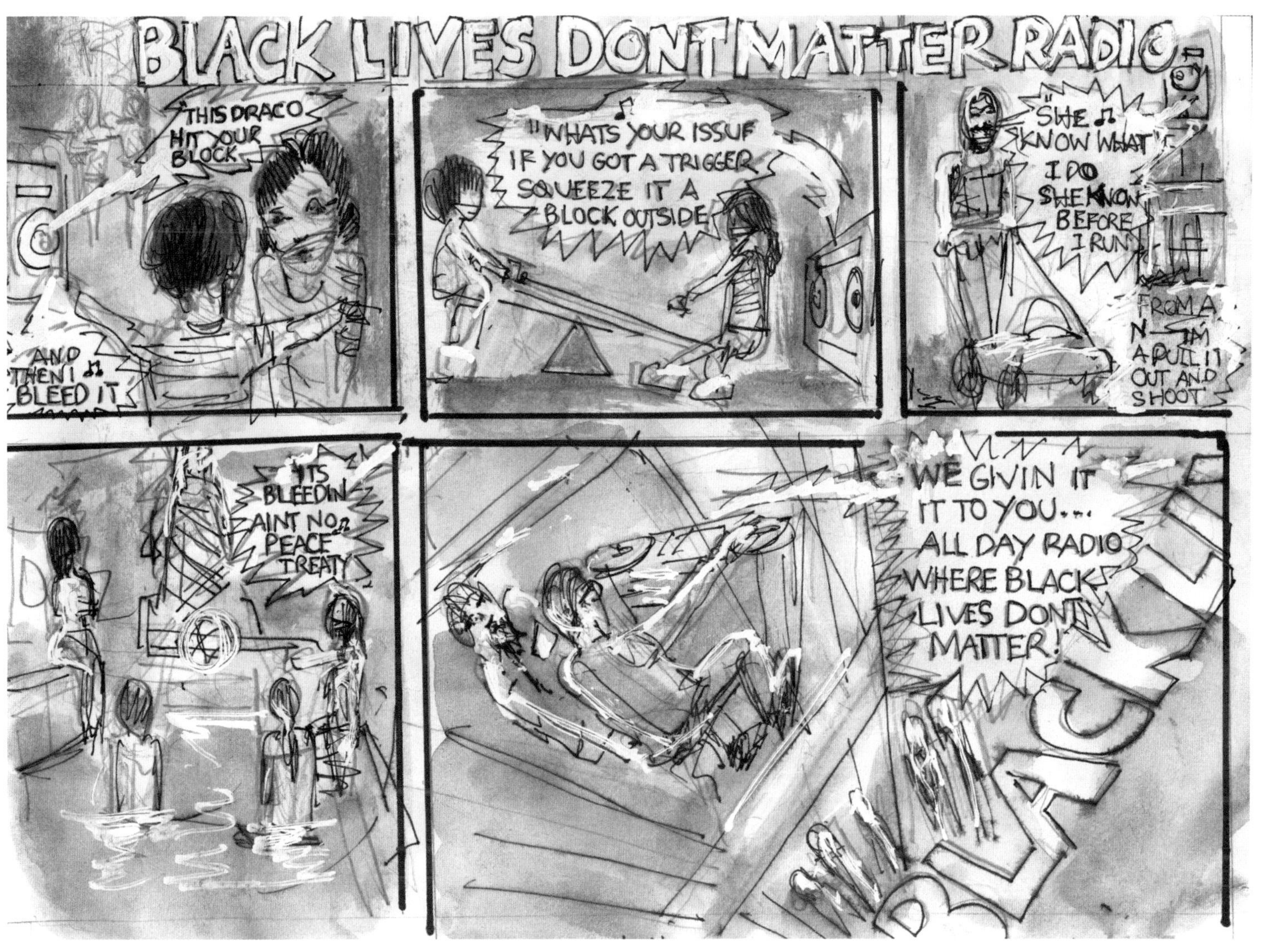

Black Lives Matter is beyond an organisation.

It's a movement like the National Urban League or the NAACP, which were also up against a society that considered black lives to not matter. The new hyperbole they're throwing in – that Black Lives Matter is an antifa terrorist movement – shows that some ears are always going to be shut down to our logic, wisdom, understanding and delivery.

Dr Martin Luther King wanted to put pressure on the government so that it lived up to what it put on paper. Even there, they were fronting. That was more than 50 years ago. Now, you have an arrogant authority that is positioning Black Lives Matter as radical, fundamentalist and crazy so they can push their agenda for the few at the expense of the many.

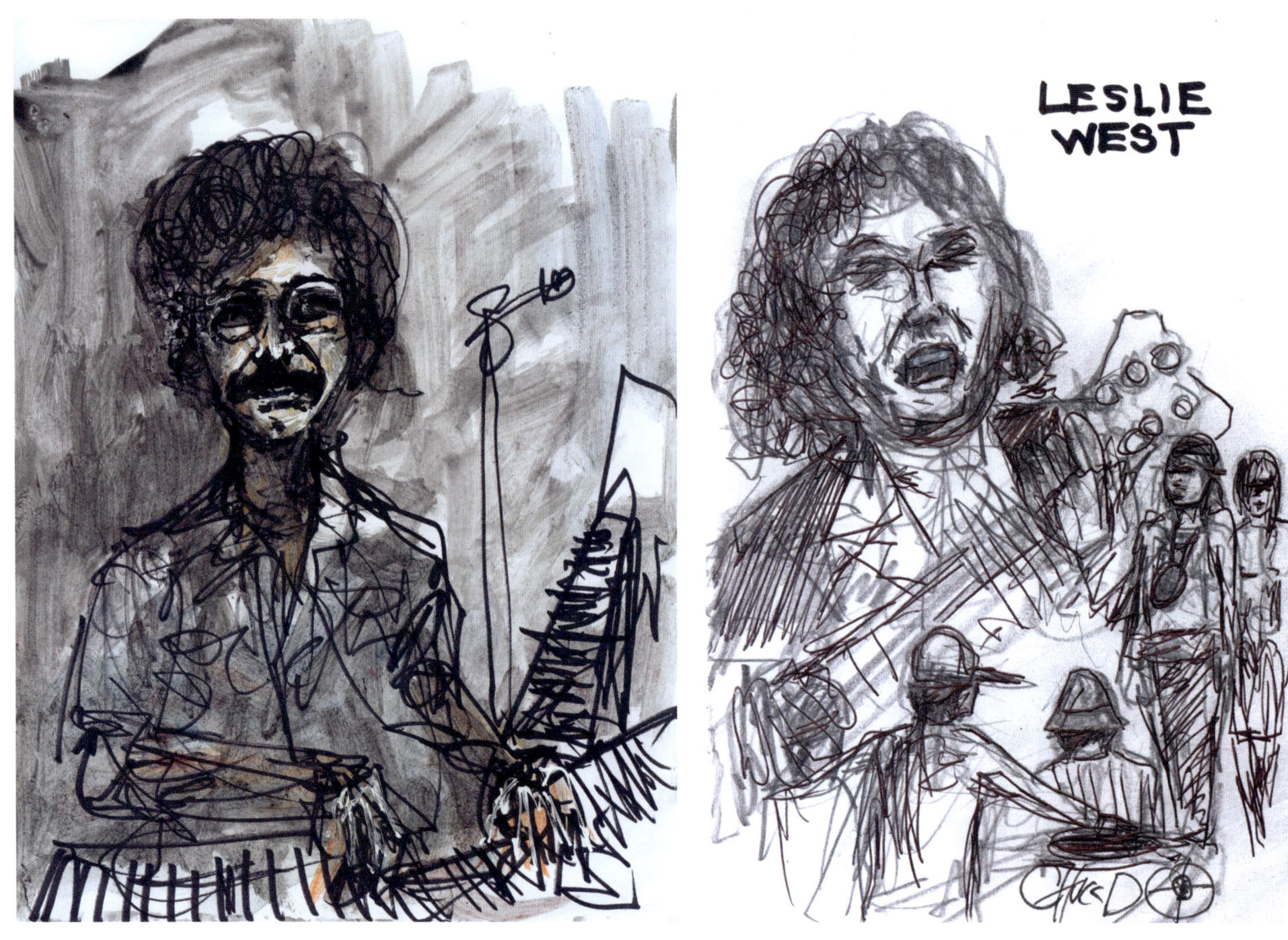

When Chick Corea passed away, I automatically paid homage.

Public Enemy has the utmost respect for music from the Sixties and Seventies. We've been doing music for the last three decades, so we know. If someone asks you when the best music was recorded, you've gotta say the Sixties and Seventies if you have any sense in you! George Clinton told me that.

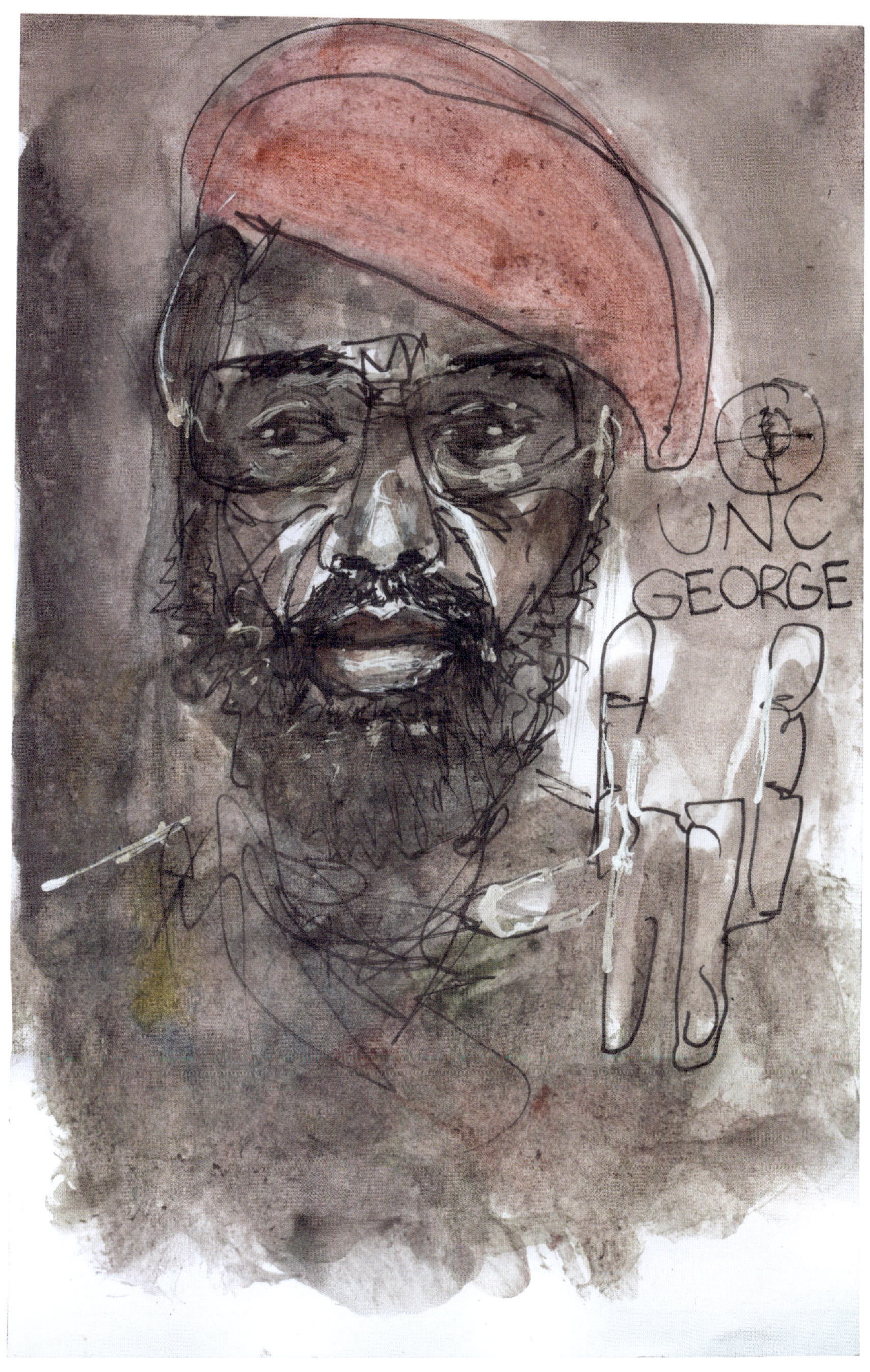

George Clinton appeared on our album *What You Gonna Do When the Grid Goes Down?* I asked Uncle George to just be himself, and we really thanked him for that blessing. A lot of people go to George Clinton for his funk and that's the no-brainer, but we also went to him for his visionary and futuristic ideas. It's his funkolosophy that we wanted to go forward with.

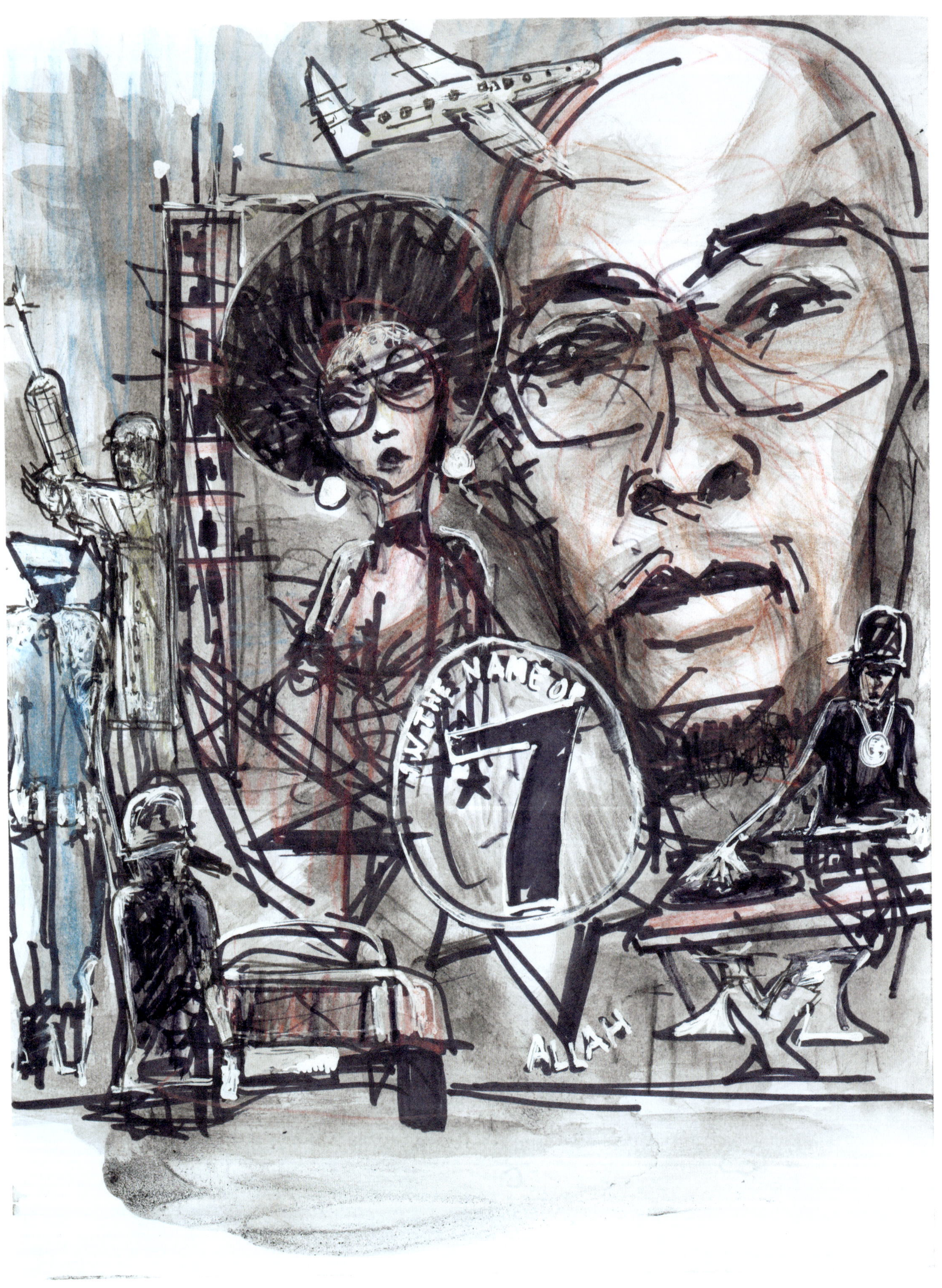
IN THE NAME OF
7
ALLAH

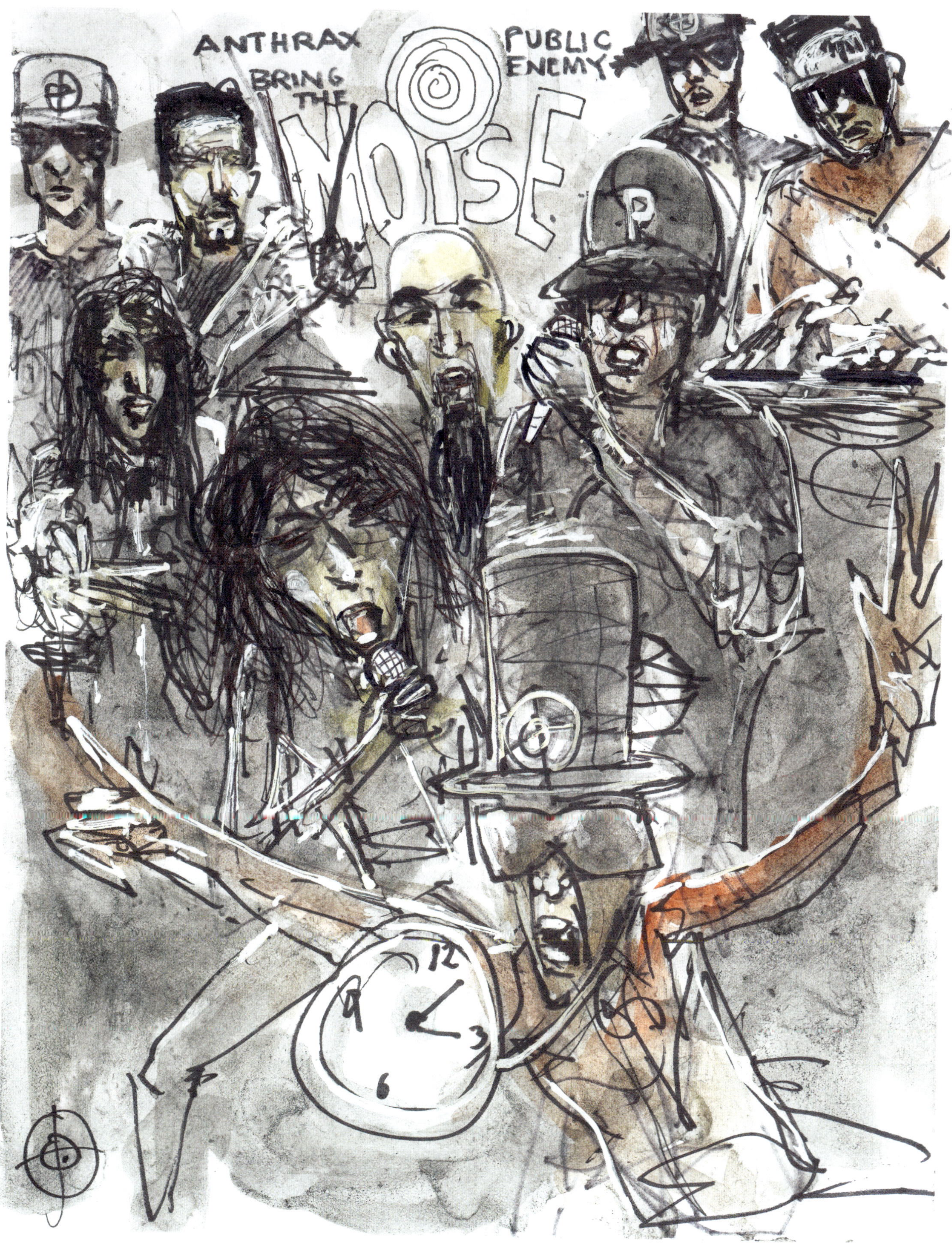
ANTHRAX
PUBLIC ENEMY
BRING THE NOISE

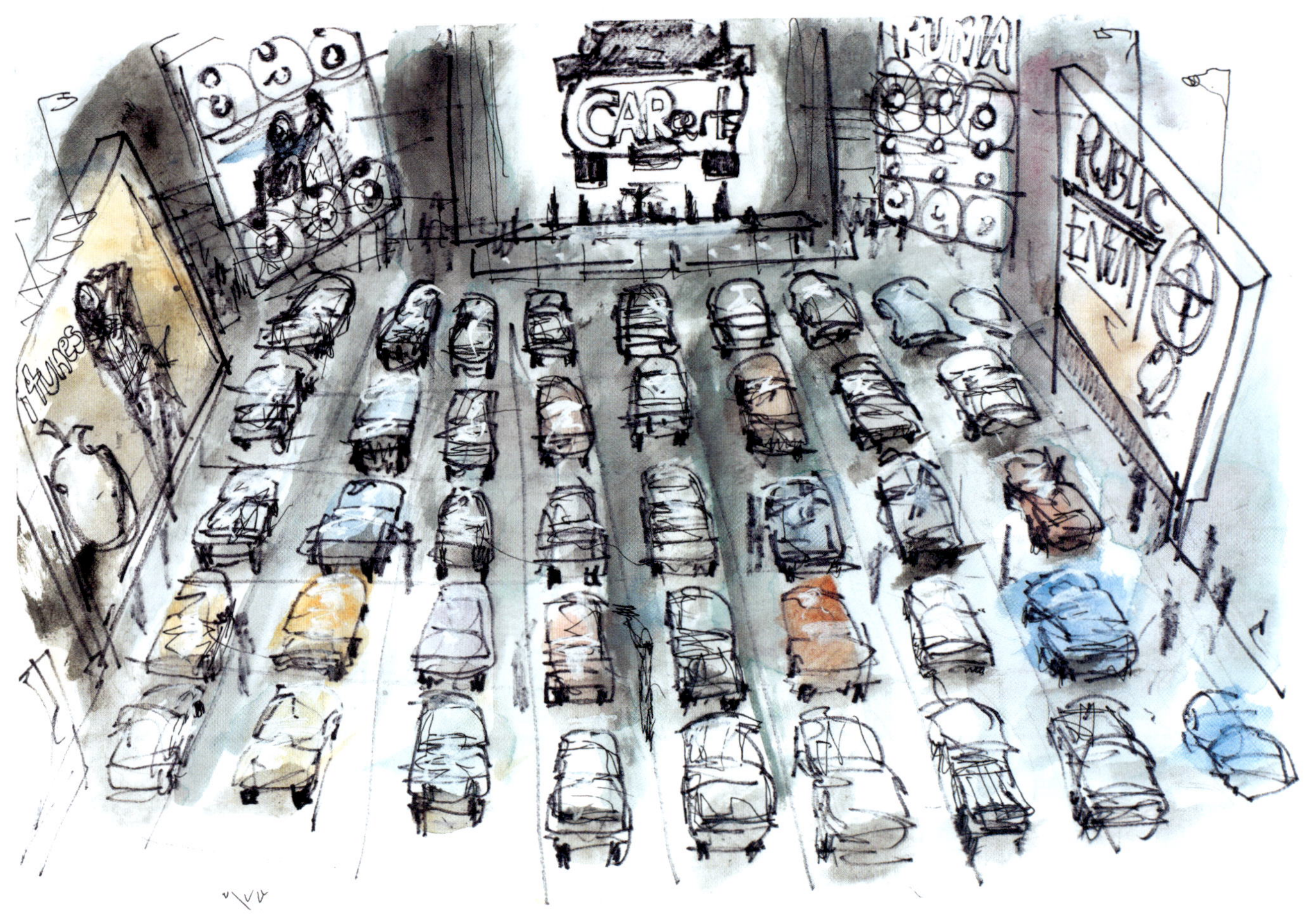

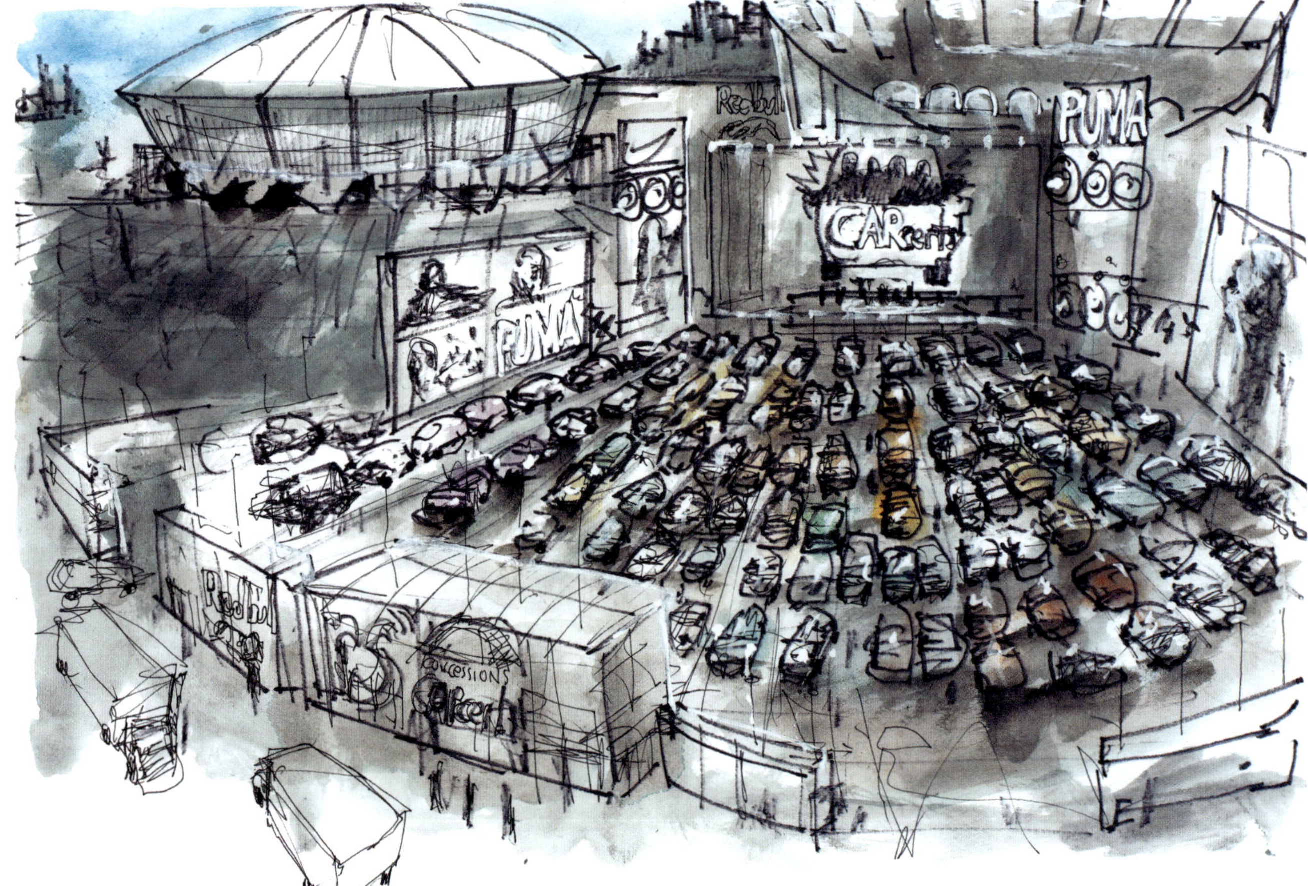

At the beginning of the pandemic, I had an idea for parking lot concerts called Carcerts.

HOMEDRANT

About 15 years ago I designed a home hydrant system with fellow Long Islander Norm Levy and his engineers, in the wake of serious wildfires in California. It would take water from a swimming pool or a tank and pump it out. Unfortunately, we faced massive insurance obstacles and so it never got made.

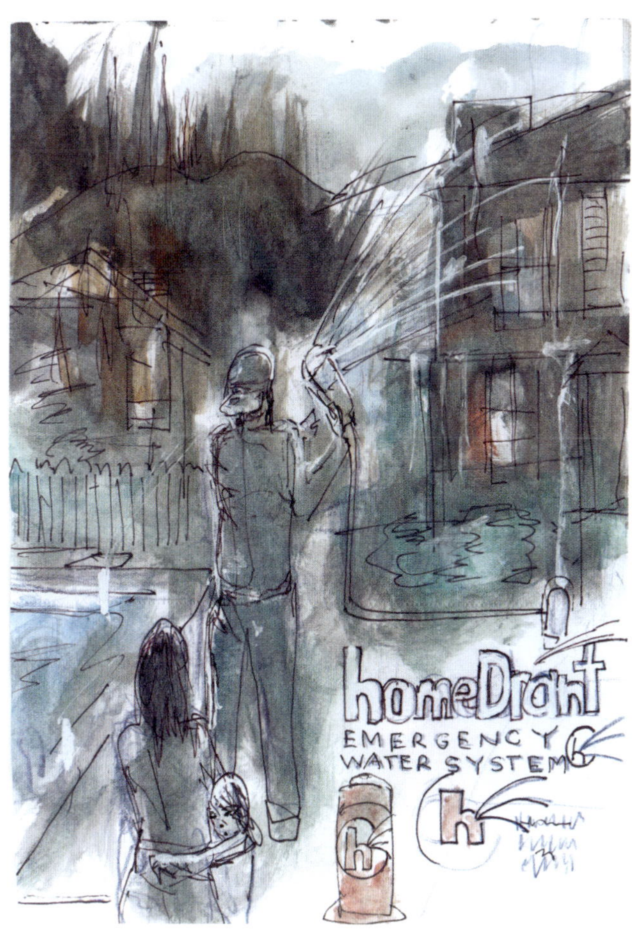

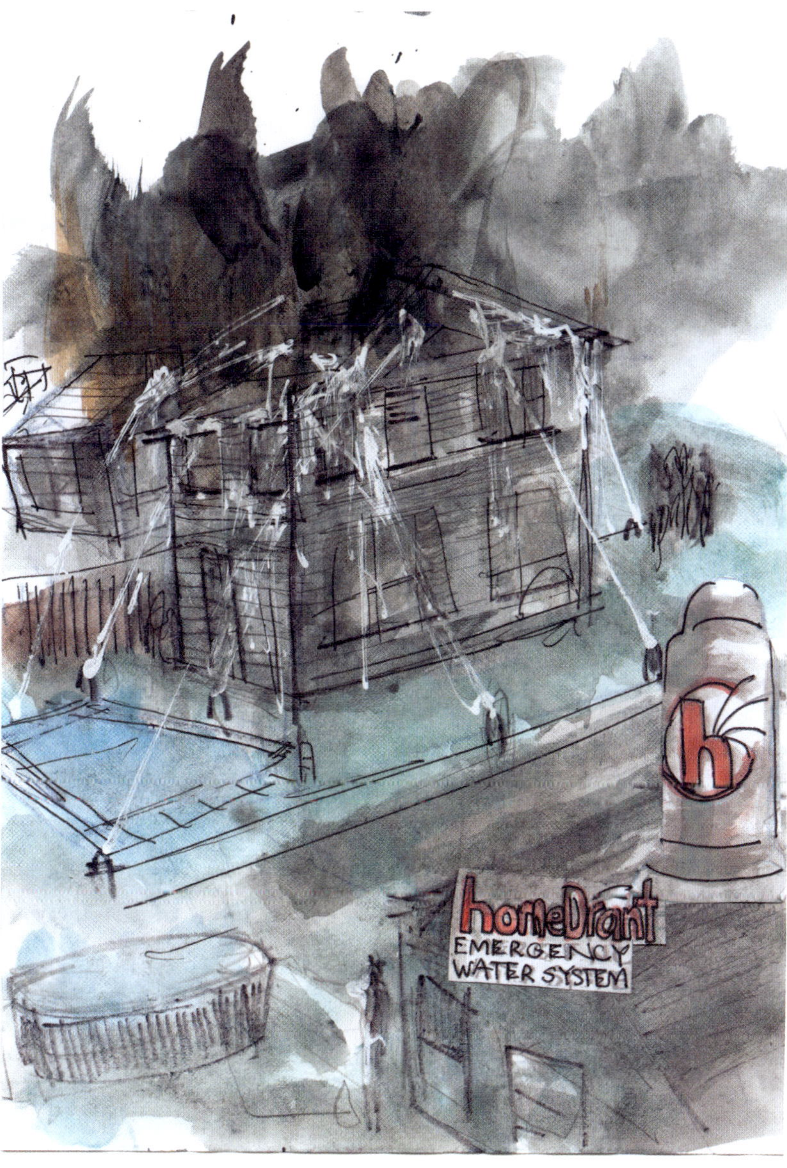

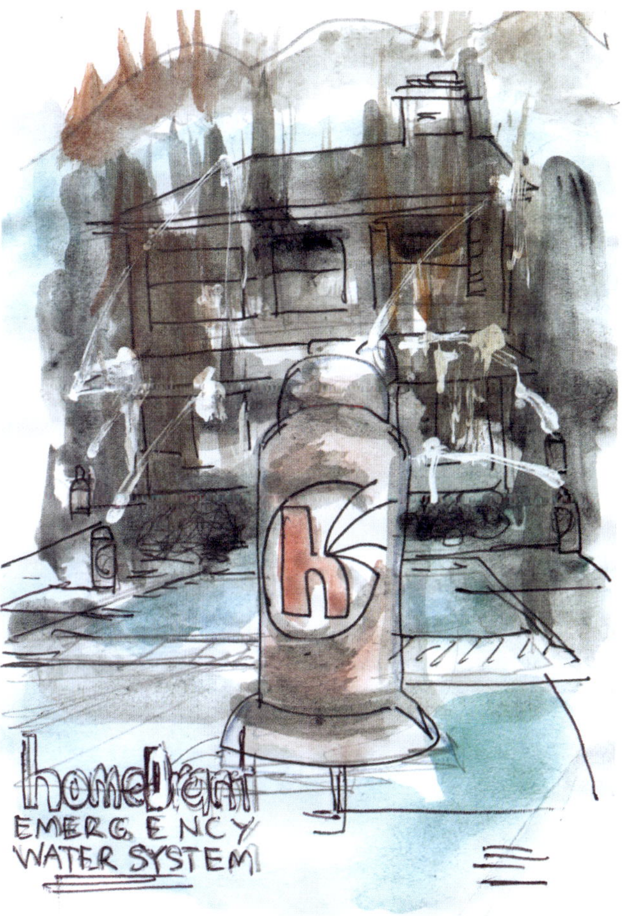

Mr William Marsella, who taught my high school architecture class, gave me the confidence to really go into my art and be something.

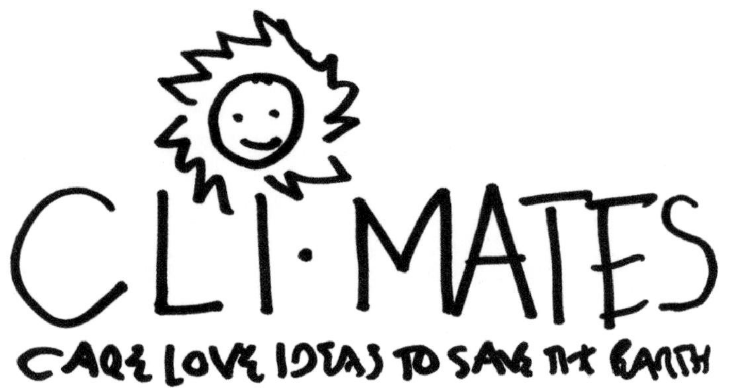

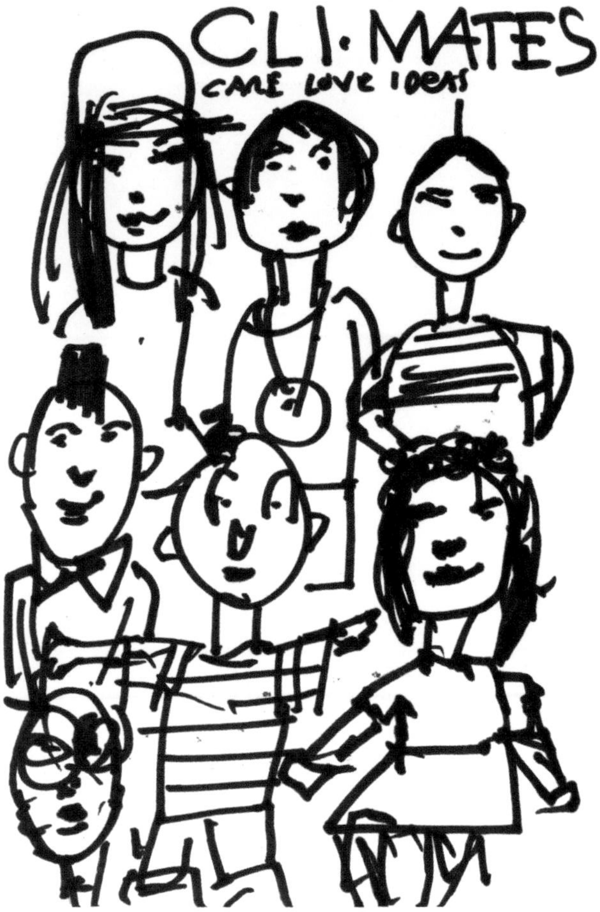

This is an idea for a children's book about kids dealing with climate change.

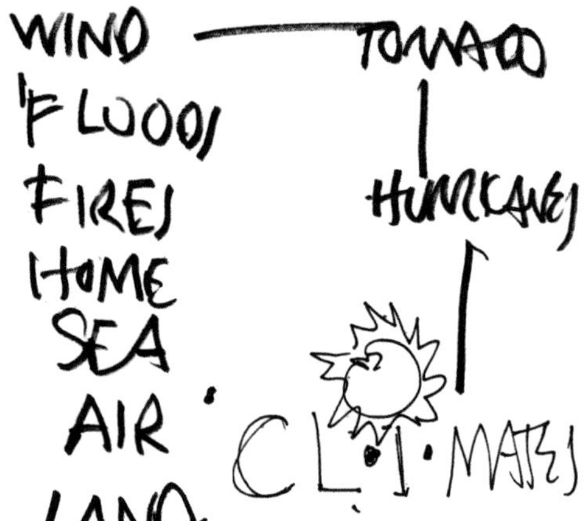

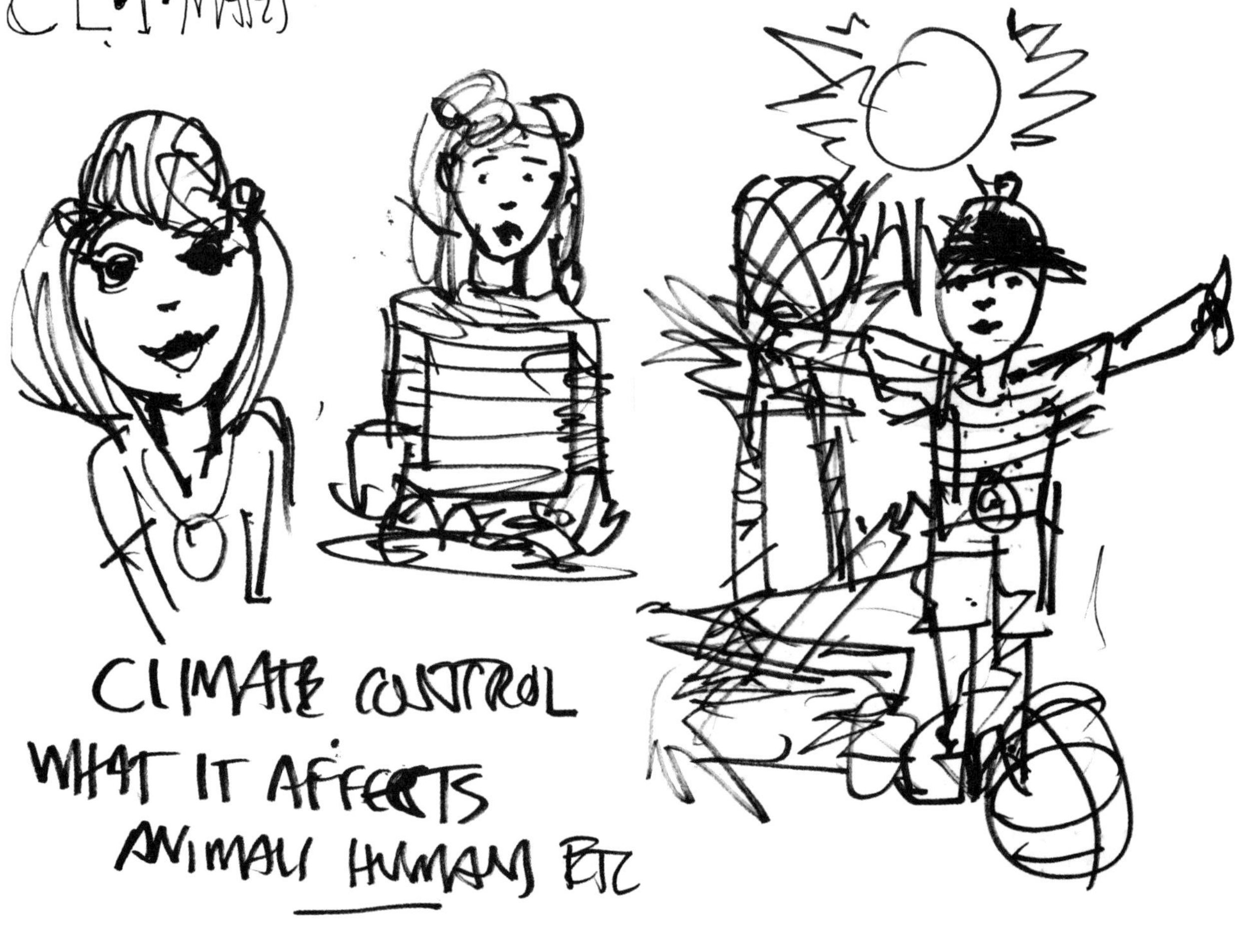

WIND — TORNADO
FLOODS
FIRES — HURRICANES
HOME
SEA
AIR
LAND
WATER
FOOD
FISH

CLI·MATES

CLI·MATES
CARE LOVE IDEAS

CLIMATE CONTROL
WHAT IT AFFECTS
ANIMALS HUMANS ETC

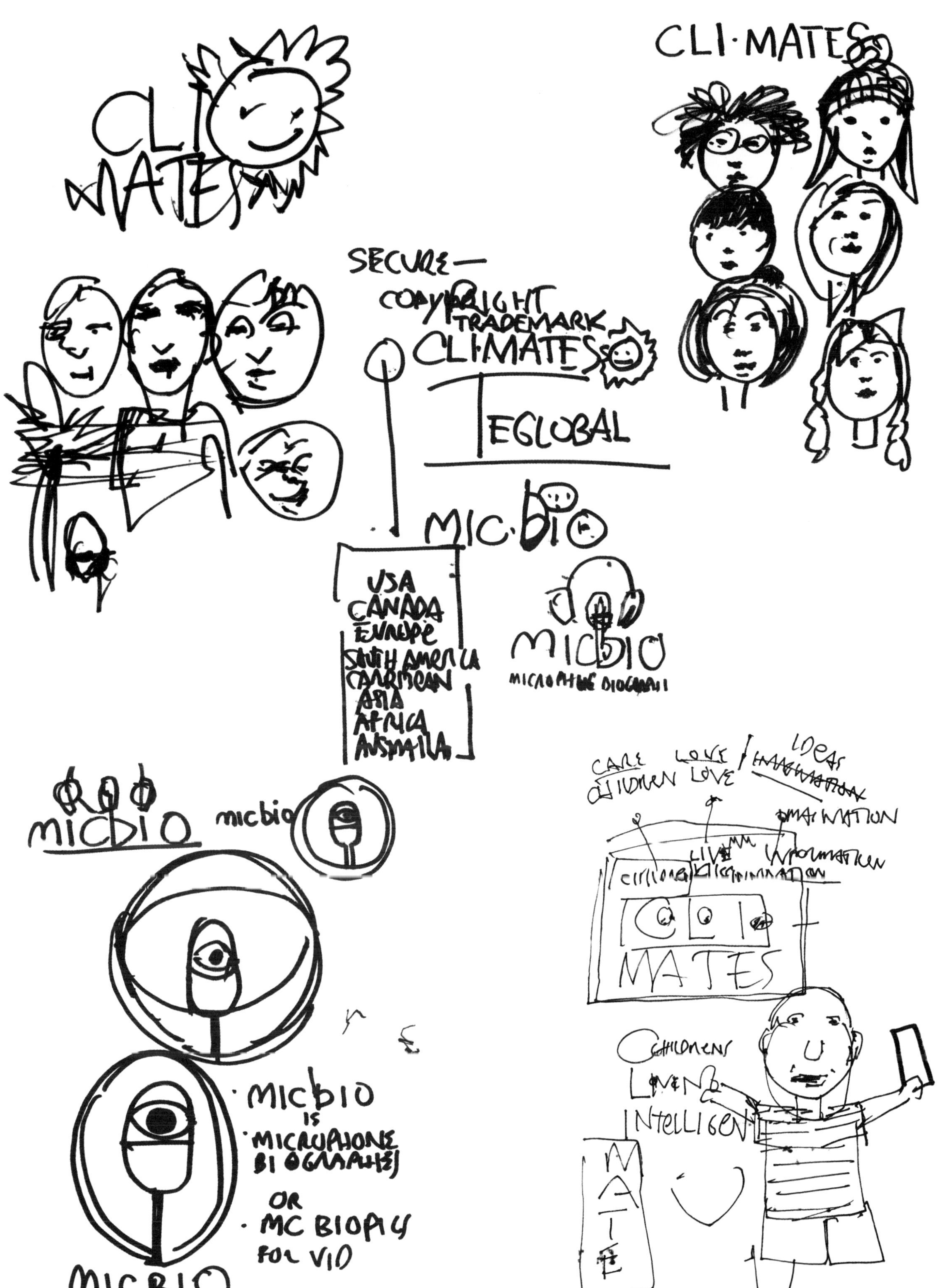
CLI MATES
CLI·MATES
SECURE—
COPYRIGHT
TRADEMARK
CLIMATES
TEGLOBAL
MIC·BIO
USA
CANADA
EUROPE
SOUTH AMERICA
CARIBBEAN
ASIA
AFRICA
AUSTRALIA
MICBIO
MICBIO
micbio
CARE LOVE
CHILDREN LOVE
IDEAS
IMAGINATION
LIVE
INFORMATION
CLI
MATES
CHILDRENS
LOVE
INTELLIGEN
MICBIO
IS
MICROPHONE
BIOGRAPHIES
OR
MC BIOPICS
FOR VID
MICBIO

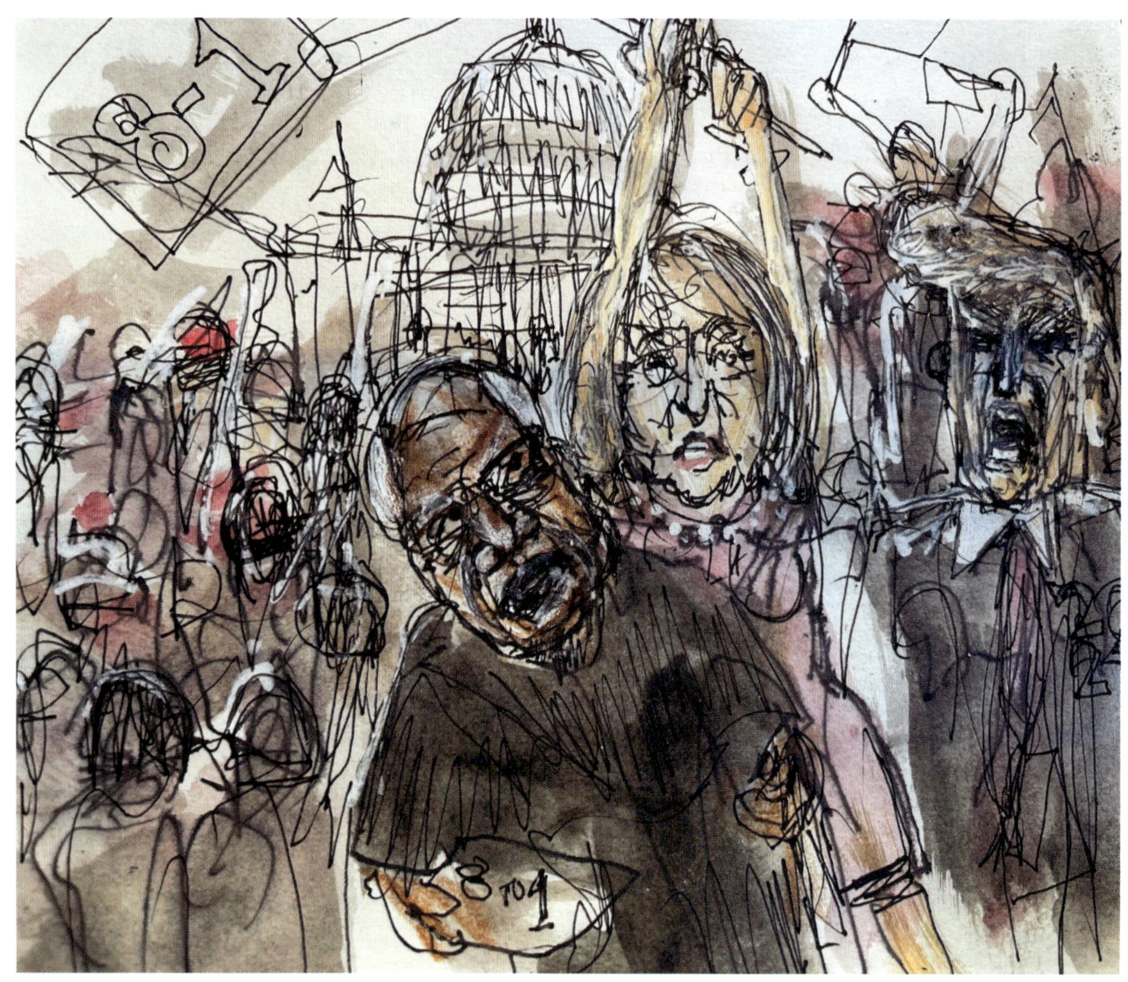

The state of America right now is leaning heavily in the direction of the white, rich, powerful, imperialist, exploitive, money-grabbing, opportunity-seizing capitalists. We have to save ourselves and stop relying on other people to come up with great answers for us.

We have to look within ourselves and our own community.

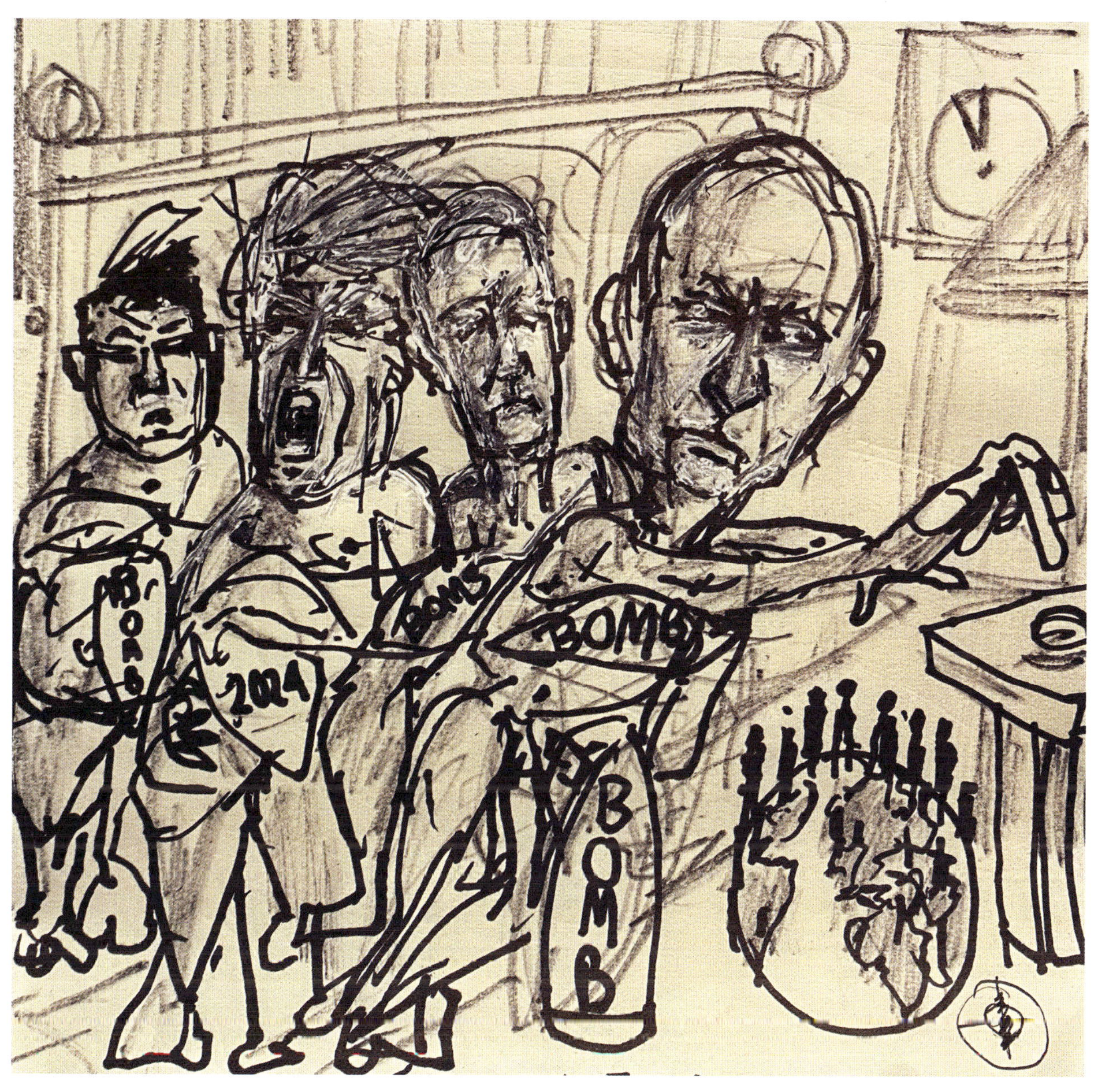

War is a testosterone-filled event. Muhammad Ali set the standard for black people to say, 'Fuck the war and screw the government if they don't give a damn about us.' That was always my stance.

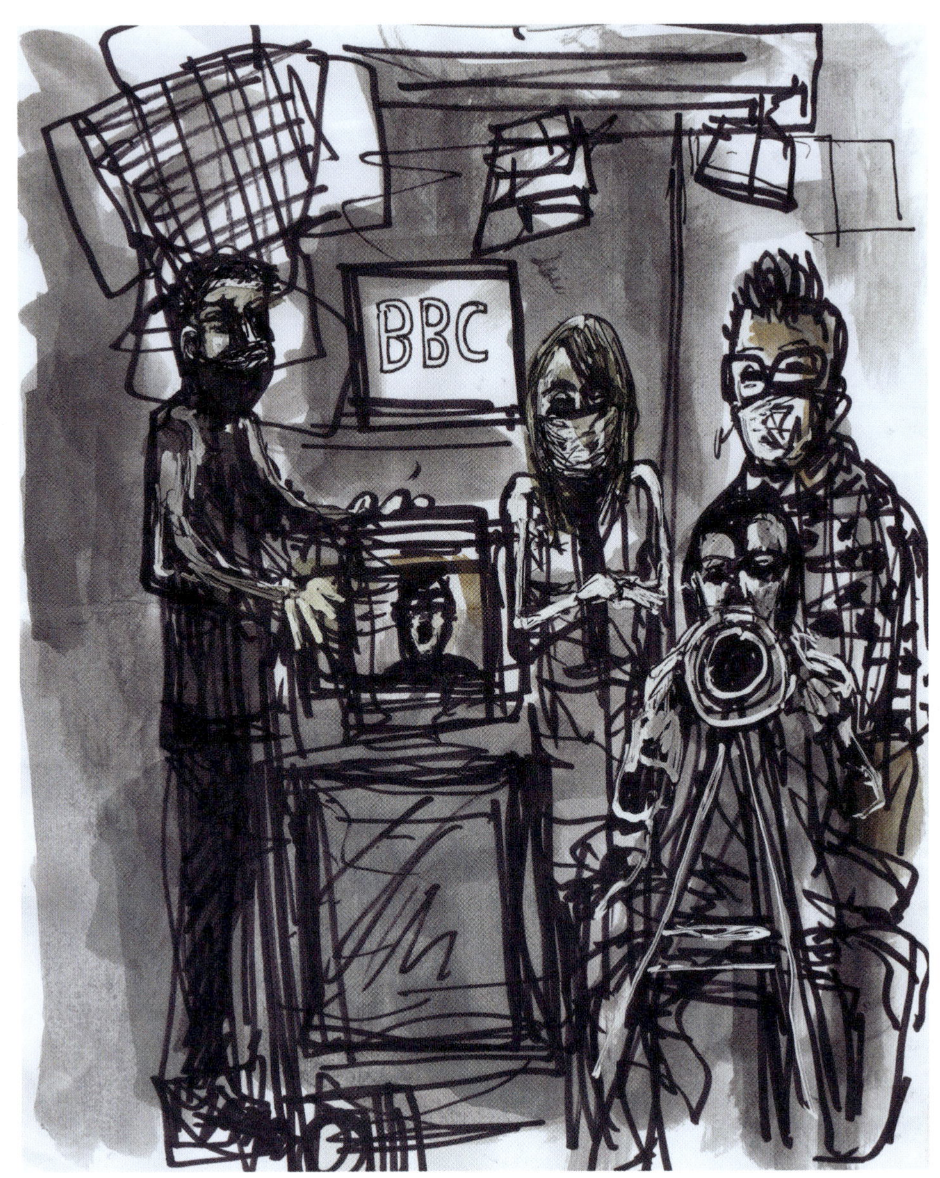

Rappers get knocked for saying rebellious things, but what the fuck is the average R&B singer saying? It's cool to play at Live Aid and other benefit concerts, but these concepts are devised by white people who say, 'I think something should be done.'

Whatever rappers feel, we'll say it – whether it's regarding police brutality with NWA's 'Fuck tha Police' or giving our mothers their respect with Tupac's 'Dear Mama'. In 1992 when the rebellion took place in South Central Los Angeles, rappers came out and expressed an opinion but spineless black singers and athletes were silent.

My work throughout my life is always representative of the time we live in. I always want to move forward with everything I am doing. So, I do the radio show, speak at universities and other social institutions around the world, appear on television, and continue to create music, all to keep the struggle alive.

Most other artists are always fighting for their fame. They have that fear – like the saying goes, 'out of sight, out of mind'. They need to keep themselves out there. I have never had that fear.

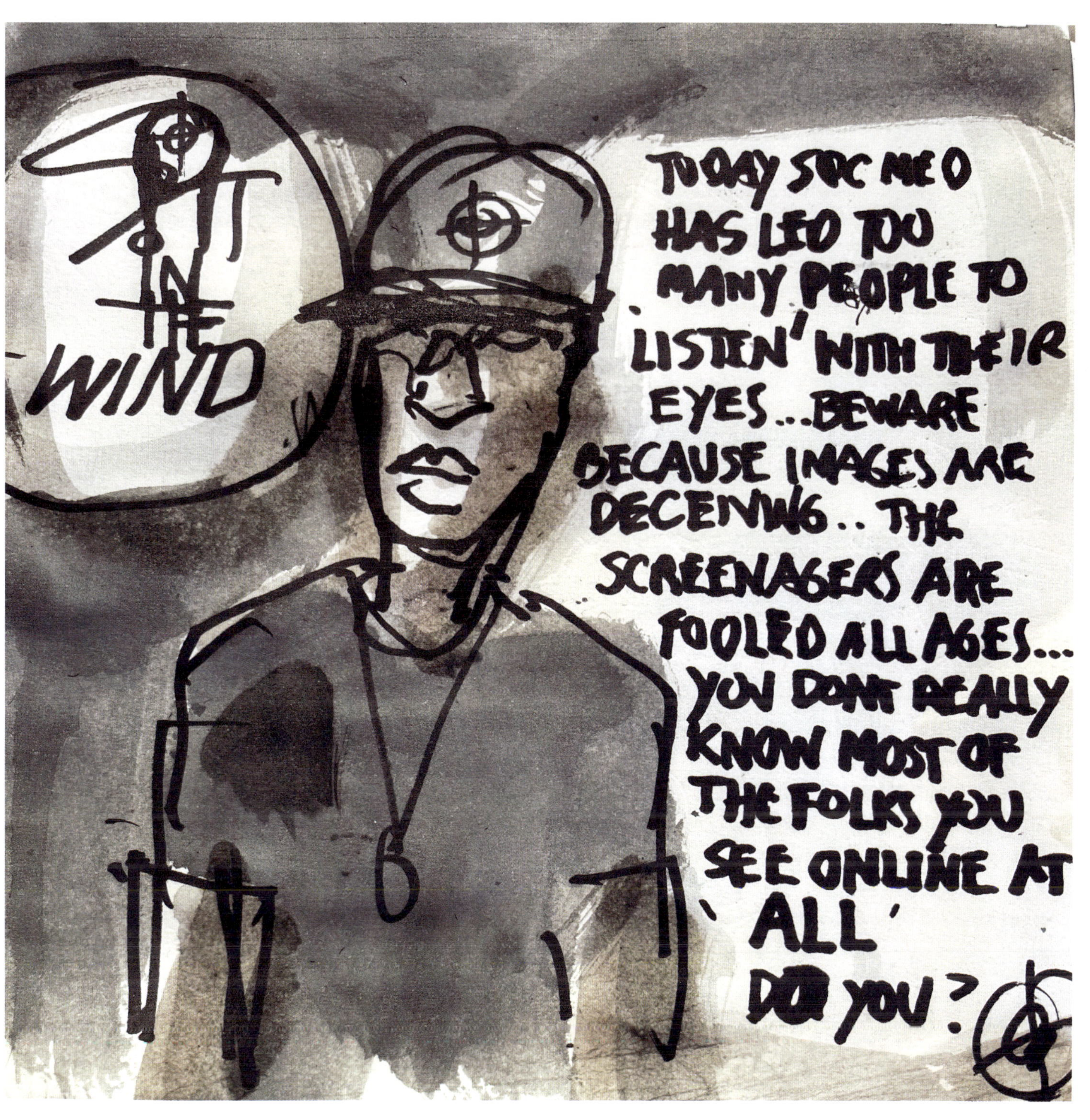

If I have any fear, it's not doing enough to reach people.

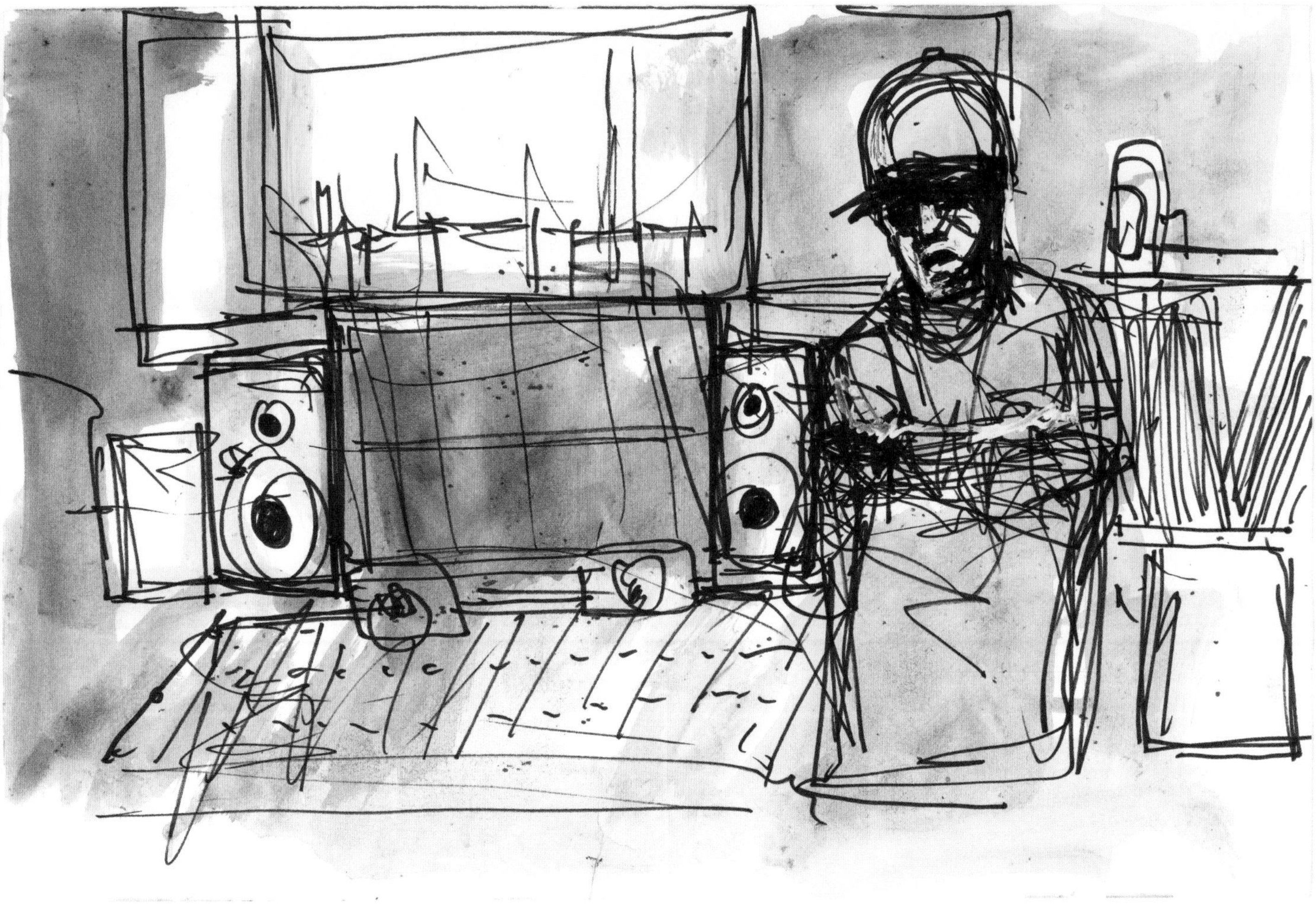

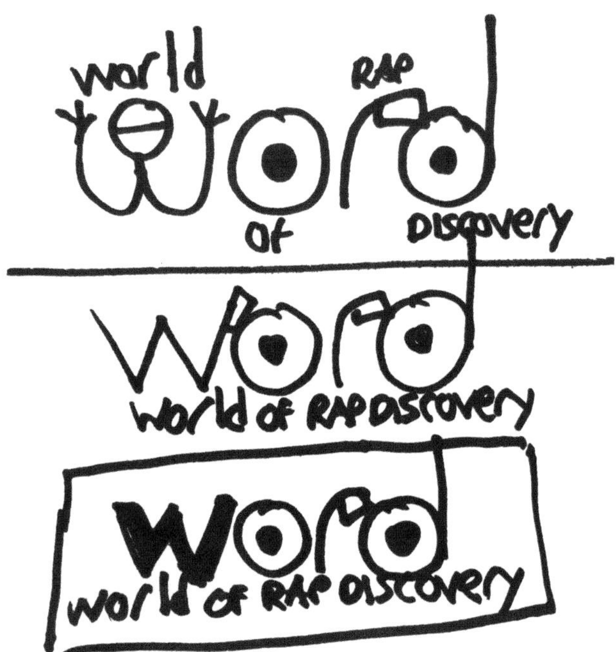

As Public Enemy, our collective voice keeps getting louder. The rest of the planet is on our side. But it's not enough to talk about change. You have to show up and demand change.

The biggest difference between now and 1990, when we made *Fear of a Black Planet*, is that a lot of the people who are speaking out now weren't even born back then. We can't say, 'Haven't we been through all this before?' because somebody who's 26 years old has not been through all this before. Every generation has to be able to find its own way through these issues, but also build systemically on what has gone before. We have to keep working on the '-isms', like racism and sexism, at an institutional level. We can't fall back and say, 'OK we won the battle, so who cares about the war?' The war is to continue to strive for peace and love in a society of -isms and hate.

We're at war with our own ghosts. I don't want a person to come up to me before a show and say, 'Yo man, you blew me away in '96, best show I've ever seen.' When that happens I know I have to try to obliterate myself. Obliterate that piece of history out of your mind.

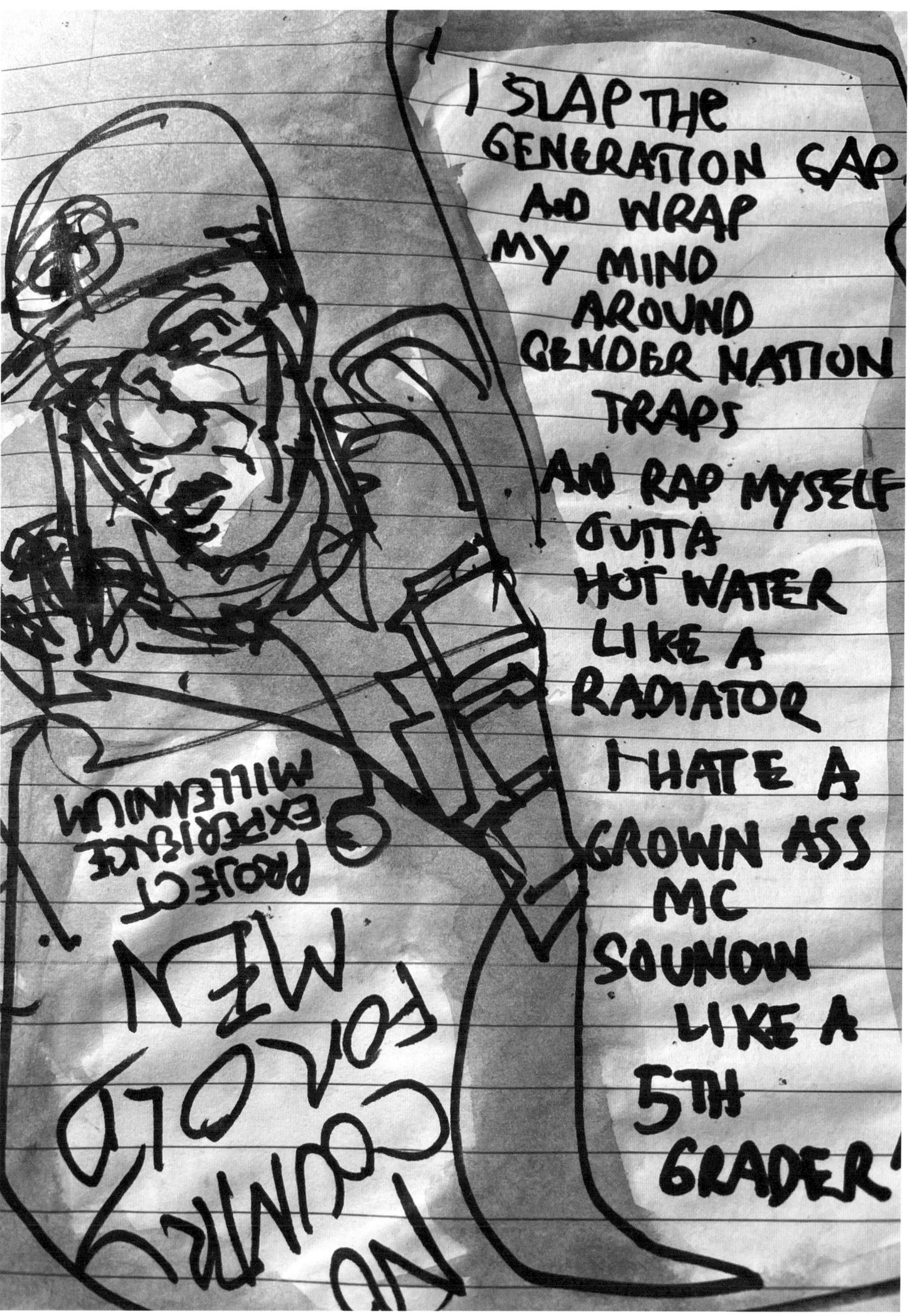
I SLAP THE GENERATION GAP AND WRAP MY MIND AROUND GENDER NATION TRAPS AND RAP MYSELF OUTTA HOT WATER LIKE A RADIATOR I HATE A GROWN ASS MC SOUNDIN LIKE A 5TH GRADER
PROJECT EXPERIENCE MILLENNIUM
NO COUNTRY FOR OLD MEN

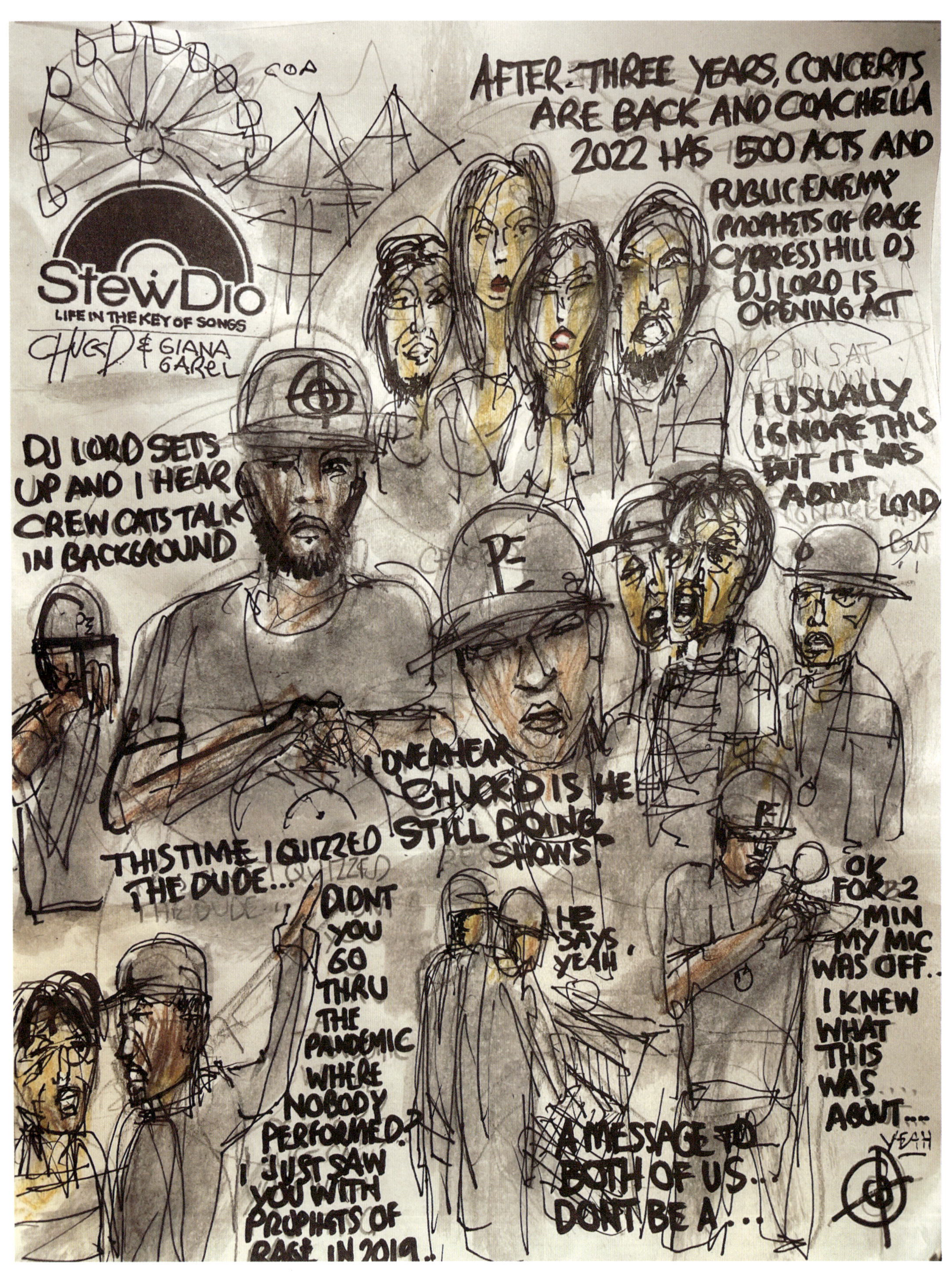

People have decided that 'Fight the Power' speaks to now. I'd be a fool not to recognise that.

Our thanks to Chuck D for allowing us to present his paintings to Genesis readers and the world for the first time. Working with Chuck D has been an exciting creative collaboration and we are incredibly grateful for the energy and insight he has given to every stage of the project.

ACKNOWLEDGEMENTS

Thank you to Tom Morello for his great foreword.

The team at Soul Kitchen Music, Lorrie Boula and Kevin Abrantes.

The Genesis team, with a special mention for Megan Lily Large and Katy Baker.

Additional thanks to Dominique Ridenhour and Giana Garel of SoundSpeak for facilitating me.

MADurgency Chairman Malcolm Riddle, Andy Katz, Craig Kriendler, Adam Illus Wallenta, Carole McCoy, Kate Kelton, Ernie Barnes, Mr Bill Marcella (WT Clarke), Professors Jennerjahn Cantone and Davies (Adelphi U), Cey Adams, Steve Carr, Kenny Gravallis, DefJam and Dr Frank Frazier for further inspiration.

Kyle T. Moser, Myron Adinig, Mark Culmer - Madina, Tony Coppin, Sage Gallon, Amy Cinnamon, Christian Cordes - Confuse Art, Baron Walton, Darren Holtom, Miho Michelet, Hieram Weintraub, Sally Murrow, Damien Van Der Meer, Louise Barnes, Yann Demierre, Tommy the Animator, Bill Ladson.

LOUD IS THE LIVIN
OF THE LIFE
I LEAD
COMIN
LIVE
WITH
THE VOLUME
THE SPEED Y'ALL NEED
TOP OF THE WORLD
SMACK THE BOTTOM OF HELL

STEP BACK AT THE DEMACIBEL

CUTTIN
TURNIN
THE
SHOTS
CUTS
ROCKIN
THE
KNIFE

LIVIN
LOUD IS THE WAY OF THE LIFE